To the Highlands in 1786

*THE INQUISITIVE JOURNEY OF A YOUNG
FRENCH ARISTOCRAT*

Drawn on stone by J.D.Harding.   Printed by C.Hullmandel.

Recess in the Saloon,
Alnwick Castle.

Alnwick Castle: recess in the Salon, an example of the Gothick decoration that impressed Alexandre so favourably. It is now replaced throughout the castle by no less impressive Victorian Gothic decoration. Printed by O. Hullmar from J. D. Harding's lithograph. Collection of the Duke of Northumberland.

To the Highlands in 1786

THE INQUISITIVE JOURNEY OF A YOUNG FRENCH ARISTOCRAT

NORMAN SCARFE

with a Foreword by François Crouzet
Professor Emeritus at the Sorbonne

North of Aberdeen, the single-arched, early fourteenth-century bridge spans the Don at Balgownie. Aquatint from William Daniell's Voyage round Great Britain *in 1813.*

THE BOYDELL PRESS

First published 2001
The Boydell Press, Woodbridge

ISBN 0 85115 843 9

The Boydell Press is an imprint of Boydell & Brewer Ltd
PO Box 9, Woodbridge, Suffolk IP12 3DF, UK
and of Boydell & Brewer Inc.
PO Box 41026, Rochester, NY 14604–4126, USA
website: http: //www.boydell.co.uk

A catalogue record for this book is available
from the British Library

Library of Congress Cataloging-in-Publication Data
La Rochefoucauld, Alexandre de.
    To the highlands in 1786 : the inquisitive journey of a young French aristocrat /
[edited and translated by] Norman Scarfe.
        p. cm.
    Includes bibliographical references and index.
    Based on the travel journals of Alexandre de La Rochefouchauld and Maximilien
de Lazowski.
    ISBN 0–85115–843–9 (alk. paper)
    1. Highlands (Scotland) – Description and travel – Early works to 1800.   2. La
Rochefoucauld, Alexandre de – Journeys – Scotland – Highlands.   3. Lazowski,
Maximilien de – Journeys – Scotland – Highlands.   4. French – Scotland –
Highlands – History – 18th century.   I. Lazowski, Maximilien de.   II. Scarfe,
Norman.   III. Title.
DA880.H7 L25 2002
914.11'50473 – dc21   2001035618

This publication is printed on acid-free paper

Printed in Great Britain by
St Edmundsbury Press Ltd, Bury St Edmunds, Suffolk

Contents

Two young Frenchmen, friends of Arthur Young, tour and record Britain's economic landscape, from the Fens to the Moray Firth and the Great Glen; home via the Boyne, Dublin and North Wales

The Fens in winter from Denver Sluice to Wisbech and Peterborough, where Alexandre was game to climb one of the cathedral towers for the view of Fen landscape; great embankments and serried drainage-windpumps; a drowned landscape drained

Tantalising views of the FitzWilliam house at Milton, and Burghley House at Stamford; a spectacular marble in St Martin's, Stamford; Leicestershire stallions on the Great North Road; the splendid Angel at Grantham; Nottingham's new General Hospital; Thoresby, Clumber, Welbeck and Worksop; the Roche Abbey idyll

Bog-reclamation at Doncaster; the Walker foundries at Rotherham; Wentworth Woodhouse and Wentworth Castle; Leeds, the General Infirmary and the Cloth Halls

York's walls, castle, Assembly Rooms, Minster and (keeping the best to the last!) Dr Hunter's Asylum; Harrogate; the extraordinary beauty of Fountains Abbey; the cattle of Bakewell's disciples near Northallerton; Durham's grandeur concealed by fog

Newcastle, the coal metropolis, its river and its chaldron-wagons; Morpeth; Caucot beside the Coquet; Alnwick Castle, its battlements and Georgian

'Travel in the younger sort is a part of education;
in the older, a part of experience.'

Francis Bacon: 'Of Travel'

'He did not crawl through museums
as if preparing for an examination.'

Cyril Connolly on 'The Grand Tour'

Illustrations

Below, sample page from Alexander's first notebook, cf p. 10 for translation, the last nine lines or so above the sketch of Denver Sluice.

Credits

The author and publishers are very grateful to the following owners and trustees of copyright for permission to publish:

Dust jacket: The Duke of Argyll's Estate

Frontispiece: The Duke of Northumberland and his Trustees

Title-page, 4, 5, 6, 8, 10, 11, 14, 15, 20, 21, 22, 27, 31, 33, 34, 41, 43, 46, 49, 52, 58, 59, 62, 66, 67, 69:   G. F. Cordy

1:   Mme G Etienne, Directeur des Archives départementales de l'Oise, Beauvais

2:   Le Marquis de Amodio, Verteuil

3:   Mme Sonia Matossian, La Rochefoucauld

7, 12, 13, 16, 19, 26, 28, 29, 32, 35, 38, 50, 51, 54, 55, 57:   the author

9:   The Bodleian Library, University of Oxford (Gough Maps 26, fol 6)

17:   Doncaster Metropolitan Borough Council

18:   Sheffield City Council

23:   York City Council

24:   Oblong Creative Ltd, Mary Wragg and Giles Worsley

25:   The Walker-Neesam Archive

30:   Newcastle City Council

36, 40:   City of Edinburgh Council

37, 39, 53:   National Galleries of Scotland

42:   Perth & Kinross Council

44:   Aberdeen City Council

45:   Priscilla, Lady Burton

47:   Mrs Edwin Smith

60, 61:   Glasgow City Council

63, 64, 65:   Renfrewshire Council

68:   Birmingham University Library

70, 71:   Le Duc de La Rochefoucauld d'Estissac

Notes on the Translation and Bibliography

As with my two earlier books of La Rochefoucauld travels, I have not thought it desirable to create some notional 1780s English: where 'it is' seems too formal, I have invariably preferred 'it's' to ''tis'. Within the limits of 18th-century manners, their travel notebooks are very informal. In chapters 6, 7, 8 and 9, Lazowski's letter-book (of letters from Scotland to the duc de Liancourt), the manner is slightly tutorial, as if he were addressing Alexandre, instead of his father: but how very well informed he made himself.

I have deposited at Ipswich, in the Suffolk Record Office, the complete microfilm of the 1786 travel notebooks of Alexandre de La Rochefoucauld, so generously made available to me by his direct descendant, the Duke d'Estissac.

As I explain early on in the Preface, Sir John Sinclair's *Statistical Account of Scotland* covers, in 21 volumes published between 1791 and 1799, the state of the individual parishes of Scotland in the decade immediately following the visit of these two enquiring Frenchmen. Naturally, there are references to these volumes on many of the pages on Scotland at the heart of this book. The *Statistical Account of Scotland* is as clumsy a title to the eye as it is to the tongue. I therefore draw attention, here at the outset, to the fact that I have generally shortened it to its simple initials, *SAS*.

My most frequent references to contemporary diaries are to John Byng's *The Torrington Diaries, Tours through England and Wales, 1781–1794*, 4 vols, 1934, reprinted 1970: often here abbreviated to Byng.

I also refer frequently to Howard Colvin's *Dictionary of British Architects, 1600–1840*, 3rd edn 1995: here often abridged to Colvin.

Other architectural references are to John Harvey's *English Medieval Architects to 1550*, 1984, and to Pevsner, short-hand for the 'Buildings of England' series, founded by Nikolaus Pevsner, many vols now revised by Bridget Cherry. They are being supplemented by three comparably valuable series: the 'Buildings of Scotland', 'Buildings of Wales' and 'Buildings of Ireland', Total so far, almost 60 vols.

Notes on Measurements and Currency Values

Arthur Young travelled extensively in France in 1787–90, and his observations are invaluable in interpreting the prices and measurements noted by his three French friends during their English tour in 1785. Constantia Maxwell grouped Young's reckonings in her edition of his *Travels in France* (CUP, 1929), on pp. 405–07.

Currency

In Young's day the *livre*, which equalled 20 *sous*, or *sols*, was worth $10^{1}/2$d ($10^{1}/2$ 'old' English pennies, before the decimalization of our coinage). A *livre* was thus worth seven-eighths of one English shilling. The three Frenchmen used the English word 'shilling' instead of trying to convert it into the precise French equivalent. And a *sou* was equal approximately to a halfpenny (half of one 'old' penny).

24 livres	=	the French *louis d'or* (or the English guinea).
23 livres	=	the English pound sterling.
6 livres	=	the French *louis d'argent*, or *écu*, which was equal to the English crown, or 5 shillings (25 'new' pence).

How many debased modern English pounds a 1785 pound sterling was worth is hard to calculate.

Measures

Young wrote: 'In France, the infinite perplexity of the measures exceeds all comprehension. They differ not only in every province but in every district, and almost in every town, and these tormenting variations are found equally in the denominations and contents of the measures of land and corn.'

In these journals of their English tour, it is clear that the Frenchmen, well aware of the variations (which were not confined to France), tended to equate the *arpent* with the acre, and use the French and English words interchangeably, though at one point (*A Frenchman's Year in Suffolk, 1784*, p. 27) François reckoned an *arpent* varied between $1/2$ and $5/6$ of an acre.

In linear measurement, these are the basic measures (variable, of course):

1 *pied de roi*	=	.3267 of a metre = (roughly) 1 foot
6 *pieds*	=	1 *toise* (a fairly common measure)
20 *pieds*	=	1 *perche*
2,200 *toises*	=	1 *lieu* (or league)
1 *lieu*	=	4,400 yards = $2^{1}/2$ miles

And in 1790, Dorothy Wordsworth and her brother, walking through France, reckoned one lieu (or league) = 3 miles (E. de Selincourt, *Dorothy Wordsworth*, Oxford, 1933, p. 27).

Foreword

Readers who enjoyed *A Frenchman's Year in Suffolk* and *Innocent Espionage* had been eagerly expecting the last part of the La Rochefoucauld trilogy. They will not be disappointed by the present volume, even though the previous trio of travellers has been reduced to two: Alexandre de La Rochefoucauld and his Polish mentor, Maximilien de Lazowski. The former's travel notes make up most of the travel book, though Lazowski comes into his own while they're in Scotland: both are published here for the first time. They will be a mine of data for historians and a source of pleasure for general readers. Moreover, thanks to Norman Scarfe's prodigious industry, copious footnotes supply much additional and useful information, on the towns – and villages – which the two Frenchmen visited, the monuments and country houses they contemplated, the people they met – and the inns where they stayed (it is amazing how many of them have survived).

The stereotype about the frivolity of 18th century French noblemen does not fit Alexandre de La Rochefoucauld (though he was only 18 in 1786), except for a few brief remarks about the prettiness (or plainness) of young women. Indeed, the two travellers had a hard time. They started their journey on 14 March, in snow and frost, and discovered too late that 'the only practicable season for visiting the North [of Britain] is midsummer'; on 9 April, Alexandre felt 'frozen to the bone'. Some of the roads they followed were pretty bad (the gig which accompanied them must have been strongly-built!); Lazowski and his boatmen had a narrow escape from drowning in the rapids of Loch Etive.[1] Nonetheless, the two men progressed very fast: 'we run, instead of travelling, complained Lazowski. My companion wishes only to move from place to place'. And Alexandre admitted, after covering 39 miles within one day, that it was 'a long haul'. Moreover, the travellers spent much time upon recording their journey; one can wonder when Lazowski claims: 'I write four hours at least every day', but, in Glasgow, on 7 May, Alexandre noted: 'We scarcely went out and spent most of our time writing up our journals'. Admirable serious-ness![2]

On the other hand, the Frenchmen had no complaints about lodgings and food, even in Northern Scotland, inasmuch as innkeepers did not overcharge. At The Ship, in Inverbervie, north of Montrose, Lazowski wrote: 'compared with the English inns this is pitiful, but it's very much better than the great majority of those on the Continent that are away from the main roads. Here we have good bread, game, good beer, wine, and even a sweet course . . . this is a Scottish usage . . . For

---

[1] Infra, pp. 96, 98, 186.
[2] Pp. 222, 219, 204.

xv

breakfast we are given various kinds of dry cakes [scones], with butter and jam, usually orange [marmalade].' The next day, between Stonehaven and Aberdeen, the only inn was 'less a house than a cabin . . . a poor inn, unsupplied with bread, so that we had to make do with oat-cakes. And yet there wasn't too much to complain of: one can dine well enough, with veal cutlets, fresh eggs and slices of grilled beef'.[3]

In the Highlands, there was 'no choice of inns . . . Obviously they aren't very sophisticated, but it's impossible to find them wretched or inadequate. You always seem to be able to find tea, sugar, rum and wine; and to eat, as we did here [Portnacroish], fresh eggs, calf's head ragoût, boiled chicken, and an excellent bullock's tongue, with a potato cake'.[4]

Actually, the only unpleasant experience the travellers had was at the General's Hut, on the shore of Loch Ness, where the kitchen was 'at the same time the family's parlour and bedroom . . . The light gets in only through a door which serves as door, chimney and window'; moreover, 'our great horror was to find that the whole family had scabies. However, one has to eat; but we couldn't face the oat cake [kneaded by their hands]; after putting on a pair of gloves, I was ready to eat fresh eggs', plus tea, milk, cheese and some very good rum. Alexandre added: 'I daresay this description makes you feel sorry for us, but good travellers feel challenged rather than discouraged when they are exploring enthralled'.[5]

The purpose of Alexandre's and Lazowski's journey was to study Scottish agriculture. Actually, as Scotland is only reached on p. 101 of this book, it also contains much information about farming in England. The tourists lost no opportunity to enquire about the rotations of crops which were practised in the areas they went through (and also about rentals). Indeed, the traditional three-field rotation had disappeared, to the benefit of varied, longer and more complex systems, even though periods of fallow survived in some places. One feels the influence of Arthur Young in the not unfrequent praise of enclosures. In Scotland, they found farming backward relatively to England, at least in two of the three 'divisions', which Alexandre – quite accurately – distinguished. Along most of the Eastern and South-Western coasts, 'the land is ungrateful, but the peasant gives everything to clear a part of it', and Alexandre thought he had achieved some progress. As for the Highlands, 'for arable purposes [they] are virtually unclearable'. In the third division, however, i.e. the Lowlands, from the Clyde estuary to the Firth of Forth, 'the people have proved themselves. They've cleared their lands, working daily to improve them . . . In these richer parts, one has a sense of real opulence'.[6]

An interesting point is that, both in England and in Scotland, the kind of landscape which most appealed to Alexandre and Lazowski was a densely populated and well-cultivated countryside (and better still if it also had some industry). When

3 Pp. 144, 147. However, Alexandre found the meat 'wretched'.
4 Pp. 184. Other good meals: in Aberdeen, 'a roast chicken, a lobster, veal cutlets, potatoes and carrots'; at Bonawe, 'very good dinner: an entire pig . . . and the best port wine I've ever drunk' (pp. 152, 179).
5 Pp. 166–67.
6 P. 223.

approaching Dumbarton, 'the route is superb on account of the goodness of the soil . . . The whole country is enclosed and well farmed', with, in addition, 'an abundance of manufactures'. The next day, the way to Glasgow was 'charming': 'You go through farmlands, almost all of them enclosed, with very good soil and equally good farming, and with a large number of houses, mills and manufactures. Nothing could be finer than the whole of this route'.[7] Earlier in the tour, as they approached Leeds, Alexandre had admired 'a beautiful valley that contains both a canal and a river and is built over with immense numbers of houses. I think it's the richest view I can remember looking at. This derives from the abundance of coal mines, which fuel the manufacturing that makes people so comfortably off . . .'.[8]

Alexandre's attitude is typical with men of the Enlightenment, to whom economic development was the pre-condition for human happiness. A point of view which also explains Alexandre's reaction when visiting a cotton mill, near Paisley, where the many machines were 'worked only by children, of whom some work all day, and others all night'; he stressed 'the value of employing numbers of children, who couldn't make another industry thrive . . . in the year or so that this mill has been working it has been able to provide itself with a small village of 2 or 300 houses'.[9]

On the other hand, the two travellers were rather repelled – at first – by wild, uncultivated scenery and by mountains, which later romantic writers were to admire so much; they are likely to have read Jean-Jacques Rousseau, but they did not share his taste for wilderness. North of Aberdeen, 'the whole aspect of the country is so awful that the pleasure of travelling is nil . . . The views over the landscape are very melancholy, almost wholly uncultivated and extremely hilly'. Between Elgin and Nairn, 'there is no point in my detailing the route for it is all disagreeable . . . Without agriculture or trade, everything seems impoverished'. A few days later, however, feelings changed. Alexandre was much impressed by the waterfall of Foyers, near Loch Ness, 'in the most romantic scenery'; it was 'much more beautiful than I have been able to describe: it is a combination of wilderness, a beauty rarely found, the fall itself, and the abundance of water'; then, in mountainous country, 'you come upon delightful view-points'. Nonetheless, Alexandre added: 'The bareness of great areas of these mountains . . . is a sad and wretched story'.[10]

A similar mixture of feelings emerged during the days which followed. Lazowski wrote of 'the enjoyment of great landscapes . . . the views are large and often very imposing'; to Alexandre, 'the horror of this route [to Tarbet] contains beauty of a kind' and he found Loch Lomond 'more beautiful than I can say . . . the scenery is magnificent'. But his 'General Observations' on Scotland show that his conversion from utilitarian to romantic was not complete . . . 'The main aspect of Scotland is

---

7   Pp. 196, 199.
8   P. 54; this mention of coal gives me the opportunity of joining Norman Scarfe in his tribute to our common friend, the late Professor John Harris, who stressed the importance of coal-fuel technology as a factor of the Industrial Revolution.
9   P. 214.
10   Pp. 154, 155, 158, 159, 167–68, 169.

discouraging: a mountain Kingdom . . . It seems a land of great sadness . . . Scotland could never become what one would call "pretty" country, *un joli pays* . . . Yet the Highlands . . . are certainly wonderfully agreeable for their beautiful variety, their setting among the lochs and the rivers: most delightful'.[11]

As far as architecture was concerned, the two travellers had rather conventional tastes – of their times. They liked palladian and neo-classical buildings and did not much admire medieval churches, especially those which, unlike in France, had wooden roofs instead of stone vaults. In Glasgow, Lazowski wrote: 'The cathedral is an old Gothic building not worth going to find. But two modern churches are of a taste that pleased me infinitely', especially St. Andrew's, which is 'modelled on the antique classical style'. As for Gloucester cathedral, it is 'a fine old building but too long, and the pillars are much too stout'.[12]

To return to Scotland, as soon as the Frenchmen had entered it, they felt it was poorer than England. Near Dunbar, 'the farmhouses . . . lack the prosperous, comfortable air of English farms'; in the town, houses were not well kept, 'everything suggests meanness', in contrast with English towns, 'so neat and often looking so prosperous'. Around Edinburgh, things were different, houses were again 'clean and well-built', like in England; and Alexandre was pleased by Perth: 'I'd love to live here if I lived in Scotland – a country I would not chose for my domicile'. But later on, there was again deterioration. After passing Montrose, Alexandre wrote: 'The further we go north, the fewer the signs of comfort; or, to be blunt, the more signs of poverty . . . The people live miserably'. Fish is 'their staple food, with potatoes and oat-cakes'. From Nairn to Inverness, 'none of the land . . . is cultivated, all of it underpopulated. The dwellings are made of earth, with clods of turf for roofing; the bleakest picture of poverty'. Near Fort William, things may have been worse; people lived in 'primitive houses which are all but unspeakable, the picture of poverty, inside as well as out . . . The usual sustenance . . . is oat-cakes, instead of bread, and potatoes during the summer. To which they add milk and butter . . . The women work, usually in rather dirty work . . . One of their jobs is spreading manure on the land with their hands'.[13]

In his 'General Observations', Alexandre stressed again 'Scotland's poverty': it was 'mainly a wild, uncivilized land, some of it scarcely able to support the lives of its people, but in many parts working their hardest to transform it', so that 'in 20 years' time, the country will be unrecognisable and very comfortably off'. We have already mentioned his praise of farmers' efforts to improve their land; he also observed progress in other sectors. 'It's lovely to see quite a thriving commerce in the various places where it is now established; and to find in a land so empty and desolate, so sparsely endowed, towns as robustly commercial as Glasgow and Paisley'. It is remarkable that, on the base of information from Professor John Millar, Alexandre mentions that the merchants of Glasgow, after American independence had destroyed their large tobacco trade, 'poured their energies' and their capital 'into manufactures' and

[11] Pp. 181, 195, 196, 224–25.
[12] Pp. 199 n. 13, 243.
[13] Pp. 102–103, 104, 132 n. 20, 144, 172.

specially in the cotton industry – a problem which modern economic historians have much discussed. And he wisely observed: 'This leads me to think that the loss of America has not damaged England's purse so much as her pride'.[14]

Alexandre had a favourable opinion of Scotsmen: 'The character of this nation is tremendously enterprising . . . They are straightforward . . . fundamentally trustworthy and open, hard working and intelligent . . . a fine, good people, fit for anything'. His only reservations were that the Scots were 'perhaps a shade less polished than the English . . . not so clean as the English . . . and generally keener on drinking than the English'. One cannot refrain from quoting him: 'The Scots would do anything for what they call "a dram of whiskey", that is, about two glasses of whiskey, which is distilled from grain and of such potency that I could only manage half a glass. But the Scots drink great quantities and can do nothing without "a drop". Here they start drinking from the moment they wake up; a stable-boy can't start working with his horses until he's drunk the usual "drop" '.[15]

Alexandre and Lazowski took a special interest in the Highlanders, 'a people apart', 'of unique culture' – a culture which, they guessed, would be 'spoiled all too quickly, by the alien world, and possibly by themselves'. They were impressed by their 'wretched deprivation': 'They live on little. The idea of liberty makes them live'. Still the two travellers mention serious shortcomings: Highlanders were 'given to theft', 'notably lazy'; they drank 'truly unbelievable quantities' of whiskey, plus brandy and rum. Though the tourists understood 'how important the question of *breeches* is', they were rather shocked when they did see men in traditional dress: 'The knees and part of the thighs are bare, which seems very indecent to us'. Nonetheless, Alexandre wrote: 'Now I'm leaving these people I truly love: I'm perhaps biased towards them by their beauty and the simplicity of their manners'.[16]

An additional reason is that the travellers discovered – at least among a few men they met – an attachment to the Jacobite cause, which they probably overestimated, but which was attractive to Frenchmen. They report that Highlanders 'speak of the present king of England only with contempt and will never call him king, referring to him merely as *George*, or even *The Governor*. When they spoke of the Old Pretender, it was only as "king James" . . . [they] show you the wounds they received in his service . . . They can't speak of Culloden without getting heated'. Actually, two eyewitnesses are specifically mentioned: their innkeeper at Fort William, who 'served under the flag of Prince Charles Edward, and was at the battle of Culloden', and a boatman, whom Lazowski questioned about the prince: 'His first response was to raise the sleeve of his jacket and show me a long scar on his wrist: "My memento of Culloden" '. Indeed, the battle had been fought just forty years earlier, and the two veterans must have been close to sixty . . . at least.[17]

The liking which the travellers felt for Scotsmen did not extend to the inhabit-

---

14 Pp. 224, 226; also 205, 210.
15 Pp. 224, 225, 226.
16 Pp. 161, 175, 176, 197, 198, 223, 226.
17 Pp. 178, 181.

ants of Ireland, to which they paid a brief visit in May 1786. They were struck by the country's poverty, but it seemed to them 'the result of the great idleness, and even more of the stupid simplicity, of the inhabitants. I have never yet seen a man here working what I call hard . . . It's unfortunate that a people so stupid and idle goes with such lovely land'; their 'sole aptitude is evidently drinking'. Obviously, Alexandre and Lazowski had no idea that Ireland had serious political problems.[18]

Indeed, this travel account does not include any comment of a political nature (except those on Jacobite feelings which have just been mentioned). Possibly Alexandre was not interested in politics; unlike his father and his elder brother, he was not to side clearly during the French Revolution. But this gap is largely made up by his gift as an observer and by the many intelligent remarks he made during his tour. Moreover, this book is full of interesting and/or amusing details: the hygienic 'English privvies' at Nottingham hospital, the railway – 'specially constructed tracks' for coal wagons – at Newcastle, the 'paltry salaries' of Edinburgh professors, who were paid so much per pupil ('if a professor's lectures are dull, his class dwindles and his salary is reduced to nothing'), the large exports of carriages from Edinburgh to France are only a few examples among many gems.[19]

However, the climax of the tour was certainly the meeting in Edinburgh with Adam Smith, 'a man of prodigious knowledge', whose *Wealth of Nations* 'is known in Europe as marking an epoch in the understanding of the principles of trade and finance' (a penetrating remark, just ten years after the famous book's publication). A. Smith took the travellers to meet the Principal of the University, William Robertson, and he also had them to dinner, with the chemist Joseph Black. It is a pity that Lazowski gives no details about the conversation on those occasions; he only mentions he told A. Smith that his own 'greatest desire is that he [Smith] should carry through "une histoire philosophique" which he is in a better position than any other author to do and which he intends to write'.[20] Alas, the Master died three years later. As for the most moving passage in this remarkable volume, it comes right at the beginning (p. 7): when he left Bury St. Edmunds, Alexandre had the 'tremendous pleasure . . . to find that I felt as completely at home in some English houses as I did in my father's home: always welcome, and able to come and go as I pleased.'

François Crouzet
Professor Emeritus
The Sorbonne

---

[18] P. 228.
[19] Pp. 24–25, 83–84, 114, 118.
[20] Pp. 121, 123, 124.

Preface and Acknowledgements

Richard Ollard, reviewing *Innocent Espionage* with his observant, expert eye, noticed the way 'its generous type area with footnotes reflects the 18th century at its best'. Others mentioned the interesting contents of the footnotes. Editors and translators of travel-journals, or of almost any text, have to choose between two ways of serving it up: either with commentary from the foot of the page, or with linking-passages that share the whole page with the original text, but tend thereby to interfere with its continuity. The choice, in this case, is fairly evenly balanced. I have generally chosen to supply my commentary and notes from the foot of the page. (Neither I nor my publishers gave a thought to hiding footnotes away at the end of each chapter or of the book; a convenience to no one.) With commentary at the foot of the page in numbered notes, the reader can ignore or read them in a way that causes least interruption of the main narrative. Sometimes, usually at the beginning of a chapter, I have varied the general practice, and moved on to the main area of the page with the young Frenchmen.

A lot of what merit my commentary may possess we owe to my friend Richard Wilson, Professor of History at the University of East Anglia. Six years ago he contributed indispensably to the Appendix on the Norwich Textile Industry, included in the 1995 reprint of *A Frenchman's Year in Suffolk, 1784*, drawing attention to the exceptional acuteness of Lazowski on the Norwich industry. At about the same time, I mentioned to him that the core of this present volume was an account, by Lazowski and Alexandre, of a 5-week tour of Scotland in 1786. He instantly told me of the enormous advantage I would have in being able to make use of Sir John Sinclair's *Statistical Account of Scotland*: and sure enough, the initials *SAS*, to which I have shortened the title, appear in notes on very many of the pages on Scotland at the heart of this book. Twenty-one stout (and beautifully bound) volumes of Sinclair's work appeared over the years 1791–9, containing detailed descriptions of the economic and social state of Scotland's 938 parishes. They were drawn up by him from the reports of the different ministers (or occasionally the schoolmasters) over those years, which of course were close enough to 1786 to yield extremely useful comparative and supplementary material for me to set the observations of Alexandre and Lazowski against.

The ministers of the parochial districts were supplied with a list of no fewer than 63 subjects to try to cover in their replies. (If Alexandre and Lazowski had toured Scotland a dozen years later, most of their questions would have been answered in these compendious volumes, but of course their object was to see for themselves.) The questions included description of soil, mode of cultivation, number of proprietors and whether resident, implements of husbandry, manures, quantity and value of each crop, price of grain and provisions, wages and price of labour, commerce, manufactures, inns, roads and bridges, harbours, ferries, and so on: the very subjects the keen-eyed Frenchmen were looking out for, including 'character of the people'. The volumes of the *SAS* have almost always enabled me to make good the late M Marchand's excisions in Lazowski's enthusiastic descriptions of Scottish farming improvements, which seemed, alas, to him, librarian of the *Assemblée Nationale*, intolerably tedious. Scotland, alone in the British Isles and probably in the world, has this remarkably complete statistical record of its economic condition in the 1790s. There is nothing comparable for England. Arthur Young, when he was Secretary to the Board of Agriculture in 1794–6, tried to achieve something comprehensive in the way merely of local Reports on English farming. They fell hopelessly short of Sir John Sinclair's *SAS* (ironically, for their comparative failure derived from the discordant personalities of Sinclair and Young: as President of the Board of Agriculture, Sinclair treated Young, according to Young, as 'nothing more than a first clerk'). Young's *Travels in France* did much to even the score.

Other printed sources that have been useful in this edition start with *The Beauties of Scotland* (5 vols, 1805–8, edited by Robert Forsyth). Unusually for such series, it included, as well as many beauties, accounts of local farming and manufacture; and its 5th volume was dedicated to Sir John Sinclair. Boswell's *Journal of a Tour to the Hebrides* (brilliantly combined with Johnson's *Journey to the Western Islands of Scotland*, in a Folio Society volume, in 1990, and edited by Peter Levi) is really more an illustration of the beginnings of Boswell's incomparable *Life of Johnson* than it is about Scotland, where Boswell was largely 'at home'. Where they coincided with my Frenchmen, though thirteen years earlier, in 1773, Boswell arranged VIP treatment for Johnson: at Fort George, Sir Eyre Coote and his agreeable wife gave them a 3pm dinner party in the Governor's house. After saving Madras at Wandewash in 1759, Coote had returned home in 1770. He gave them 'a dinner of two complete courses, variety of wines and the regimental band playing outside in the square after dinner'. Johnson: 'I shall always remember this fort with gratitude.' The Frenchmen's visit to Fort George was more incognito and 'low key' by design: they could not have wandered round observantly, as they certainly did here, if they were being treated like the celebrity Dr Johnson had already become. Lazowski formed an unfavourable opinion of Dr Johnson: 'well treated and kindly received everywhere, he can only speak ill'. That this opinion was too quickly formed may be judged from Lazowski's reproach that Johnson had never gone to Edinburgh: yet *A Journey to the Western Isles* actually starts with Johnson leaving Edinburgh after a 4-day stay. Even their fascination with the Highlands sprang from different causes, and produced very different effects.

Thomas Pennant set out from N Wales on a first *Tour in Scotland* in 1769; a second, in 1772, included the Hebrides. He was accompanied by an excellent draughtsman, Moses Griffiths, many of whose drawings were engraved by P. Mazell (see Pl 43 and ch 7, fns 44 and 76). He supplied evidence of the incomplete success of the 1746 proscription of the tartan (see ch 7, fn 105), and had Joseph Banks's permission to publish the celebrated drawings of Staffa by a member of Banks's team. In 1780, the Rev Charles Cordiner published *Antiquities & Scenery of the North of Scotland in a series of letters to Thomas Pennant* (Pl 46). In 1778, when a bishop decried Pennant for inaccuracy, Johnson defended him warmly: 'He's a whig, sir; a sad dog. But he's the best traveller I ever read; he observes more things than anyone else does.' Neither Alexandre nor Lazowski makes reference to Pennant, but like the later *SAS*, he serves as a valuable editorial check on their descriptions in 1786. So does Jabez Maude Fisher (1775–9), *An American Quaker in the British Isles* (ed K. Morgan, 1992). Marc de Bombelles, whose *Journal de Voyage en Grande Bretagne et en Irlande, 1784* was published by the Voltaire Foundation at Oxford in 1989 and whose title naturally took my interest, turned out to be an unemployably boring minor diplomat who was sent to Britain for a few months in 1784 to get him out of the Abbé de Breteuil's way. He served only to make me even prouder of Alexandre and Lazowski.

Among the most enjoyable of the later Georgian travellers in Scotland are a Frenchman, Louis Simond; Dorothy Wordsworth; and Robert Southey. Of Simond I need only say that, after living twenty years in the USA, he brought his English wife to spend 1810 and 1811 in Britain, and published a *Journal of a Tour and Residence in Great Britain* in Edinburgh, by 'A French Traveller', in 1815, and under his own name in 1817. He has written it in his own good English. The Scottish visit was spent mostly in Edinburgh and Glasgow. They got as far north as Dalmally, where Simond described the wheel-less carts (two poles dragged behind a horse) that Alexandre saw and sketched 25 years earlier between Fort Augustus and Fort William (see p. 171, pl 52). Dorothy Wordsworth's *Recollections of a Tour Made in Scotland* (1803) and *Journal of my Second Tour in Scotland* (1822, made with Joanna Hutchinson, her younger sister-in-law) appear in *Journals of Dorothy Wordsworth*, Vols I and II, 1959, edited by E de Selincourt. Southey's *Journal of a Tour in Scotland in 1819* (accompanied by Thomas Telford, the gifted canal-builder and engineer, and their friend John Rickman, the statistician, who brought his wife and two children), like Dorothy Wordsworth's writing, I hope, scarcely needs my recommendation. The latest edition of this delightful work of Southey appears to be C. H. Herford's, back in 1929. A new edition is overdue.

The 3rd edition of Sir Howard Colvin's *Biographical Dictionary of British Architects, 1600–1840*, one of the most perfect works of its kind, has proved endlessly invaluable. In following these Frenchmen in their 1786 tour, I have met with even more kindness from Museum and Gallery directors and their staffs and Archivists and Librarians and their staffs, than I did when I was following their 1785 travels. For, since *Innocent Espionage* appeared in 1995, there has been more wholesale cutting of expert museum, library and archive staff, often in the current belief that 'Leisure' is more important than Learning and Culture, and that management skills should take priority over professional understanding of what is being managed. The help I've received from so many kind and expert archivists, Local Studies librarians and Museum and Gallery curators, makes me the more indebted, and profoundly grateful, for their dedication.

My detailed obligations to scholars are recorded in the text and footnotes, and I can only express my general thanks to all of them here. But some historians, librarians, archivists and curators have been exceptionally kind. I must mention the steady encouragement of John Rogister, of Durham University, most particularly for revealing to me, at Versailles, Lazowski's substantial manuscript *Tour of Switzerland in 1786*; Sir Howard Colvin, not only for his incomparable *Biographical Dictionary of British Architects*, but for showing me the correct architectural term to describe the front double staircase at Wentworth Woodhouse; John Harris, Roy Young and Ruth Harman too, for being so helpful over Wentworth; in Edinburgh, Nick Phillipson's warm encouragement on the whole Enlightenment background to the La Rochefoucauld visit, and Andrew Bethune's help in the Edinburgh Room in the Central Library; Christopher Fleet, of Scotland's National Map Library; Robert and Katrina Clow of Aiket Castle, Dunlop, for unstinted hospitality and most expert guidance to Glasgow and its treasures; in Paisley Museum and Art Gallery, Dan Coughlan matched Alexandre's enthusiasm for Paisley's textile products, particularly their machine-embroidered gauzes, with his own devotion to the historic looms and textile-collections in his care; it was he who identified Johnston as the 'latest' textile mill with its own small but burgeoning new town, 3 miles from Paisley.

As to the production of the book, I am, over the decades, much indebted to Geoff Cordy for his unfailing kindness and expertise in translating my microfilm and some very challenging prints into delightful illustrations; equally to Richard and Helen Barber and their Boydell staff, especially Caroline Palmer, Pam Cope, Elaine Townsend and Pru Harrison for the magic transformation from typescript into book, I'm immeasurably grateful; my friend the distinguished typographer Jeremy Greenwood has done me the kindness of reading and commenting on all the proofs; most of all I owe to Paul Fincham, for his constant companionship on the trail of those young Frenchmen, for his patience with the temperamental word-processor, to say nothing of the temperamental author. In her index, Meg Davies has admirably interpreted the dual rôle of the footnotes, as commentary on the narrative and on the sources of that commentary.

My thanks to the La Rochefoucauld family I have tried to indicate in the book's dedication. François Crouzet, of The Sorbonne, foremost authority on the relative prosperity of Britain and France in the 18th century and doyen of economic historians of the period, has interrupted his formidably full programme and, with characteristic kindness, contributed the Foreword to this book. I am profoundly grateful to him.

Introduction

This book is based on the travel-journals of two Frenchmen: one of them Alexandre de La Rochefoucauld, 18, the second son of the Duc de La Rochefoucauld-Liancourt, an enlightened benefactor of France; the other Maximilien de Lazowski, son of a court official of King Stanislas at Lunéville in Lorraine: there he was noticed by the duke, who was so struck with his manner and conversation that he at once engaged him as *précepteur* for his two sons, 'not for the common purposes of education but to travel with them'. This had little to do with 'the Grand Tour'. The duke believed in a practical education: he had already in 1780 begun to found the earliest *écoles des arts et métiers* at home in Liancourt, in Châlons-sur-Marne, and further afield. At 14 and 16 his own two eldest boys set out with Lazowski to look at France for 18 months, more at her farming and trade than her architecture and art. Then, after a brief break, they arrived here in Britain. 'At Dover I first noticed the air of contentment of the country I was entering: I saw that all kinds of people – the neighbouring countrymen, even the servants – were well clothed and, above all, very clean: that the furniture of their houses was all made of mahogany, even in our inn, including tables, which are so dear in France. I saw several carts, all harnessed to good horses with good trappings. I felt myself transported into another world.' As Voltaire had been, in England in the 1730s.

For the whole of 1784 they were based on Bury St Edmunds in Suffolk, where they soon fell in with Arthur Young, a famous agronomist (farming expert), and the four of them soon began to transform one another's lives and a good deal of history. Young told them how and where to study 'improved' farming in Great Britain: and this is what Lazowski, now 38, and the duke's second son, Alexandre, are still doing in this volume, in 1786, in a great sweep up through north-east England and, anticlockwise, right round Scotland as far as the Moray Firth and the Great Glen, and down to Glasgow and Paisley; and briefly over to the Boyne and Dublin; then home through North Wales and the Cotswolds and (presumably) Dover.

So this is the third volume of a trilogy. The first was largely written by the elder brother, François, then 18 and the most gifted writer of the three travellers. As it's largely one man's work, I called it *A Frenchman's Year in Suffolk, 1784*. As it was based on their stay of fourteen months in Bury, François felt able to get, and give, the measure of the pleasant hierarchic society around Bury, and even a sense of the wider society of Suffolk. (In a delightful excursion they inspected north Norfolk, and the Norfolk coast; and in another they ventured south with Arthur Young to the Stour valley and, *very* briefly, to north Suffolk, where they were determined to look at Heveningham Hall, the last word in interiors by James Wyatt and exteriors by Sir Robert Taylor and Capability Brown. Their visit there on 25 July coincided beautifully with the completion of almost every detail of that superb interior, so that their

1

1. *Ancestral home, Liancourt, before the Revolution, engraved by Née, from a drawing by Tavernier. A one-horse gig such as Alexandre and Lazowski used in Britain stands on the right. On the left, the* laiterie *built for Alexandre's mother alone survives: see* A Frenchman's Year in Suffolk, *Pl 6.*

full descriptions are very useful to the present owners, and their professional advisers.) The longish stay at Bury enabled François to venture several essays on general topics: tea-drinking, servants, the apportionment of the day, an Election dinner, young people in society, our special friends, and so on. His observations are shrewd and usefully angled by an intelligent young Frenchman: readable, and indeed re-readable.

The second volume is a very notable travel-journal, based on the notes of the two brothers and their tutor. In February 1785 they left Bury on a well-planned journey of discovery of – among other things of more usual interest – the state of industrial technology in midland England. I called the book *Innocent Espionage*, which was a deliberately challenging title. This was a trip of an 'improving' kind for the useful technological and economic education of the two boys. Their youthful enthusiasm and diligence in observing and recording new industrial and agricultural processes, which might be of use to France, counts, for me, as innocent patriotism until it gets harnessed to an official government, or commercial, organisation. The late Professor J. R. Harris, in his definitive book on *Industrial Espionage and Technology Transfer: Britain and France in the Eighteenth Century* (1998), fairly pointed out that the investigations of these two boys, though in no way government-sponsored, were perhaps not perfectly disinterested.

For instance, a cousin of their father's, whose title their father inherited when the cousin was murdered by a Revolutionary mob in 1794, was trying to 'acclimatize', at

2. *Sophie de Lannion, duchesse de La Rochefoucauld-Liancourt, Alexandre's mother.*

3. *Le duc de La Rochefoucauld-Liancourt, Alexandre's father. Detail from portrait attributed to the Baron Gros.*

3

home in France, the latest improvements in the English stocking manufacture. Passing through Leicester on their way to Derby, the boys looked hard at the Leicester stocking-frames: the elder brother gave up, baffled; 'yet I examined it for half an hour with the greatest attention'. Four days later (after visiting Mr Bakewell the great stock-breeder), they found they managed to follow the workings of Mr Swift's silk and cotton mills at Derby, and François made some intelligible sketches of 'doffer cylinders carrying strips of card clothing'. Then, while the workpeople broke off for their dinner, the Frenchmen made haste to see Lord Scarsdale's superb country house at Kedleston, making notes on its interior and its park before heading for Matlock, and noting some rich artificial meadows.

Do they seem like professional industrial spies? Their enthusiasm's palpable: it's hard to believe these young patriots were being taken advantage of and used by Lazowski or their father, though it can't be denied that the duke had a cotton mill and a calico factory on his own estate, nor that Alexandre set up his own cotton mill ten years later.

Coming to the present book, their principal interest was improved farming, particularly in the different regions of Scotland. On the strength of the farming statistics Lazowski had gathered during their 1785 tour of the industrial Midlands and south-west England, the duke, who was a member of a pretentious and unimpressively 'academic' committee of the French equivalent of a national Board of Agriculture, presented them with Lazowski's 'memorial' of that 1785 tour. He was vexed and mortified by the other members, who thought they knew everything worth knowing about English agriculture, and waved the duke's offering away.

Instead of turning his back on them after this fiasco, his reaction was to expand his friend Lazowski's understanding of Britain's agriculture to include the whole of Scotland and a part of Ireland between Armagh and Dublin, and risk another snub.

In November 1785, Lazowski and Alexandre returned to Bury for a 3-month stay at the comfortable Angel Hotel facing the great 14th-century abbots' gatehouse and the abbey ruins; here Lazowski settled down to a study of farming in Caledonia and a corner of Ireland, and Alexandre renewed and strengthened his Bury friendships. This time, the choice of Bury was obviously determined by Arthur Young's home being at Bradfield, only four miles away; there, at Lazowski's disposal, was Young's remarkable working library and his prodigious working knowledge. I've found no specific reference to Young's help with Lazowski's studies over these three months, beyond Alexandre's remark as they set out for the north: 'Mr Young made us several notes for our tour.' But what could be more interesting and valuable?

There is no mention of this Bury stay by Alexandre and Lazowski in Young's *Autobiography*: though their friendship was close, that delightful work is regrettably patchy. Among their other friends in Bury, John Symonds, Professor of History at Cambridge, was certainly in Bury. He'd been in Paris and reported on the duke's débâcle with that unsatisfactory committee. They had then travelled back to Bury with him in November. On 19 January 1786, they came as his guests to James

Oakes's private ball in the Guildhall (*Innocent Espionage*, p. 237: Dr Jane Fiske's kind information). It's easy to see how Alexandre came to feel 'as completely at home in some English houses as I did in my father's', and how he felt as they left in thick snow and frost on 14 March. (They encountered a heat-wave in the Conway valley later in their tour.)

A letter to Young written by the duke in Paris says that Lazowski, shortly before leaving Bury for Scotland, had sent him 'the most superb memorial on the agriculture of the two kingdoms'. Perhaps the tour's object was partly to check the accuracy of this Bury document? Fortunately the tour you have before you doesn't seem unbalanced in the interests of farming: easily the greatest excitement for them was watching the making of machine-embroidered gauzes at Paisley (Pl 65). For Alexandre, more natural excitement presented itself three days after landing in Ireland. With minor exceptions around Old Meldrum and Banff, he had found the looks of the young Scotswomen disappointing. Things were altogether different as they drove from Lisburn to Hillsborough: 'The girls here are all beautiful, fresh-complexioned and cheerful. They want nothing more than to laugh, with all their hearts . . . they are entirely appetising. We were followed along the road by one who was pretty and *assez x x x* [*sic*!].'

What is harder to understand is why the duke presented Lazowski's 'most superb memorial on the agriculture of the *two* kingdoms' to that 'academic' committee of their Agricultural Board (*l'Administration d'Agriculture*) on 9 June 1786, three weeks or so before Lazowski and Alexandre got back from their 3-month tour. Could he not have waited? It may be that he knew, as I suppose his position (Grand Master of the Wardrobe) at Louis XVI's court at Versailles ensured that he would, that the government of Calonne was in trouble. Once again the duke was unlucky: the memorial actually reached Calonne, but on the brink of his disgrace and fall from power. When he found refuge in England, he brought with him an enormous trunkful of unsorted papers, including Lazowski's 'memorial', presumably unread. There it lies now, securely among *our* Public Records in Chancery Lane; filed under PC 1/123 2946.

The duke's eagerness to present it was certainly not matched by the Controller-General's to receive it. There can be no suggestion that Lazowski's memorial on English and Scottish agriculture was any sort of government-inspired espionage. The promoter was the duke and his interest in bringing improved British farming to Calonne's attention was no more a matter of espionage than it would have been for someone to draw Young's *Travels in France* to the notice of Mr Pitt. The question was put finally into perspective when the French government themselves published this most famous book (more fully entitled *Travels with a View to ascertaining the Cultivation, Wealth, Resources . . . of the Kingdom of France*), together with other helpful items from Young's *Annals of Agriculture*.

So there was no serious question that the duc de Liancourt was implicating his sons, or their *précepteur*, Lazowski, in industrial espionage. They were all of them committed to travelling as education. The boys were interested in seeing for themselves, and reporting to their public-spirited father, the many ways in which English technology, in industry and agriculture, and indeed the manifest condition of defences in English garrisons and ports, had a bearing on the economic and military prosperity of France. They were seriously interested in the ways hospitals in Britain were run, in comparison with their own: in 1785 in Leicester, and in 1786 very notably in Nottingham and York. Friends of a deeply patriotic English publicist and propagandist on British farming, they were thoroughly patriotic young Frenchmen. It was part of their very well attested charm.

Alnwick Castle's defenders

1

Leaving Home

During the winter months in Bury, Alexandre had strengthened friendships and found it painful to leave. As they headed north through snow and frost, one of his Bury friends rode with them, determined to show them the management of his uncle's farm in the Fen, between Downham and Denver. After Brandon, they passed a Lynn merchant's farmhouse with a stable of hunters (and a notable sundial specifying former links with both East and West Indies); also Lord Mountrath's large new house, dismissed by Alexandre as 'small', presumably remembering his own enormous house at Liancourt. He made a simple sketch of Denver Sluice (1750), the first navigation lock in use in the Fen; also a minute sketch of a marsh drainage mill with encased scoop wheel. His friend, Wollaston, left them to return to Bury, while he and Lazowski stayed at Wisbech Rose and Crown in horrible weather: 'slept well, without picking up pen or pencil'.

To Peterborough along the straight bank of the Nene, pausing for food at the Cross Guns Inn, a name that refers to the old punt guns used for Fen fowling: a 2-inch bore and a barrel up to 10 ft! Alexandre sketched one of these, too. He was tremendously impressed by this landscape of great embankments and serried drainage-windmills. By the time he reached Peterborough he was ready to climb one of the cathedral towers for the view, but was perhaps rather jaded by the weather sweeping across the black fen. 'For the farmer in this drowned landscape, the best years are the driest.'

On [Tuesday] 14 March   we were leaving Bury again, to my great regret: more keenly felt than last year, for we'd lived longer in the town, and (if it were possible) we'd been made even more welcome. There, among my close friends, something gave me tremendous pleasure, a pleasure I was aware of this year for the first time in my life: it was to find that I felt as completely at home in some English houses as I did in my father's house: always welcome, and able to come and go as I pleased. More than that, even, if I dare say so, I had made uncomplicated friendships [*amitiés sans intrigue*] which held me in spite of myself and which imposed on me the sadness always experienced when one leaves behind what one loves, or at least what one thought one loved. I've known this feeling only on leaving Paris to come over to this country; and I feel it now very acutely on leaving something [*un objét: it is vexing that, after his recent course of novel-reading he gives no hint whether he's missing a person or a place: it's probably just Bury*] so perfect and that I cannot see it again at all soon.

I'd better admit to anyone who does me the honour of reading this that, towards the end of my stay in Bury, I read some novels: otherwise he may be astounded by my language and alarmed for me. [*I am sure that his father is the first reader he had in mind: it seems ungrateful to wish that Alexandre wrote more to astonish and even alarm him.*] I hope that this confession may reassure him a little on my account and dispose him to read me with the necessary indulgence and patience, but I think he will need to spend his time on something more interesting.

So, we left Bury on the 14th. Mr Young, whom I often mentioned last year, made us several notes for our tour, and our plan was to go to Ely and on to Peterborough. But the weather had grown so appalling, the snow and frost so thick, that that route was no longer thought practicable. We had therefore changed our plan, and decided to go via Newmarket, when Dr Wollaston arrived to say goodbye. Mr Lazowski seemed very fed up because we would not now be going through what in England are called the Fens, and in French *marais* [morass *is the nearest English word*]. He complained so much about the wretched weather that the doctor devised another route. This would enable us after all to see the Fen, which was so interesting both in its natural state and in its methods of cultivation. This route wouldn't be as long as the one we originally planned. We immediately sent after our servants to divert them via Brandon. When we finally got away, it was getting on for 4 o'clock. Mr Lazowski and I rode on horseback, alongside Dr Wollaston's son (a friend of mine who came along to show us an estate his uncle owned). Our two servants rode in the gig. We slept at Brandon, where we arrived rather late.

You cross a landscape quite uncultivated and almost uncultivable. I say 'almost' because Lord Cornwallis, who lives quite near our road,[1] has cleared part of his estate and farmed it. His return is only 3 or 4 shillings an acre, and I think if he were not so good and so disinterested a man he wouldn't do it. But he is so honourable and virtuous that he would act for the benefit of others even if it ended in his own ruin. From Bury to Brandon is 13 miles. Three miles from Bury, you pass Sir Charles Kent's house.[2] Lord Cornwallis's a mile further on, and Lord Keppel's six miles from Brandon – well-built and beautiful.[3]

However, there is nowhere fine in these 3 miles of flat lands[4] to Brandon: only sheep and scrub. You go through a warren: I've never seen so many rabbits. The proprietor claims to make more profit from the sale of them than he would if the land were properly cultivable.

1 At Culford: a handsome house of 1586–91 till remodelled in white mathematical tiles by Samuel Wyatt for Cornwallis, 1790–96. Grounds apparently embellished by Thos. Wright (1711–86), Colvin, *Dict. Brit. Architects*, 1995, p. 1100; and E. Harris, ed, *Thomas Wright's Arbours and Grottos*, 1979. For Cornwallis's kindness to Alexandre and his brother two years earlier, see *A Frenchman's Year in Suffolk, 1784*, pp. 103–5.
2 Fornham St Geneviève: new-built c1785 by Jas Wyatt, Colvin, *Dict Brit Architects*, 1995, p. 1116; H. Davy, *Views of Seats in Suffolk*, 1827; pulled down c1951.
3 Elveden: see H. Davy.
4 Now known as Breckland: see W. G. Clarke, *In Breckland Wilds*, 1926, and Olive Cook, *Breckland*, 1956.

Brandon Chequers   This town sits beside the Little Ouse, navigable as I mentioned when
we were at Thetford in September '84: it also passes Cambridge,[5] contributing to its
beauty. Brandon has nothing worth noting, no commerce, a small town but pretty.[6]
No market. No members of Parliament. We left Brandon on the 15th, arriving at

Downham Crown   (17 miles) going through a little town called Stoke [Ferry] on our
way. Soon after leaving Brandon we found a pleasant house belonging to a Mr
Denton, a farmer and now a merchant, newly enriched, so that he has a house at
[Kings] Lynn, as well as this one. He has a stable of hunters and a number of sad-
dle-horses.[7] The country to Stoke Ferry is just as open and uncultivated as it was the
other side of Brandon. You can tell by looking at the soil, which is full of shells, that the
water once covered it. I forgot to say that, two miles after crossing Brandon Bridge, we
passed in front of Lord Montross's house – newly and very well built, and with an air of
comfort, despite being small.[8] Nothing worthy of remark between here and Stoke:[9]
from Stoke to Downham the road's good, the countryside enclosed and looks
well-farmed. Downham is 17 miles from Bury – long miles.

As soon as we reached Downham, we found out how far it was to Mr Canham's
house, who farmed one of Dr Wollaston's properties. Our plan in coming here was
to see a part of these enormous fens, drained by windmills. We had already provided

5   Easily mis-remembered: both the Cam and the Little Ouse join the Great Ouse.
6   He naturally missed seeing the oldest of industries, flint-knapping, and the wrecking of the
town by motor-traffic in our time. The Chequers has gone.
7   Denton Lodge, Feltwell, built c1770 by Osbert Denton, stands just off their road where a
gibbet stood and a branch leads to Feltwell village. Their eye may have been caught by the
Mansard roof, or the pretty 2-storey bay windows, or the horses. The stables are walled with chalk
and handsome flint (Grimes Graves are close by). Dr John Barney, chief authority on Lynn's
18th-century trade, thinks there were two Osbert Dentons, father and son, by no means in the
front rank of Lynn's merchants, but leaders in corn-export coastwise to Newcastle and Scotland.
This is disappointing, for the most beguiling and remarkable feature of his house is a sundial set in
place of a porch-window, and inscribed with what looks like a significant string of sea-ports
stretching from Bantam (Java), Surat (which Bombay overtook only during the 19th century as
the greatest trading city in W India), and Diu (a Portuguese island just opposite Surat, so close to
it as almost to share its time). When it was midday at Denton Lodge (between the longitudes of
Amsterdam and Lisbon) it was approx VI hours later in Bantam, IV hours back in the Bermudas.
These far-flung trading-posts patently were *not* importers of E Anglian corn! They look more like
17th-century British trading-posts, and one wonders if Osbert Denton was commemorating
either much earlier connections of his family business or, perhaps, early and romantic world-wide
travels of his youth. Bill Wilson is including the list of them in the 2nd vol of his magnificent revi-
sion of Pevsner's *Norfolk*.
8   This is Weeting Hall, seat of the 7th and last earl of Mountrath. Dr Alan Mackley kindly refers
me to Armstrong's *Norfolk*, 1781, vol 6, p. 125: 'Lord M has built a large house in which he
resides. His lordship has also enclosed a park, made many plantations, roads and other valuable
improvements.' Sold in 1808 and much remodelled; demolished 1952. Lynn Lodge survives, the
porter's house that would have greeted them on their way to Downham. *Paterson's Roads*, 1786, p.
151, said 'Near the Cliff [at Hunstanton] is a bathing seat of the Earl of Mountrath.'
9   The small former market-town of Stoke Ferry, still quietly handsome, with late-17th-century
and 18th-century houses, was worthy of a mention; but they were in a great hurry.

ourselves with a letter of introduction to Mr Canham, with the hope that he would demonstrate these drainage-works. We took a post-chaise (Mr Lazowski, my friend Wollaston and me), and found Mr Canham at home. We handed him our letter, soon got talking, and found that he was not only a farmer but also the agent (*homme d'affaires*) of Dr Wollaston. Evidently the proprietor discovered that he had too lively a spirit (*trop d'esprit*) for this employment and had complained of him. Mr Canham's high spirits were no concern of ours, and he was most helpful to us in showing us what we had come to see.

THE FENLAND

We set out from his house on foot, and there we were, right among these mills: on the way he told us many things about this fenland that I will report on my return to Downham.[10] Here we are in what was a drowned countryside: a lost land, barren and nowhere cultivated, until this drainage by means of windmills was undertaken. Every year there are floods; but, provided they don't come in the middle of April, the land yields a good harvest. Dozens of small drains [*saignes*] have been dug to feed the greater surrounding dykes. These come together to form a river, on the banks of which the drainage-mills are established. The rivers feed the two major river-systems, the Ouse and the Nene, which enter the sea not many miles away. They've built great embankments along all the rivers and dykes to prevent them from flooding back across the fenland.[11] The greatest difficulty comes about here, where the sea is close, with its tidal rise and fall. They have had to find a way of regulating the outflow of the river against differences in level caused by the tides. The weight of the river can be built up to give it greater strength to enter the sea: then when the tide rises and the river flows back, the sluice automatically closes against it. There is little fear that the gates won't work adequately without loss of time; but a man is at hand to assist with the opening and closing of the gates, just in case.

4. *Denver Sluice*
(Alexandre's sketch).

10 This reads as if he was making notes as they walked.
11 He was probably looking south from Denver Sluice to the Old Bedford River that had been dug parallel with it in 1651. At Denver Sluice both Bedford rivers rejoined the Great Ouse. The gap between the parallel rivers was a safety reservoir that could be flooded at times of exceptional high water-levels. Denver Sluice's mechanism interested Alexandre so much that he sketched it, rather unsatisfactorily: it serves as a sluice between the tidal mouth of the Ouse and the Bedford rivers.

Alexandre's drawing of the sluice at Denver is opposite. The first one was constructed by Vermuyden in 1651, but would have enabled vessels to pass through only when the waters reached the same level on each side of the sluice. What Alexandre was seeing was the first navigation lock in action, built by Labelye in 1750, effectively 11 metres long and 4 wide, affording a means of transition by the craft from one level to the other. This was replaced by Rennie's lock (23 × 5.5 m) in 1834, the essential structure of which survives today. A sluice for flood-water from the Cam was built in 1957, and more complex arrangements 1959–70 are well explained on a display-board beside the sluices. Alexandre wrote: 'This is so badly drawn that I'm afraid it won't convey anything to anyone.'

To come back to our original subject, when they've remedied the effect of the tidal flow, they've established these mills. Here's a description. They're exactly like an ordinary windmill, their sails perhaps slightly larger. They're always set up beside one of the main drainage dykes, and there doesn't seem to be much difference in size between the big rivers and those cut for the purpose of flood-prevention. Beside the dyke is a canal at a lower level, and at the junction of canal and river is a sluice-gate that shuts when the river-level is higher than that of the canal, and which opens when the water from the mill is higher than the river-level. You notice that the mills can only work when the waters are in their last state heavier than those of the canal. The sluice can't open 2 inches, for if it opens, the waters flood in and destroy the mill. They have to keep the most careful watch on the water-levels, and as soon as they find there's a mere one-inch difference in height, they risk saying goodbye to the mills.

These mills are set up as high as possible, on land capable of bearing the weight of the building: failing that, piles are constructed, which is the best and surest method. These mills are of timber, clad in little planks [clap boarding] much like ours. The only external difference is that you notice, on the side facing the canal and the river, a protrusion, standing about 10ft high and two ft wide, attached to the side of the mill, and clad in the same materials. It contains the scoop-wheel. You see it in this scrap of a drawing. The protrusion marked A is the casing in which a great wheel turns as it scoops up the water, which then leaves the wheel at a higher level. When you go inside, you see this novel construction, something I've never seen. In my various travels I'm very happy when I find remarkable new mechanical techniques. It must be a new idea for anyone who hasn't been here to imagine that, in the small confined space of a windmill, wheels have been devised that, in the end, drain a whole countryside.

5.   *Marsh drainage mill (Alexandre's sketch).*

Here is a rough idea of how it works. The water drained from the fen is led down a steady slope to the mill. A sluice-gate is raised, allowing the water to rush into the mill. [*He then explains the simple principles of mill-races and sluice cut-offs applicable to water-mills through all the centuries. He goes on to explain in detail: the windmill-sails are joined by a cog-wheel to the top of the oak post that rises from the floor to the top of the mill. The water-wheel, or scoop-wheel, was about 27 or 30 ft in circumference, and of course worked from gears connected to the central post. The wheel with its scoops fitted tightly into its walling, spilling none, or very little, of the water. As it turned, it lifted the water 5 ft, and ejected it into a channel specially angled with a slope tilting straight into the river.*]

One of these mills costs as much as 500 *louis* to build [*c1786, 500 louis d'argent* equalled approximately £125]. The great central post requires a tree of real splendour: it must be 14 ft long, about 2.5 ft in diameter at the base, and a foot at the top. I'm told that one would change hands at 30 *louis* [£7.50].

Here we are really only at the beginning of the fens: I need to go further to give you more detail and to be able to talk about their ways of life.

After seeing that great sluice and drainage-system, we returned to Downham for dinner.[12] There we parted from my friend Wollaston, who left for Bury. The weather was detestable. The snow and sleet accompanied us to Wisbech and prevented me from paying much attention to what little of the landscape I could see. Which was that we were following a river along the top of a very high bank.[13] The further we went, the more we found ourselves in lands partly enclosed.

Wisbech, The Rose   [and Crown].[14] Arrived late, in more horrible weather: not tempted to look at the town. So we supped very well and, after that, slept well without picking up pen or pencil. Next morning, Thursday the 16th, we set out in the morning to reach Peterborough for the night. On the way we dined at a little inn called *The Cross Gun;*[15] and beyond and all around, I shall try to give you a general idea of this

12 Downham Crown, c1700, still looks in structure rather as it did during their two visits on that crowded day, Wednesday 15 March: getting 17 miles from Brandon to Downham, being shown Denver Sluice, sketching the sluice, scribbling 16 pages and dining here before covering 12 more miles through the snow to Wisbech. They would recognise the hipped roof and the wrought-iron bracket for inn-sign, and the archway through to a 4-step mounting-block in the stable yard.
13 They presumably followed the New Podyke to Nordelph, then along Well Creek as far as the Middle Level Main Drain, which they crossed into the more cultivated district round Outwell and Wisbech.
14 Grander than Downham Crown: 7-bay brickfront with stucco quoins, late 18th-century; arch leading into charming yard backed by 1601 pedimented gable painted with hunting-horn and ?pheasant: faces corner of Market Place, now exclusively pedestrian.
15 In fact The Cross Gun inn is remembered only by name in the Cross Guns Pumping Station on the north bank of the Nene, 1.5 miles down a straight lane opposite the Black Hart pub, which stands opposite the Thorney Toll petrol station on the Guyhirn to Peterborough road (A47). The 'Old Cross Guns' was affectionately remembered by H. W. Wheelwright in *Sporting Sketches from Home and Abroad* and quoted by the irrepressible J Wentworth Day in his evocative *History of the Fens* (1954, republished 1970), p. 182. (The Cross Guns Pumping Station is a mile further than the 2 miles along the Nene bank that Alexandre reckoned.) Cross Guns is presumably a reference

immense landscape I've just been through: it is so remarkable for its difference of land use.

For this first part of the route you were always on one side or the other of the river Nene on a causeway raised by the duke of Bedford, to whom all this level land belongs.[16] Seven miles from Wisbech, at Guyhirn, carriage-traffic is obliged to use this causeway, which runs straight as a die[17] for 14 miles. I should think the causeway's raised a good 20 ft above the river. The carriageway's about 7 ft wide up there, a gentle slope running right down to the river:[18] it's a magnificent work of engineering, doing honour to its designers. These great embankments, together with a great number of drainage-mills, have succeeded in draining these thousands of acres that were not very long ago water-logged, or under water.

Before the invention of these mills, the fens were being lost again to the waters[19] and impossible to cultivate. The area is perhaps as much as a hundred miles round, as you can see from the map, and is crossed by the rivers Ouse and Nene; and many of the canals dug to drain the land are navigable. Much of the land is divided up in squares and rectangles of, often, about 20 acres, surrounded by a dyke, and the holdings themselves drained by a great many little streams and watercourses. These all lead into one large drain that runs to the scoop-mill. As I said earlier, provided these fields are dry in April, the year's not lost, and it's time for seed-sowing. They take off three harvests in succession and then have one year fallow. They told me they'd seen as much as 10 comb of oats on an acre, but the usual yield is 7. When the water stands too long on the ground, it ruins it, and the following year isn't good. The best

to the old, long punt-guns used by fenland wildfowlers down to the middle of the 20th century, muzzle-loaded.

16 He's referring to Francis, 4th earl of Bedford (1593–1641), and a number of speculators, known as Adventurers, who also gave their name to these levels. Bishop Morton of Ely had made a beginning in this Guyhirn-Peterborough stretch.

17 Alexandre says '*droite comme un i.*' From his description, it is clear that they were using the bank of the unwaveringly straight river Nene, *not* the present desolate equally straight course of the A47. The position of the old Cross Guns pub beside the Nene river indicates the riverside route.

18 This description of 'a gentle slope running down to the river' makes me wonder if they were on the carriageway above Morton's Leam (1478), which runs more or less parallel to the Nene in its present cut (1728) from Guyhirn to Peterborough. That 1478 carriageway has crumbled a bit, and is now part of a designated long-distance Walk called Nene Way, coming from beyond Wisbech and continuing beyond Peterborough: its gentle slope down to the one major late-medieval drainage achievement is utterly idyllic. But I think they must have followed a carriageway along the bank of the present (1728) course of the Nene itself, beside which stood the little Cross Guns inn where they stopped for dinner.

19 What he may not quite have understood is that the very success of the drainage schemes in the 1650s caused a shrinkage of the peat. By the beginning of the 18th century the wastage had become very alarming, spoiling the system of natural gravity drainage from the fields down into the drains that led into the rivers. It was this shrinkage that caused the introduction of those ingenious pumps that so much interested Alexandre; it was also the reason for Humphrey Smith's 1728 Nene cut from Guyhirn to Peterborough, supplementing Morton's Leam, but providing no remedy for the obstructed outfall between Wisbech and the Wash.

years are the driest. In a really wet year, the farmer loses his whole crop, isn't even able to sow it. These lands are worth about 9 shillings an acre.

They are composed of a sort of thick peat, and sometimes clay. The farmers are obliged to have Lincolnshire sheep, which don't leap about. The local breed at once destroys the dykes where they are put to pasture: in putting them to pasture they are careful to see that the meadows are well drained. For anyone who has once caught a glimpse of this landscape, it becomes necessary to survey much more closely these immense unending flat lands, half covered by water, with hardly a house, enough cattle, all intersected by rivers and drains and a large number of causeways at various heights above the waterways. This Bedford [North] Level I've just been describing would astonish you: it has succeeded in draining all the lands to the right [North], by sacrificing to the waters a strip of land to the left. [*'The Wash', a safety reservoir, almost a mile at its widest, between the straightened Nene, alongside which they travelled to Peterborough, and the late-15th-century Morton's Leam running parallel for nearly 10 miles.*]

One may easily argue that at least these unoccupied lands are inhabited by enormous numbers of wildfowl. They shoot them with great punt-guns, 6½ ft long, of a very wide calibre, and weighing at least 30 *livres*.[20] The fowler sets out on his own in a small specially designed boat, and the gun fixed in place.[21] You can kill a duck at 100 *toises* [300 yards]. And of course you can fish from the same boat. From the Cross Gun[s] Inn we arrived at Peterborough, continuing along the top of the

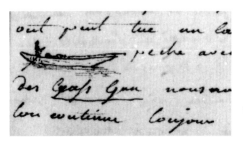

6. *Alexandre's sketch of a punt-gun, or cross-gun.*

[20] James Wentworth Day (1899–1983), a great Fenman and sportsman, described a flintlock punt-gun 8 ft 6 in. long in his gun-room at Wicken; also a sledge-gun of his, 7 ft long, bell-mouthed at the muzzle, one-inch in bore, firing rather more than a half-pound of shot, and itself weighing about 35 lb. But he recorded that his were old Fen fowlers with muzzle-loading punt-guns up to 2 in. in bore, and weighing 150 lb. A friend of his, a well-known agricultural engineer, had a punt-gun 'about 2 ins in bore and 10 ft in length, making his own punt-gun look like a pocket pistol'. Rather alarming for the fellow-fowlers, let alone the fowl (*A History of the Fens*, 1970, pp. 88–91).

[21] He didn't explain that, once he'd located a flock of wildfowl feeding, the 'art' of the punt-gunner consisted of manoeuvring the punt from a prone position, legs stretched out behind to steady it, a stalking-stick in each hand to edge the punt forward through the reeds until his prey was, if possible, within about 100 yards. The gun, flat in the punt, protruded only a couple of inches forward: the gunner aimed solely by shifting his weight, so aiming the punt itself. After firing, the gun was supposed to recoil under his right arm, but often collar-bones must have been broken and shoulders dislocated in these excitements (J. Wentworth Day, pp. 184–5).

causeway, 21 miles from Wisbech and very well built all the way. There was just one occasion when it burst open and drowned the entire countryside.[22]

[Alexandre obviously saw this as the end of a chapter and turned to a new page.]

PETERBOROUGH

Peterborough Angel[23]　　　This town grew up on firm land at the very edge of the Fen that I've just passed through and that I've been at such pains to describe. The town: terribly unattractive, with nothing whatever worth looking at.[24] It's a cathedral town. The bishop's palace is very ugly, and has no more of a presence than any small private house.[25] The church is beautiful, 600 ft long and tall in proportion.[26] Unfortunately it isn't vaulted.[27] Also it isn't quite broad enough for its length and height.[28] At the far east end, which serves as a library, the vaulting is pretty well carved, but still there is nothing of real beauty.[29] I climbed to the top of the tower which, though it isn't enormously high, does enable you to see a great area of the surrounding country: 26 miles they reckon, and scarcely a hill to impede the view. From here we could see the whole of the Fen we'd just crossed, as well as a lot of Norfolk, of Northamptonshire, and bits of several other counties. The soil round the town is good, especially that to the north. It's worth about 30 shillings an acre.

[22] H. C. Darby (*The Draining of the Fens*, 1956, p. 142) notes breaches in the north bank (along which they were travelling), with consequent 'great inundations', in 1763, 1764, 1767 and 1770. Troubles were still being reported in 1782.

[23] The Angel, in Georgian brick, stood at the corner of Bridge Street with Priestgate in the 1960s: swallowed up in comprehensive redevelopments.

[24] Two centuries later, Pevsner concurred: 'There is surprisingly little of interest in the town' (1968).

[25] It contains medieval undercrofts, but now makes a rather dull Victorian-Gothic appearance.

[26] In fact, only 481 ft long and 81 ft high, but it does convey a memorable sense of length.

[27] Well, the chancel-aisles *are* rib-vaulted, among the earliest examples, after Durham, and some in France. Alexandre was thinking of France's great Gothic cathedrals and failed to understand what a remarkable survival from c1220 this canted nave ceiling is, with many of its lozenge-patterns retaining the original colours.

[28] One wonders what he would have made of Saint-Savin-sur-Gartempe in Poitou: long, canted like this, and marvellously painted.

[29] The fan-vaulting of this 'retro-choir' or 'ambulatory' at the east end of Peterborough cathedral is perhaps one of the most beautiful stone vaults in Europe; not as grand as King's College Chapel at Cambridge, of course, but somehow on a slightly more human scale. John Harvey saw that the design bears 'an exact correspondence' with other work by the great John Wastell, and assumed that he worked here c1496–1509, before going on to complete the glorious chapel for King's College. Of the Peterborough work, John Harvey wrote: 'The beauty of this eastern ambulatory . . . and the technical mastery of fan-vault design make this one of the most notable examples of late Perpendicular architecture' (*English Medieval Architects*, 1984 edn, pp. 320–1). Alexandre's elder brother François, when they were shown Cambridge two years earlier, wrote that the chapel of King's College 'is utterly beautiful; vast and raised to a prodigious height, the vault borne aloft solely by the two side walls'. Alexandre clearly didn't remember those fan-vaults. He seems to have been looking out for the soaring vaults of early medieval France, or perhaps their Romanesque achievements. He may very well have been jaded by wintry travel across the dark Fen.

2

The East Midlands and the Dukeries

The old road ran west from Peterborough to Wansford, lord FitzWilliam's 'fine but simple' house to the north, and the beautiful bow of the Nene to the south (the story of the house closely linked with Wentworth Woodhouse in the next chapter). Could the forebears of the present Jacobs sheep already have been grazing here in 1786? Alexandre was affronted at being denied admission to Burghley House. In St Martin's church, Stamford, he thought little of lord Burghley's grand tomb, and naturally admired the white marble monument, by Monnot, to his descendant, at ease in Rome. It's been reckoned 'the most spectacular classicist monument in Britain'. What also pleased him on the Great North Road was a large number of stallions he recognised as Leicestershire horses from his visit in '85 to Mr Bakewell. The Old Black Bull where they ate at Witham still stands (beside the southbound carriageway). He seems to have been unaware of the remarkable 'political connections' of the splendid Grantham Angel.

Alexandre was naturally peeved at being taken round by Newark instead of through the pleasant Vale of Belvoir, to Nottingham. Here he came into his own by giving so full a description of Dr Thomas Wright's Nottingham General Hospital, with rough plans of each floor, that it has lately been printed in the Transactions of the Thoroton Society. *We reproduce his description. He and Lazowski joined Dr Wright's dinner-party, fifteen couples that evening. Alexandre didn't find the Nottingham women very pretty: in this we shall find him hard to please until he reaches Aberdeenshire and Ulster. At Mansfield, in one of his rare references to Lazowski, he admits that their travel-journals are in arrears. At Thoresby he admired the music saloon and the landscaping, and at Clumber the great plantations of woodland, the library, and especially the model farm. Welbeck seemed awful: Worksop, a great palace begun, but never finished: Roche Abbey, tall ruined arches in a Capability Brown idyll.*

We left Peterborough on Friday the 17th and slept at Stamford. It's only 14 miles, and we made the trip without a halt. The countryside was enclosed all the way, and for a great part of the journey you are riding through the estates of Lord Exeter[1] and Lord Fitzwilliam.[2] Lord Fitzwilliam's house is more beautiful in its situation than in

---

1 Brownlow Cecil, 9th earl of Exeter (1725–93) lived at Burghley House, 2 miles outside Stamford.
2 William, 2nd earl FitzWilliam (1748–1833) lived at Milton Park, just west of Peterborough. In 1782, on the death of his maternal uncle, Charles Watson-Wentworth, marquess of Rock-

its design: the house looked fine enough but very simple.[3] The great beauty lies in the park, very splendid and surrounded by plantations.[4] The view of the river, the Nene, which here flows in a bold semi-circular curve along the south end of the park, forms a remarkable picture with its meadows and a framework of wooded slopes.

The farmland is let at an average 9 shillings an acre. They have here the custom of giving their landlord, once every 4 years, a fallow field ready for sowing. Their land, so they say, is too strong for growing turnips. Their usual crop rotation is

                  1. wheat
                  2. peas
                  3. barley or oats
                  4. pasture

They do sometimes fallow between grass and wheat, and this is when they manure the fields. They keep their meadows for 2 years and sow them with barley and sometimes mow them the first year, when the yield is poor. They feed their cattle the second year.

Their ploughs are very like the Suffolk ploughs, and they draw with one horse behind the other, which shows how heavy the soil is. It is true that all their land is good for wheat-growing.

Just as we reached Lord Exeter's park at Burghley, we came to land half enclosed and half open-field. Arrived at Burghley, we sent our horses on to Stamford, only a mile or two further on, and we went on foot. As we crossed the park we saw what we were told were Spanish sheep.[5] They're a very curious colour, what one might describe as a deep [*foncé*] flesh colour. Their wool looked to me very fine.

What we had come to see was the house, the finest monument in England to the time of Queen Elizabeth. It was built by Cecil who, as everyone knows, played the leading part in the Queen's reign. We were unable to enter, for no one may see the house without Lord Exeter's permission. We had to make do with seeing almost nothing. The house seemed enormous and very well looked after; the park very grand, and a piece of water that crosses it is as beautiful as anything I could describe. All we could do was go on into the town, pretty mortified, and find our inn. We had seen nothing, and felt resentful and affronted at the meanness of that *Lord* in not allowing strangers to admire so beautiful a house. His only conceivable excuse, in

---

ingham, he succeeded to the vast estates of the Wentworths near Rotherham, in Yorkshire, which Alexandre and Lazowski visited nine days later.
3 It's not clear what view of the house they had: the Elizabethan north front is embattled, the south front Palladian by Flitcroft, nine bays wide, c1745–50.
4 Repton seems to have been called in later, in 1791.
5 The present house-manager at Burghley, Jon Culverhouse, very kindly writes to say they unluckily have no record of the breed of sheep grazing in the park at that time, and agrees that they sound almost like Jacobs. Arthur Young seems not to have noticed them, which is remiss; his letter II in *A 6-Months Tour Through the North of England* starts with a description of Burghley House and *22 pages* of description of the pictures 1770, 2nd edn 1771. No wonder Alexandre was miffed at their exclusion from the house.

7. *St Martin's, Stamford: Pierre Monnot's monument 'in white marble, very well carved', to Lord Exeter, c1700, Roman to the life.*

my eyes, might be that he has recently been robbed, and so might have some reason to mistrust anyone he doesn't know.[6]

STAMFORD

Stamford Angel[7]   As soon as we reached our inn in Stamford, we ordered our dinner, which I badly needed, and stepped just down the road to see Cecil's tomb. It's in the little church of St Martin, Burghley's parish church, and conveniently near the inn. It's not a very remarkable tomb, all in stone and painted like all the others of that age.[8] In

---

6   A not unreasonable explanation might have been their appearance on foot, after a cold crossing of the Fens, speaking with marked French accents and, for once, apparently without a letter of introduction. Mr Culverhouse kindly comments (9 July 1998) that Brownlow, the 9th earl (1725–93) was not known to be averse to travellers, but he might have been away, and it's known that in 1786 his health was not good: he adds that 'there is certainly no remaining record of a theft'. Exeter himself may easily have been at his London house, and the servant opening the door at Burghley might conceivably have invented a diplomatic, if unacceptable, excuse.

7   Now very widely known and respected as The George, before Hanoverian times it was The Angel, certainly as early as the 1440s. With the arrival of George I, it became The Angel and George (an unlikely combination), and Alexandre was using an abbreviation of that. By 1826, Paterson's *Roads* was listing it with George's name coming first. The good old inn stands just below St Martin's church, south of the Welland, as The George, its old double name forgotten.

8   It's humped up in the north side of the choir: 1598, and possibly made by Cornelius Cure, who

the same church is the monument to his grandson[9] in white marble, very well carved. In the evening we didn't leave our hotel, the town not worth the trouble: it is frightful. A river runs through it, the Welland, bringing its provisions. I was behind with my journal, and this pause was just what I needed.[10]

On Saturday 18th March   we left Stamford and dined at Witham Common (11 miles).[11] You find some commons that aren't in cultivation, but one must be fair: much the greatest part of our route was in a pretty good state of cultivation. We met on the road a large number of stallions on their way to Stamford, and I recognised them, from our visit to Mr Bakewell, as belonging to the Leicestershire breed.[12] I imagine they are being brought in to perfect the breed of the horses around here, which look to me in pretty poor shape. On from Witham Common to sleep at Grantham, the whole journey from Stamford only 21 miles. I saw nothing else to interest anyone reading this, so I'll turn at once to Grantham.

GRANTHAM

Grantham Angel   Grantham's quite a large town in Lincolnshire. The most curious thing I've discovered about it is the active rivalry between the two chief inns of the town. One, the *George*, has the enormous advantages of having been built by the lord of the manor: it is truly magnificent. It cost 14,000 *louis* to build [presumably *louis d'argent*, so £3,500 in 1786 values], and is a lavish and unforgettable extravagance: certainly it's elegant and very pretty. The other, the *Angel*, where we're staying, prides

was responsible for Mary, Queen of Scots' fine monument in Westminster Abbey [N. Pevsner, revised by Bridget Cherry, *London and Westminster*, 1985, p. 442]: alabaster, painted and gilded. A fine 6-poster under 2 tunnel-vaults north–south. He lies in state without either of his two wives, wearing his Garter robes over his armour, all surmounted proudly by an elaborately carved coat-of-arms.

9   This is the splendid white marble to John Cecil, 5th earl of Exeter, died 1700, the great Burghley's self-indulgent descendant, by Pierre Monnot, who signed himself, proudly, 'Petrus Stephanus Monnot, *Bisuntinus*: fecit ROMAE'. John Lord has fairly described it as 'the most spectacular classicist monument in Britain': *Church Monuments*, I part 2, 1986, p. 98. Cecil was tremendously impressed by Monnot's tomb for Cardinal Millini in S Maria del Popolo. The Cecils, in Roman dress, recline, completely at home, Romans to the life, flanked by Minerva and another goddess of the arts with her L-square, hammer, palette and brushes.

10   The need to stay indoors to write up his travel-notes may a little excuse the obtuseness of his comment on this town, which remains wonderfully well preserved despite all the onslaughts of our own times: the best possible tribute to its citizens, medieval, Elizabethan and Hanoverian, including those who have helped it survive the 20th century. Arthur Young, in 1770, thought it 'a pretty well-built town all of stone, a quarry lying under the whole county'. But he was severe about the bad state of the road at the north entrance to the town: 'the pavement, if such it is to be called, is nothing but deep holes'.

11   The Old Black Bull still stands beside the southbound carriageway of Ermine Street at the north end of Witham Common, facing south: a well-established Georgian coaching inn, now providing bed-and-breakfast. Villages of South and North Witham are near the start of the river Witham that runs north to Lincoln and then south to the Wash at Boston.

12   See *Innocent Espionage*, p. 24, fn 45.

itself on its excellence and above all on its competitive prices: also on its political connexions. At the Angel, I promise, they leave nothing to be desired: the service we had was above everything we'd been led to expect.[13]

Sunday the 19th   We left Grantham for Nottingham. Our plan was to take the more direct minor road across the Vale of Belvoir, only 24 miles. But before we left, the *maitre d'auberge* told us it would be much better to go via Newark, though that would make a journey to Nottingham of 34 miles – too much for our horses who have just completed 5 days without a break. However, we reached the decision to go the long way round: 14 miles to Newark followed by 20 across to Nottingham, instead of 20 miles from Grantham direct to Nottingham across the Vale of Belvoir. That would have enabled us to acquire some knowledge of the countryside by talking with the peasant farmers we would meet on the way, who are usually so instructive in everything one wants to learn about their farming.

Off we went on the 14 miles to Newark, along a road I found ugly and boring. The land seemed to be newly enclosed, yet very badly farmed; much of it fallow, as the land is wet. They work it, as I remember we noticed last year as we came through Huntingdonshire,[14] ignoring the natural slope for land-drainage. Here, with the land very low and wet, you can't achieve good meadow grassland. They take care to have, with their saddle-back ridges, one slope always under grass, and the other arable.

I have nothing else to say about the road from Grantham to Newark except that, near Newark, you see some square meadows of 10 to 15 acres where the cattle are put to graze as I remember seeing last year at Derby. In each field there's a rather pretty little house.

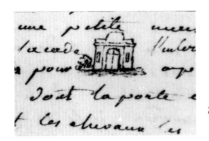

8. *Unusual cattle-byre (Alexandre's sketch).*

---

13 Byng, who stayed at the Angel in July 1791, recorded the experience in his own way: 'It bears a most venerable front, with an angel crowned in stone on the top. We occupied a very old room, and there are large ranges of rooms and of stabling behind. Our evening stroll was around the newly-built cross in the market-place; to survey the George, a great staring new inn . . .', II, p. 404. Byng, no great antiquary, knew a venerable building when he saw one. Alexandre missed not only the angel supporting the central oriel but also the carved heads of Edward III and Philippa, those doughty competitors for the French kingdom. They may be forgiven for not knowing, nor perhaps caring, that King Richard III, an earlier traveller at this inn, used his time under this roof by ordering the death of the too-competitive duke of Buckingham. For Byng, see note on p. xii.
14 *Innocent Espionage*, p. 14, and n 6.

Here's a sketch of the façade: the interior is nothing more than a cattle-byre, for about 5 or 6 cows or horses.[15] In the meadows are horses, cattle and pigs.

NEWARK[16]

Newark is small and pleasant, its market-place quite grand, its town-hall stone built and very grand.[17] I won't nag my tutor any more about the monotony of the road from Newark to Nottingham: I'll just content myself with saying that in all this district limestone is so easily available that the peasants' houses are built of it. To within 9 miles of Nottingham it's all sand, and for the rest of the way you follow the river Trent to Nottingham. It is flanked by water-meadows, but flows over a sandy bed. Below that are beds of red sandstone, a workable freestone, as we saw in some parts of Derbyshire.[18]

NOTTINGHAM

You cross the river before you reach the town you see in front of you, situated in a recess [enfoncement], raised above the watermeadows, and built on a low hill.[19] In fact you have to climb to quite a height in order to arrive. The town's built on the solid rock. I am leaving till tomorrow my description of this town, a very important one.

[15] Robert Lowe, in his *General View of the Agriculture of the County of Nottingham*, 1798, described some enterprising experiments in the design of cattle-byres, but not in the Newark area, nor charmingly disguised as small villas. Tim Warner, of the Local Studies section of the Newark library, knows of no survival of what *looks* like model farming on one of the neighbouring ducal estates.

[16] They didn't stay here, but probably dined before heading for Nottingham.

[17] The Market Place contains the extraordinary 14th-century White Hart Inn as well as the Great North Road staging establishments, the Saracen's Head and the Clinton (formerly Kingston) Arms. Arthur Young in Newark noticed the great steeple, 'which for some miles appears very light and beautiful'. He also recorded a notably early terrace development: 'a new street worth viewing: although the houses are very small, yet each side of the whole street forms but one front, and in a very pretty neat taste. How much it is to be lamented that this is not the method in all the towns of England': *A 6-Months Tour Through the North of England*, 1770, I, p. 102. This is Wilson Street, near the church, begun on Old May Day, 1766, to a uniform plan by the vicar, Rev Bernard Wilson. It was thought not impossible at the time that the street was built to increase Wilson's voting influence. One side of Wilson Street was destroyed in the 1960s, the other remains in good order. The Town Hall *is* very grand. See B. Wragg, *John Carr of York*, York, 2000, pp. 180–2.

[18] He is remembering accurately the way the New (Triassic) Red Sandstone covers South Derbyshire as well as Nottinghamshire: see Alec Clifton-Taylor, *The Pattern of English Building*, 1962, p. 133.

[19] In fact, two hills: St Mary's church on one, the castle on the other. The curving street that links them starts as High Pavement, continues as Middle and Low Pavement, and ends as Castle Gate, with buildings that should have pleased them. In S and N Buck's *South Prospect of Nottingham* in 1743, the castle is shown surprisingly isolated on top of a great bare rock like, as Alexandre noticed, a petrified sugar-loaf. Kip's engraving of Knyff's drawing of *Nottingham from the East* beautifully related the castle on its hill to St Mary's on its, in *Britannia Illustrata*, 1707; see pp. 26–7 below.

Nottingham White Lion,[20] *Monday 20th March*   We went out before 10 o'clock to call on Dr White[21] at his house. He wasn't at home but we were not long back in our inn when he called to see us. We attempted a kind of general conversation, and from that we advanced to something more particular. To me he seemed very well-informed, modest, and most of all interested in chemistry and natural history. He said that, from the letter he'd received, he could see that our plan was to see the local manufactures: but that, for the last 3 months or so, the local chambers of commerce had resolved to keep everyone, foreign or native, from seeing their manufacturing processes. There was no way of getting in, and so he was very embarrassed to have to tell us the bad news that we could see nothing. At the same time, he offered to go with us and show us the town and the hospital and we accepted with pleasure.

We walked through the whole town, which is large but not well built, the roads narrow, ill-paved and tortuous. The ancient parish church didn't seem very remarkable.[22] The market-place is enormous, and in the form of a sharp-pointed triangle. At the base were the exchange and the market-house. I've been able to learn nothing about the value of the business of this town, but it must be very considerable. There are silk mills and cotton mills, as at Derby; and, among other commodities, one of the biggest makers of stockings one could ever see or even imagine. I've seen the frame in which the latest, most fashionable, silk stockings are made, not liable to ladder like the rest. The frame was so complicated that I didn't begin to understand its complexities. I know it required an enormous amount of care and a great deal of time.[23]

[20] *Paterson's Roads*, 1811, lists two inns at Nottingham: the Blackamoor's Head and the White Lion: gone. Adrian Henstock kindly located the White Lion: it stood at the corner of Long Row East and Clumber Street (formerly Cow Lane) and near enough to the Market Place. Looking at Thomas Sandby's ravishing drawing of the buildings lining the Market Place's great broad curving triangle, you wonder what could possibly have damped Alexandre's admiration. Sandby's drawing, in Nottingham City Museums, appeared in Mark Girouard's *The English Town* (Yale UP, 1990, pl 13).

[21] This is Dr Thomas *Wright*, surgeon to the Nottingham General Hospital 1782–1819. Again I owe the identification to Adrian Henstock, also the reference to F. H. Jacob, whose *History of the Nottingham General Hospital*, 1951, shows that Dr Thomas Wright was followed by three other members of his family down to 1905, an outstanding record of service to local medicine. It is the more surprising to learn that Thomas Wright features in none of the biographies of Nottingham's worthies. It is clear from what follows that he was not only an ingenious hospital-designer, but also a very sociable character. As nothing was previously known of Dr Wright's part as designer and founder-physician, Adrian Henstock has published Alexandre's account of it, with my translation and notes, in *Transactions of the Thoroton Society of Nottinghamshire*, vol 103, 1999, pp. 141–7. Sir Howard Colvin has shown me that John Simpson was the architect responsible for giving Wright's plan such a respectable appearance. The engraving (Pl 9) in the Bodleian, Gough Maps 26, fol 6, shows up the inaccuracies of Alexandre's rough sketch of the elevation and illuminates his useful rough sketches of the plan on p. 25.

[22] He is likely to have been referring to St Mary's, as the most obviously imposing, but Alexandre was at sea in English parish churches. He had no standards. In Peterborough Cathedral and in York Minster he was properly observant, though keener on buildings of his own day.

[23] For the remarkable account by his brother François of the mills at Derby, see *Innocent Espionage*, 1995, pp. 38–45, and of the hosiery frames at Leicester, pp. 27–8. Adrian Henstock notes

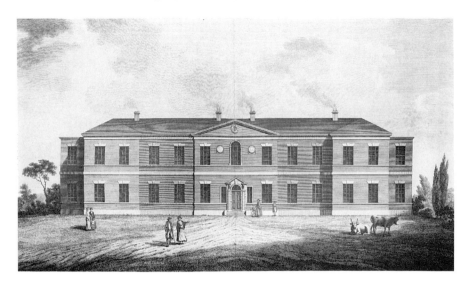

9.   *Nottingham General Hospital: James Newton's engraving of the front elevation in 1782, drawn by its architect, John Simpson, working with Dr Wright (pp. 22–6). This is better than Alexandre's sketch of the front, which we omit.*

So we went on with Mr Wright to the hospital where he is the doctor. It stands on a hill to the west of the town, behind the castle what we shall come to later. The hospital's a very simple brick building, erected by the subscription of several gentlemen who each have the right to the admission of so many patients. The good fortune of this hospital is that nowhere in Derbyshire is there any establishment of this kind, while in Lincolnshire[24] there is only a hospital with 20 beds, so that those two counties by themselves have enough people to raise the very large subscription needed when the necessary capital has been raised and the site chosen. The subscribers have set up a kind of committee of management to represent everyone. And the committee chose, for its physician, this Mr Wright, who told us he wouldn't have the post if he hadn't been given the entire responsibility for the layout of the interior. They agreed, and all that I shall describe of the building is of his choosing, and often of his invention.

The dukes of Portland and Newcastle gave the site for the building, naturally: they could hardly have done less, I suppose, for both were subscribers. But that's scarcely to the point. The front of the building is quite simple and here it is: one can't help seeing that there's nothing very magnificent about it.

that the Nottingham hosiery was largely organised on a domestic basis with framework knitters (out-workers operating stocking-frames in their own homes) working to warehouses maintained by merchant hosiers. The stocking-frame had some 2,000 separate components and is illustrated in C. Deering, *Nottinghamia Vetus et Nova . . .*, 1751. M Bruno Jacomy pointed out that the only *Arts et Métiers* item in the *Encyclopédie* that Diderot insisted on writing himself was that on the knitting-frame: he trusted no one else to do it.
[24] He means Nottinghamshire.

Behind that elevation of the house one can make out the arrangement of the two storeys within.

Column 1 lists the lower storey, column 2 the upper.

	1		2
A	assembly hall (if it's built)	A	operating room
B	linen	B	post-operative rooms
C	kitchen	C	wards for the sick
D	wash-house	D	stairs
E	water-closets, privies [*commodités*]	E	closets
F	stairs	F	washrooms
G	surgery	G	passages
K	surgeon's apartment		
L	apothecary's store		
M	matron's room		
N	dispensary		
O	consulting-room [no door!]		
P	where the cups are kept		
q	baths		
R	passages		

You see on the plan the letter q which marks the place where the steam baths are. They should really be nearer the necessary coal supply, but their construction makes them a little more economic by their all being in the same small room. There are two steam baths and one with running hot water. [He goes on to describe at length and in rather confused detail the way the supply of steam and hot water is kept without supervision from being dangerously hot.] The same coal that serves to heat the water serves also to provide underfloor heating for the invalids when they come out of the bath. Everything in this hospital has been carefully thought through. Above the doors is a gap through which the rooms are ventilated by air neither too warm nor too cold: what serves as current to the fire also disperses all unpleasant odours and freshens the air which might otherwise get stuffy. This warm air is led into the house by an underground flue, and outside the house is a sort of column through which the fresh air enters and is at once circulated throughout. Another of the ways in which they have planned to eliminate hospital smells is by making sure there are never too many beds in one room, and that the rooms are always kept scrupulously clean. They reckon that all kinds of smell and infection are lighter than air, and so tend to rise. To safeguard the fireplace and prevent a draught in the room, they have made a space, parallel to the ceiling and no more than 3 inches below it, and covered it in with planking, so that the smells etc pass through this small space, which is quite large enough for the purpose. At any rate, I've been in all the rooms and I can assure you I sensed not the least odour.

The last precaution against insalubrious smells is in the water-closets. You know the necessary rooms we call English privies [*commodités anglois*] in which they are

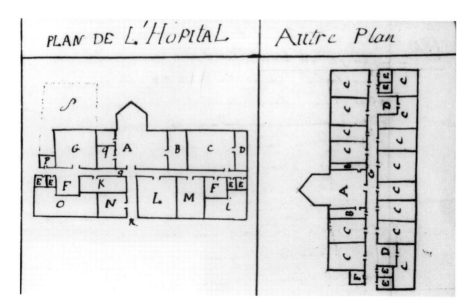

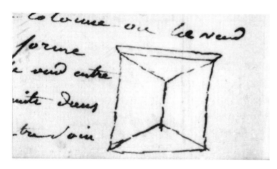

10/11. *Plans of Nottingham General Hospital, drawn by Alexandre. 10: Plan of ground floor and first floor. 11: Small sketch of fresh-air inlet: see middle of long paragraph opposite, and p. 26, lines 14–16.*

flushed clean by the turning of a tap. Here, when you close the lid [*en fermant la planche*], it releases a flushing of water powerful enough to wash everything clean: which is how we can be sure that they are always clean and cannot infect the house in the way one sees too often.

Then there is a special kind of bed in each room to ease and soothe the invalid with every device for preventing discomfort and pain, even restlessness. In the end, this house reflects great honour on Dr Wright, for the enormous care taken with the patients here, and the lack of waste on external show.

Each subscription brings the right to places for patients, but they can't be admitted without permission and the examination of a doctor, and there's one day a week when they consider who should be discharged. Also they are careful not to admit anyone suffering from a contagious disease that might spread to other patients.

Then there's a day when the doctor is available in the hospital to see outpatients, and to prescribe and issue free drugs. The doctors and surgeons receive nothing at all for their services: it is all done voluntarily. At the head of it all, in maintaining this large hospital, there is just one matron in charge, with three women and two men to assist her. And they show that this small staff manages: for in the smallest of corners one saw nothing but scrupulous cleanliness.

I've seen many hospitals, but I had no notion that the ideal of a hospital could be taken so far. I don't think that we were at all mistaken in going miles out of our way to see how much can be done in caring for the poor. Finally we were able to see the place where people in easier circumstances come for nursing through quite small ailments. Perhaps I didn't make enough of that invention of the little column for ventilation. It is square. The inside of each side is in the form of a triangle and the bottom is perforated so that from whichever side the wind's blowing it's bound to enter, and from there it's at once circulated through every room in the house.

At present they are putting up a new building at the back to make room for more beds. I've marked it with the letter S on my plan. This will give them 14 more beds, a substantial addition to their present 52.

After seeing the hospital we went home with Mr Wright. He pressed us, in so friendly a way, to stay for dinner that we found we couldn't refuse, though we badly needed the time to write our journal. As we'd accepted his kindly invitation we made a hurried visit to the castle, which stands in front of the hospital, built up on the rock like a sugar-loaf, and very high up. It appears perfectly square,[25] and belongs to the duke of Newcastle, though he doesn't live there. His father lived there solely in the interests of his popularity in the town. But the son, finding that the advantages didn't outweigh the disadvantages of living in a commercial town, where he was reduced to acknowledging the humblest workman, doesn't even keep the house furnished. It looks very well built and has wonderful views. From the top you can see into five counties: Derbyshire, Yorkshire, Lincolnshire, Leicestershire and of course Nottinghamshire. The view reaches over about 30 miles. You see over the Trent valley, with its meadows that can never fail to enhance the view, and the hill opposite is well wooded. The castle has obviously been well fortified. It was built in William III's reign,[26] and is at present completely unfortified, though its position gives it great strength.

---

[25] In fact it's a strongly pilastered and rusticated horizontal rectangle, but with projecting wings in rear. The duke's father recorded that he'd 'laid and designed' the model of the castle himself. It was built in the years 1674–9 under the direction of the Lincolnshire mason, Samuel Marsh, who had built Bolsover Castle, in all its baroque splendour, for the duke. Summerson (*Architecture in Britain*, 1953, p. 104) noted detailed influences on its composition from Rubens' book on the palaces of Genoa: see pl 59A in Summerson, which is an engraving after Thomas Sandby for Deering's *History of Nottingham*.

[26] No, it was just a decade earlier than William III's accession, but over a century before this visit. Only with unnaturally powerful eyes could you expect to see into Yorkshire.

We went back to dine with Mr Wright and to our surprise found ourselves joining a dinner-party of fifteen, and all men, but we very soon felt at home. There was discussion of politics and trade, and what was said on this issue seemed agreeable. After dinner we took tea and we found in the other room as many ladies as we were men. What seemed rather more important was that we were in our boots! We played at *Wisk* [whist]. When the party was over, we returned to our inn. From all the company we met at Mr Wright's house, I have the impression that the people of this town are excellent and that one would find here a very agreeable society. The women here aren't very pretty, so something is missing from the pleasure of life.

The town's prominent position above the valley is curious, for it is said never to have as much snow as the rest of the country for 5 or 6 miles round. This seems extraordinary, and is thought to be something to do with the Forest and with the way the town on its protruding rock divides the valley. I'm only reporting what they tell me in this neighbourhood.

The commerce here, though very considerable, isn't enterprising [*hardy*]: in this whole town there are only two merchants exporting to foreign parts, and in their own ships. All the others use agents in London, to whom they send all their goods for export: and what is amazing is that, from Nottingham, they actually send all their merchandise to London by land. They say that's a better deal for them than sending it all by boat on the river Trent to Hull and then re-loading it on shipping for London and foreign parts.[27]

Tuesday 21 March   We left Nottingham and dined at Mansfield on our way to York. The distance is 14 miles, and along perhaps the most tedious road I've ever travelled. You cross a part of what is called the Forest, yet there isn't a tree to be seen.[28] In the middle of this lost country, the first thing you come upon is the house that seemed to me that of a gentleman-farmer who by his persistence and skill has created a very fine farm, well cultivated. It was a pleasure to see turnips, and sheep walking about eating them, which will help fertilise all these light lands. Among other things, what has given me the biggest pleasure are the superb artificial meadows. Also, here is a place that can show a very good husbandry, and I find that I'm most content when I see, where one would scarcely have believed it possible, finding everything that tells you it must be an improving estate: this is an immense land-clearance of lord *Byron*. Some of it is far

---

[27] Adrian Henstock has kindly suggested that this may have been partly as a result of a restrictive private monopoly exercised over the river-trade, and partly because the Nottingham merchants found the London carriers' inns useful as markets and distributing warehouses (see his and J. Beckett's article in J. Beckett, ed, *A Centenary History of Nottingham*, Manchester UP, 1997).
[28] Sherwood, like most forests, has been dogged by the misconception that Alexandre illustrates here. It arose from the fact that the word forest has acquired two distinct meanings: one, an actual belt of woodland, the other an area, whether wooded or partly wooded, or just heath, in which the Forest Law applies, a law designed to preserve the king's hunting in a particular area by such technical rules as trespass on 'vert and venison'. Here Alexandre is describing a fairly characteristic stretch of Sherwood Forest. J. Chapman in *Nottinghamshire, survey'd in 1774*, London 1776, showed the Forest area as heathland, embracing numerous woods and the parks of 'the Dukeries', itself a word coined in the 18th century.

from new, but some of it has been created this year, and it has now to be burnt and afterwards ploughed.

After arriving in Mansfield you drive between two woods that seemed to me pretty big and which belonged to the government which has acquired great estates round here.[29]

Mansfield, The Swan[30]   Mansfield lies in a bottom, in the middle of farm lands, although it is surrounded by the forest.[31] After leaving the town you cover two miles of enclosed arable lands. I noticed a number of artificial meadows, and I think there may be two explanations of this. The first is that in land like this – that is, in sandy or light land – they are bound to provide the kind of solid consistency that such meadows create. The second is that, as they fatten sheep that come here on their way from Scotland, they must have plenty of good meadows for them all to graze. Otherwise, I have a poor opinion of what I've seen of this district.

Leaving these enclosed fields, you cross about two miles of open country and then ride through 'real forest' belonging to the government.[32] It's very extensive and will be an extremely handsome wood if the oaks haven't all died from neglect. You may have heard of land that Parliament has need, at present, to sell off to individuals who would cultivate it well: this is it. For almost all these wretched lands belong to Parliament.[33] In the middle of all this you come upon a delightful house, belonging to a gentleman; one that would be reckoned a house of distinction if it were in any other position than the edge of the forest.[34] It's the house of lord Kingston,[35] at a place called Thoresby where we shall sleep tonight. We arrived in good time but I shall leave my description till tomorrow.

We slept at a little inn built by the lord about half a mile from his house.[36] We sat down to try to catch up with our travels in arrears, but I'd better admit that I was in no position to catch up, however fast I scribbled or how hard I worked.

[29] See J. Chapman, *op cit* in footnote 28 above.

[30] They merely stopped for lunch: see p. 27. It is now rather near the famous railway viaduct that crosses the town.

[31] '*au milieu de la fôret.*' Here again he seems to be expecting the old legalistic name, the forest, to mean actual woodland.

[32] This shows that he was aware of the difference between woodland and what is legally 'forest'.

[33] Adrian Henstock says this would probably have been Budby Forest, still unenclosed and unimproved as late as 1832. It had been acquired by the Pierrepont family, presumably from the Crown, some years before this. Alexandre is confused about the Crown's involvement.

[34] About its situation, Alexandre soon becomes less critical, as we shall see. It's very possible Capability Brown had landscaped the park, presumably pre-1773: Stroud, *Capability Brown*, 1995, p. 242.

[35] The ancient Nottinghamshire family of Pierrepont were earls and dukes of Kingston-upon-Hull. The 2nd (and last) duke had died in 1773 and was succeeded in 1788 by his nephew, Charles Medows (created Earl Manvers 1806). Thoresby is still lived in by the family. It is open to the public on certain days in summer.

[36] And no longer there.

THORESBY

Thoresby Kingston Arms. On Wednesday the 22nd   we left early and went up to see Lady Kingston's house.[37] Milord died some years ago. The house, which is called Thoresby, is built of freestone, simple but beautiful. The interior is elegant, without magnificence.[38] The one thing that really struck me is the grace and style and decoration in what they call the music saloon. There's a superb room that must be intended for public receptions [*les jours publiques*], but which has scarcely been begun.[39] What really distinguishes this house is its river and the beauty of its courses. The river at Thoresby comes from the duke of Portland's house at Welbeck, 7 miles away: 2 miles from here it forms a really superb piece of water.[40] From this end, its great length, and fine width, forms a number of ox-bows and loops along its edges: all uniformity is discarded. Some talented painter has painted these slopes a lovely green as they lose themselves down in the water. Here is the true magnificence. The making of this stretch of ornamental water has cost 12 thousand *louis*.[41] From the house it makes the most wonderful effect.

From this large area of water, enough runs off to form another small arrangement

[37] The 'notorious' duchess of Kingston had in 1744 married a Hervey (later 6th earl of Bristol) who divorced her in 1769. In the Lords she was found guilty of bigamy in 1776, pleaded privilege as a peeress, and went to live in St Petersburg. When Byng was here in 1789, the duchess had died and the house was open for viewing the contents in a 10-day sale. To Byng it seemed like a house 'in St James's Square, fitted up with French furniture; all for shew, as if the Dss and Mrs Cornellis [who ran a well-known London night-club] had clubb'd tastes . . . To view which were assembled the neighbourhood, gaping about at the mock marble, the gilding, the shells . . . The foolish expense and vanity of this dutchess is visible in every room.'

[38] Presumably the French taste that disagreed with Byng rather appealed to Alexandre. The first house here, designed by Wm Talman in 1685, was one of those seminal houses like the Queen's House at Greenwich, and Coleshill: John Harris, 'Thoresby House, Notts', *Architectural History*, 4, 1961, pp. 11–21. Unluckily it was burnt down in 1745, and what Alexandre was admiring was 'a compact redbrick, stone based house, with Ionic columns' (Hy Thorold), by Carr of York: see 'The Building and Alteration of the Second Thoresby House, 1767–1804', Thoroton Society Record Series, XXII, 1962, pp. 16–20. This in turn has been replaced by Anthony Salvin's romantic design of 1865, with almost modest references to the magnificence at Burghley, Wollaton, etc. B. Wragg, *John Carr of York*, York, 2000, pp. 211–13.

[39] With the duke dead in 1773 and the duchess abroad from 1776, the saloon had been discontinued.

[40] The waterways here are more complicated than Alexandre had fathomed. The rivers Meden and Poulter that supply Welbeck, Thoresby and Clumber with their ornamental waters are easily confused. Here at Thoresby, it's the Meden river, flowing north-east into the Idle river as its meanders north. A mere 350 yards north of where Meden and Idle join, the Poulter runs into the Idle from the duke of Portland's Welbeck, where it formed a fine long lake on its way east to make another handsome lake at Clumber. Before the house at Clumber was pulled down in 1938, its south front faced this lake, separated from it only by a narrow garden terrace. (The Idle slides on into the Trent: on its east bank in the year 616, a decisive battle was fought. The king of East Anglia (Raedwald, whose burial-ship was found at Sutton Hoo in 1939) slew the king of Northumbria and set up king Edwin there in his place.)

[41] £3,000 sterling: the louis d'argent equalled the English crown, or 5 shillings. Very possibly Capability Brown's work: Stroud, *Capability Brown*, 1975, p. 242.

with cascade and fountain.[42] Further off there's another straight canal, a quarter of a mile long, stocked with fish, and entirely devoted to this use. The rest of the park, though small, is very well planted: most notably a great wood to the north, which makes an excellent effect. The opening in front of the house is remarkable both for its elegance and for the beauty of the woods terminating the view.

CLUMBER

From Thoresby we came on 3 miles to Clumber, the country seat of the duke of Newcastle: one of the miles in Thoresby's park and the other two in Clumber's, which is famous for its enormous plantations: the oldest trees looked about twenty years old; later on, we came to trees of all ages. They're looked after with the greatest care: all of them are wrapped in straw, and all the clumps are surrounded by a double wooden palisade, stout timber to protect them from the damaging attentions of deer, sheep and cattle generally. You see nothing but plantations, of great variety, and some of them very handsome indeed. It is extraordinary what a great improvement this has made to the face of the country. They claim to have planted such a huge number of trees that it's now impossible to know precisely how many trees have become woodland.[43]

Here Alexandre confessed: 'I was so far behind with my journal that I've had to skip: you will find the continuation of p. 79 on p. 113. The reason for all this is that I found that what followed p. 81 was so interesting that I had to double what I'd written.' This is all now sorted out.

You arrive at the house in the middle of all these plantations. Suddenly you find yourself at a river, bridged very elegantly,[44] and there it is. The house itself is beautiful, its interior magnificent. Only the lower part is furnished, but there it's

---

[42] Byng (II, p. 7) in June 1789, thought little of the water 'about and near the house: it runs in ditches and canals except where forming a paltry (playhouse) cascade in front of the south aspect'.

[43] It's unlikely that the duke of Newcastle and his estate manager didn't know the exact extent of their woodland. Alexandre's details of the protection of the young trees indicates a programme of wood-pasture, 'the art of growing trees in the presence of grazing animals'. (O. Rackham, *Trees and Woodland in the British Landscape*, 1976, p. 18.) It was presumably combined with a campaign of forestry – 'growing trees in plantations like an arable crop'. Byng (*Torrington Diaries*, II, p. 9, 9 June 1789) was equally admiring: 'Clumber Park is in wonderful, and hourly, improvement. What can be so useful, so noble, or so gratifying as this farming, from sterility, a charmingly cultivated wooded domain?'

[44] By Stephen Wright, protégé of William Kent and the duke of Newcastle (he contributed the Palladian front to Cambridge's old university library): here he designed the house c1768–78, now gone, the elegant 3-arched bridge over the Poulter, and other agreeable surviving features. The Frenchmen clearly entered the park directly from the Thoresby Park boundary at South Lodge. From there, the drive leads north in less than a mile to the bridge, then across the river and round to the house, destroyed in 1938; but which they saw standing before the fine long lake into which the river had been translated since it went under the bridge. They saw the lake as a strip of water that widens and narrows, with bends such as the elbow at Hardwick Grange.

12. *Clumber. Stephen Wright's handsome bridge over the Poulter.*

well-furnished. The rooms are large and well-proportioned. The library is the best room in the house,[45] beautifully designed and full of well-chosen books. It is said to be one of the best collections in this part of England. The front of the house is simple and good, a strip of water of small width but some length, losing itself in these immense plantations, leaves no possible way of improving the view. This house certainly has the air of belonging to a *grand seigneur*, quite the equal of that of the duke of Kingston. They rejoice equally in the magnificence of the river, the vastness of the plantations, and in their houses.

---

[45] Byng was equally impressed: 'I think it the best house I ever entered . . . the library and the great dining-room are of the most spacious dimensions, and furnished with all the proprieties of such rooms of enjoyment.'

The garden in front of the house is planted to admirable effect. After seeing the house, we went to look at the farm: we were attracted to it by its name, 'the pleasure ground'. It gave us a chance to follow the various twists and bends of the river.[46] From the park you enter the adjoining farmland. The whole park is kept in hand by the duke, who himself farms, to keep his eye in.

He has built a superb farmhouse, to make for most convenient management, without excess. You can see from my plan, though it's very badly drawn.

A is the yard in which cattle, pigs and young animals roam freely all day. B is part of the main yard that's fenced off, merely by a wooden palisade, for cows giving milk and being fed on straw. C is the farmhouse, solid and very simple. D dovecote. E the wash-house, known as the office, and where butter's made and pigeons fed: stalls and general stores. F stables, roomy and fine, to hold I dare say 50 horses. G where the pigs are fattened up. H, where the beer is brewed, is next to G I suppose because, for pig-swill, the remains from brewing mixed with the whey is one of the best recipes. K are the barns, three of them, all communicating with the yard I where they put the pigs that are being prepared for fattening or sows that are pregnant. L byres for the young beasts or for deserving cows. M byres for 31 cows from the yard B for milking. N where the bullocks are fattened. O land enclosed for the grain that can't be brought in to the barns. P tradesman's house and shop.

One sees at once that this farm is run on the grandest lines, and that it must have cost a small fortune. They fatten a great many cattle, making them work for their first seven years: then the fattening. They bring in their beautiful breed of Scottish bullocks. The whole farm covers, I suppose, 3,000 *arpents* (4,500 English acres). All I can tell you is what we're seeing on this farm in March: in springtime they sow 200 *arpents* with barley and oats. The soil isn't quite good enough for wheat: or at least there isn't very much land up that quality. Generally the rotation of their harvest is:

1. barley
2. oats
3. fallow
4. barley
5. oats
6. grass

They declare that they do much better by sowing oats than barley after hay harvest. They grow turnips but only small quantities. The whole park and plantation extends over no more than 5,000 *arpents* (7,500 acres), and the amount of woodland

---

46 'The pleasure ground' was the name of the gardens that had been laid out immediately east of the house by 1774. The model farm they describe is a good mile further east, round the end of the lake's arm. The farm's outlines can still be seen at Hardwick Grange with the farmhouse itself standing pleasantly above the weir where the Poulter continues on beyond the lake's elbow. The large dovecote, too, survives, related to the house exactly as in Alexandre's drawing. I think the lower parts of the brick walls of the 'byres for 31 cows from the yard' were unchanged in alterations to the farm-buildings in the 1850s and c1890. It is remarkable that Arthur Young wrote of a cowhouse 'with 31 stalls in a line' in 1771. One wonders if Alexandre got the number from that oracle.

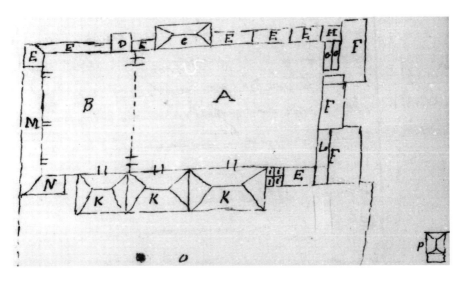

13/14. *The model farm at Clumber, sketched in plan by Alexandre, is now called Hardwick Grange. 13: The dovecote and farmhouse. 14: Alexandre's sketch: D marks the dovecote; C, the farmhouse, stands 'solid and simple', beyond.*

you see all round makes you think the estate's double that acreage.[47] What's clear is that their huge outlay on the farm and on the young plantations of woods will be amply repaid by the efficient cultivation of the woodland that already makes the reputation of the place.

WELBECK

The same day [22nd March] we came to the duke of Portland's country house, riding through 5 more miles of Clumber's park before leaving it, and then through the park of Welbeck. We saw the house, grand but fearfully ugly.[48] The park could be handsome if it were well maintained, but it's entirely neglected.[49] It's famous for the great amount of straight timber [*bois de charpente*] it produces. In front of the house is a superb stretch of grass, cut through by a small river, and ending in a wood of mixed oak and pine which makes a very fine impression. I could see nothing else worth mentioning, and can't imagine why we should have been recommended to see this house: it seemed to me awful.[50]

[47] There seems to be a discrepancy between this figure and the 3,000 *arpents* at the beginning of the paragraph. It's also puzzling to square the rotation with preference for oats after hay. Mr Andrew Barber, the Historic Buildings Representative of the National Trust at Clumber, and his colleague Mr J. Fletcher, were pleased with Alexandre's plan, 'badly drawn' though it was. They have kindly commented on his notes. They say that the poverty of the land, noted by Alexandre, was later in the century the very expensive ruin of the duke's agricultural plans. But the plantations proved to be a great commercial success as well as an aesthetic one. And they report that the cossetting of the young trees in straw and with double palisades is confirmed in the Newcastle papers at Nottingham University Library.

[48] Byng's verdict was 'mean, ugly and ill-built' (II, p. 13). He couldn't think why the duke of Portland should neglect Welbeck for politics: he was 1st Lord of the Treasury (Prime Minister) in 1783. Burke called him a 'virtuous, calm, sturdy character', rare qualifications in politics.

[49] Byng was scathing about this too: 'We entered a pinery, but it was the pinery of a private gentleman: nor is there any pleasure-ground, or roses, or flowers, or orange-trees for my lady Dutchess.'

[50] Byng went on: 'The inside of the house is of no account. What has been done by the present duke are three respectable modern rooms, the great hall is fitted up in the most contemptible attempt at antiquity, being stuck over with a white trimming, just like the sugar ornaments of a second-course cake.' The bogus fan-vaulting which pleased Horace Walpole – 'so much of everything I like' – was part of 'a Gothic tour-de-force that had no equal' in 1751, done for the duke's predecessor, Lady Oxford; he himself got Carr of York in for the 'three respectable modern rooms', but most of the exterior remained gabled and castellated. A century later egregious additions were made, underground, by the eccentric 5th duke (d1879). House and park are now in excellent order as Welbeck College, a pre-Sandhurst establishment. The pity is that Alexandre failed to notice the great riding-school built for a Royalist duke in 1623. It all still belongs to the Cavendish-Bentincks, and is closed to the public. Like Thoresby, it is a subject of one of Henry Thorold's delightful essay-entries in his *Shell Guide to Nottinghamshire*, 1984.

WORKSOP MANOR

From Welbeck we came to Worksop, the duke of Norfolk's house. We didn't leave their two parks, which are separated only by a road: the first is full of handsome woods which continue right up to the park boundaries, and even beyond them. For I was told that the duke of Portland cleared a great deal of the forest he had planted, and that it had grown into handsome woods.

The other park (*Worksop Manor*) is greener, really only the edge of a plantation. It enables you to see the house the moment you enter, through a gate built in the shape of a fortification: adjoining the wood, it creates a very pretty first view of the house.

What there is of the house is remarkable only for the grandeur which was planned for it. A massive quadrangular house was designed, of which the one wing complete forms a very good house, already grand enough for a great lord. What's built is only the back range, and this façade facing north is [23] windows wide. But it looks as if it will never be finished: a great pity, for you can see in its palatial size something very remarkably interesting, and it would have shown what one English nobleman could accomplish for his own habitation.[51]

From Worksop Manor we went into the town, a mile away. The entire road runs through the park. You have on your right a view of fine meadows, ending in woods, which advance and retire. You seem never to get a straight trunk forming in a mixture of trees of all species. There you can make out a scattering of several small houses. On a limited scale this is one of the prettiest views I've seen. Worksop is a very small town built on the slope of a hill. It is unsightly, yet there are several attractive houses. Part of the main road is well constructed.

---

[51] Alexandre perhaps had the royal grandeur at Versailles in his mind. English country houses didn't run to that massive scale. But Norfolk had bought the big Elizabethan house of the Shrewsburys in 1740, and already had James Paine redecorating it in 1761, when it was burnt down. Paine was instructed to build a huge quadrangular house in its place, spanning the inner quadrangle with an Egyptian Hall on the lines of the York Assembly Rooms, and approached through a 2-storey circular tribune. You would arrive at the south front under a fine *porte-cochère*, almost the first of its kind. They began building at once, apparently with 500 workmen, working chiefly under the supervision of the duchess, herself an amateur architect. The roof was on the north wing after a year, and the wing was occupied. But in 1767 their nephew and heir died at 22, and with him died their resolution. Paine's grandiose designs survive, and an extraordinary oil painting, by William Hodges, in 1777, shows the north front with its statuary and urns along a skyline, and with its other three sides seen through the painter's imagination. It does look to us unescapably like a great Whitehall administrative building. Only the stable yard now survives and has been compared with the court of a Cambridge college. For Hodges' painting, see John Harris, *The Artist and the Country House*, 1979, revised 1985, pl 302. I have based my account of the detailed plans on Peter Leach's fine book, *James Paine*, 1988, pp. 27, 77–9.

SANDBECK PARK

On [Thursday] the 23rd   we left Worksop for Doncaster. On the way we stopped at *Lord Scarbrough's house*[52] – about half-way. You enter his park through a beautiful freestone gateway, simple, but exactly right. From there to the house you follow a ride which is almost straight although you can't see the end: it's lined with rare trees, of all ages, and some of them extremely handsome.

You arrive at the house through this woodland. It is beautiful, but simple,[53] built in freestone. The interior is gracefully decorated, the saloon fine, but nothing that makes me want to single it out. After mentioning the art of the house and giving a brief description, my spirit really isn't up to presenting it to its advantage, nor perhaps to mine.

In the front of the house and in the bottom of the valley runs a river that widens in view of the house but without enough width to seem natural: you're aware that it must have been an expensive business, for it is all contrived. The other facade is plain, but the view is extensive and lovely. A great lawn of which you can scarcely see the end, adorned with cattle and deer, and ending near a fine wood of great maturity, almost touching the sky.

After leaving the house we came to what is called *Roche Abbey*, 3 miles from the house, and a part of its estate. You travel through the park and come upon some superb trees, some of them enormous. I measured one – an evergreen – which was nine feet round.

You leave the park by a gateway to the west of the house, and cross a bit of country all enclosed: I'll come back to its farming methods. You reach the park we were making for by following the edge of a very deep valley, where you hear the very audible noises of a running stream. The valley's full of fair-sized trees. For the first time you realise what very hilly country you're in. We halted at a little inn near the old abbey, and from there we went down to see it on foot.

ROCHE ABBEY

We went through a gate and descended the steep hillside by a pretty tree-covered zig-zag path which brings you to the bottom, beside the little stream. From there

52 Sandbeck Park. The Scarbroughs regarded Lumley Castle, Co Durham, as their ancient seat, and Sandbeck as a mere villa before James Paine remodelled it for them c1763, the year after the palatial Worksop Manor for the Norfolks.
53 It could only seem 'simple' because they'd come straight from the grandeur of Worksop. At Sandbeck, Paine worked in the framework of an existing rectangle, unusually tall. Wings and central portico are pedimented. The two lower storeys are clad in rusticated stone (perhaps to reduce the sense of height: why?): under the portico, the upper ground floor is a very severely rusticated arcaded loggia. Behind the portico, running right across the piano nobile, the saloon has a very fine coved ceiling by Paine.

you see the mass of the ruins of the ancient abbey. You see two gatehouses[54] which I suppose led into the church, and various fragments of the abbey survive.

At the bottom of this tree-clad valley, the stream is of no great width but of very clear water and – often finding quite large stones in its way – forms several cascades, of which both the sight and the sound are very agreeable.[55] The whole valley seems smiling between two very tall slopes, a carpet of green arranged with trees and the ruined arches of this abbey. The stream waters the garden of the gardener's cottage, which is built very simply, rather in the ancient style.[56] Near the house is a stone bridge, built high and covered in branches. Under it, the river forms a pretty cascade. You go through a small wood and arrive at the edge of a beautiful river at a much higher level than the stream. It must be 300 feet across and a quarter of a mile long.[57] River and stream share the same source, and separate off from one another at

[54] The lower storey of the medieval inner gatehouse remains to the north-west of the ruins of the church: there was an outer gatehouse near the present car-park. You can see a few surviving stretches of the 10-ft stone wall that surrounded the 31-acre site, which spread more or less equally on both sides of the stream.

[55] This was part of Capability Brown's work over the years 1774–81, for the 4th earl of Scarbrough at Sandbeck Park. Dorothy Stroud (*Capability Brown*, 1975, p. 139) showed that 'the course of the stream which flowed past the cloisters was altered and dammed to form shallow cascades'. The low footings that outlined the accurate and complete plan of the church were all grassed over to form 'a neat bowling green'. These detailed footings were revealed again in the late 19th century, and you can now follow the lines of the buildings with unusual clarity. The blissful scene is shown from the air (Stroud, pl 51B), and she gives Brown's detailed proposals 'fixed on with Lord Scarbrough (With Poet's feeling and with Painter's eye)', which quotation was a reference to William Mason's *The English Garden*, 1772. Lionel Butler and Chris Given-Wilson, *Medieval Monasteries of Great Britain*, 2nd imp, 1983, 324–5, includes another excellent air-photo and a plan of the monastery of Cistercian monks, founded in 1147 and more or less completed in the 1160s. The tall twin eastern arches of the north and south transepts survive and show how remarkably far English Gothic had developed here. Apparently the whole church was vaulted in stone (unlike York's great Minster). The proximity of the white limestone rock in the hillside close to the north wall of the church makes this fine ruin look almost as if it's carved directly from the rock-bed, like Petra. The rock gave its name to Roche Abbey, which in turn gave its name to the local quarries of handsome magnesium limestone. See Clifton-Taylor, *Patterns of English Building*, 1962, p. 109.

[56] Alexandre's sketch didn't do justice to the very pleasant castellated Gothick cottage, in Roche stone. In 1998 it serves as English Heritage's ticket-office. It would make a most attractive curator's house. It is not clear what purpose it served in Brown's day, or whether he designed it: it was well within his capabilities.

[57] This is Laughton Pond, as shown on the English Heritage *Roche Abbey* booklet, p. 4. In 1774, in Article 5 of Brown's contract for Sandbeck (Stroud, *Capability Brown*, 1975, p. 139), Stroud doesn't make clear whether the contract is preserved in Brown's surviving account-book, deposited with the Royal Horticultural Society: see p. 9. Brown undertook 'to finish all the valley of Roach Abbey . . . beginning at the head of the Hammer Pond, and continuing up the valley towards Loton in the Morn . . . and to continue the Water and Dress the Valley up by the Present Farm House'. Fees of £3,000 were agreed, but only a little over £1,000 was received. 'Laughton in the Morn' was an abbreviation of Laughton-en-le-Morthen, which is distinguished by what Pevsner reckoned one of the finest spires in the West Riding. William Gilpin noticed already in 1776 that Brown's valley with the lake looked towards Laughton spire (Stroud, *loc cit*). But ten years later, Alexandre seems not to have had his eye 'caught' by it.

a weir on the stream. After separating, the river broadens until it reaches a dam of some considerable height. It forms a waterfall with a 12-foot drop, passing over rocks on either side adding extra enchantment to the view. This piece of water made a deep impression on me, on account of its position.

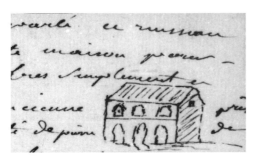

15. *The gardener's cottage at Roche Abbey (Alexandre's sketch).*

As you stand at the waterfall, you see this stretch of water, caressed on both sides by very high slopes that are beautifully covered with all kinds of woods. These slopes seem often to advance, or to withdraw, to make room for the water, and thus they prevent the formation of any suggestion of a straight line. You lose sight of it among the trees. Then when it narrows at the bottom of the valley it contrasts with smooth slopes. All that makes for a very beautiful land-surface, combining lake waters that come right along the valley and up to your feet. This is one of the most beautiful views I've ever experienced. The water of the cascade mingles with that of the stream, and together they form quite a wide river; it runs over the rocks, a source of unceasing pleasure. This whole area is perhaps two or three miles long. It is intersected by a number of carefully designed walks, and maintained by lord Scarbrough as a continuation of his park at Sandbeck.[58]

After Roche Abbey, we went on to dine at Tickhill, where you find the ruins of a castle, a formidable landmark that once dominated all the country around. There are extensive earthworks, and a tremendous hill.[59] From there we went on to sleep at Doncaster. The road was pleasant and the country undulating, with mostly meadowland, which they need for the large number of beasts they fatten. Their rotation of arable crops is:

1. oats   2. beans   3. barley   4. fallow   5. barley   6. grass

---

[58] Alexandre makes an excellent guide: most visitors venture no further than the lower stream and the fine ruins.

[59] Byng, too, on leaving Roche Abbey, 'came into the turnpike that soon brought us to Tickhill, and glad we were to partake of cold lamb, eggs and bacon (and some had collops at the young man's desire), when we ate as for a wager. Unluckily we are too early for beans and peas [11 June 1789]. Our dinner finished and some Burton ale drunk (but not by me).' Byng's bill at the Tickhill Red Lion for himself and two friends and their horses came to 7s 6d (37.5 modern pence). It is vexatious that Alexandre practised a self-denying ordinance, generally abstaining from descriptions of the food and general hospitality of inns.

16. *Roche Abbey: the gardener's cottage itself, serving as a ticket-office for English Heritage in 1998. It would make a pleasant curator's house.*

It's astonishing that they sow the barley after the beans and after the fallow year, but that's the rotation that serves them best. They deserve to have a really good harvest after the fallow year: it hurts me to say so, as a declared enemy of fallowing, but I'm glad to say that they use that year to manure the fallow ground.

3

Ambitious Enterprises: Doncaster to Leeds

At Doncaster, a 'very pretty' town, the most enterprising farming included bog-reclamation at Pawtrick Carr, pioneered by Edward Miller, Doncaster's organist-historian; and flax-growing. Messrs Walker's iron-furnaces and cannon foundries at Rotherham called for a sketch of a water-powered bellows furnace. The approach to the great east front of Wentworth Woodhouse, 600 ft wide, up through the park from Greasborough, was spoilt for them by driving rain, but they seem to have made out the 'Bean Seat' and Flitcroft's Doric temple. Alexandre thought the great double outside staircase, folded back on itself under the central portico, the best he'd seen in England. He showed off, calling it an Escalier en fer à cheval, which sounds like some kind of iron staircase for horses, and is in fact circular, as at Fontainebleau. He was naturally full of admiration for 'the Whistle-jacket room', and the great marble saloon, which wasn't quite finished. At Wentworth Castle, they were impressed by the Long Gallery and the 'pleasure garden', leading up to a fine folly, a large sham castle, now often called Stainborough Castle. Leeds was pronounced beautiful, its streets well designed, though the General Infirmary 'inclined more to magnificence than utility': it was one of Carr of York's distinguished designs. Alexandre described the White Cloth Hall and the Mixed Cloth Hall, and liked all the cloth he saw except what was made in Halifax; he admired the moderation of the Leeds merchants in contrast with those he remembered at Liverpool.

You reach Doncaster by a beautiful route and very well-made road.[1] The town's on a rise. It seems large but has only one parish. The country round has plenty of people and the town looks pleasant to live in. A river brings its provisions and one part of its trade.

DONCASTER

Friday the 24th, Doncaster Angel   On the morning of the 24th we asked our landlord[2] if he could find us someone who would show us the farming of the neighbourhood. The

---

[1] Byng concurred when he came 8 years later, 2 June 1792: 'Doncaster looks well in approach; and is a well-built, well-paved and wide-streeted town. The Angel where I expected everything comfortable I found to be nasty, insolent, and with city stabling . . . In a sad room, after my long ride, I could not eat what they brought: a dirty bit of salmon, that had been dress'd before, with 2 lumps of boil'd beef: I sent them both out, and then could not get a waiter near me.'
[2] 'I long'd to be able to kick the landlord, to whom I complain'd in vain' (Byng). The landlord then was Thomas Foster.

17. Doncaster. Merchants' houses beside the Roman road south. Obelisk, 1792, replaced the medieval cross of the Steward of Conisborough Castle, which stood where F. Nash stood to draw this. It appears in Edward Miller's fine History of Doncaster.

person he came up with had the appearance of a small farmer. We left on our little excursion on foot by half-past ten, crossing the town, which is very pretty.[3] It has a very rich corporation, which has added much to the beauty of the town and its environs. The main street, a mile long, is delightfully broad and well-built about the middle; you notice a building in freestone where the Corporation meets.[4] The stone is common locally, and I have seen ordinary houses built of it.[5]

---

[3] Arthur Young in 1770 used these same words: they would not occur to any visitor to Doncaster today.

[4] The Mansion House, James Paine's first urban commission, now looks completely out of place, virtually the only building in Doncaster worth notice. Not one of his very distinguished designs, it was 'borrowed' from Inigo Jones (Peter Leach, *James Paine*, 1988, p. 99). It had been built 1744–50 and temporarily interrupted by the presence of government troops during the 1745 Jacobite Rebellion. Alexandre and Lazowski glanced at it before the giant pediment had been replaced (in 1800) by an attic storey with parapet. Paine's proposed Palladian wings were not built (see Leach *op cit*, pl 93, p. 100). If they'd taken a little more time, Alexandre might have recognised the source of the stone.

[5] Paine used Roche Abbey stone here, which Wren is alleged to have thought the best building stone after Portland: Paine also used it in Sandbeck Park but, as Alec Clifton-Taylor pointed out (in *Pattern of English Building*, p. 109), it has the disadvantage of turning a dark grey, and failing to resist the chemicals in coal smoke.

To get back to our farm-walk, we left the town on foot. We were off to the left of the London road.[6] In these very low-lying lands of the poorest quality, we came first to a swamp [*marais*]: at present it scarcely merits any other name. however, they do manage to harvest some grain. The ground is a peaty turf, apparently bottomless, for you could drive a pole down without meeting any obstruction.[7] These lands you leave as meadows for as long as possible, but the wetness of the soil involves a great deal of work. You are reduced to burning the turf if you want wheat to grow, and this is ordinarily the rotation:

        1. turnips   2. wheat   3. turf

As I say, they burn the turf before the ground's prepared for turnips. They turn their sheep on to graze the turnips and manure the land. Then, before April, when the land's apt to be dry, they sow their wheat. Their grass they sow by drawing a stick to score lightly across the ground, and they leave it as meadowlands up to the point when the roots show signs of rot.

These lands fetch nine shillings an acre. The reason for this high price is the nearness of the town, and those with cattle send them down here to graze in preference to the better land. Sometimes they feed cattle and sometimes they grow flax in these places. But half of the land is useless and breaks up when you try to work it.

You need to have a good understanding of these poor lands, which scarcely repay outgoings. But all that springs from a cause which is all too foreign to us: a love of the public good. It's very clear that if these lands are let solely according to a

---

6   It's clear from their itinerary that Alexandre was thinking of the road they'd arrived on from Tickhill as 'the London Road'; the present A60, which is very close to the present A1. The old Great North Road, the Roman road south from Doncaster through Bawtry, wasn't in his mind, though it was the continuation of that broad Doncaster High Street he admired.

7   They have ventured into Doncaster Carr, which on Thomas Jefferys' *County of York Survey'd*, 1775, is labelled PAWTRICK CARR. Carr is 'now usually wet, boggy ground, a meadow recovered from the bog' – *Oxford English Dictionary*. The modern spelling of Pawtrick is Potteric. The Carr was drained by John Smeaton in 1764 and it was enclosed in 1771. The west side of the Carr is now obscured by railway sidings and yards. Even the Nature Reserve near Balby Carr Farm is enmeshed in railways. There were once no fewer than 60 miles of sidings, and 'the Plant' was the chief locomotive works of the Great Northern, later the LNER. The works were closed for a week in September to clear the sidings for St Leger horses and race-goers. (See an exciting account of all this in Jack Simmons and Gordon Biddle, *Oxford Companion to British Railway History*, 1997, p. 129.) Then there was the enormous coal traffic. One sees why Doncaster's no longer the pretty town Arthur Young, Alexandre and the others saw.

Edward Miller, the organist-historian of Doncaster (1804) was the pioneer of the cultivation of the Carrs. He wrote: 'Soon after the Act of 1771 I rented of the Corporation 65 acres of Carr land and had a lease of 21 years, average 9 shillings an acre. At the expiry of the lease, the Corporation let it for more than treble the price. I bought 20 acres for £7 an acre and sold for £40. The first process was pare and burn the soil. On ploughing afterwards for a crop of rape, the horses sunk up to the middle and my men were often seen drawing their legs out of the bog with ropes. After a tolerable crop of rape, I was encouraged to try wheat but had only a single sack from 10 acres. Mr Francis Elwiss of Loversall [on the west side of the Carr] knew more about the Carrs than any man of his day. He received from other owners 10s an acre for paring and 10 for ploughing.' He lived to behold the Carrs 'waving with corn and luxuriant in the highest degree'. I have found no reference to flax in Miller.

common average value – 6 shillings an acre – one would have to adjust the sum that a great number of these acres would fetch to relate to the nation as a whole.

We turn now to the kind of soils that are suitable for flax-growing. They should consist of a loamy sand[8] to a depth of between 6 inches and a foot of sand, to keep them dry. In this rather wet land, the deeper the sandy soil the better, remembering the importance of keeping the flax dry. They never sow flax until the field has been worked with the greatest care, and it takes at least ten years for the land to be at its best. The field is prepared before winter so that the snow and frost can make it more friable. For, with the sandy soil underneath, you can only plough it once for fear of bringing the sand up on to the surface: that would ruin it. They generally sow two bushells of seed to the acre. This is the general rotation in these parts:

       1. flax   2. wheat   3. beans   4. wheat   5. grass

If the soil is well worked, the wheat crop is fairly good, especially after flax. The usual yield of flax is 70 tons (28 *livres* weight) per acre. They have harvested as much as 200 tons, but that's very rare. They extract from these 70 tons something between a quarter and three-quarters of linseed oil, from which one-quarter goes to fatten the bullocks. One quarter of linseed costs between 2 and 3 *louis* [between 5 and ten shillings; or between quarter and half of one pound sterling], and a ton of linseed costs about 5 shillings. You can see the benefit to the farmer of a good harvest, but it's so risky a crop that a great many farmers dislike it. [The chief hazards are, and presumably were, a particular vulnerability to birds and to summer hailstorms.] They reckon the best flax is that which stands no higher than 2 to 2.5 feet high, but the taller variety's more common.

When they sow grass seed, its always the hayseed of *regrasse* [presumably a mis-hearing of rib-grass] and white clover. They always leave their meadows 14 or 15 years before breaking them up.

They sow the linseed in May and, at the end of 3 months, it is cut. It is then put into water for a fortnight or three weeks.[9] After that, it's spread out over a meadow and then collected into little heaps and left to dry.[10] Once it's dry, it's spun into yarn in the way everyone knows. All these operations are worth to the farmer 36 *sols*

---

8 What Arthur Young called 'sandy loam'. Prescribing the land favoured for hemp (it's odd that he scarcely mentions flax) in his *General View of the Agriculture of Suffolk* (1797, pp. 119–37) he associates it with the 10 miles from Eye to Beccles along the Waveney valley: 'it does well on old meadow and bottoms near rivers. They manure it with great attention.' It also favours the Fen-edge of west Norfolk and Cambridgeshire. J. R. Ravensdale refers to small quantities of hemp and flax growing on the Chamberlains manor in Landbeach in the 14th century: *Liable to Floods*, Cambridge UP, 1974, p. 117. The lands there are like the carrs, the edges of boggy land such as Alexandre describes here at the southern edge of Doncaster. In 1758, *Sir William Burrell's Northern Tour* (ed G. Dunbar, Edinburgh 1997, p. 30), in north Lincolnshire, near Brigg, noted: 'All sorts of grain grows here and large quantities of hemp and flax. A great extent of land now unprofitable might be made fit for cultivation at a very small expence . . . for want of which 22,000 acres remain fenny and useless which may easily be drained . . . into the Humber.'

9 This process is known as retting, or water-retting. An alternative method was dew-retting, leaving it spread.

10 In June 1785 and January 1786 the children of two flax-dressers were baptised in St George's, Doncaster.

[about 19 English pence] *la ton* [he must mean per stone]. In these lands suitable for sowing linseed, when the farmer decides against going on with it, this is the rotation one of them has adopted, tilling and sowing over 14 years, in which he has prospered:[11]

1. oats 2. wheat and rye 3. oats 4. wheat and rye 5. turnips 6. fallow 7. grass They plough only once. In sowing their oats, they merely draw a stick over the ground for a seed-furrow. They harvest oats up to 3 quarters to the acre, which is an immense yield.[12] As I understand it, wheat and rye is quite a common arable crop and one that combines, they think, for the making of better and more wholesome bread. Combining them doesn't affect the yield of the rye; nor, scarcely, that of the wheat.

When the turnips are small, they clean them of weeds by hoeing, and repeat the process a little later, which works very well.[13] But what grieves me is that year lost when they fallow. I've seen so many districts where they don't even know the meaning of this word that I can no more accustom myself to it than to the run of four grain harvests they gather in, which is every bit as harmful: what exhausts the land is worse, if anything. Their excuse is that otherwise they wouldn't easily discover the roots of the old grasses. With their lands in such good condition, they can't take much harm. After the fallow year, they fertilise their land, and sow more grass, as I said earlier, and prove thereby that the great advantage of ploughing up the meadows comes from what they put back in the new seed. All these good lands are worth 3 *louis* [15 shillings] an acre,[14] and I believe that is not too high. The cattle feed on these good meadows until April, so that their dung is spread thoroughly.

The sheep here are not native: they don't raise them, but merely import them for fattening – which they do on turnips. As to the bullocks, they are also brought in, generally from Scotland, and fed on turnips or on *linseed-oil cakes*. The first method is much more advantageous to the farmer, and also to the meat, which is good, but apparently not so fat as by the second method of feeding. To fatten a bullock you need nearly a load of these oil-cakes, which cost about 4 *louis* [£1 sterling]. Now, in this bad year, they cost twice as much.

There are other farmlands around the town of Doncaster, both worse and better than those I've just described. You get an idea of the good that this farming has achieved when you see that the day's work of a farm-labourer costs in winter 32–36

---

11 Presumably he was their guide. It would have been good to know who he was, which farm, etc, but I suppose unnecessary in the interests of Mr Lazowski's fact-finding.
12 He probably means 'by local standards'. In 1797, Arthur Young reckoned 'the average produce of this grain [in Suffolk] at four quarters, possibly four and a half': *General View of the Agriculture of Suffolk*, 1797, p. 56.
13 Young, *op cit*, p. 79: 'The second hoeing is given about a fortnight or three weeks after the first, at half the expense – 25s an acre: it answers exceedingly well'.
14 Cf Arthur Young's Section VIII on 'political agriculture', statistics of the produce of land in Suffolk: *General View*, 1797, pp. 266–78.

sols [16–17 English pence pre-decimalisation], and in summer board and keep are added.[15]

About a mile from the town is the course where the races are held sometime in September. The whole of the nobility of the area meets here. The Corporation has laid out a course precisely two miles long and 200 yards in breadth in a state of such perfection that it's regarded as the best in England after Newmarket.[16]

After completing our tour we returned to the inn. We had dined with our farmer, who was brimming with intelligence and instruction.[17] This evening we are busy writing up everything he has told us.

[Saturday] *25 March*   we left Doncaster for *Rotherham*: it was only 12 miles, but we knew we'd be finding forges and furnaces and so left before 9 in the morning and made the journey without a stop. The countryside was beautiful, up hill and down dale [*assez coupé et montagneux*], and after two miles left the Doncaster soils and entered a district of red sand, above red sandstone in the valleys. You run along above the little river Don, the one that goes to Doncaster, and all along the road you see a great many country houses, some of them very pretty. And all the countryside seemed well peopled[18] and well stocked with cattle. Just as we were entering *Rotherham* we came to a farm that a gentleman farmer was managing for himself: it had all the appearance of being productively and very carefully farmed.

ROTHERHAM

Rotherham Red Lion   We got to Rotherham at about 1 in the afternoon. We had some dinner and went to see the furnaces. It's a small town, and scarcely warrants the name. It's badly built and badly paved.[19] I saw some pretty houses on the edges of the town,

[15] Arthur Young in Suffolk (*General View*, 1797, p. 202) reckoned labour by the day, beer included, was 16 pence in winter, 18 pence in summer, and 34 pence in harvest.
[16] They probably didn't see the course or he would have mentioned the superb grandstand designed by John Carr of York, 1777–81. It was altered in 1804 and 1824, and demolished in 1969. (Pevsner's *West Riding*, 1959, pl 63a reproduced R. G. Reeve's engraving of J. Pollard's exciting painting.) For the Victorian popularisation of Doncaster Races, especially the St Leger, see footnote 7 to p. 42 above. See also B. Wragg's *John Carr of York*, 2000, Pl 133, p. 138.
[17] It is maddening not to be told his name. It seems doubtful whether he was Mr Miller, the historian: see footnote 7 above.
[18] Arriving in Rotherham from the village of Maltby, just south of the road the Frenchmen took, Byng (II, 22) couldn't resist saying: 'Finer children than in this country I never saw; and such white curling polls cost me many a halfpenny, thinking of my Frek [Frederick was his 4-and-a-half year old son] and wishing he was here to walk with and talk to me. The happiness and growth of these children depend upon their having the nourishment of warmth.' Staying in the tumbledown Rotherham Crown (June 1789) he walked down and looked across the river to a 'new-built, flourishing town arising from the cannon-foundries and great ironworks established by Mr Walker, who not only maintains the neighbourhood, but has so honourably enriched himself that he and [three of] his sons live in magnificent villas built on several eminences about the town. They ought to invent signals for invitations and announcements of all kinds.'
[19] It's extraordinary that their inn faced straight onto what Pevsner rightly calls 'one of the largest

but none in the middle. The most striking houses had been recently built by the Messrs Walker, the three brothers who are masters of these foundries I'm about to describe. Their forebears amassed a very big fortune in this branch of industry, and they are continuing in it. Their houses are near the ironworks, well designed and handsome.[20]

The town is supplied with iron and heavy goods by the river Don, which washes its walls and is wide enough to carry very stout vessels. This same river, part of which is used as navigation canal,[21] also works corn mills. A wheel to power a forge is of a different kind. The forge, which stands on the river, didn't seem to be distinguished from any other by any new invention. They flatten the iron, a small piece, to make it more pliable and suitable for small products.

Now, to get back to describing our visit. We had set out in the afternoon to see the furnaces belonging to Messrs Walker. They are more than a mile outside the town on a small tributary of the Don.[22] We arrived at the workshop just as they were about to cast [*fondre*]. After we'd asked several layman's questions about the process, we had a discussion with one of the workmen who was very bright. Soon after, the smelting was done, and perhaps in a manner we won't see again. The molten iron flows, as we remembered seeing in France and in Coalbrookdale, from the great furnace along a channel especially shaped in sand and which goes into another furnace held expressly in lime. From there it was carried on shovels to wherever it had to go. I saw some very fine pieces they'd cast in the other furnaces, very well finished. The grain of the metal must be very fine to make such beautiful pieces.[23]

and stateliest parish churches in Yorkshire'. Its central spire rises, with pride and elegance, to 180 ft. Yet they were in such a hurry to get to the foundries that they ignored it. Perhaps if they'd ventured inside, the fan-vaulting in the tower would have impressed them, as it had in Peterborough cathedral.

20 Joshua Walker got John Carr of York to design Clifton House for him 1782/3: 2 storeys of 5 bays, stone-faced, dignified, with 3 central bays coming forward under pediment, with porch on Tuscan columns under Venetian window: the 5 upstair windows neatly balustraded. The handsome curved main staircase was by John Platt, 1783–4, see below. Clifton House now serves well as Rotherham's Museum. Joshua's brother Jonathan got John Platt (1728–1810) to build Ferham House for him, beside the Kimberworth Road in September 1787, so Alexandre is unlikely to have seen it: it's more of a prospect house (though Clifton, too, stands at the head of a steep hill): Ferham has 3 storeys and 5 bays, the central 3 making a canted bay rising through the 3 storeys gracefully. In 1998 it was a retirement home. The third brother's East Wood House has gone, as have the original Walkers. Byng's description of their houses on 'several eminences about the town' is more descriptive than Alexandre's 'near their ironworks'.

21 The river Don, which they'd followed with such delight from Doncaster, was, as they should have noticed, not navigable. The Navigation ran separately and more or less parallel to the river, on the farther side of it from the town, both upstream and down. One can only guess how he imagined the Don washing the town's walls. It was never a walled town. But he may have been confused on seeing the battlements of the Bridge Chapel, c1483, on the medieval bridge.

22 In fact they are no more than a quarter of a mile from the parish church, and the Red Lion where they were staying. This discrepancy is hard to explain, for if they had been misdirected Alexandre would almost certainly have mentioned that. Nor is it possible to imagine what small tributary he refers to.

23 Is it known what pieces they were turning out in 1786?

At this site there are three furnaces: two with bellows worked by water-power, the other by a steam-pump[24] which is used only in the making of iron bars from a red ore. To make iron from this you mix charcoal, the ore – which isn't crude – and limestone all together. The proportions are 2 baskets of charcoal, 6 of ore (these aren't as big as the charcoal baskets), and 2 of the limestone. You mix these same quantities 26 times for a single smelting. When they are ready, they can cast twice a day.

The two other furnaces use only the local ore. The bellows are worked by a machine that is kept in motion by water. I think a little drawing is called for to explain it [drawing omitted since it is totally inadequate]. The lever (C) is held, on one side, in the cylinder (A) by the bar (D), to which is held suspended the weight (E). This weight is balanced at point (G) by the other bar (F), which connects at point (B) with the water-wheel. There are three of these machines and together they ensure that the bellows work very regularly and make possible two castings a day. So that you can generally count on 20 tons of casting weight a week, which means 44,800 *livres* for a single furnace. [The English £ sterling was worth approximately 23 *livres*: if Alexandre did his sums right, each furnace should have produced iron worth about £1,948 a week!] They burn coal that has already been burnt together with ore that has also been part of the process – the same as in so many furnaces. The reasons for their burning it is so that the same quantity of iron can be cast in a smaller volume. The number of times, and the method by which they load the furnace is the same as for the first furnace, which I've described.

They also cast cannon, and in the same manner. They make them in the perpendicular plane, bringing their casting into the mould where they drill the bore by means of an instrument the same calibre as the piece, turning inside it when the piece has been fixed so that it can't move. I didn't see this process but was told how it was done.[25]

The ore and the coal are brought two miles from the place where they are obtained for nothing.

The workmen are paid, the lowest at 8 shillings a week, ordinarily at 2 *sols* a day [approximately 8 'new' pence], and the best earning 4 or 5 shillings a day.

Around this town there are three furnaces, two forges, one place where iron is cut [*où l'on coupe le fer* (Is this a slitting mill, in which iron bars or plates were slit into nail-rods, etc?)],[26] 4 other flatting-mills [*où on l'aplatit*: for rolling the iron into sheets?]. Every branch of this business is growing remorselessly.

In addition, the trade of *glaces* [?looking-glass-making] occupies many of the townspeople.

---

[24] A Boulton & Watt steam engine seems to have been installed by 1782 (Judith A. Ely, *The Walkers of Rotherham*, public Borough Library, Walker Place, Rotherham, 1992).
[25] In 1773 (Ely, *op cit*), Samuel Walker's journal recorded the first construction of 2 boring-pits for cannon. In 1782, over 1,220 tons of ordnance were produced, over half the produce of the foundry, at the end of the American War of Independence.
[26] Ely mentions a river-powered slitting-mill and grinding works in the 1760s.

18. *Wentworth Woodhouse: the east front that so enchanted Alexandre with its width (42 bays) and the nobility of its double staircase and portico.*

WENTWORTH WOODHOUSE

Sunday 26 March   we left *Rotherham* to see Lord Fitzwilliam's[27] Wentworth House, another of whose houses we passed at Milton as we left Peterborough [p. 16 above]. Here his house is only four and a half miles from Rotherham, near Wentworth village. Before reaching it, you enter a park for perhaps a couple of miles: very fine, but the weather was so terrible that we could scarcely see anything. I got an impression of a great many buildings, pavilions, seats, in fact everything you could imagine as ornaments to a garden.[28]

Before reaching the house you pass, on an eminence, a small pavilion of freestone with eight columns, a rotunda *à l'italienne*, elegant.[29] The way the house comes into

27 Charles, 4th Earl FitzWilliam, had succeeded, as recently as 1782, to the enormous estates of Charles Watson-Wentworth, 2nd Marquess of Rockingham, who continued the work Thomas, 1st Marquess, had begun c1734 in building this extraordinary house – its width almost twice the span of Blenheim, where Alexandre had so unaffectedly applauded the 'great, great noble and beautiful buildings of Sir John Vanbrugh' (*Innocent Espionage*, p. 132). They had succeeded very indirectly, through a great-uncle whose grandfather was Charles I's minister Thomas Wentworth, 1st earl of Strafford. On 2 September 1789, FitzWilliam entertained the Prince of Wales and about 40,000 people here. The owner of the house since 1999 has been Mr Clifford Newbold. The well-maintained park and estate were lately inherited by Sir Philip Maylor-Leyland.

28 Arthur Young's *6 Months Tour of the North* has a full lyrical description of the park in 1770, giving the clearest overall picture of this park as it was when the two Frenchmen were here. One notable freestone 'seat' survives in the form of a simple arched shelter-recess, close to the Doric temple: it is called the Bean Seat, apparently in recollection of a former Lady FitzWilliam who liked to take a bag of beans out there to the seat, where the deer came to her to be fed.

29 The rusticated rotunda with eight columns is the Doric temple, one of the two temples

view is admirable. You don't suspect it is so near until you've come round the hummock I just mentioned:[30] suddenly, there it is, within gun-shot, and you see widespread before you one of the most beautiful façades I've ever seen, owing equally much to its grandeur and its nobility.

You walk right up to the portico unable to take your eyes off it, it so entirely commands your admiration.[31]

The front is 42 bays wide. In the middle is a great double staircase, folded back on itself and ending beneath the portico supported by 6 Corinthian columns, carved with the utmost perfection.[32] It is crowned by a pediment. This most elegant portico is the best I've seen in England. The rest of this very big frontage is relatively low, yet manages to hold together. The wings, too, terminate in slightly smaller square buildings.

recorded by Colvin (*Dictionary*, p. 367) as having been designed by Henry Flitcroft (1697–1769), who worked here from about 1734. (The other, beyond the terrace on the west side of the house, they wouldn't have seen.)

30 Despite major changes to the park landscape – notably those by Humphry Repton, who made a great fuss about enhancing the way the house was, till the last minute, hidden, as the French had already very satisfactorily found (H. Repton, *The Art of Landscape Gardening*, 1795 and 1803, ed J. Nolen, Boston and New York 1907, p. 81) and by the dire open-cast mining unleashed right up to the west front of the house by E Shinwell, Minister of Fuel and Power, c1946 (see, eg, James Lees-Milne, *Caves of Ice*, Faber, 1983, p. 53), visitors approaching the house across the old drive from Greasborough today can only enjoy most agreeably the results of the past half-century of replanting of the public approach through the park to Wentworth Woodhouse.

31 Despite the driving rain, he is naturally impressed by this enormous east front, 600 ft wide. It is based on Colen Campbell's famous Palladian house at Wanstead, c1714–20, demolished 1824. The designs of the two houses are most easily compared in John Summerson, *The Unromantic Castle*, 1990, p. 95. Wentworth Woodhouse was at least still standing in 2001. In *Country Life*, 21 January 1999, John Martin Robinson called for national action to safeguard it, and made use of the marvellous photographs of 1923, with the original furniture: his Pl 1, from a slight rise, gives the best view of the massing of the entire front (from slightly lower, photographs make it 'strag-gle'). The photograph of the Marble Saloon is sensational. In his *Dictionary*, under Ralph Tunnicliffe, Colvin shows the building begun in the 1730s under Tunnicliffe, who died in 1736. 'Henry Flitcroft was brought in to advise, and to complete the building after Tunnicliffe's death. He made minor adjustments to the elevation, including raising on pedestals the columns of the portico.' The east front is essentially Tunnicliffe's design (after Wanstead etc) with improvements by Carr of York in the 1780s, in the wings. The glories of the interior are Flitcroft's. Some were used in the TV filming, in 1999, of Mrs Gaskell's novel *Wives and Daughters*.

32 Again, I'm in Sir Howard Colvin's debt. Describing the great double staircase, Alexandre uses the historic French architectural term '*Escalier en fer à cheval*', and misleadingly he's got the wrong term. Colvin has sent me the relevant definition in A. C. Davilers, *Cours d'Architecture*, Paris 1720, II, p. 577: there, *Escalier en fer à cheval* means 'staircase projecting from a facade: its plan is circular and the steps are not parallel: for example those of the Cour du Cheval Blanc at Fontainebleau, and at the Villa Farnese at Caprarola'. (At Caprarola there is also a staircase on the same plan as Wentworth Woodhouse's: the term Alexandre needed was *Grand Perron en deux rampes de chaque coté*.) I naturally began by thinking he'd found at Wentworth 'an iron stairway for the convenience of horses'.

From straight in front of the pediment you see, as he did, 6 columns, but each of the end columns conceals another so that there are *eight* supporting the portico. It stands on rather an exposed slope, and the weather was 'terrible'.

The interior is immense, and the rooms are beautiful, though a long way short of what the outside encourages you to expect.[33] The dining-room is the most beautiful, but all the rooms are very well furnished, elegant, and full of good pictures.[34] The *halle*, which isn't completely finished, is 60 feet square [the details show that he is really describing the Marble Saloon],[35] all in stucco[36] and adorned with attached columns in antique yellow.[37] The height and proportions have a wonderful effect.[38]

I'm really vexed at seeing nothing of the park, for it seemed superb and very large. All we saw was a well-designed stretch of water, meant to be seen from the house.[39] The weather was so deplorable that we made for the inn, half a mile off, where we dined. From there we reached *Barnsley* for the night.[40] Around here you find very good farm-lands fetching at least 16 shillings an acre. This landscape has very much the feel of that of Sheffield, which we are very near.[41] The enclosures are all stone-walled, and with big stones.

We'd come to see Lord *Strafford*'s house, but as it was Sunday we left that visit till tomorrow. All today our travelling was very hilly, in country like that we found last year in *Derbyshire*. Missing the excursion today compensates us with the pleasant thought that the horses are having a rest.

Barnsley White Bear Barnsley's a very small town on high ground above some fine
meadows.

On Monday 27 March we rode out on a hired horse to see Lord *Strafford*'s house,[42] two
miles off.

---

33 The almost royal-French *scale* outside, and that portico, clearly led Alexandre to expect an interior even grander than Blenheim's. The grandeur here of Flitcroft's Marble Saloon is naturally different from Vanrugh's baroque: half a century later, Flitcroft was refining Inigo Jones and Palladio, still.

34 Ruth Harman kindly points out that the dining-room they admired is 'the Whistle-jacket room', which was the dining-room originally.

35 Athenian Stuart evidently designed the panels above the niches for the classical statues. Can he have done the very pretty garlands between the scagliola Corinthian pilasters around the gallery? The only indication that the Marble Saloon 'wasn't completely finished' seems to have been the gaps waiting for the large white-marble reliefs above the fireplaces, done c1821, by John Gibson, in Rome.

36 The flat wall-surfaces are marbled plaster, rather than the marble suggested by the Saloon's name.

37 Alexandre wrote *jaune ancient*, an early franglais phrase: they are of scagliola; attached Greek Ionic columns below the gallery, and flat pilasters with Corinthian capitals in the gallery. Pevsner called them 'brown'.

38 They do: they are based on the proportions of Inigo Jones's hall in the Queen's House at Greenwich.

39 This is puzzling: Repton wasn't here till some years later.

40 At the White Bear, now gone.

41 And which they had visited the previous year, chiefly to be shown the steel-making (*Innocent Espionage*, 51–6).

42 Charles I's minister was the 1st Wentworth Earl of Strafford: the title died with his childless son in 1695 and the estate passed through his daughter to Thos Watson of Rockingham Castle.

WENTWORTH CASTLE

This house, above a steep slope, is built of freestone and very simply, though the side facing south has a new façade that's rich and elegant.[43] The whole house forms almost a square. As I said, it occupies a height, a considerable hill, covered with woods. From the house you see over the entire countryside, for miles around, with plenty of inhabitants. A river crosses the park and – although it's fairly wide – it does little to dispel the idea of a dry countryside. The way its course is accompanied by a drive is pleasant. The view's edged by a hill for about 2 miles; part of it crowned by woods, the other part by an old castle and fortifications[44] that give it, from a distance, a misleading air of function and activity it certainly needs.

Inside the house itself, the most beautiful room is the [Long] Gallery which is 60 yards, or 180 English feet, long,[45] and which occupies the entire east side of the

Meanwhile, the title was re-created in 1711 for another Thomas Wentworth (1672–1739) – directly descended from Strafford's brother. This new 1st Earl of Strafford had been a tough young soldier in the thick of the fighting at Steinkerk when he was 20; next year he was made aide-de-camp and groom of the bedchamber to William III, and was in attendance at the king's last illness. After kissing hands on Anne's succession he returned to the war, but next year was envoy to the new kingdom of Prussia, becoming envoy-extraordinary: his popularity there seems to explain his choice of architect at Stainborough for the ambitious new east front of what till 1730 had been known as Stainborough Hall. The new front was completed to celebrate the re-creation for him of the Strafford earldom. His designer was General Jean de Bodt, a Frenchman who had created the arsenal for Frederick I in Berlin: Thomas Archer exercised some useful restraint.

[43] As centrepiece, four tall Corinthian pilasters frame these broad round-headed windows, the large spaces between window-heads and entablature filled with extraordinary carvings in very high relief; in the side panels various clusters of dangling fruit, in the middle panel his formidably elaborate coat of arms, supporters' limbs intermingled with trophies, all surmounted by the earl's coronet. According to Rupert Gunnis (*Dictionary of British Sculptors*, 1964), Joseph Bower, father and son, were the master-masons for building Wentworth Castle, 1714–22, 'and they were responsible for the carved stonework'. The younger Bower in 1725 made 'the cascade in the menagerie' and in 1725 built three miniature towers named after Strafford's daughters; in 1734 an obelisk in memory of Queen Anne, in 1734 a temple copied from one at Tivoli, in 1742 a column with carved capital. Most of those features survive, though not one designed by Horace Walpole in the Menagerie Wood. Strafford's German connections suggest the possibility of an anglicised *Bauer*. My guess is that the 'Wentworth Castle' the Bowers built was the impressive, substantial eye-catcher folly some way higher up the hill, caught romantically in 'Mr Webb's' painting of 1745 (John Harris, *The Artist and the Country House*, 1979, revised 1985, pl 285). The folly is now usually called Stainborough Castle to distinguish it from Wentworth Castle, the house Strafford was embellishing for himself for his retirement in Stainborough, separated by 6 miles (and now by the M 1 motorway) from the rivals at Wentworth Woodhouse. Strafford's house now serves as Northern College of Residential Adult Education attached to Sheffield University; the garden leading up to Stainborough Castle folly is planted with a remarkable variety of rhododendrons and azaleas, part of the National Collection. David Hey has written an excellent *Short History* of the house for English Life Publications, 1991.

[44] See footnote 43 above.

[45] Said to have been modelled on the Galleria of the Palazzo Colonna in Rome, which was finished in 1703. The windows along the 15-bay east wall, together with a fine Venetian window at the east end, now light the college library, its utility shelving set happily, if a shade incongru-

19. *Above Wentworth Castle, Stainborough Castle Folly. It appears spectacularly in a painting of 1745 by 'Mr Gill' in John Harris's* The Artist and the Country House, *1979, revised 1985.*

house. There are some good pictures, and altogether it is handsomely decorated. The furnishings of the rest of the house gave me the feeling that it was done by a gentleman who wanted to be a great lord and wasn't quite up to it. Much gilding is scattered all over the place, yet there are certain shortcomings, such as the balustrade of the great staircase in oakwood, and more disappointments of this sort.[46]

The garden they call the *pleasure Garden* is in a special genre. It is small, and it occupies the whole of the upper part of the hill I've just been describing. It includes a large number of mature trees, and some rare and beautiful ones, with walks and rides running through them in all directions. The very top of the hill is occupied by a castle with battlements and round towers for all the world as it was in the Middle Ages with courtyards and billets for troops. In overall plan, it is circular, and it is maintained in the greatest perfection. It was made with the object of creating a promenade – a walk – and its elevation, and the superb view one gets from the terrace must create a very delightful picture in summertime. The whole of the other side of the hill is a red rock, half covered with trees that are crooked and scarcely able to find a place for their roots; which gives you, if I may use this expression, a romantic feeling, quite fine. The view is a very extensive one, and you can command a countryside well covered in trees, generally well cultivated: in short, a beautiful view.[47]

After seeing Lord Strafford's house, we mounted our horses and rode to *Wakefield*, only ten miles. We arrived early. The weather was so awful that I could pay no attention to anything on the route. It was hilly, and the district notably populated, and even furnished with a good number of parks and country houses.

WAKEFIELD

Wakefield Strafford Arms   Wakefield stands on a distinct rise, enough to enable it to be seen from a distance: it slopes down to the navigable river Calder.[48] The town itself is

---

ously, in so much elegance. The Corinthian columns of shining marble had their capitals carved by the anglicised Frenchman Daniel Hervé of York, to be fitted to marble columns 'already shown to the said Daniel Harvey, in 1720'. They were to be carved in Roche Abbey stone (Rupert Gunnis, *loc cit*). Five years later he carved four more capitals, this time in wood, for the house.

[46] He has picked on this heavily voluptuous carved staircase in the north wing (cherubs trumpeting above scrolls of acanthus), not seeing that it was part of the old house Wentworth bought in 1708. And he seems not have seen the stuccoed rococo walls of the staircase leading down from the north end of the long gallery: a handsome medallion of the earl in his youth shares the walls with Fame and Perseus (? c1720), rather embarrassed by Medusa's head.

[47] The rest of the page is blank. He has paid no attention to the great variety of garden ornaments other than 'Stainborough Castle'. Nor has he mentioned the impressive, though more conventional, south front, thirteen bays, ground-floor rusticated, the 'grand pediment' supported on six detached Corinthian columns and elegantly carved ('according to the model' in 1762, by John Platt of Rotherham: Rupert Gunnis, *Dictionary*, who mentions several chimney pieces for this new wing). But the weather continued wretched.

[48] They arrived from Barnsley at the medieval bridge, with weir and wharves, dye-houses, mills etc upstream to their left, the striking 14th-century Bridge Chapel on their right, before climbing Kirkgate to the church in one corner of the triangular market-place. This was already entirely

very attractive: the principal street is one of the most handsome I've seen,[49] on account of its length, and fine breadth, adorned with merchants' houses, all of them well built, and charming. The overall appearance is very good to look at, but there's nothing else: the rest of the town's a mess, little lanes, yards, nothing.[50]

The town is famous for its trade in narrow cloth. The cloths are brought in from neighbouring villages and sold at the market. I'll explain all that at Leeds, where we're going tomorrow.

The canal navigation[51] serves to carry the fleeces in from the different counties to be sold and turned into cloth. The boats are quite big, drawing 4 to 5 feet of water, and can carry 40 or 50 tons of goods. They go regularly from here to *Lincoln*, a journey of 4 days. Descending the Calder, they join the *Humber*, then turn up into the *Trent* and come to Lincoln. There they pick up their fleeces[52] and bring them here for distribution to the clothiers.

On the 28th we left Wakefield   reaching Leeds towards midday. The road was hilly all the way, and the countryside occupied by a great many cattle. The crops were geared partly to feeding them, so there's a lot of grass.

Three miles from Leeds you see it in the middle of a beautiful valley that contains both a canal and a river and is built over with immense numbers of houses: I think it's the richest view I ever remember looking at. This derives from the abundance of coal mines, which fuel the manufacturing that makes people so comfortably off: they are encouraged to build and furnish pleasant houses according to their means.

surrounded by market-cross, shambles, corn exchange, Rotten Row, etc. The Strafford Arms had been conspicuously established at a cost of £800 in 1737 by Lord Strafford at the north corner of the Market Place, where Northgate enters it. In 1776 an American Quaker visiting Britain stayed here: 'one of the best Inns in England. The Front is very grand and the back buildings are like a little City' (*An American Quaker in the British Isles, 1775–79*, ed K. Morgan, 1992, p. 155). Four new rooms were added in 1784, with extra stabling. It was the chief posting house. All replaced by something suited to present ways.

49 This is Westgate, sweeping down now to the bluntest railway bridge.

50 This may have been a bit hard. Some of the best bits now are beside old former inn-yards off Westgate, and they are clearly marked on J. Walker's beautifully detailed map of the town in 1823. Up Wood Street he shows the elegant Public Rooms (Library, Newsroom, Dispensary and Assembly Room), and beyond that the Court House, with grand pillared and pedimented portico: they were built in 1820 and 1810 respectively, but probably replaced decent 18th-century buildings. Away to the south of Westgate, Market Street and Queen Street lead to South Parade (c1775), but alas, it's no longer possible to share the delight Alexandre felt in this town in 1786. In 1776, the American Jabez Maud Fisher's view of Wakefield was: 'a beautiful town, wide commodious Streets, elegantly paved, good houses and a thriving situation' (*loc cit*, p. 43).

51 Aire and Calder; Calder and Hebble.

52 Reckoned in general the best.

LEEDS

Leeds Old Kings Arms[53]   The town itself is very large and full of people, its streets well designed, altogether a beautiful town. The greater part is new, showing the advantages trade has produced. We brought a letter of introduction for Mr *Read*, who is a banker, I believe.[54] He showed us great politeness, receiving us kindly, and even showing us over the whole town. I was astonished at the quantity of pretty houses we found there among the several major buildings.

The hospital, of which you can see elevations on the next two pages, isn't nearly as good as the one at *Nottingham*. It holds 65–70 patients, who are very properly and well looked after, but they are admitted in consideration of the subscription they've paid: the doctor should alone control admissions. The hospital does also treat sick people in the town with free remedies: these are those who can't be admitted because the hospital's already full. Admissions and discharges are on Wednesdays.[55] I haven't time to describe the hospital's working in detail. My impression is that the building's inclined more to magnificence than utility.[56] It was established by the generous contribution of various individuals, and is kept going by annual subscription that can scarcely be less than substantial. The North Front (Pl 21, p. 57) gives on to a pleasant large square that unluckily belongs to separate owners, and so lacks unity: it is used for drying the cloths being made there.[57]

I've mentioned the river and the canal, the one communicating with the Humber, the other going to Liverpool. This last can never be completed, for there

53 Now gone, it stood on Briggate, above Duncan Street, a continuation of White Cloth Hall Street, handy for seeing the White Cloth Hall in the south-east quarter of the old town: what survives of this hall is in Crown Street. Arthur Young in 1770 found this inn 'Dirty and Disagreeable: veal cutlets, tarts and cheese for supper'.
54 *Bailey's British Directory*, for *1784*, in its Leeds section (pp. 560–4) contains no reference to a Mr Read, Reade, Reid or Reeve, whether as a banker or in any other condition. This is disappointing: Alexandre names all too few acquaintances and informants.
55 S. T. Anning (*General Infirmary at Leeds, Vol I, 1767–1869*, 1963, p. 81) recorded that the first Rules of 1767 named Friday for the admission and discharge of patients by the Weekly Board, between 3 and 5pm. 'These patients were examined by the Physician and Surgeon of the Week but only those suitably recommended were considered for admission as either in- or out-patients. To become a patient it was necessary to have a recommendation of a subscriber. Those who subscribed one guinea annually had the right to recommend one out-patient at a time. Two guineas secured one in-patient or two out-patients at a time. Any person who gave 10 guineas and subscribed a guinea a year was considered a Trustee and could recommend an in-patient so long as the annual subscription continued.' (There were certain exceptions – the mentally disordered, epileptics, TB, VD, etc. In chapter X, Anning gives very interesting examples.) In the two decades between 1767 and 1786, mid-week change-over seems to have been found more convenient than the weekends that were originally tried.
56 The American Quaker, writing of Leeds in August 1775: 'Here is the greatest Cloth Market in England. Mixt Cloth Hall, White Cloth Hall and one famous new building, a beautiful infirmary': *An American Quaker in the British Isles, 1775–1779*, ed K. Morgan, 1992, p. 42. John Carr of York was its fine architect (Colvin, p. 219).
57 See footnote 56 above.

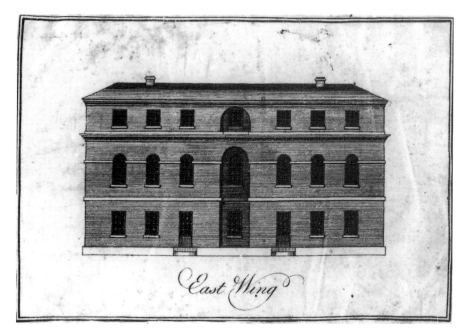

East Wing

20. *Leeds General Infirmary, East Wing. Among J. Carr of York's distinguished public buildings, the General Infirmary at Leeds was begun 1768–71; the wings were added in 1782 and 1786, of which Alexandre pasted this engraving, and one of the North Front, into his travel-notebook. N. and F. Giles' Plan of Leeds and Environs, 1825, shows this East Wing facing, across the Dissenters' Burying Ground, the back of the Mixed Cloth Hall, with which it was squarely aligned; its West Wing faced the terraces round Park Square at 45 degrees. (They were probably aligned with Park Lane and Upper Head Row.) In his sketch of the Mixed Cloth Hall (p. 58), Alexandre shows it with a round end: it had become square-ended in Giles' 1825 plan.*

are 20 miles to go overland between here and Manchester.[58] From there to Liverpool is so quick that the double road and canal journey takes less time than the complete journey by water, which would be 120 miles. But they have to load on to a boat, then on to carts, and finally to load back on to other boats – which makes the price of carriage very dear. The canal here has never paid its way, and probably will never pay its costs of construction.

[58] In the end, Alexandre was proved wrong; the Leeds and Liverpool Canal was finished but only after 46 years, 1770–1816. As Jack Simmons observed, it was the longest single line of canal ever constructed by one company in Britain: 127 miles by canal as against 75 by road (*Transport*, 1962, p. 35). Alexandre recited the advantages of not having to divide the carriage between road and water. In the end what paid was the local traffic, not the loads going right through from Leeds to Liverpool. But it was an admirably ambitious scheme. An engraved plan was published (in January 1772) in the *Gentleman's Magazine*, showing the whole meandering route: first north-westwards up the Aire valley to Skipton and 'the Pennine Way' at Gargrave, then turning south-west and

21. *Leeds General Infirmary, North Front. N. and F. Giles'* Plan of Leeds and Environs, *1825, shows this North Front looking out, across West Street, into an open area framed on three sides by East Parade, South Parade and Park Road. He shows the small enclosures Alexandre grumbled about, 'in separate ownership, lacking unity and used for drying cloths'. Dr J. Aikin,* A Description of the Country . . . round Manchester, 1795, *mentions this area north of the infirmary as 'partly laid out in gardens and partly as tenter ground', ie ground used for stretching cloth on tenter-hooks, a common sight in all clothing districts from the Middle Ages into the 19th century.*

Whereas the river carries ships as hefty as those at Wakefield: it's larger, and is called the Aire. It carries the cloths to Hull, where they're transferred to ships bound all over the world. I hope you can already judge of the wealth that must govern this town. One sees everyone in movement – upwards – and busy for good reasons: in other towns comparable incentives are missing.

After seeing the town, we took tea with *Mr Read* and later returned to our hotel [*chez nous*]. Now I want to describe the way business is done here, very different from the way it's done elsewhere. Every workman seems to work for himself; by which I mean that a man, even a working man, perhaps a shade older than the rest, has under him two or three others who, with him, make cloth after he has made the capital outlay. He has put up the wool and the tools, and makes the cloth of white

through the Fenridge (?Foulridge) Tunnel to the 'Bason' near Colne. The distance so far was reckoned just over 42 miles. Joseph Priestley (not the famous scientist they had met in Birmingham) was Superintendent of the canal in all its development during the year after its completion, being depicted (very probably) at one end of this tunnel on his monument in Barnsley cathedral. From Colne the route planned in 1772 was another 66 miles – 108 miles all told, too optimistic by 19 miles but it did, in the end, heroically reach the Mersey. In France, alas, such an enterprise would only have been carried through by Louis XIV's or Napoleon's government.

wool, which he buys simply spun, or – if it's to be coloured cloth – buys it already dyed.

When all these men have made their cloths, they bring them into town on the two market-days, Tuesdays[59] and Saturdays. There are specially designed market buildings where they bring their wares, one for White Cloths, the other for Mixed Cloths [*draps de couleur*]: they were built by subscription.

22. *Leeds, Mixed Cloth Hall (Alexandre's sketch).*

In plan the Mixed Cloth Hall is shaped like this. The place lettered A is the courtyard. B indicates the places where the traders set up their sales stands. The hall is roofed over. Each person stands beside the table displaying his merchandise. Each person is entitled to a place big enough for his piece of cloth: those with the broadest pieces can, for 3 *louis* a year [15 shillings or 75 new pence] have a position running right back to the wall. And there are 4,692 of these places in the whole hall. Those who haven't paid their 3 *louis* are obliged to give 12 shillings [60 new pence] for each piece they sell. The White Cloth Hall is entirely similar, though not so large.[60]

The Coloured-Cloth Hall is open from 11 o'clock to midday. At midday they ring a bell to warn everyone that they have only 25 minutes to conclude their transactions. At 12.25 they ring the bell again, and everyone has to leave, or be fined.[61] The White Cloth Hall runs from

---

59 Luckily they were in Leeds on Tuesday 28 March; and luckily also, the timing of the Market in the Mixed Cloth Hall had slipped from daybreak in 1745 to 11am. Yet Alexandre doesn't catch the excitement Defoe felt here in the 1720s. On the other hand, the number of clothiers marketing their cloth seems to have risen from something over 3,000 to very nearly 5,000. And the selling-time seems to have slipped from one hour sharp to 1 hour and 25 minutes!

60 It was built in 1775, with Assembly Rooms on the north side, and survives in modified form and in lively use as a collection of boutiques, east of the Corn Exchange, in Crown Street. The Mixed Cloth Hall has been replaced by the Head Post Office, between Infirmary Street and Quebec Street, just north-west of the City Square.

61 Saml & Nathnl Buck's well-known panorama of *The South-East Prospect of Leeds* was published in 1745 with this caption, bringing to life their stately model of 'this rich and populous town, divided by a spacious stone Bridge, formerly remarkable for the Mixt Cloth Market being held upon it until removed in 1684 to the east side of Briggate [the broad street running due south to the Bridge and the now tranquil former quayside still known, evocatively, as The Calls]. In Briggate it is yet held [1745] and is so much increased that upwards of 3,000 clothiers expose their manufactures to sale there every Tuesday and Saturday in the open air; the cloths being laid on trustles neatly ranged for the purpose. The time for the Market is limited to one hour, and begins in summertime at 6 o'clock and in winter as soon as the Merchants can see to distinguish the Colours. The signal is given by the ringing of a bell at an old Chapel at the Bridge-foot, which is

1pm to 2.25, following the same rules. The cloths they sell range from 2 shillings to 12 shillings: there are very few at the higher price. All the cloths are beautiful, with the exception of those made in a small town called *Halifax*,[62] where they mix wool from *Spain* in with the wool from hereabouts. Here they use only the local wool. All the little merchants who bring their cloth here live out in the country, but close to the town.[63] They live, in general, very poorly [*très mal*]. They bring in their merchandise on horseback.

In the Cloth Halls, where the place of each is marked out, the dealers walk between two rows of tables, and each merchant cries the price of his cloth. You see if the price and quality suit you, then buy or refuse accordingly.

Not all the cloths brought in are immediately sold. Indeed, they are often unsold for as long as 2 or 3 years before they find a purchaser. At present business is slow. People aren't buying. There is always a bale of each colour, containing, before it comes to the hall, two pieces. There is a stamp that the officials affix to tell how many ells the piece contains, and its width, which they note, together with the merchant's name. These stamps are amalgamated so that it can be calculated how many cloths are made in each district.

The traders come to this White Cloth Hall to buy their cloths, then hand over

rung again after 1 hour. It is almost incredible what large sums of money are laid out every Market-day in so short a space of time, and that with so profound a silence that surprises all Strangers.' (Defoe II, pp. 205–6, described, 20 years earlier, how the buyers 'come along the spaces between the rows of boards, some with foreign letters of order, with patterns sealed on them, in rows, in their hands; and with those they match colours, and when they see any cloths that suit their occasions, they reach over to the clothier and whisper . . . and 'tis agree or not agree, in a moment'. Defoe added: 'the reason for this silence is that the clothiers stand so near to one another, and that one should not know what another does'.) By 1745 the Bucks could add: 'There is, besides, a handsome well-built Hall for the White Cloth, under which are very convenient cell[ar]s, where clothiers may deposit the cloth remaining unsold from one market-day to another.' 'Thus you see', Defoe added, 'ten or twenty thousand pounds value in cloth, and sometimes much more, bought and sold in little more than an hour: the laws of the market the most strictly observed as ever I saw . . . And this done twice a week. By this quick return, the clothiers are constantly supplied with money, their workmen are duly paid, and a prodigious sum circulates through the county every week.' He goes on to consider the local consumption, the London buyers for America and the Baltic, and the foreign merchants over from Holland, Hamburg and 'the farthest provinces of Germany'.

[62] Defoe (Everyman, II, p. 198), c1724, found Halifax covering a rough circle 12 miles in diameter with 13 chapels of ease and 12 meeting-houses. He reckoned that the town increased by at least one-fourth in forty years through the great demand for kersies for clothing the armies abroad. He then described the new manufacture of shalloons, of which they are reported to make 100,000 pieces a year without reducing the output in kersies. One Halifax man was said to trade, by commission, for £60,000 a year in kersies only to Holland and Hamburg. Alexandre might sniff at the beauty of Halifax's products.

[63] Steven Burt and Dr K. Grady, in their *Illustrated History of Leeds* (p. 59) show Leeds as the chief market of the West Riding broad cloths. 'The coloured, or "mixed" broad cloth area began on the W outskirts of Leeds, the white broad cloth area 6 miles to SW from Burstall to E edge of Halifax.' They show 18th-century statutes fixing width of broad cloth at 49.5 inches (125 cm) with maximum length 46 yards (42 m). Narrow cloths were usually 27–30 inches wide. Defoe reckoned West Riding broadcloth was thought 'narrow' by old West Country traditions.

their purchases to the dyer and to whoever will be dressing [*appretant*] the cloth. For the whole year they prepare the cloths for sale. They dye them, then they put them on wooden posts in order to give them the proper width.

When the cloths are finally ready for shipment, the merchants load them on to river-boats, and from them on to ships going all over the world. A great many go to France and to the north. I was told that, since the end of the American War, demand has been considerably lower, which has given me at least a hint that this country lost a little in this branch of its industry. In general, these prosperous merchants seem not to aspire above the heights of practical ambition; a form of delusion and deception the Liverpool merchants, for example, seemed very often prone to.

4

York to Durham

They stayed at Bluitt's Hotel, which stood on Museum Street, backing on to the Assembly Rooms, which greatly impressed them. So did the Minster, its only shortcoming that its handsome vault is made of timber: a perceptive criticism; but not a word said about York's glorious stained glass. After looking at the whole town, they went to see Dr Hunter and his asylum; Alexandre saved it up 'to keep the best to the last' for his father! At Harrogate Green Dragon, they took tea with a lady and gentleman, which 'has taken care of the whole evening'. 'The almost completely preserved ruins of Fountains Abbey offer the most magic view from different standpoints in the park and garden . . . it was clearly extraordinarily large and extraordinarily beautiful. This is certainly the most beautiful place of its kind I have ever seen.' A fair judgment. At Northallerton, the Frenchmen made a short detour to Ketton and Bampton to see the cattle of the Colling brothers who had studied under Bakewell in 1783. Durham was spoilt for them by 'fog so thick we could only just make out our horses' heads'. They failed to appreciate the massive quality of the Norman piers in the cathedral, as they did again at Gloucester. The whole grandeur of Durham was lost in the fog.

On the 29th we left Leeds and dined at *Tadcaster*. The road is always the same: what I mean is that these fields, however variously cultivated, do look depressingly alike. The cropping reflects some differences: the wheat-lands are the best and strongest, and the others are too light to compete with them. The wheat-lands have this rotation: 1 oats; 2 beans; 3 wheat; 4 beans; 5 oats; 6 barley; 7 pasture; 8 wheat. These farmers never create meadowlands; they merely put down grass to give the soil a year off. Also *clover's* sown with barley, just for one year. Here, beans are reckoned an excellent crop, and I do believe they yield a much better return than can be got by exhausting the land for a great many harvests of what they call white corn.[1] Here are permanent meadows, only ever ploughed, of course, when they would grow grain of any value. The usual rotation is 1 oats; 2 oats; 3 fallow; 4 barley; 5 meadow. One sees that a series of fat harvests is bound to exhaust the soil and ruin its owner so that he won't cover his expenses. Of course, each district has its habits and each believes its own ways are best.

---

[1] *Grains blancs.* I've never seen another reference to white corn, nor to 'white grain'.

Tadcaster White Horse[2]   We left Leeds in time to dine here, an unremarkable little village with its own harbour on a navigable river. After Tadcaster, you cross a lot of common land and open country until you are 3 or 4 miles from York. Then you pass large enclosed farms, their fields well looked after, but cultivated always in the same way I've been describing. I imagine that the approach to this great city must be very fine, but the fog was so thick that I could scarcely see anything as we entered. I'll leave description till tomorrow.

York, Bluitts[3]   On 30 March we looked at the town. It's still surrounded by an ancient wall,[4] and you can't leave without passing through one of the stone gateways, now half dilapidated. As often in fortified towns, the castle, guarding the east side,[5] stands within the town walls. It serves now as prison, with Assize Courts. The old keep is round. In its bailey you confront the prison for all the worst criminals, entering it through a formidable freestone doorway,[6] where you find yourself inside a square tower. Flanking this gaol on the left is the Debtors' Prison, a new freestone building, well designed. Those are the prisons. Forming the west flank of this group of three is the Courthouse for the Assizes of the whole county, in rather an elegant building. It contains two courts, one for criminal and one for civil cases.[7] These buildings are very

---

2   Later amalgamated with the Angel, it still presents a fair Georgian stone front to the Leeds–York road, with front door balanced on either side by a modest canted window-bay lighting all 3 storeys.
3   Bluitts stood on Museum Street, backing on to the Assembly Rooms, and with extensive stabling where the present Central Library stands (Thomas's Hotel looks as if it occupies some of Bluitts' site). In 1768 the King of Denmark and his suite lodged at Bluitts (C. B. Knight, *History of York*, 1944, p. 546). Later on, it became Ettridges, with a large posting business.
4   Part Roman, most medieval, York's city wall is the longest in the kingdom: 2¾ miles, its only gap where the King's Fishpond, of c1068, occupied a boggy area on the east side. Four of the principal medieval gateways into the town are substantially intact – certainly in their main structures – and, well-restored; they no longer look 'dilapidated'. The tall, top-heavy outlines of Monk Bar stay in the mind, the 14th-century entrance surmounted by a late-15th-century storey, its outer round turrets (bartizans) rising high above its parapet, each turret displaying, above its battlements, carved-stone symbolic defenders ready with boulders, probably going back to the 17th century (?post Civil War). On Micklegate, similar small figures of knights were replaced by new carvings in 1950; on Bootham Bar, the 1894 renewals have weathered well. Such amiable defenders haunt other northern bastions, including Alnwick, as we shall see.
5   In fact it dominates the south side, and is additionally protected on a narrow peninsula between the rivers Ouse and Foss.
6   Pevsner and Neave (*York and the East Riding*, 1997 reprint, p. 191) call this the Debtors' Prison, but rightly proclaim it as architecture 'next after the Minster the most monumental of York'. It was built 1701–5 as the County Gaol and described by Defoe as 'a prison the most stately and complete in the kingdom'. Its designer isn't recorded: the great rusticated pilasters flanking the entrances could be Vanbrugh, the broad, rounded pediments suggest Hawksmoor: that it may be the work of an amiable local gentleman-amateur is not rejected by Colvin (*Dictionary*, 1995, p. 1016). The Female Prison, now Castle Museum, is by Carr: see Wragg, *Carr of York*, pl 56 and p. 232.
7   John Carr's design of 1773–7 retains its original façade: the two court rooms have been named 'perhaps the finest rooms in York' (Pevsner and Neave). Wragg, *op cit*, pl 60 and p. 230.

23. *York. A Noble Terras Walk, engraving by C. Grignion after N. Drake. 'Along this river for a mile and a half runs an attractive public walk, planted with well grown elms on* cercaux *(?hoops)', 1756.*

well maintained.[8] The only nourishment the prisoners are allowed is bread and water – at least, those with no money. Those who can afford it have what they want. They sleep on straw. Those who have committed the greatest crimes are kept underground, manacled hand and foot. Opposite are the remains of an ancient keep, ruined and half-demolished, and standing on a mound: they say it was destroyed in Cromwell's time.[9]

The town is large but not largely populated: it has only 70,000[10] souls, which is nothing for a place of great distinction. The streets are winding and not well-paved, but there are a great many good houses.

The river Ouse which crosses the town carries some fairly large boats for which there isn't really enough trade.[11] The population is certainly important enough to keep the river fully occupied in supplying all its needs. Along this river for a mile and

[8] I never see this trio of handsome buildings without wondering whether their grouping at the Norman and Georgian hub of a Roman town was suggested by a visitor to the Campidoglio in late-17th-century Rome.

[9] Clifford's Tower, pleasantly quatrefoil in plan, like Aldeburgh's Martello Tower in Suffolk, served ignominiously as a garden ornament in the 18th century to a house that stood on its north side. That was worse than being 'slighted' by Cromwell. Colchester's castle survived a similar decorative use much more successfully.

[10] Presumably a slip for 17,000?

[11] Sir William Burrell, 1758, said merely, 'Trade: iron and deal from Hamburgh': *Burrell's Northern Tour, 1758*, ed Dunbar, Edinburgh 1997, p. 36.

a half runs an attractive public walk, planted with well-grown elms on hoops,[12] which will be very pleasant on a fine summer's day.

The Assembly Rooms are very well designed. They were built by public subscription,[13] and each month the subscribers choose 12 persons to manage their affairs and enforce their rules if the need arises.[14] The room is 112 ft long, 40 wide and 40 tall, and designed in an Egyptophile manner,[15] with two tiers of columns; the upper range attached[16] to the wall, the columns below detached by 4 ft from the outer wall. Facing into the room, along the front of these columns is the benching for the ladies to sit on.

These columns are smooth[17] and of the Corinthian order. The frieze and the entablature are magnificently carved and coloured, and at the ceiling-level the simple garlands between the pilasters have a beautiful effect.[18] There are, in the four corners of the room, *des tuyaux de chaleur* – stoves.[19]

The Cathedral is a superb building, immensely old. It was burnt, but later

[12] Alexandre has written '*arbres d'orange sur cerceau*. I assume that *orange* is one of his not uncommon phonetic slips: here, for *orme* (elm). The walk was planned in 1730 with 66 limes and 64 elms. So popular, it was extended by ¾ of a mile in 1740, with 340 elms from Telford's nursery (*York Through the Eyes of the Artist*, York City Art Gallery, 1990, p. 136, pl 120, engr by C. Grignion after Nathan Drake, 1756; it shows trees like tall telegraph poles along each side of the walk, each topped by a light balloon of foliage, the trunks carefully trimmed to secure neatness, and presumably lightness and room to promenade). I cannot explain *cerceau*, a hoop, which scarcely describes the 'balloon' of foliage on top of each tree: nor can one see how any hoop-like espalier might have been employed. See previous page.

[13] 190 subscribed.

[14] One of the purposes of such assembly rooms was the encouragement of manners, which, as Burke reckoned, were more important than laws (*Letters on a Regicide Peace*, 1796).

[15] 'Egyptophile' is a misunderstanding. Lord Burlington, who designed and erected the Assembly Rooms (1730–2), took his design directly from Palladio's drawing of 'The Egyptian Hall' as it appeared in *The Four Books of Architecture*, 1738 (see pl 154 in Giles Worsley, *Classical Architecture in Britain*). He also reproduces, as pl 153, Wm Lindley's Perspective View of the interior in 1759, with the benching Alexandre described, and that had been moved in front of the columns so that they could be sat on by ladies whose hooped skirts prevented them from moving comfortably between the (rather close-set) columns. The fine rococo benches have since been removed to reveal the architecture properly, which Giles Worsley regards as 'the perfection of Burlington's neo-Classical manner' (*op cit*, 1995, p. 126).

[16] ie pilasters, between the clerestory windows.

[17] Painted and marbled.

[18] Lord Burlington would have been delighted by Alexandre's observations. He felt that at York he'd done his best for the new classical architecture in what had once, briefly, been the capital of the Roman empire. It is extraordinary how faithfully he copied Andrea Palladio's elevation of the interior of 'the Egyptian Hall' in *The Four Books of Architecture* (published only later, in 1738). The frieze in the ground-floor entablature is precisely based on Palladio's detailed drawing; and what, apparently, impressed Alexandre was an effective design of a continuous cable of evergreen foliage bound, at intervals, by a circling gold cord. Clearly, something in Burlington's academic approach to classical architecture struck a chord in Alexandre's own interest in buildings: we don't often find him referring to entablatures and friezes.

[19] To ensure a warm start to the assemblies on cold days. They also had smaller public rooms for use during winter.

repaired and was as fine as before.[20] The interior's magnificent: 325 ft long,[21] 220 wide,[22] and of very great height,[23] and the breadth of the vault gives it great beauty. The only slight shortcoming is that this handsome vault is made of timber.[24]

The choir stalls are of oak, carved very delicately, and the sort of thing one finds in so many ancient churches.[25] Close by is a chapel,[26] superbly vaulted, an octagon of considerable diameter yet its vault stands without the aid of any central pillar, an extremely bold design. The exterior forms of this church are like those of all ancient churches of their day.[27]

After looking at the whole town, we went to see Dr Hunter,[28] a famous writer and a considerable farmer. He received us with great politeness. He seemed open, unreserved. He's a physician, but not, I think, particularly famous on that account. He showed us a book, or rather some notes, he intended to publish on plants.[29] We chatted together about our travels, and he told us about the country round here,

---

[20] This is unlikely to refer to the fire of 1069 which damaged an earlier building. John Carr had repaired the choir roof in 1770, but that was the result of a routine survey. The major fires occurred in 1829, 1840 and 1984, but Alexandre wasn't being prescient.

[21] In fact, from east wall to west wall the interior length is 486 ft, the nave being a little shorter than the choir.

[22] 222 ft was, by coincidence, the width of the HQ building of the 1st-century legionary fortress that underlies the Minster, but at an alignment differing by about 48 degrees from the Minster's east–west line.

[23] The height of the choir is 102 ft, only a foot short of Westminster Abbey's: but small beer compared with the vaults of the choir at Beauvais, soaring up 157 ft above the floor. No wonder some vaults collapsed in 1284, and others look alarmingly in need of extra buttressing. Nor is York quite in the same league as the Sainte Chapelle, which Alexandre would have known: 138 ft, and without Beauvais' overstrained look.

[24] Roger North, here on circuit c1680 with his brother Francis, reacted more strongly, finding the church 'stately indeed, only disgraced by a wooden roof framed archwise' (*Lives of the Norths*). The wooden roofs of York Minster naturally represent less weight than stone roofs, such as Frenchmen expect to see; they also present a greater fire risk, as was seen in 1984 when lightning struck the south transept. Most of the roof-timbering is now concealed beneath lath-and-plaster, except in the north transept, above the Five Sisters window, where the timbers are seen, as the medieval architect intended. Alexandre's disappointment is understandable.

[25] Alas, what Alexandre saw was destroyed in the 1829 fire; all replaced in Sir Robert Smirke's Gothic.

[26] This is the chapter-house, c1275–90, its amazing design now demonstrated in a useful model: one or two of the great painted sections of boarded ceiling are also shown. Seen in position by Alexandre, they were replaced by lath-and-plaster in 1798.

[27] Interested as he is in this great church, Alexandre seems not even to have noticed its medieval glass, some of the finest in England: in terms of quantity, unsurpassed in England, and with only a few exceptions in Europe. The great west window, with its striking tracery, and the east window, are almost impossible not to notice. Nor was the glass being neglected at that time. William Peckitt, the local glass-painter, had worked in the north aisle in 1782, and the on great west window in 1757.

[28] Alexander Hunter, MD, 1729–1809.

[29] He'd taken an active part in founding the Agricultural Society at York in 1770, and edited *Georgical Essays*, 4 vols on plants, composts etc, reprinted once in London and twice in York. It was perhaps one of these reprints that he showed Lazowski and Alexandre. Lazowski would have been particularly interested in an essay he published in York in 1796, *A New Method of Raising Wheat*

24. *York. Bootham Park Hospital, designed by John Carr for Dr Hunter, 1774–5.*

strongly decrying the bad ways they have of farming their land. After conversing for quite a long time, he asked us if we would like to see the lunatic asylum. It is completely different from all the other asylums I've ever seen or heard of.

This hospital is the one thing left in York for me to tell you about, and I've saved it up, to keep the best for the last (*pour la bonne bouche!*). It stands outside the town,[30] and is in redbrick, designed very simply. Its façade is very like that of the Leeds hospital.[31] The building stands apart from the town to get the best possible air. The surrounding meadows belong to it. The hospital has been built by subscription, but it has a régime that is entirely its own.[32] The subscriptions were calculated

---

for a Series of Years on the Same Land. He had also edited Evelyn's *Sylva* and *Terra*, with notes, and made various other observations on rural economy.

[30] A short walk outside the Bootham Bar, standing back beyond a sort of parkland meadow.

[31] It was designed by the same excellent York architect, John Carr, and more simply than the Leeds hospital, which Alexandre may have forgotten he found 'more inclined to magnificence than utility' (pl 21, p. 57 above): here classical references are confined to four tall attached Tuscan columns supporting a modest pediment at roof-level. Wragg, *Carr of York*, pp. 231–2.

[32] Alexandre doesn't explain that Dr Hunter was one of the earliest supporters of the project in 1772. Born in Edinburgh, he studied medicine there and in London, Rome and Paris. He came to York as a GP in 1763, and when the Lunatic Asylum was finally opened in 1777, became its sole Physician, and still held that post 32 years later, when he died. The whole history of this asylum, now Bootham Park Hospital, has been compressed into a 50-page essay, one of the Borthwick Papers published in York, and written by Anne Digby of York University, 1986. She explains that most of the records for the early years, 1777–88, covering Alexandre's visit, have been destroyed. Here, the interest he had always shown in our hospitals is abundantly vindicated. Anne Digby shows how the initial subscriptions included 25 guineas from the Social Club at the Black Dog, as

on what was needed to make a good start. After that, the house was kept going because the patients were charged. In this way, each month one saw the running costs and shared them out in proportion to the patients' ability to pay when they were well. The tariffs of charges are 6 shillings a week, or 8 shillings, 10 shillings, 12 shillings, and so on, according to their means. The hospital provides the patients with their food, which is excellent. They have meat 3 times a week, and puddings (*poudings*) or eggs the rest of the time. And they are supplied with their house-room, their beds, their laundry, and their medicine. Those who pay more than eight shillings a week are admitted without certificates. Those who give more than 7 shillings a week can have their servants (*domestiques*) for whom they must pay 6 shillings a week.

Each patient has a small room with a good bed, the door shut at night. But during the day the patients are all in one room together, and never quarrel, nor do they come to blows. They are never physically beaten, and the only accepted punishment is to be sent back to their bedrooms for a greater or less time. There's a place for the men, and one for the women, and they walk or stroll whenever the weather allows. They are given drugs only during the first week after their admission, in order to discover which they never react against, and which they can safely take.

Here is the statement of their results to date:

Total of admissions into the hospital	<u>315</u>
Cured	137
Physically well	76
Incurable and ordered to be taken home	34
Died	25
At present in the hospital	43
	315

well as country gentry and prosperous citizens, including several women. She shows that the promoters were greatly concerned in establishing an asylum 'under men of principles and honour' to enable people of modest means to avoid the clutches of mercenary keepers of private madhouses, inclined to prolong the treatment. In the first year, 1777, a flat charge of 8 shillings a week for each patient should be made. It was soon found that, to pay its way, persons of varying means must be admitted, and a sliding scale be charged. As might be expected, a clerical critic objected that the charitable intentions of the original subscribers were being betrayed. This is where the objective good sense of young Alexandre is so useful. Without him we should know nothing, in these formative years, of the life of the patients, what they ate, how they slept and spent the day, how little they squabbled, and how punishment for unacceptable behaviour was limited to being sent to one's bedroom. Hunter was not of a retiring disposition, continuing in charge till he was 77! His successor coincided with hard times; and distressing discoveries were made in 1814 in the conditions in which a number of the women were living. My feeling is that Hunter did well by the city of his adoption. What Alexandre doesn't mention is the subject of all their conversations: it must have stemmed from his part in founding the York Agricultural Society in 1770, and from his experiences as a farmer in Lincolnshire (Digby, *op cit*, p. 12).

Of these 43, 20 are men, 23 women. No one has been refused admission, nor has anyone had to be sent home, which speaks even better for the management.

After seeing the hospital, we had dinner and spent the evening at Dr Hunter's house, where we conversed a great deal more.

Friday 31 March   We left York and slept at *Harrogate*, 23 miles: the first six cross land that about 12 years ago was a common, completely wasted, but now it's very well cultivated and brings in 15 shillings the *arpent* [1.5 acres]. As you leave York, the land's light but productive, the arable arrangements good (wheat, turnips, barley, grass). But then you come to rather poor-looking peat, where wheat's followed by barley and then 3 fallow years.[33] That's followed by a common which is about to be enclosed next year, and promises to be as good as anything else we saw on the way to Harrogate. The landscape becomes hilly and agreeable, along the edge of a narrow valley, green and cut by a beautiful river.[34] We went through Knaresborough, a small town but well-situated and pretty, and across the bridge with its view of the river flowing over great big stones:[35] one bank is protected by ancient woods, tall and vertical above the river, while on the other side houses look as if they're built one above another, and make a very pretty view. The rest of the way was along a plateau, at the end of which we found *Harrogate*. There are two, as I shall explain.

Harrogate, The Dragon   Harrogate's the Bath of all this part of England: it's here that one comes to drink the waters. There are two Harrogates[36] – one which is higher up on the slope, and where most people stay; and the other lower down. I hope I'll have a chance to describe it in the morning.

We're lodging at an inn where two people were already staying, a lady and a gentleman who are taking the waters. All we have is one wretched room.[37] The lady

---

33 This is Marston Moor.

34 The Nidd.

35 Byng (*Diaries*, 1792, III, p. 4) writes of 'the river Nidd, wide, shallow and brawling'. He thought Knaresborough 'would be a sweet place if quietly situated; but it is in everlasting gape from Harrogate. The men of the town diverted both me and themselves by playing leap-frog.' At the bridge, they resisted the allurements of Mother Shipton's Cave, with its literally petrifying well. Byng described the effect of its dripping: 'One year will dress a wig in stone.'

36 Upper and Low Harrogate. Fisher, the American Quaker, here briefly on 7 September 1775, wrote: 'Here there are one or two good inns. But at upper Harrogate are the most Capital, where the better sort station themselves' (*op cit*, p. 44).

37 The Dragon was established pleasantly near the northern tip of High Harrogate, beside the Skipton road, c1690. During 'the season' which didn't start till late June, it was popular with rather an exclusive and fast set. To reach it, the French visitors had just driven past the stuffier and grander Granby (see Malcolm Neesam, *Exclusively Harrogate*, Otley 1989, pp. 22–4, and W. Grainge, *History and Topography of Harrogate*, 1871, reprinted 1989). It may be that they closed most of their rooms out of season. The fact that the Dragon, large and successful under Joseph Goodlad from 1775 to 1796, had only one other couple staying, and yet could only let one room to the Frenchmen, certainly makes it look as if he was content just to 'tick over' in March, a sensible policy in any seasonal resort.

25. *Harrogate. The Dragon, where Alexandre stayed 31 March 1786. (To the left, boyhood home of the painter W. P. Frith.) Victorian photograph by kind permission of the Walker-Neesam Archive.*

has asked us to take tea, and also to supper. I accepted with great pleasure, and that has taken care of the whole evening.

On 1 April   we left there, and went to look at the other Harrogate I mentioned – a little village made up of no more than about a dozen houses, and all of them new[38] and resulting from a recent land-clearance.[39] It's about a mile and a half from the other

---

[38] A map by Charles Greeves shows Low Harrogate with perhaps 4 dozen buildings in 1821. The dozen or so new ones Alexandre mentioned may be those most closely grouped close to the sulphur springs.

[39] Alexandre's referring to the Award by the Duchy of Lancaster in 1778, which wasn't so much responsible for 'land clearance' as for preserving 200 acres 'for ever open and unenclosed'. These 200 acres are shown clearly in Charles Greeves' map of 1821: they are shaped in the form of a U, or more fancifully in the form of a swan swimming vigorously from east to west (see map of Harrogate in 1821, Neesam, *op cit*, p. 28), one tip of the U representing its tail, incorrectly but elegantly aloft, with the Dragon Inn near that tip, and including the little village of High Harrogate, the Granby Hotel, and the chalcybeate spring known as St John's Well, or the Sweet Well, the spa's original mainstay, at the base of the tail, where the swan's feet, in rear, would have been paddling. This shapely strip of common followed the line of the Skipton road from its junction with the Knaresborough and York road in front of the still – very – grand Granby Hotel. There, where it meets the Knaresborough road, it bends round to the SW, following the line of Otley Road, which in this stretch is called York Place, and has beside it the fine range of the former Queen, or Queen's Head, Inn, established c1687, a year or two before the Dragon. This overlooks the longest stretch of the open land (known as The Stray), apparently a northern term for land on which animals graze untethered, each end of which was marked by a chalcybeate spring: St John's to the east, the Tewit Well (found in 1571) to the west. The Queen, equidistant from these two

Harrogate, and in the middle of the area where the springs have been found.[40] They rise in four different wells, two clear, two cloudy. The first are for drinks, the second for bathing. The water's like those all over Europe, running very vigorously and with an air of having passed through volcanoes, vestiges of which one would probably find. What has surprised me is the dirt[41] that has to be cleaned out of these wells: where the exterior is so well cared for, one might not have noticed all that.

From there we crossed two different landscapes to *Ripon*, 11 miles away. The first, newly cleared, is very hilly and the other is charming garden.[42] The hills are steep and stony. The stones are used for walling (2 shillings) and those left over are piled up and used later. The grass has all been burnt off to help enrich the soil. Their usual rotation is: 1 wheat; 2 beans; 3 barley; 4 turnips; 5 barley; 6 meadow-grass. Neither the beans nor the turnips are hoed, and what is particularly bad is the way they usually leave their grass down for 3 years. It's because they must feed their cattle, very numerous round here. But then you come to a landscape like a garden, you are travelling through the most beautiful countryside in the world, fairly level, very well cultivated, and soon Ripon comes into view, so admirably situated.[43]

Ripon White Hart[44]   Ripon overlooks the little valley of the Ure, which is not navigable but gives life to the whole of the surrounding landscape. The town itself is pretty, with interesting street-scenes, and quite well built. The church is beautiful, but the market-place seems more so: oblong, and the middle occupied by a fine, tall, freestone obelisk raised by Mr [blank], the lord of the town.[45]

wells, closely overlooked the racecourse in the 19th century. York Place is crossed by the Leeds – Ripon road, and here the common curves up along the Ripon road to the north-west, forming the swan's neck, and the west-facing swan's head. This takes its shape from the little village of Low Harrogate, and its *raison d'être* from the discovery of sulphur wells. Disgusting to both taste and smell, they nevertheless overtook the chalybeate waters as a fashionable treatment. These sulphur wells, for drinking and bathing, are shown in use in a drawing of 1772 by Moses Griffiths. Happily they are now decently contained beneath the Royal Pump Room, designed as an octagon by a local architect, Isaac Thomas Shutt, and opened in 1842.

[40] A mile and a half as the crow flies, but three by road. He is referring to the sulphur springs: he'd passed the chalybeate wells near the Granby and the Queen.

[41] *saleté*. Malcolm Neesam says this may refer to the natural gravel that sometimes filled the basin of the sulphur wells, or is the result of vandalism that sometimes occurred before these wells were housed beneath the Pump Room.

[42] They began by re-crossing the valley of the Nidd, where Byng described 'many fine views with some sweet stretches' south of the river and the little market town of Ripley. Then the road itself improved as it headed north for Ripon, with the dales away to the left and the hills and woods around Fountains Abbey. Alexandre found these newly-cleared fields interesting because they'd been made by dry-stone walling, with stones gathered from the hillsides. He records a cost of 2 shillings (3 *livres français*) but doesn't say what for.

[43] At the south-east edge of the Pennine dales.

[44] The Unicorn and the Howard Arms were Ripon's two inns: they perhaps mistook the Unicorn's sign for a white hart, but Alexandre seldom slipped in such matters. The Howard Arms bore nothing like a hart. See plate opposite.

[45] It's disappointing to find Alexandre preferring the market-place to the Minster, even at a super-ficial glance, after his keen appreciation of York Minster. But it says much for his eye that he

26. *Ripon, the unicorn (which Alexandre mistook for a white hart).*

picked out the obelisk, based entirely on Nicholas Hawksmoor's design of 1702, and lately built (1781) to celebrate William Aislabie's death, after 68 years as MP for Ripon. (Pevsner, in 1959, referred to it merely as a 'tall obelisk, on the market square'.) William was the son of John Aislabie, Chancellor of the Exchequer and crooked promoter of the infamous South Sea scheme 'with a view to his own Exhorbitant [*sic*] Profit' (*Report* of Commons' secret committee), who was disgraced, but allowed to retain his estate here at Studley Royal. He made up for it, occupying his last 21 years improving Studley and Fountains Abbey, one of the finest landscapes of its kind anywhere. One sees how Alexandre *could* prefer the square (especially as, unlike Byng, they missed the cattle fair) to the 13th-century west front of St Wilfred's Minster. In our day, its arrangement of lancet windows is unforgettable, 'a composition as serene and restrained as that of a classical temple' (Edwin Smith and Olive Cook, *English Cathedrals*, 1989, p. 66). It's ultimately French Gothic from St Denis, via William of Sens, but Alexandre saw it when its tracery was still over-elaborate in consequence of a 14th-century 'improvement' from which Sir G. G. Scott rescued it in the 1860s. It obviously wasn't looking its best in 1786; anyway, Alexandre preferred the square. And Byng, who visited Ripon in 1792, referred twice to the 'old black Minster' and to its interior 'all in dirty decay'. (Apart from a few years in the 7th century, the church became a cathedral only in 1836.)

71

We left our men here, and set out on our horses to see the famous house at Studley, returning for the night to Ripon.

Studley   Only 3 miles along a very beautiful road. You enter the park,[46] and soon come to the house, built of freestone, but small and not measuring up to someone with 20,000 *louis* in rents (£5,000 a year in 1780s sterling) lying all round his estate.[47] Beside the house is a small garden or, rather, a poultry-run, nothing at all worth talking about.

The park struck me as being superb and very extensive indeed – 1,650 acres (1,100 *arpents*). Not an inch of it is flat, and therein lies its beauty. It is adorned by many small pavilions; and time, which presses us, has not let us go and look at everything I should like to have told you about, to give you some idea of the magnificence that unfolds all over this great park. Only deer graze in it, so the profit's nil. There can be very few people who would sacrifice 5 or 600 *louis* in rents (£125–£150 sterling a year) in order to keep a park full of deer, when venison's being eaten ever more rarely.

At the far end of the park stands *Fountains Abbey*. It is what the English call '*un pleasure-ground*'. It covers 600 acres, all maintained in the most magnificent condition. They employ, all told, 14 workmen all the year round: 6 of them are paid by the year, the rest by the day.[48] The [landscape] garden was begun 30 years ago and is composed of very agreeable mature woodland. It is separated from the park and from the higher slopes by hedging and from the river by a very beautiful iron gate. The whole garden is a valley bounded by two wooded hills. Where the bottom of the valley starts, the river cuts through it in a straight line[49] which has, in my view, an ugly effect. Further on, you come to a piece of water[50] which unluckily was drying

---

[46] Through an impressively rusticated stone gateway of c1729, conceivably by, or approved by, Colen Campbell, who died that year and was advising on the stables. These survive (privately owned) and make a grand enough house in themselves.

[47] John Aislabie had replaced a house burnt down in 1716, very possibly with Colen Campbell's advice: it was demolished soon after another fire in 1946. Judging by the surviving stables, it is difficult to understand Alexandre's disparaging remarks.

[48] About a hundred men were involved in the early construction work under John Aislabie, working seasonally (National Trust booklet, 1988: text on Studley Royal by Lydia Greeves). The formative influences, a combination of French formality and English waywardness, and the more secluded walks at Wrest Park, in Bedfordshire, come to mind, created in the early Georgian decades, both interrupted by the bursting of the South Sea Bubble. Where Wrest Park has Archer's breathtaking baroque pavilion, Studley Royal has the most disturbingly complete of all our ruined abbeys. Both have extraordinary tranquillity (out of season), despite Alexandre's stress on the beauty of Studley Royal's 'unflatness'. Marchioness Grey's Chinese pavilion at Wrest Park may have been inspired by Mr Aislabie's though his had been built high on a wooded ridge, and no longer survives.

[49] He's referring to 'the canal', designed to run straight to the lake as it still does, falling into it in the form of a cascade between two pavilions. Alexandre hasn't quite adjusted to the mixture of formality and informality, and the absence of 'Gardeners' Dogma' that characterises this most gratifying 'garden'.

[50] This is the Half Moon Pond. It curved round Tent Hill, a tall, conical artificial mound rather like a Norman baronial motte, crowned when they saw it by an octagonal Temple of Venus, the

27. *Fountains Abbey: west view of abbey church and cellarer's range, drawn 2 May 1785 for Grose's* Antiquities.

28. *Fountains Abbey: same view in 1998, showing how much lay concealed in the 1780s.*

up when we were there, but you could easily guess what a charming effect it creates; grandly and beautifully shaped. The steep eye-catcher is exactly right.[51] This beautiful piece of water is kept full [except, clearly, in an unseasonable early April] by the river[52] which runs here past the remains of a superb abbey standing in the bottom of the valley. These almost completely preserved ruins offer the most magic view from different standpoints in the park and the garden.

This garden is adorned with an unusual number of small pavilions and temples and seats from which you can enjoy these very delightful views.[53] Most of them are set fairly high up, and are of very different forms of construction. Several of them I admired, but others didn't please me at all: all that depends so much on one's tastes.[54]

The abbey I mentioned earlier is the best preserved I have ever seen. It is built beside the river, with four arches through which it runs.[55] One sees the convent's entire building. in this valley, its size declaring its great wealth. All the walls are remarkably well preserved. It was clearly extraordinarily large and extraordinarily

steep slopes around it wooded. The Half Moon Pond was fed by the Skell Beck flowing from the abbey and forming here a reservoir for the 'canal'. Unusual weather for this reservoir to be dry on 1 April.

51 Tent Hill, with its Temple of Venus which, like the Chinese temple, has long disappeared.

52 The Skell, running through Skelldale: the very name suggests the unflatness.

53 Four can still be enjoyed. Near the Canal Gate entrance (the end remote from the abbey), the Banquetting House, not far from the Aislabies' own house that was destroyed in the late 1940s, they presumably used as a summer-house for entertaining friends to semi-al fresco meals. Its rusticated Palladian work, probably by Colen Campbell, c1729: the tent-like plaster design in the coving of the apse is taken direct from an engraving of an ancient Roman apse published by Bartoli in 1704 and reproduced in Giles Worsley, *op cit*, pl 172. The Temple of Piety, which stands so chastely beyond the great calm sky-reflecting circle of the Moon Pond, with its supporting crescents, has simple Doric columns derived from those of the similarly six-columned ancient Temple of Piety, part of which one still sees embedded in the church of San Nichola in Carcere in Rome. This version is based on the original *via* Palladio and Lord Burlington (Worsley, *op cit*, p. 219). At the top of a steep slope, the path leads to the Octagon Tower, Gothic, from the top of which the Frenchmen would have been able to see Ripon Minster though today the trees conceal that view. It was Aislabie's plan to combine the Minster with Fountains Abbey as eye-catchers from his gardens, the noblest possible 'garden-ornaments'. Passing the Temple of Fame, an open Adam-esque rotunda, wood dressed as stone, you reach what is fondly called Anne Boleyn's seat and a surprise view of the greatest of our ruined abbeys. Louis Simond, a Frenchman who wrote observantly about almost everything and in admirable English, was here in 1811 with his English wife and felt that these ruins were 'the most striking thing of this kind we have seen'. He also noted, with truth: 'A high tower remains entire; too much so for beauty' (*Journal of a Tour and Residence in Great Britain*, by a French Traveller, Edinburgh 1815, II, 65).

54 He may have been thinking of the Chinese temple and various other eye-catchers now gone, and of some sculpture that still seems out of scale and oddly sited.

55 He had noticed that it flowed beneath the lay-brothers' infirmary and their large dormitory (over their refectory) and the reredorter (privies) built between refectory and infirmary: by c1200, there were probably more than 50 monks and 200 lay-brothers, who worked the surrounding estates, leaving the monks free to devote their days to the service of God in prayer. The size of the lay-brotherhood explains the extraordinary size of the nave and the length of the range running south from the west end of the nave.

beautiful. One easily makes out the standing remains of the cloisters, the dormitories, the kitchen and the refectory which was enormous, and served what must have been a very big community. There are many more remains that I'm unable to interpret.[56] To give you an idea of the grandeur, the ruins themselves cover about 4 *arpents* – 6 acres. The abbey was built in 1155, as you can discover by reading that date over the main entrance.[57] It completes this end of the gardens I've been describing.

A proper description of this enchanting place would take much too long. I will try to summarise, in the hope of giving you what I can, something of the feel of it all. It is grotesque and magnificent.[58] The varying slopes of the hills, the natural setting for different trees, serenity in nature set against the rough, broken outlines of crag and rock; some valleys with gentle sides, some precipitous; the murmur of streams, the smooth green of sloping lawns, a scatter of cottages: there you have what constitutes the beauty of all English gardens. What especially distinguishes them is that nothing is uniform, nothing is too beautiful, but everything, in the end, is natural. This is certainly the most beautiful place of its kind that I've ever seen, and I doubt if it would be possible to find one more agreeable. If you think of making the tour, you must be ready for a 2-mile walk in the course of which you will find yourself sometimes in a wilderness, sometimes in a garden; and everywhere what's extraordinary is the great variety of viewpoints and vistas.[59]

We returned from Fountains Abbey to Ripon for the night.

[56] He has done well for a layman. It's curious that he doesn't mention the church itself, and particularly its great tower.
[57] Perhaps needless to say, abbeys did not carry the date of foundation over their entrances. Alexandre was taken in by the guess of a later owner. Temporary buildings must have been started in 1132, and more permanent ones in 1135. 'By 1150, Fountains had sent out no fewer than 91 professed monks to colonize 6 new abbeys in England and one in Norway' (L. Butler and C. Given-Wilson, *Medieval Monasteries in Great Britain*, 1979, p. 237).
[58] He may have thought grotesque what he didn't specifically mention, but what Philip Yorke noted in 1744 when he was working on his own gardens at Wrest Park: 'Mr Aislabie designs to erect a Chinese house of a pyramidical form, with a gallery encircling every storey, upon the point of a ridge which encloses on each hand a valley finely wooded and worked by a rivulet. One side is formed into a number of small terraces interspersed with rock, which makes a Chinese landscape' (M. Batey and D. Lambert, *The English Garden Tour*, 1990, p. 163).
[59] In that same note, quoted immediately before, Yorke wrote: 'What seems peculiar to Studley is that the same object, taken at a different point of view, is surprisingly diversified and has all the grace of novelty.' Jabez Maude Fisher, the American Quaker, here on 8 September 1775, was appropriately economical with his lyric, and adds something thereby. 'The Cascades, natural and artificial, Canals, Lakes, Walks, Views, Groves, Shrubberies, Obelisks, temples, Rotundos, Images, Urns, Seats, Towers, Fields, Gardens, hedges, Lawns, [more] Fields, Hills, Vallies, Rocks, Mountains, Islands, Avenues and Banqueting House are astonishingly beautiful. The Variety of Trees of various sorts and the grandeur of the whole is past all possible Description. Art and Nature have combined to make it an entire Elysium. The former has brought the latter out of Chaos and has given Mechanism to the whole Scene. There are also the Ruins of Fountains Abbey, the venerable appearance whereof beggars Description.'

On 2 April (Sunday)   we slept at *Northallerton*. We lost our way and went through Thirsk, adding three miles to the journey. From Ripon to Thirsk everywhere was well cultivated, but, near the town, we crossed a very large common and then, further on, we came to a warren and saw an enormous number of rabbits. This common and warren lasted only 2½ miles, and we were back in as fine farming country as before, which brought us to Thirsk. Thirsk's a very pleasant little town making common cloths but in small quantities. There's a stream that turns a flour-mill: the stream crosses the whole town and waters the meadows all round it.

From Thirsk to *Northallerton* is truly superb country, skirting the high hills[60] below which Thirsk is built. Here the sheep are splendid, large as donkeys and very well covered with wool. The land soon levels out, though you are soon in view of the hills of Durham.[61] This is excellent country.

Northallerton Golden Lion[62]   The town is situated on rather an eminence: it consists only of one long, broad street, well enough built, and I saw several gentlemen's houses looking very attractive.

3 April [Monday]   We left Northallerton and reached Darlington, where we stayed: only 17 miles. We stopped to talk to a labourer about the farm and farming methods.

Around here the land, in general, is good: worth a *louis* an *arpent*.[63] Some land lets much more favourably. The farms are all down to pasture, and we were told that here they breed and rear, and have many cows and other animals, which obliges the farmers to extend their pastures. Cows make up the great majority of their cattle. A great part of the meadow-land is never ploughed, or never more than once in twenty years, which is almost the same thing. When they can't turn the cattle on to meadow-land, they have to feed them on turnips, which gives a bad flavour to the butter.

The cows here are very beautiful and, above all, all the animals in this area are larger and more handsome than in the rest of England:[64] in Yorkshire, for example,

---

60 Hambleton Hills. The sheep are no longer donkey-sized, and more than half the land is arable.

61 A bit premature: the hills of Durham do begin to spread out when you get to the Tees, near Darlington: he may have spotted the Cleveland Hills.

62 The Golden Lion was built c1726 as a coaching inn when the Great North Road ran through. A Doric porte-cochère juts out over the pavement; on its roof a jolly couchant lion welcomes visitors with tail waving. Near the reception desk, G. Hurst's receipt on 19 June 1794 for 26 'Tennants Dinners' & Ale and punch is framed alongside a printed notice: 'Hoof & Horn Manures: Apply to Yard'.

63 The *louis d'argent*, or *écu*, was roughly equal to the English crown, or 5 shillings. The *arpent* was 1.5 acres.

64 A decade later (though Arthur Young *should* already have been well aware of the point), in his *General View of the Agriculture of Suffolk*, 1797, pp. 184–5, Young published the observations of Mrs Chevallier, of Aspall, in the middle of the High Suffolk claylands district that had specialised in dairying from the 16th century till Arthur Young's own day (when much of it converted to corn-growing to survive Napoleon's war menace). Mrs Chevallier wrote to Young: 'In the conver-

if one may generalise, I've seen the most handsome horses, and owned by all and sundry. Certainly, in the parts we are just leaving, the pigs, cows and sheep seem even handsomer than those we've seen elsewhere.

To return to these cows: they commonly give two gallons of milk, but a very good cow will give 5 gallons, which is a great quantity. As I say, they are fed only in the meadows, and never on clover, which is thought to be pernicious: they say that dew on the clover leads to distension and illness and the death of many cattle. On a farm of 100 *louis*' rent,[65] they feed between 12 and 20 cows, according to the land, and each cow may be worth 8 *louis*[66] a year.

Their usual crop-rotation is: 1. wheat; 2. beans or oats; 3. fallow; 4. turnips; 5. barley; 6. meadow. They sow their beans by hand, and don't weed them. The meadow is sown, as a rule, with barley[67] and some clover: it is cut and given to horses and sheep, which are fattened with turnips.

A handsome cow is worth 10 *louis*;[68] and handsome bull 20 to 25.[69]

Our whole route was very agreeable, first because the countryside was so beautiful – not level, yet not really hilly – everywhere well farmed and with an air of prosperity created by the great quantities of cattle covering every field. Apart from that you find increasing numbers of houses and several streams. Finally, for a good long time you follow a sturdy river, not navigable, but which looked as if it might be subject to flooding; for the valley isn't cultivated and the river is full of great round stones.[70] You cross the river on an uneventful bridge (Pl 29, over), and then follow it into Darlington, through pleasant country with fine cattle.

sation I heard on your purchasing cows, I observed that you inquired after large and handsome ones; but I have often known little cows, not at all remarkable for beauty, give more milk than the greatest; for instance, at present, the smallest cow we have, a cream-coloured polled one [ie one without horns] gives more milk than any of the rest, though some are almost double the size. This cow last summer, for some time in the height of the season, gave four gallons of milk twice a day; three gallons for the rest of the summer, and has given more than two gallons within two months of calving. This vast quantity of milk is not uncommon [in this district].' Four gallons once a day was the high standard reached by Robert Bakewell's famous cows (and all the cows of his area) in 1785 when Alexandre and his brother visited him (*Innocent Espionage*, p. 30).

65 £25.
66 £2.
67 Did he mean oats?
68 £2.50.
69 £5 to £6.25.
70 This is the Tees, where it marks the southern boundary of the former Durham palatinate. Croft Bridge crosses to the Durham side at Hurworth. From their horses it looked 'uneventful', but if they'd dismounted they'd have seen seven stout ribbed stone arches built by an early 14th-century bishop. From then right up till 1832, the Prince Bishops crossed here into their palatinate with a curious ceremony that had earlier been performed when they had crossed by ford into nearby Neasham.

29. *'You cross the river on an uneventful bridge, and then follow it into Darlington through pleasant country with fine cattle.' If they had dismounted they would have seen quite an eventful bridge on which the medieval prince-bishops crossed the Tees ceremoniously into their palatinate.*

Darlington, Talbot Inn[71]   Darlington sits on a small rise, forming an amphitheatre. The river, which crosses it,[72] and the width of the streets, should render it very healthy. It is a small manufacturer of broad cloth, but nothing to speak of. There is nothing in the whole town to make it remarkable. We dined very fully, and afterwards went on foot to see a farm with the finest cattle in the neighbourhood. It stands 1½ miles out of the town, the farmhouse one of the most elegant we've so far visited. But it was the cattle we had come to see.[73]

The farmer has only 12 or 14 cows, several of them very young. They are

71 The Talbot, last tenanted in 1864, stood in the corner of High Row and Post House Wynd: a plan of it in 1833 is preserved in the Library in Crown Street. Darlington's welcome in 1825 to the railway age (see North Road Station) led to the supplanting of most of its 18th-century features: a few survive in Houndgate. Alexandre characteristically failed to remark on St Cuthbert's noble 13th-century parish church beside the river, and to name the farm 1½ miles out, to which they walked so cheerfully after dinner.

72 It's the Skerne, a tributary of the Tees, that crosses Darlington.

73 Mrs K. Bennett, of the Darlington Library, has kindly informed me that two brothers, Charles and Robert Colling, were famous cattle breeders locally. Charles, who had actually studied under Robert Bakewell at Dishley in 1783, farmed at Ketton, 3 miles north of Darlington, his brother in Bampton, the next village. It seems possible that the Frenchmen were put on to the brothers by Bakewell. I've noticed elsewhere that Alexandre makes an (unusual) underestimate of distances walked.

big-built, with good flat backs and very small heads, and clearly of a good breed. Yet I find *Mr Bakewell*'s celebrated breed of cows, which I described last year,[74] looked very much better, with smaller back in relation to height. All through the winter, these cows are fed on hay; but that's been very scarce this year, so they had to be fed on linseed oil-cake, which is very expensive. They are very well-fattened, even though the scarcity and dearness of hay has prevented them from being fed as they really should be. We saw one animal that was the local prize-winner two years ago: the prize was awarded for the cow with the best all-round features, and whose calves fattened up most quickly. This cow is a real beauty, and notable for the width between the rear legs, something one looks for particularly in animals.

We've seen some good first-year calves, fine and handsome, especially those being kept for breeding as bulls. All the calves are fed on milk and water till the spring, and then they are put out to graze in the fields. Those earmarked to serve as bulls are fed by a cow bought by the farmer expressly to feed them for at least 6 months, and whenever they feel thirsty.

These young cows receive the bull at 2 years old, but their first calf isn't much good: the second is altogether better.

At present, they have only one one-year-old bull, a very fine creature but still small. The farmer, naturally keen to maintain his fine breed, sends his cows to another bull, as his own's still too young. The one he had, he sold last summer – 60 *louis*[75] – to an Irishman. He was reputed one of the most handsome beasts anyone had ever seen.

We also saw some fat bullocks. There were only three, and one of them was about to be sent to the butcher. I'd swear he stood 16 hands high, and weighed at least 364 *livres*.[76] He was fattened only on hay and a very small amount of oil-cakes. He's certainly one of the most beautiful beasts I've seen. I believe the bullocks and cattle are cleaned up twice a day, and the bull once a week. He never grazes with the cows; always by himself. As for the sheep, they are fed, as everywhere, on limitless turnips.

That evening, back from the farm, I saw in the market-place a painted notice of a cow with two heads. It was a curiosity advertised by two men who make their living by showing such oddities. I went to look and there it was. It was a white cow, and a fine animal. One of its heads was like that of any other cow, though pointing slightly to the left: the other looked to the right and was the head of a bull! The animal had two mouths and four eyes, of which three seemed to see normally. It breathed through its four nostrils, and ate and drank with both mouths at the same time. This cow at six years old had been sold for 100 *louis*. It is kept in a small covered cart, seated, and doesn't walk, and is certainly the most extraordinary animal I ever saw.[77]

---

[74] See *Innocent Espionage*, p. 30, for his brother's slightly fuller description.

[75] £15.

[76] At 52 stone, he compared with Galloways in Suffolk in 1849 (where Shorthorns reached 70 stone): Raynbird, *Agriculture of Suffolk*, 1849, p. 144.

[77] Happily, Darlington has no newspapers as early as 1786; we are spared any further details about this distressing peep-show.

4 April [Tuesday]   We left *Darlington*, dined at *Durham*, and went on to sleep at *Newcastle*: 34 miles. Now the country gets very much hillier. I can't say anything about the route: the fog was so thick that we could only just make out our horses' heads. So you mustn't be surprised to find I've written nothing until we reached Newcastle.

Durham, Green Dragon[78]   Durham's perched up on top of two hills separated by a very narrow valley, in the bottom of which an unnavigable torrent[79] flows past, encircling the town and overhung by great trees that grow right up to its sheer banks. The castle is built on its high hill, dominating everything around: what a view it must present. The castle contains the bishop's palace, but is more of a fortress than anything, itself dominated by a taller keep. The cathedral is in excellent order: built, I imagine, two centuries before the Reformation.[80] It is extremely large for its period, but I've never before seen such a heavy church: the supporting pillars are enormous, and all carved differently, without symmetry.[81] They were at work on repairing the church, renewing a chimney-stack:[82] they were being careful to rebuild it in the original style. We didn't see the library: *it's said* that, on his appointment, each dean has to present 25 *louis'* worth of books, the custom going back to the foundation of the chapter.

The rest of the town is terrible, climbing up and descending narrow and ill-constructed streets. The two bridges over the river are narrow and ugly: altogether an ugly old town.[83]

---

[78] The Green Dragon's name here presumably means that that was where they left their horses to make the ascent to cathedral and palace on foot, as people do with their cars today. The Green Dragon stood in Old Elvet, which runs due east from Elvet Bridge: no 61 occupies the site (K Proud, *Durham City*, 1992, p. 108). There they presumably ate their dinner.

[79] The river Wear. It is a terrible disappointment that they rode into Durham's splendid city in a fog and pressed on, with little pause, to Newcastle.

[80] He's a clear two centuries adrift for this massively Norman building: no budding architectural historian!

[81] The round piers are boldly carved, each a randomly chosen pattern, lozenge-shaped, chevrons, zig-zags, etc, doubtless each originally coloured, and the round pillars alternate with the major piers supporting the earliest of all the rib vaults of Europe.

[82] *Cheminée*. I think he must have seen one of the turrets under repair. But he may have been referring to the palace or one of the houses of the canons round what is now College Green.

[83] They were there in fog and too much haste: one can see how Durham made such a bad impression.

5

Newcastle to Berwick-upon-Tweed

Newcastle is 'one of the most commercial places in all England. Their first article of trade is coal. Here they're all set to flourish in trade and to see that this lasts into eternity.' Coal was measured by the chaldron, and chaldron wagons were a symbol of the town: one, fully laden, is boldly outlined in the foreground of James Fittler's effective drawing and engraving of Newcastle from the south *in May 1783. (Pl 30, over) Alexandre did his own drawing of one, and one is on show at the Beamish Museum. Alexandre was in his element in describing this historical trade, and he managed to find space for the glass-factories. He and Lazowski took a sail down the river, noticing some 3-masters. Good farming on the road to Morpeth, and splendid sheep. They ate at Caucot, beside the Coquet, 'a romantic sight flowing over and around its rocks'. This is the duke of Northumberland's territory. Visiting his castle they noticed that 'the towers are covered with stone statues in imitation of warriors, all in fighting postures'. Their small stature may have added to the illusion of the height of the gates and towers. Alexandre commended the* goût ancien *in the Georgian restoration and redecoration of the castle. After seeing the castle they walked in the park, went back to the White Swan, wrote up their journals, and after supper engaged the innkeeper in conversation about the local farming.*

At Bamburgh they ate at the Swan and were delighted in the castle to find only the square keep restored and the whole place given over to saving the lives of sailors wrecked on this rocky coast; with a surgeon maintained, and an elaborate system of signals. Alexandre goes fully into the lifesaving arrangements. Back on the main Berwick road, they made for the Bluebell Inn at Belford, alongside the little market-place. Arriving, Alexandre was driving the gig with Lazowski's servant as passenger: turning it too tightly, he managed to tip them both into a muck-heap, before a big and cheerful crowd. The pleasant inn was fairly new in 1786, and has undergone very little structural change to this day. Next morning they left for Berwick in a north-easterly gale.

Newcastle, Turk's Head [1]   The 5th [April] we spent looking at Newcastle. It occupies a steepish rise, a hill really, that flanks the river Tyne, and slopes down to it. It's a very broad river, crossed by a very handsome bridge, which also has the merit of being flat. [2]

---

[1]   The Royal Turks Head Hotel stood on the west side of Grey Street near the corner of High Bridge: it closed in the early 1980s, and now houses a financial body.
[2]   The medieval bridge had replaced a Roman one and, like London's, had been lined with houses. It was badly damaged by flood in 1771. Alexandre was admiring Robert Mylne's joint

81

30. *Newcastle-on-Tyne from the south, with characteristic chaldron wagon prominent in the foreground. Detail from James Fittler's drawing and engraving of May 1783.*

There are no remarkable monuments in the town, and no street vistas; but much uphill and downhill walking. There is one new street being created, which will be very pleasant.[3] In the middle of it there's to be a comedy-theatre, a playhouse, but it looks small,[4] and I think it will prove to be too small in relation to the size of this town and

design of 1774–8, in turn replaced by the present serviceable swing bridge of 1876. It brings the motorist conveniently across to Sandhill, the waterfront, at the point where the bridge crossed in Fittler's beautiful engraving of 1783 for John Brand's invaluable 2-vol *History and Antiquities of Newcastle-upon-Tyne*, 1789, frontispiece to vol II. For the visitor, it's now one of the most lively parts of the town, with comfortable hotels and attractive restaurants.

3   Dean Street and Mosley Street were being built in the years 1784–86 by David Stephenson, who was also building the very handsome church of All Saints, behind the Quayside, in 1786. Unluckily, it is now divided from Dean Street and Mosley Street by the Central Motorway East, with a great roundabout blighting Mosley Street; but All Saints was described by Thomas Sharp as 'probably the best individual building in the whole of Northumberland'. Howard Colvin thinks it 'one of the most striking and original churches built in England in the 18th century'. Stephenson's pupil, John Dobson, was responsible for the remarkable designs with which he and Richard Grainger transformed the commercial centre of Newcastle in the six years 1835–40, working out northwards and westwards from David Stephenson's beginnings. He soon switched to what mainly interested him: Newcastle's business. Defoe had described the town's situation to landward as 'exceeding unpleasant, and the buildings very close and old'.

4   He is probably referring to the theatre John Dobson pulled down, to get the best line for Grey Street. Alexandre didn't refer to the very elegant Palladian Assembly House, 1774–6, by Wm Newton in Fenkle Street, off the Westgate Road, now a conference and banquetting centre; nor, curiously, to the Infirmary of 1751. He was right about the size of the theatre: the new Theatre Royal of 1837 (by Benjamin Green) verges on the noble.

its reputation, for it's over 100,000 souls. It's a very large town, and in general it's inhabited by merchants: there's little sign of the nobility, for here – just as it is everywhere else – gentlefolk live separately from the merchants.[5] Here we've arrived in one of the most commercial places in all England. Their first article of trade is coal. It is from here that the whole of London and many of the provinces are supplied; some of it also goes to foreign parts, but it's fair to say that here they're all set to flourish in trade and to see that this lasts into eternity.

As I said, the town's built beside the river Tyne, which is navigable from the sea as high as Newcastle (only 7 miles) by ships of 2 or 300 tons (the ton is 2,420 *livres*). Almost all the ships make their way back upstream to the town, delivering everything they bring from London in return for the coal – such heavy goods as sugar, hay, iron, etc. But one would like to know in detail how such a complex, large-scale commercial operation works.

Above the bridge, the biggest ships can't sail, though the river is still navigable by flat-bottomed craft up to 10 more miles: that far, and along both banks, the entire trade is in coal, of which there appears to be no shortage. Here there are two kinds of merchants – those who work the mines for the coal, and those with the ships to convey it where required. The first run the land operations, the second the whole operation on water. The production of the coal depends on the first; from the mines it is drawn on an extraordinary kind of tumbril.

These wagons have two iron wheels and two wooden ones: they are very short (from front to back), and the horse may be harnessed to either end, as required. They run always on specially constructed tracks, which are wooden for going downhill, and iron for level ground. That's to say that at the place where the wheels pass over there's a band either of iron or of wood which is about 4 inches wide; and the

---

5   Things weren't quite as they were in France: some merchants were also gentlefolk. Roger North, accompanying his brother the Lord Chief Justice to Newcastle c1680, listened to stories of their coal-works told by the aldermen (*Lives of the Norths*, 1890, I, p. 175). One of them, Sir William Blackett, Bart, had cut into a hill to drain water from his mines, finally found the *clay* too hard for him, and had lost £20,000 in the attempt. Blackett's house, home of the leading merchant's family (engraved by Kip and published in 1707) is shown amid pretty but not enormous gardens, sandwiched between the town-wall and the houses of the rest of the town. Celia Fiennes described it in delightful detail in 1698. In their notes on Kip (*Britannia Illustrata*, publ privately for the National Trust, 1984, and ed by John Harris and Gervase Jackson-Stops, pl 54), the editors summarised the Blackett family fortunes: founded on coal, lead and property in the early 17th century, by Sir Walter, 1st Bart; he left one fortune and his title to Edward (who acquired Newby, which Alexandre failed to notice just outside Ripon); another fortune to William, who inherited the Newcastle house, achieved the mayoralty and a baronetcy of his own, and a considerable reputation in the Commons. Their mother was a merchant's daughter. William bought Wallington, formerly owned by the Fenwicks, fellow merchants in Newcastle. (Later, Wallington was bought by the Trevelyans, who helped found the National Trust with it.) William's family left the Newcastle house in 1783, the year in which it appeared prominently on the horizon beyond the Castle in James Fittler's marvellous engraving, of the town seen across the Tyne, which he dedicated to Sir Matthew White Ridley, Bart, Mayor that year. Alas, the house was pulled down in the 1830s in order to make Hood Street.

31. *'An extraordinary kind of tumbril' (Alexandre's sketch of a chaldron wagon).*

two iron wheels have rims on the outside, to prevent the wheels from leaving the tracks. The roads run from the mine to the riverside, always following *either* a smooth surface or a descent, but a gentle one. For one horse, singly, couldn't draw uphill one of these wagons full of coal. When you get down to details, the horse, and the man seated on the piece of wood (A) [clearly a curved, and perhaps sprung, wooden brake exerting pressure on the top of the back wheel] holds back the wagon as it goes downhill. The piece of wood's very strong, to retain so heavy a vehicle. Often it breaks, or catches fire with the sustained friction, and that's very dangerous. When the wagons have reached the river-bank, there are men ready to manhandle them on to a ship, purpose-built, with a lot of chutes [*conduits*] which, from the covered container, tip the coal into ships already at the loading-place. Thus one doesn't have to load a second time, between the mine and the collier.

You use only one wagon. The boats to which you bring the coal are big in propor-tion to the trade of the place. The business we visited was very big, with 30 of these wagons to serve its mines. Each of the wagons holds almost a *chaldron*: in fact 9 wagons carry 8 chaldron. At this point the merchants dealing with the land opera-tions finish the job begun by the merchants ships. All the costs of what I've described belong to the first group: those that follow belong to the second.

The merchant sells the coal loaded on the boat at 14 shillings a *chaldron*. The boats that come for the coal and are, as I've described, able to navigate about 10 miles above the town, are flat-bottomed, draw about 3 feet of water and are usually managed by 4 men, 3 rowing and the other manning the tiller. Often they are able to hoist sail. They can carry 9 of these wagons. This kind of boat is called a *Keel*.[6]

6   *OED* gives 'keel, a flat-bottomed vessel, especially the kind used on the Tyne'.

32. *Here is a chaldron wagon preserved in the Beamish Museum. One appears prominently in James Fittler's great panorama of Newcastle in 1783.*

The port officials check them every year, reckoning 21 tons for 3 feet of water. If they don't pass the test, then they are fined. These Keels carry the coals from where they are loaded to where the bigger ships are moored. When they've discharged their load they return to the dêpot to re-load: that's the routine all the year round for a total of 500 of these flat-bottomed boats. The sea-going ships carry the contents of anything between 15 and 24 *Keels*, and they usually moor as far downstream as they can, and set sail the moment they're loaded.

They make from 10 to 12 voyages a year from here to London, returning with other merchandise in exchange. [Alexandre changes to a thinner, finer quill at this point.] This one trade brings in a great return to this town, and its exclusiveness is the circumstance that makes it extremely profitable. The merchants risk almost nothing, and they can't, as in other towns, venture more than they have. Another advantage in this business is the preference given to Newcastle's coal for its hardness, requiring less coal for the same heat. One asks how it happens that London provisions itself so much from the north when coalmines are to be found so much nearer inland. But the quality of the coal resolves this question and seems to guarantee this branch of trade to Newcastle for ever.

There are glass-factories here; indeed three kinds: makers of ordinary bottles, those of drinking-glasses, and those who make window-glass. The first two are like those I described last year at *Warrington*,[7] but the last is altogether different.

The window-glass is made by Scots settled here, all members of one family; they all work in the factory and at the same time have an interest in it. So it was enough that one member of the family came to explain the work to us. He was perspiring like a workman. He didn't admit anyone else. They employ only women and old men to prepare the charcoal. The place where they work is arranged so that they can combine being both merchants and workmen.

This is how they make their glass. The material is thrown so that it's deposited in large troughs in the shape of bath-tubs of varying sizes, the fire arranged on all sides. When it's ready, a workman comes to remove the dross; and they mayn't start production until a customs officer arrives to judge, by the specifications of the trough (which they measure with a semi-circular tool) what quantity of drinking-glasses they should make: anyone going ahead and turning out as many as they can sell is in the business of contraband: they mustn't do that.

It's worth noting what big business this nation thrives on for it to submit to such a heavy yoke as this: always to have to put up with an official following every one of your business operations, with power to control them if necessary; yet, despite that, to be the first in the world for the beauty of its glassware, and for its relative cheapness and its quality.

When the glass is ready, a workman comes with an iron bow, bored through the middle, and takes from the glass two or three times until he has enough. Then he puts it into another kiln. He blows it into the shape of a ball, and returns it to the fire two or three times. Then he places it in a lime kiln [*four les chaux*], cutting it by means of a very cold steel. He makes a smooth surface in this shape. The place where the letter A is is where the iron bow [*la bot de fer*] was which forms a semi-circle, cutting it when all that is done. This piece of glass is put in another kiln, but not so hot [*chaux!*]. By degrees it is cooled and lifted out ready. [Small sketch omitted.]

All that remains to be done is the polishing, and that process I didn't see. This trade is never less than considerable. It concentrates on portable goods. All the furnaces are built beside the river, so as to be well-placed for loading the goods on to boats, and at the same time for the delivery of materials by water, not to mention the supply of water itself, the coal and the stone; in short everything they need.

We went down the river by boat, seeing some very fair-sized ships: some

7   Alexandre's account was less detailed than his brother's, doubtless because he seemed to have a touch of 'flu: they were in Warrington on 9 March 1785 and François was particularly interested in the method of making twist glasses (*Innocent Espionage*, p. 83).

three-masters, for instance, capable of sailing everywhere.[8] Ships are built here. We've seen some fine shipyards, all along the waterfront for at least a mile.

The poor-rate is 3 shillings in the pound, which isn't much considering the size of the population, and the tremendous trade that so much augments it.

On (Thursday) the 6th (April) we left Newcastle   and reached *Morpeth* – 14 miles – without stopping. The countryside is enclosed. For the first 3 miles, the road is paved, as in France, except that it's much worse and beset with a great many deep holes.[9] However, after those first three miles, the route becomes part of a garden, running often between two plantations, as welcoming as a park. The farms good, well-cultivated, the land lets at above 30 shillings, the pasture up to 15 shillings. Their rotation: 1) barley 2) wheat 3) oats 4) turnips 5) wheat 6) grass. Hereabouts they are famous for the breed of their cattle, of which they raise large numbers. For example, on a farm of about 400 acres, they support 18 cows and 10 horses: they don't fatten beef, which is another branch of the business.

Their pasture lasts 3 or 4 years; they go off, after that, and need new grass. And they then have a long spell of corn crops. It's good to see that they don't sow the meadows with barley. Following our route is like riding between two parks belonging to gentlemen farmers whose farms appear to me to be superbly maintained.[10] We've seen a great many splendid sheep coming down from the north to the Newcastle market. They're of a beautiful breed, rather like those of Durham. The whole of the way was hilly and I would say agreeable.

Morpeth, Queen's Head[11]   A pretty town, down in a valley so that you don't really see it while you're in it. It's on the Wansbeck, which isn't navigable,[12] but provides a charming view. And from the top of the hill on the other side of the river, you get a good view of the town, the surrounding fields and the river itself.

8   The Bucks' caption to their fine *SE Prospect of Newcastle*, 1745, described 'one of the most beautiful and spacious keys in the kingdom, where ships of considerable Burden may load and unload with pleasure'.
9   A Young, *A 6-Months Tour through the North of England*, 1770, IV, letter XLIII, contains comparisons of roads. Describing the road to Morpeth, he found 'a pavement for a mile or 2 out of Newcastle, which is tolerable: all the rest vile'. Then, on to Alnwick, he found the road better; Alnwick to Belford 'better still'; finally to Berwick, 'part good, but some very bad'. The Newcastle–Morpeth road-surface had declined 1770–86.
10   In Northumberland, as in Scotland, landowners under the Hanoverians no longer needed large retinues for battle: they turned to building, enclosing, draining, planting woodland and parkland: and eviction. These are empty lands still, with sheep providing the life and movement.
11   It survives as Queen's Head Hotel in the main street, with carriage-way through, and a Georgian lustre chandelier on the staircase: front given bogus geometrical 'half-timbers'.
12   *Paterson's Roads*, 1811, explains 'not navigable beyond the Town, owing to a Cataract at the Bridge. An ancient Borough with a good market and Free School'.

On 7 April we left Morpeth   We dined [lunched] at Caucot,[13] and went on from there to
Alnwick: the distance only 19 miles. After you've left Morpeth and climbed a very
steep hill, you look back to see the town in what is partly a sort of amphitheatre with
the river flowing through, fine meadowlands on either side, contrasting with the arid
commons beyond the meadows. Further on, you come to large enclosures. Quite
often you get a view of the sea to your right, and to the left, woods and great fields
enclosed by dry-walling in a stone[14] that is used in the construction of all sorts of
things.

Caucot lies among all these hills in a very narrow valley. Through it, in the
bottom of the valley, comes the river *Coquet*, a romantic sight as it flows around and
over the rocks, but after it has passed under a nice bridge which is in the village, it
runs through some meadowland, and that's pleasant to see. The village itself is a
poor place, but one sees two or three good houses in it. We stopped there only on
account of our horses, not to look at the place.

From *Caucot* to *Alnwick* the land belongs almost entirely to the duke of
Northumberland, who in these parts is regarded as lord of the whole county. There
is more enclosure along the road, but further away it's open. Here the hills are very
frequent, and tiring to man and beast: they are both high and steep. The only drawback is the steepness of the roads, which in these two last counties have been excellent.[15]

Alnwick White Swan   Alnwick stands fairly high above its river, which flows past the foot
of the town and is narrow, but endlessly attractive. The town's surrounded by old
walls: the only exits are through very heavy stone gateways.[16] It contains no remarkable antiquities. The castle, which adjoins it, is magnificent both in situation and
construction. As in all old castles, you enter through an oppressive stone gateway[17]

---

[13] In the 6th edn of *Paterson's Roads*, 1784, Caucot is 9 miles from Morpeth and a mile short of
Felton Bridge on the Great North Road. In later editions Caucot's name disappeared, nor is it on
contemporary road-maps. It may have become part of Felton, 'a bare village above the banks of the
Coquet', which shares Caucot's name, and where the medieval bridge is by-passed and preserved.
They would perhaps have dined at The Northumberland Arms, pleasantly double-bow-fronted,
and now rather too opened up inside. It faces the bridge they crossed over the Coquet.
[14] I suppose these must be the cementstones of the Whittingham Vale, through which Alnwick's
river cut its way down to the sea. The better building-stone, a carboniferous sandstone, occurs
farther north at Doddington, near Belford, and is well presented in the National Trust's
Wallington Hall.
[15] Cf Young's verdict in 1770, footnote 9 above.
[16] To reach the White Swan, in Bondgate Within, they would have passed through the Hotspur
Tower, the most prominent part of the town's 15th-century defences: the line of the walls can still
be made out on Thomas Wilkins's map of 1774 in the castle. Several Alnwick street-names end in
-gate (Scandinavian word for 'street'), not necessarily implying the existence of a gatehouse. A
Borough was chartered in the 12th century.
[17] This is the main entrance gateway, itself protected by a turreted castellated barbican, from the
early 14th century, possibly the most formidable survival of its kind. Stone figures of soldiers guard
these battlements, 'very striking, yet ridiculous' according to Louis Simon, in his usually very intelligent commentary on his tour in Britain in 1810–11. He was misled by the way the 18th-century

into an outer court, fairly large, in which the stables stand in great magnificence. They hold 30 horses, and are designed in the grandest manner: you find even the nails are gilded: these are dream-stables.[18] Once you are in this court, you are in full view of the château, on its slightly raised platform. It has been extensively restored, but always in the medieval taste. It confronts you in the form of a half-circle with three towers. You have to go through another stone gateway,[19] to arrive in a very large court (the Middle Bailey) enclosed along the side away from the town by a tall wall, and enclosing square towers over on the far side and also in the middle of this court; also a lion carved in white marble which is the supporter of this family's arms.[20]

You still have to go through one of these gates[21] to enter the castle. You find yourself in a courtyard of much smaller proportions. The interior of the house is very well furnished, but I found its decoration too much changed. The dining-room is more or less in its ancient state, large and very handsome. All the other rooms have been modernised, but always in the medieval taste.[22] The castle occupies 5 acres or

replacements of the earlier figures light-heartedly included Hercules and Apollo among British crossbowmen and arquebusiers who had originally been set up to add to the apparent numbers of defenders during the various times of siege and attack. Original medieval figures survive on the Octagonal Towers. In World War II, a friend of mine, Mervyn Bell, defending a stretch of the Sudan frontier with 55 Arabs against 800 Italians from Ethiopia, placed gourds on makeshift walls, with sticks to make the gourds look like men with rifles. It worked; and I'm sure the stone figures at Alnwick seemed to add numbers to the defenders in the confusion of an attack. Their apparently small stature might have been intended to emphasise the height of the battlements under assault. So much for (the admirable) Louis Simon's 'puppet-show castle': he himself noted that some of the figures had been weathered to half their size. It is strange that he didn't notice the similar figures manning the main gates at York: on the Bootham, Micklegate, and Monk Bars. The re-modelling of most of the figures by the Georgian masons was part of the *goût ancien* Alexandre commended at Alnwick, expressing as it did a civilised elegance in the rearrangement and delicate decoration of the neglected comparatively barbarous baronial apartments.

[18] It is extraordinary that *all* the identifiably Georgian work of Paine and Robert Adam for the 1st duke of Northumberland in the 1750s and '60s, including even the stables and the broad terrace along the north wall of the castle, was destroyed and remodelled a century later by the 4th duke.

[19] The Middle Gateway; it leads through to the Middle Bailey and the twin Octagonal Towers which give access to the Courtyard of the central Keep.

[20] No: this lion *statant*, with tail extended, is the familiar Northumberland crest. The supporters are lions rampant. For a duke's son, Alexandre is disappointingly vague about heraldry.

[21] The Octagonal Towers (P. Leach's pl 160 shows them in 1825, but much as they were in 1786).

[22] Louis Simond's observation, in 1811, that some of the small stone figures were badly weathered but others 'quite whole and fresh', led to the discovery that this apparently old castle was in fact built only sixty years ago'. He was exaggerating. But it was true that, c1754, the 1st Smithson duke of Northumberland, who was responsible for Robert Adam's remodelling of Syon House in the 1760s, commissioned James Paine to reconstruct Alnwick's Keep as a suitable residence. As Paine's biographer Peter Leach (1988) says, 'the changes made to the basic form of the building were much less extensive than those carried out by Salvin' for the Victorian 4th duke. Leach says 'the most remarkable feature of Paine's work was the skill with which he fitted the accommodation into the existing irregular shell, exploiting its potential for spacial effect: the dining-room, the former great hall' was given a symmetrical appearance that persuaded Alexandre that it was more or less in its ancient state: Paine's drawing (P. Leach, pl 162) says much about Alexandre's ideas of the Middle Ages. Adam had taken over from Paine and decorated the saloon, drawing-room and library in his version of Gothick: Robert Adam's brother John, in Spring 1759, found the

33. *Alnwick Castle, 'like many others in the north, was anciently ornamented with figures of warriors distributed round the battlements. The present noble proprietors have allowed them to be continued and have supplied some that have been destroyed. To show what they once were, and that this is no innovation, they have retained the ancient ones, though defaced, which have been placed on the top of the two octagon towers.' F. Grose,* Antiquities of England and Wales, *IV, pl 3, by S. Hooper, December 1784, and p. 47.*

more, all enclosed by a skirting-wall built out of the rock. All the towers around the house are covered with stone statues in imitation of warriors, all of them in fighting postures, creating an impression of small-scale combatants.

dining-room and drawing-room 'extremely noble and elegant in the Gothick taste, but the drawing-room pleased me most' (John Fleming, 'Adam Gothic', *Connoisseur*, Oct 1958, p. 75). A Georgian lithograph by J. D. Harding serves as frontispiece to this book, giving a very rare picture of the charming Gothick decoration of a recess in the Saloon. Arthur Young, not easily carried away by the flimsy, wrote of Alnwick (*Tour of North*, 1770, III, p. 39): 'The apartments are all fitted in the Gothic taste and ornamented in a very light and elegant style. The architecture of the new buildings is quite in the castle stile, and very light and pleasing.' Perhaps this was what Alexandre meant by 'too much change'. It was certainly too much for the 4th duke, who got Salvin in and gave the house essentially its present appearance. Salvin and his Italian colleagues swept away almost everything Paine and Adam had contributed: he himself gave a more plausible, irregular medieval appearance to the exterior, while Adam's delicate Gothick gave way to the opulent Italian Renaissance interiors of Commendatore Canina, Director of the Capitoline Museum from 1854; on his death in 1856 he was succeeded by his assistant, Giovanni Montirole. The 4th duke died in 1865, leaving the drawing-room and library to be furnished by the 6th duke (1867–99). Around 1885, when the Record Tower needed repair, it was done in a 14th-century style that involved the sacrifice of 'a fine Adam ceiling'.

Here, then, you see a castle as it was in the time of the Barons' Wars, and looking at it gives you a most impressive idea of what they were like. Its position was immensely strong, standing over 200 feet above the river, and dominating the rest of the country around. On top of that, remember that the castle went with the ownership of the whole, or almost the whole, county.

This is the cradle of the great English family of Percy, familiar in the story of this country's wars. It's the present duke who has restored the whole castle and put it into its present fine condition.[23] To give you an idea of the expense he has incurred in this, and in the improvement of his plantations and his whole estate, his agent has said that £26,000 have passed through his hands, all of it revenue from this region.[24]

After seeing the house we looked for a while at the park. It's very large and forms a beautiful view from the castle, with the river winding through, widened to show to best effect, and passing under a bridge he's had built in the medieval style, but handsome.[25] Soon after it has gone beyond the bridge, it loses itself among rocky banks covered with fine, mature woods.

After walking through the park, we went to the inn, wrote up our journals and had our supper. Our inn-keeper came and talked, and from his conversation we learnt something of the local farming. The farms are mostly very large, and belong to the duke of Northumberland, who has lately been reducing the size of those he owns and leases out to round about 100 *arpents*.[26] It's good land and worth 130 shillings[27] an arpent. Their crop rotation is: 1) oats   2) turnips   3) barley   4) beans   5) fallow   6) wheat   7) grass [*prairies*]. Here they sow their grazing-land with wheat: it is the only place where I've come across such a practice. These grazing-lands continue for three years: in one year they are mown; in the other two they are turned over to the cattle. It seems to be the general practice here to feed turnips underfoot to the animals: in England, common practice, but not universal.

As for their oats, they send for the Poland oats,[28] believing them to be much the best on recent results; yielding three times the quantity, with oats of this seed, than they had been getting with their own.

---

[23] Hugh Smithson (afterwards Percy), created duke of Northumberland 1766, died 6 June 1786.

[24] GEC, *The Complete Peerage*, IX, 1936, p. 744 note (c) records: 'He is said to have planted above 12,000 trees annually in Northumberland, and to have increased his revenues from £8,000 to £50,000 a year, while Alnwick Castle, Stanwick in Yorkshire, Sion House (Isleworth), and Northumberland House in the Strand, were adequately restored.' In *The Complete Peerage*, 1775, he is described as 'one of the most polite and accomplished men of the present age, an excellent judge of the fine arts', and his wife as possessing 'a noble and beneficent spirit'.

[25] The park, as will have been guessed, was the creation of Capability Brown (D. Stroud, 1974, pp. 103–4 and pl 94B). The bridge is round-arched, but self-consciously battlemented. Beyond it the river curves, and disappears, romantically, as Alexandre recorded, into woods coming right down to its banks.

[26] An *arpent* seems to vary from an acre to an acre and a half.

[27] £1.30.

[28] 'Most of my neighbours prefer the white Poland oat': *Museum rusticum, Select Papers on Agriculture*, 1964.

A very big farmer often has 2,000 *arpents*,[29] the lands are strong, and yet, although they are themselves rich men, I can't make out how they manage to farm so successfully over such an extended area. This puzzles me, because they are rather neglectful of their farming-practice. In fact, it isn't really as good as it is in the other parts of England.

They don't introduce the Poland wheat or barley; only the Poland oats. With the wheat it's often possible to get back 30 seeds for one; yet their oats return only 10 seeds for each one sown. What makes a great difference is that they sow 2 bushells to the *arpent*. That I find very good, and I have seen it sown profitably in other parts of England – for example in lower Yorkshire.

8 April, Bamborough Castle, The Swan   We had dinner at Bamburgh, the road in sight of the sea all the way. You leave the main road 6 miles from Alnwick and fork right on to a very stony road,[30] bad but passable. The farming here looks rather neglected; however, I met one of the gentlemen farmers who are the friends of English agriculture. This poor cultivation is enclosed in dry-stone walling. The walling doesn't leave you with much of a view. Apart from that, the land is so rough as to be almost inaccessible. It's very hilly and the road is often bare rock. You can see up to your left, some ten miles from the road, the hills are all covered with snow, as I suppose they may be for much of the year.

You see ahead from a long way off the outlines of *Bamburgh Castle*, built up on a high rock beside the sea.[31] A little village lies half a mile away on the landward side, composed of only one street and a few houses. But it's the castle that attracted us here, and that's what I want to describe.

The castle is not remarkable for its buildings, nor even for its situation, but for the good it achieves and the great number of lives it saves. It is perched on a steep outcrop above the sea, in the middle of desolate country. The rock has a reddish tinge, and is immensely hard. On the seaward side its ruins are covered with sand at high tides: it stands about 150 feet above sea-level. From what remains of these

---

[29] See footnote 26 above.

[30] They seem to have struck off from the North Road at about North Charlton instead of staying on the better surface as far as Adderstone. *Paterson's Roads* disdained to mention Bamburgh, nor was it marked on their maps. Alexandre's must be a very early reference to The Swan.

[31] Its outline as you approach is now its main attraction. What you see is largely the formidable creation of the 1st Lord Armstrong (1810–1900), and his great-nephew who succeeded him; Armstrong, a remarkable engineer and inventor, was employing 25,028 workmen at his great plant near Newcastle at the time of his death. He lived at Cragside, near Rothbury, now National Trust. He bought Bamburgh Castle in 1894, apparently meaning to create a convalescent home there. That would have seemed a natural sequel to the lifesaving foundation Alexandre and Lazowski came out of their way to see in 1786. But between 1894 and 1905, Lord Armstrong and his successor got carried away, creating almost from scratch a huge impregnable-looking strong-hold on the scale of Dover, perhaps with the idea of eclipsing Alnwick. When Alexandre was here, the square keep was in repair and good use (schools, infirmary, life-saving activities) and two or three buildings for lodging the shipwrecked sailors between the keep and the present main entrance, but contemporary paintings show the rest as rubble and ruin. The Armstrongs spared no expense but the results, apart from the keep, are impressive mainly at a distance.

34. Bamborough Castle *by S. Hooper, 1 January 1785 (F. Grose,* Antiquities of England and Wales, *IV, facing p. 49). Grose noted that 'a constant watch was kept from the top of the tower, whence signals are given to the fishermen of Holy Island when any ship is discovered in distress – these fishermen being able to put off in their boats when none from the mainland can get over the breakers. The signals are so regulated as to point out to the particular place where the distressed vessel lies.'*

ruins, plainly the castle was large and powerful in its hey-day. At present it's abandoned, and they've put up new buildings within the walls to accommodate sailors who've been shipwrecked: also to house the equipment used to help in the rescue of ships, and of course to house the people living and working here in the castle.

They have lately repaired and rebuilt a square tower for storing all the machines and tackle.[32] The Master's lodgings are high up in two towers, from which ships in peril can be signalled. The castle was uninhabited when *Lord Crew*[33] saw the

[32] The ground floor of the keep displays some of the great chains used in the 18th-century rescue and salvage work organised by Dr John Sharp.

[33] This Lord Crew (whom Alexandre called Lord Gore, through misreading his own notes) was the celebrated Nathaniel Crew, barefaced Anglican collaborator with James II, as Roman Catholic duke of York and King, who helped him to the bishopric of Oxford (1671). In 1674 he bought the bishopric of Durham from Nell Gwynne (GEC, *Complete Peerage*, III, 1913, p. 534), and became dean of the Chapel Royal after James's accession. When James fled, he managed to hang on to the bishopric of Durham, though shorn of his right to appoint prebends. In 1700 he married Dorothy, daughter of Sir William Forster of Bamburgh; when Forster was reduced to selling that estate in 1704, Crew was able to buy it for £20,679. Dorothy's nephew Thomas was the hapless

appalling numbers of the ships that perished on this coast and, in humanity, left all his estates in the hands of 12 Trustees. Their responsibility is to maintain the house, to give help to those needing it, and to establish a free grammar school, for Latin and Greek, where the scholars are lodged and fed.

Dr Sharp, one of the Trustees, runs it all. He lives here in the castle during the summer, and is at Durham in the winter, which here is very bleak. He has an apartment in the tower, and even rooms for his friends.

The castle is thus by Trust Deed dedicated to helping ships in danger. For not only, as I've said, is it standing upon a very dangerous shore, the place itself is surrounded by rocks[34] reaching 2 miles out into the sea, providing a firm foothold for signal-lights.[35] Despite all their preparations and precautions here, a great many ships perish with their crew and cargo every year. Those who effectively warn a ship of its dangers are rewarded; and the first boat putting out to sea to help with the rescue takes some of the tackle provided for these emergencies. If the ship is wrecked, rooms and food are prepared for those sailors who are saved. Storerooms hold merchandise and goods over a period until someone reclaims them. As soon as

---

Jacobite commander in 1715, news of whose capitulation seems to have caused her death from convulsions. Crew died childless, leaving considerable estates to trustees through whose wisdom, as the *DNB* observed, Crew enjoys a reputation as a farseeing philanthropist. Crew's most indefatigable trustee was Dr John Sharp, who died in 1792, and whose youngest brother was Granville Sharp (1735–1813), largely responsible for winning the crucial case of James Somersett in the movement for the abolition of slavery; and who went on to join the crusade against the press-gang.

In the keep at Bamburgh, as well as some of the apparatus of ship-salvage, a very interesting document recreates the kind of rescue-work promoted by Sharp and his fellow trustees here. It is headed *An Account of the Signals made Use of at Bamburgh Castle, in case ships or vessels are perceiv'd in distress, and of the charitable institutions established there for their assistance and relief*, now published by direction of the Trustees of Nathaniel, late Lord Crew, with the approbation of the Master, Pilots and Seamen of the Trinity House in Newcastle-upon-Tyne: signed 24 December 1771, Thomas Aubone, Secretary at Trinity House, Newcastle.

1. A 9-pounder is fired as signal when any ship is observed in distress.
2. In every storm, 2 men on horseback are sent to patrol the coast.

I   Rooms and beds are prepared for seamen ship-wreck'd who will be maintained for a week or more.

II   Cellars for wine, etc, are to be deposited for a year.

III A storehouse for wrecked goods.

IV   4 pairs of screws for raising ships that are stranded, in order to their being repair'd. Blocks, tackles, handspokes, cables, ropes, pumps and iron ready for use of shipwreck'd vessels. NB, but if taken away, to be paid for at prime cost.

V   A pair of chains with large rings and swivels made on purpose for weighting ships (of 1000 tons Burthen) sunk upon rocks or in deep water. NB, to be lent gratis to any person having occasion for them within 40 or 50 miles along the coast on giving proper security.

VI   Whenever dead bodies are cast on shore, coffins etc will be provided gratis and funeral expenses found.

34 The formation is called the Whin Sill, composed of 'dolerite', a kind of basalt. The Farne Islands include the most spectacular examples, covered with kittiwakes, puffins, eider-duck, etc.

35 The furthest out into the sea, the Longstone, bore the lighthouse from which Grace Darling rowed out with her father on their heroic act of rescue in September 1838: a Bamburgh family, they are commemorated in the churchyard.

35. *The Belford Bluebell faces the little triangular market-place beside the Great North Road. It was probably fairly newly built in 1786: the bedroom doors still hang from the local blacksmith's hinges. This is just where Alexandre brought the gig round in too tight a turn, tipping himself and Mr Lazowski's servant into a muck-heap. 'Very rarely has such a tumble been performed before so big and cheerful a crowd.'*

a ship is seen to be in danger, signals are made to reassure them that they've been sighted, and that help will be on its way. This castle has succeeded in saving ships, and has saved above all a great many sailors. In brief, they provide for men and ships everything they may need by way of help, and that's one of the most impressive signs of a reflective and useful humanity.

During the war, troops were stationed here. One finds cannon of all calibres, held in the castle and belonging to it: their gun-fire is often used as signals to warn ships.

A surgeon is maintained here on an annual fee, to heal injured sailors and bring them back to life. A paper is displayed showing methods of artificial resuscitation of those who appear to be drowned; also showing methods in use that are harmful and to be avoided. The surgeon needs drugs for his treatment, and these are supplied free for patients unable to afford them.

Belford Bluebell   From the castle we went on to Belford, where we slept: only 5 miles. Half the route passes through a common beside the sea; then you pass through a beautiful plantation, and arrive at Belford on the rise beyond the stream. Nothing remarkable. On arriving in the little town, I had the gig in hand, turned too abruptly, and over we went, right in the middle of the market-place, and tipped straight into a heap

95

of muck. There we were, in front of the inn. I was with Mr de Lazowski's servant, and we were both besmirched from head to foot. Only my shoulder was slightly damaged, but I can assure you, very rarely has such a tumble [*culbute*] been performed before so big and cheerful a crowd.

On the 9th we left Belford[36]   and dined and slept at *Berwick*, 13 miles off. The road was very hilly, and the wind hurled itself at us. Here we're back in winter, and it's very hard to keep going. I begin to think that the only practicable season for visiting the north is midsummer. I already feel we may be beginning to jettison some of our plans for the rest of our journey.

As for what we see of the country itself, we keep within sight of the sea, and go through a farming landscape that looks not very keenly cultivated. The strongest impression is of a great many young cattle and a lot of gentlemen's houses round which the owners have done a lot of tree-planting.

It's up and down all the way until you find yourself facing Berwick, presenting itself as a form of amphitheatre.[37]

[36] 9 April was Palm Sunday. It fell on 20 March the previous year, and found them in Birmingham. They walked 2 miles out to the Mass House at Edgbaston: 'too great a feast of the church for us not to go to Mass'. It looks as if, in religion, they were propelled by François. At Belford they seem not to have enquired after a Roman Catholic chapel.

The Bluebell Hotel at Belford, alongside the little market-place, is today remarkably as Alexandre and Lazowski saw it in 1786; even the bedroom doors hang on their old blacksmith's hinges. It is disappointing that they hurried away from Belford – probably from the combination of wintry weather and the indignity with the gig; and surprising, in view of Arthur Young's admiration for all the improvements promoted here by Abraham Dickson. He gives them eleven pages (*Tour of the North*, 1770, III, 50–61). 'That gentleman's father procured a market and 2 fairs, but the spirited conduct of the present owner is what has brought it to the condition so flourishing – compared to what it formerly was: 13 years ago, not above 100 souls, but now over 6 times that number. Mr D has established a woollen manufacture already employing 16 looms, and the spinning business – a noble acquisition, where a spinning-wheel was not seen a few years ago. Another important establishment is a tannery: the nearest were at Berwick and Alnwick. The distance halfway between Berwick and Alnwick was very advantageous for fixing a good inn with post-chaises and accommodation for travellers and of benefit to the town. Mr D applied himself to rendering the roads north and south as good as possible. He discovered a seam of coal, which led to burning lime for agriculture: 3 new limekilns. He has built a very handsome mansion house for his own residence.' (The architect, c1755, was James Paine, no less, working at Alnwick, and here composing a very mature Palladian villa, 'one of Paine's most satisfying designs, a wonderfully complete and subtle essay in movement': Peter Leach, *James Paine*, 1988, p. 64 and plates 33 and 34. The wings were, alas, never built, and the fine main block is now divided up.) 'Mr Clarke of Belford, one of Mr D's tenants, is very famous in the North from his knowledge of mechanics. His invention of a draining plough won him a premium of £50 from the Society. The grand machine on which he most builds his reputation is one for the threshing of corn. Mr Clarke's method of cultivating turnips is peculiar; and the effect of electricity on turnips deserves attention.' That last sentence is one of Arthur Young's most riveting.

[37] '*Enfiliateatre*' in Alexandre's erratic phonetic spelling. I see that the Bucks' *South Prospect of Berwick*', in 1745, confirms the sense of amphitheatre as you arrived at the south end of the long bridge: the town seems to be closely set within a curve of hills, and within the Elizabethan walls round the south front.

Berwick Red Lion   Berwick's built beside the sea and at the mouth of the Tweed, which for much of its length divides Scotland from England.[38] The river can carry up as high as the bridge ships of all sizes. The town stands on both sides of the river.[39] The main town, to the north, is the better-looking: it has two good streets, the rest ugly.[40] Its trade is scarcely considerable, though its fishery was until recently.[41] That has slumped badly, especially when the winters are cold, for the principal fish is the salmon, which stays out at sea until the warm weather begins. I've seen only three ships in the harbour, and little under construction. The town's garrisoned by pensioners. Its fortification is irregular and not kept in good repair. There's a regular garrison in wartime, occupying some extensive barracks.

Berwick is England's last town before Scotland. It doesn't surprise me that the English haven't been willing to cede it[42] to the Scots, for the Scots side of the river on which it stands dominates the south bank. Once you were master of the bridge, you could very quickly be master of the rest. Berwick is closely attached to the principality of the bishop of Durham, which long had a role in governing this border.

On the 10th we left Berwick   and took the road to Edinburgh, which we must reach in 2 days. We had our dinner at Press,[43] a mere isolated house on uncultivated commons. Three miles north of Berwick,[44] we left England.

---

[38] From just west of Berwick to just beyond Coldstream, the Tweed serves as boundary, which then climbs south for the Cheviot and across to the Solway.

[39] Tweedmouth, Berwick's Southwark, looked more prosperous in the 18th century than it does today.

[40] Defoe's comment was 'old, decayed, neither populous nor rich'.

[41] The Bucks said in their caption: 'The Tweed produces abundance of the finest Salmon, with which London and other places are supplied.' In the river, a long raft with nets attached is captioned 'The Batt where salmon are taken'.

[42] Here are more examples of Alexandre's phonetic spelling: *saider* for *céder*, *mettre* for *maitre*, *la plus moyain* for *la plus moindre*.

[43] Press Inn is shown on Taylor and Skinner's road map, *From Edinburgh to Berwick-on-Tweed*, 1775, on the right of the road one mile into the 4½ mile waste of Coldingham Moor. It is also marked on Paterson's Road maps, 1811, 1826, etc, and stood on what is now the minor road from Cairncross that joins the A1107 a mile or two north. With the A1107 they joined the line of the present A1, along the coast to Thorntonloch, then keeping north of the A1 for Broxburn, leaving the duke of Roxburgh's Broxmouth Park (c1774) on the sea side before entering Dunbar.

[44] They had crossed the Scottish border into Berwickshire just before Lamberton, then leaving Berwickshire for East Lothian and a toll-bar a mile or so before Thorntonloch.

6

Berwick to Edinburgh

Came to Berwick on a raw Palm Sunday: no one in the fields to quiz; puzzled by town fortifications a century ahead of Vauban; farming good, not prize-winning; Dunbar their first Scottish town, its coast dangerous; Haddington beautiful, and with fat, clean bullocks; insufficiently appreciative of Musselburgh; the estuary perpetually covered by both the enormous fleet of fishing-boats and by the merchantmen; Edinburgh at Dunn's Hotel ('every magnificence'); the Castle and the Regalia; Holyrood Palace; the New Town; the Old University, matchless in Europe; the astonishing effects of the formation of the Bank of Scotland; Leith, experiments on early assault landing-craft, Tahitian model; Voltaire and Hume discussed with Principal Robertson: dine at home with old Adam Smith; fellow-guests Joseph Black and John Walker.

By good fortune, we have Lazowski's account of the Scottish section of their tour: so he takes over the main description from Alexandre until they reach Perth.

Berwick, 9 April   [Red Lion] I've little to tell you of my day today, it's Palm Sunday and there's no one out in the fields for me to question, nobody from whom I might derive any useful information.

The weather's colder than ever and to judge by the temperature we might be at the end of February; but don't judge the climate merely by what I say: the season here is extraordinary, and I hear that the farmers are in real distress. However, if you ever make this same journey, don't take this route. You could be tempted to follow the coast-road as we've done, and are doing, round to Edinburgh,[1] but if it affords pleasure, you pay for it dearly. There is no shelter of any kind, and if by ill luck the wind is set in the north-east, which it usually is at this time of year, you will be on the worst possible road and will be, as I am, frozen to the bone: not a circumstance conducive to intelligent observation.

Between Belford and Berwick there are coalmines not far beneath the surface; the coal not of good quality. They remove from the surface this stratum of fine black clay that covers the coal-beds, and burn it in great heaps before spreading it back over the land as compost, together with the cinders. In this small area they raise a great many cattle.

---

1   At Morpeth they could have taken the westerly road past the site of the ancient Northumbrian royal seat at Yeavering (long known of, but uncovered only in our time), past Flodden, crossing the Tweed at Coldstream, and on past Thirlestane castle in Lauderdale to Dalkeith and Edinburgh.

But it's Berwick's situation that has made it a town of agelong importance to the English. It stands on the left bank of the Tweed and at its mouth, covering the bridge over which one enters Scotland from England. It seems an old bridge, very long,[2] and sturdily arched to resist the current of the river that sometimes descends in spate, and to withstand the sea's high tides. The town is raised above the river; most of it is built on rock which has been steeply scarped wherever possible.

On the landward side its fortifications follow the unevenness of the hilly ground. The fortifications consist only of curtain walls, with bastions furnished with *cavaliers*, a term in fortification simply meaning raised platforms. Their covered ways are exposed in many places; and in others, entries [*coupées*] have been fashioned, rather than the usual works for the permanent defence of high-points.[3] One couldn't say that they have entirely abandoned these fortifications: I saw they had been newly repaired in some places. But in general they are neglected.[4]

Above the port and all that part which defends the seashore, they have built anew rather than repaired;[5] on the town side a raised green area backs the freestone parapet and walls. I don't know, but suppose they could only have had in mind the prevention of a sudden attack: the batteries in this area are well armed, with thirty-two guns of different calibres.

About a quarter of a mile into Scotland, there was formerly a castle to cover a passage over a small stream steeply scarped everywhere except at the road-crossing.[6] Castle and road were linked by a stone causeway, scarcely wide enough for four men abreast: the castle's now in ruins.

Berwick's port is no more than the opening of the mouth of the river Tweed as it enters the sea. It's a wide mouth, closed upstream by the bridge, beyond which there is no building.[7] The entrance to the port, apparently of such great width, is not everywhere navigable. You have to take the northern channel, then align yourself on

2   388 yards long, built over the years 1611–24, on fifteen very stout dark sandstone cutwater piers.
3   Lazowski is clearly puzzled by the famous (and uniquely well-preserved) fortifications of Berwick, which anticipated those of Vauban by a century. They were devised by Italian engineers for Mary I and Elizabeth. The narrow openings, *coupées*, between the projecting bastions and the curtain-walls, were called 'flankers', and from them guns could fire parallel to the curtain walls, covering any enemy approach to them.
4   The main risk of any attack from Scotland receded after the suppression following the 1745 rebellion.
5   This refers to the beautifully constructed mid-16th-century walls, which still look relatively new-built.
6   It is confusing that 3¾ miles beyond Berwick-on-Tweed you left 'Berwick Bounds' and entered Berwickshire in Scotland. I think he is referring to Ayton castle, though it's further into Scotland. *SAS* (I, 87), 1793, said: 'History mentions the castle of Ayton, but scarcely any vestiges of it now remain.' Another possibility is Pease Bridge.
7   That was certainly the general impression, if you overlooked the bell-tower, the school-house and a dozen or so houses within the walls (Ralph Hyde, *A Prospect of Britain: the Town Panoramas of Samuel and Nathaniel Buck*, 1994, pl 2). Alec Clifton-Taylor described Berwick in *Six More English Towns*, BBC, 1981, pp. 46–73.

the houses at the south end of the bridge: then, at about 60 yards[8] from the shore, you move to the south to follow the not-very-wide channel in which two ships could scarcely sail abreast. The port cannot take ships of any great displacement, only merchant vessels of about 200 *tonnes*.[9] Almost its only trade is with London and the north of Scotland; exporting the grain and products of the neighbourhood, and importing all the raw materials used around here.

A staple commodity of the town is its river fishery, that of salmon which they export fresh to London, and, salted and smoked, for export abroad in barrels.[10] This is a bad year; the fishery yields nothing, on account of the prolonged cold spring. There is a small boat-building yard on the quay, small in extent, but immensely useful.

The town of Berwick has none of the air of prosperity and trimness of English towns: it is built of stone – both roughstone and ashlar – but the houses are grubby, built without taste or any luxury, above all without the extreme neatness that distinguishes even the village houses. The one building of possible distinction is the Town Hall.[11]

This is a county town,[12] ruled and administered by its own peculiar laws, and sending two members to Parliament. It has a barracks,[13] garrisoned in wartime by two infantry regiments: in peacetime it is guarded by a mere handful of old pensioners who go through the military motions. The bridge can be closed by a barrier guarded by a sentry: the gates are closed at night. They preserve – one wonders why – all the outward appearances from the time when the two kingdoms were separate.

Before moving on from England, I just want for a moment to tell you of a practice I saw twenty or thirty miles before we reached Berwick: it is the way the farmers feed their horses on a journey. Instead of the usual feed of oats and straw, they give them, when they halt, a truss of it. But you can see what a false economy this is: they waste half of it, rummaging perpetually for the head of the straw in their search for the grain, and don't trouble to eat the straw-ends. I'm not saying this food is itself bad, only that this practice is, which could be put right by cutting up the chaff with the grain.

---

8   30 *toises*: a *toise* = 6 feet.

9   A *tonne* = 1000 kg.

10   Ralph Hyde, *op cit*, pl 2, depicts clearly in the foreground 'the batt where salmon are taken'. The 'batt' seems to be a form of boat, or raft, to which one end of a salmon-net is attached. An exhibit in the Berwick Main Guard museum says there were over 300 salmon fishers in the 18th century: it was not unusual for 100 salmon to be taken at one haul. From c1798, the salmon were shipped to London packed in ice brought from local ponds in winter and stored in icehouses, some of which still survive.

11   It is not a very agreeable building, designed 1754–60 by S. and J. Worrell of London.

12   The old county of Berwickshire is now the mere district of Berwickshire in the Strathclyde region.

13   Now a fine museum, not only of the military history of the King's Own Scottish Borderers, and generally, but containing a remarkable branch of the Burrell Collection, begun here in Sir William Burrell's lifetime: mainly porcelain and paintings, eg two Boudins, and a Daubigny.

Dunbar[14] *10 April [1786]*   Here we are in Scotland, as from today, and we've stopped for the night at the first Scottish town on our route. We mustn't judge Scotland on this first appearance, but if one hadn't any high idea of the kingdom, one certainly had good ideas about the diligence and workmanship of the Scots.

Around Berwick, all is cultivated; and if it isn't in a state of great perfection, the farming is good, the lands are let out at high prices and those that are brought into cultivation beside the sea let at up to fifty shillings, further proof that the salt is not destructive of all vegetation, as was all-too-commonly supposed.

This was perhaps all English territory, and I want to tell you only of Scotland. I'll say only that they cultivate their potatoes by hand, with the spade, and that they also weed by hand, without the aid of the plough. It is not prize-winning agriculture. Further on, the land gets hillier and the soil poorer; in some places the topsoil is scarcely four inches deep over an under-stratum of rocks and sometimes gravel. Many of these hills present great masses of exposed rock on which any cultivation is impossible.

You travel six miles without coming across a tree or a village. Everywhere, it's true, you see the traces of cultivation and the houses of farms with scanty crops at long intervals.

Dunbar is a neat small town, with a paper-mill[15] and some plantations of trees; the hill-slopes extend into a very considerable valley, with better soil and all of it cultivated. It is not surprising that this countryside has such a deserted appearance and is so lightly peopled: it has been so often ravaged in the interminable struggles between the two nations that I am surprised that it can be as well cultivated as it is. The men here no longer need soldiers to devour one another as men did in the time of Cadmus;[16] and the lands with such poor soil and a situation not encouraging to industry may remain deserted for a very long time.[17]

As far as Dunbar there is a mixture of lands: those that are apparently being left fallow and those in regular cultivation. Some gentlemen's houses interrupt the sad uniformity of these bare lands: they are landscaped usefully rather than ornamentally, and are reasonably extensive.

---

[14] Alexandre, too, omits to name their inn. Rev Mr George Bruce, who in 1792 contributed such a vivid picture of Dunbar to Sir John Sinclair's great *Statistical Account of Scotland* (*SAS*), V, 1793, pp. 474–87, recorded, but didn't name, 'two large inns for the accommodation of travellers'.

[15] *SAS*, V, p. 476, added: 'At the village of West Barns, a cotton and flax mill is just now begun to be erected, from which we have great expectations . . . At West Barns there are flour mills of the best sort, where a considerable quantity of wheat and barley is manufactured. There are 3 other corn mills in the parish.'

[16] The legendary founder of Thebes who, on Minerva's orders, sowed dragon's teeth from which sprang men fully armed.

[17] It was the approach that looked deserted. Dunbar itself, occupying nine miles along the coast, had 3,700 inhabitants by 1792. The *SAS* described it as 'the most fertile spot in Lothian': see below.

Here about 10 pages of detailed description of the local farming appear to have been scrapped by M Jean Marchand, who was unaware of the specifically farming-study purpose of Lazowski's 1786 tour of Scotland.[18]

The rent is high considering the nature of most of the land – from 10 to 25 or 30 shillings an acre.[19] The farmhouses are stone-built, but lack the prosperous, comfortable air of English farms. Their mills are built like those of Northumberland. The farms are stocked with a great many pigs, mostly a cross between *Tonquins*[20] and the local breed, different from the English breed: not so sturdy, standing taller on their trotters and with straight ears. The labourers during the short days are paid only at the rate of 10 pence and a shilling; during the summer in proportion to the work done.

Dunbar   a seaport and one of the Scottish burghs, would be utterly unknown were it not for the stupid defeat of the Scots by Cromwell.[21] The town is stone-built, the houses

---

18 It is possible that this cutting cost us a description of Dunglass, though it wasn't mentioned by Alexandre either. Rebuilt in 1807 and now demolished, it was the seat of Sir James Hall, whom Defoe found so courteous and 'so addicted to improve and cultivate his estate' (*Tour through the Whole Island of Great Britain*, 1724). 'We began to see that Scotland is not so naturally barren as some people represent it . . . The truth is, the soil hereabouts is very good; and tho' they have not marle, or chalk, or much lime-stone to mend and manure it, yet, the sea-ware, as they call the weeds which the sea casts up, abundantly supplies; and by laying this continually on the land, they plow every year without laying their lands fallow, as we do; and I found they had as much corn – as our plowmen express it – as could stand upon the ground.'

If only Lazowski had come to Scotland in the 1790s, he would have found that Sir John Sinclair had done his agricultural survey for him, and superlatively well: 'The parish of Dunbar is partly a rich loam, partly clay, and partly a light mould. It is well cultivated and produces great crops, chiefly wheat, barley and beans, but little oats and less rye. Rich crops of broad clover and rye-grass are raised, and the land answers well for turnips and potatoes. Sea-ware is much used for manure and with good success. Limestone is got in the E end of the parish, and there are draw-kilns for burning lime, which is used by the farmers and sold to those in the neighbourhood. The fields are inclosed, some with stone walls, some with thorn hedges, and some of them are still open. The greater part of the land is dry and the seasons are early.' *SAS* listed five villages in the parish of Dunbar: Bellhaven, West Barns, Hedderwick, East Barns and Pinkerton (*SAS*, V, 1793, p. 475).

19 *SAS* also says 'the land is, in general, high rented'. But the figures for 1792 are much higher than Lazowski's. 'The burgh acres give from £4 Sterling to above 5 guineas the English acre, and considerable farms from 30s to two guineas. The land is divided among 7 great heritors (of whom 3 reside in the parish) and about the same number of very small ones. There are 30 great farmers who pay of rent from £60 to £600 Sterling. They are generally opulent and respectable. There are 7 or 8 small ones. There is one grazier who deals to a considerable extent in breeding and feeding for the butcher market. A good many cattle are stall fed and sheep are fattened with turnips. The valued rent of the parish is £16,953 Scotch and the real rent about £8,000 sterling. The Duke of Roxburgh has a small house at Broxmouth, pleasantly situated. Sir Peter Warrender has Lochend. Nineware belongs to Mr Hamilton of Bangour, and Belton to Mr Hay. Mr Anderson has a small house beautifully situated at Winterfield, from the summer house of which there is a delightful prospect . . . The Earl of Lauderdale has built a very elegant house at the W end of Dunbar.'

20 *Tonquins* were presumably Chinese blacks.

21 3 September 1650. The Scots were impeccably, not stupidly, commanded by Leslie, and seemed to have hemmed in Cromwell with his back to Dunbar and the sea. But Cromwell's was a

would perhaps be good if they were better kept, but everything suggests meanness: perhaps my unfavourable impression merely reflects the contrast on leaving the English towns – so neat and often looking so prosperous.[22] The town's small port creates its means of living and its prosperity. Its own natural position made it habitable from early times, and although the story of its early foundation is fabulous (eleven centuries BC!) there can be no doubt that the little bay must always have been invaluable for sailing this coast.

The coast almost all the way from Berwick is rocky and without anchorage or shelter. Even Dunbar's little inlet is created only by an opening in the rocky coast; and entering the port must be, and is, dangerous in foul weather. The boats have to be towed in. It has been necessary to divide the bay to form a harbour into which boats could be brought for safety. The entrance is from the north-east; then, at fifty feet, you swing hard to the south-east into an opening cut into the rock, leaving a wall to seaward which comes forward in the form of a sheltering jetty. There, in the harbour that can scarcely pack in seven or eight small ships, the vessels are loaded and unloaded. This small port supplies coal to the town and neighbourhood, and exports the local corn and wool. There are also some fishing-boats, but the fishing is scarcely worth mentioning.[23]

At the end of the bay you see the ruins of a very ancient castle built on the rock upon an arch hollowed through naturally by the waves.[24] [The Victoria Harbour was formed immediately east of the castle ruin and west of the fort on Lower Island.]

professional army with two completely reliable subordinate generals, Lambert and Monck. Before daylight, in the rain, Lambert charged the Kirk-ridden Scottish right flank: in an hour the larger but less professional Presbyterian forces were in full retreat, out-generalled, and leaving 3,000 dead. Cromwell guessed: 'It's probable the Kirk has done their do' (Richard Ollard, *This War Without an Enemy*, 1976, p. 200).

[22] In 1793, *SAS*, V, p. 478, was able to record: 'the principal street is broad and well aired, and the houses are much improved of late, and make a very genteel appearance. There are two large inns for the accommodation of travellers. At some distance, among the rocks, there is a retired place for sea-bathing, with a room to undress . . . There are many instances of persons who have arrived at the age of 80 or 90 years and upwards. It is exposed to cold and sharp winds from the east and north, chiefly in spring . . . In 1766 a supply of good soft water was brought in leaden pipes above 2 miles, and the streets new paved. In 1758 a piece of ground wall allotted for a washing green . . . a drying house erected on it. There are in Dunbar no fewer than 46 licensed ale-houses . . . where the execrable custom of dram-drinking is practised.'

[23] This is at first sight surprising. Defoe in 1724 wrote: 'They have here a great herring-fishery, and particularly they hang herrings here as they do at Yarmouth in Norfolk for the smoking them. I cannot say they are cur'd so well as at Yarmouth . . . for keeping and sending on long voyages, as to Venice and Leghorn.' Red herring were properly regarded as 'a particular delicacy in Italy', and Leghorn was a principal importer: David Butcher, *The Ocean's Gift: Fishing in Lowestoft, 1550–1570*, 1995, p. 43. But *SAS*, in 1792, recorded 12 fishing boats for white fish and lobsters, employing about 40 men. It added: 'for several years past the herring fishery has become very precarious and uncertain'. Murray's *Hand-book: Scotland* (1884 edn) said: 'Great efforts have been made to establish a safe and commodious harbour, for Dunbar is an important rendezvous for the herring-fishers of this district, and the coast is very dangerous from sunken rocks.' This is the Victoria Harbour, entered from the north-west beside the castle.

[24] It is curious that they fail to comment on the formidable new Battery built on Lamer Island, between harbour and castle, sometime after 1781.

Edinburgh, 11 April[25]   It is not yet time to write about Edinburgh but I can describe the journey from Dunbar. As far as *Haddington*, 11 miles, where we stopped,[26] the road crosses excellent country, in many parts admirably farmed, and very adequately peopled. You might think you were in a flourishing part of England, so clean and well-built are the rural houses, and so generally well-wooded is the countryside. It's a pity that Dr Johnson didn't reach these counties during his tour of Scotland: he would not have reproached this kingdom for being parched and naked – an immense tract of country in which no tree is encountered. But without going to Edinburgh he had crossed Lothian which – they say – is superior to the countryside we've seen to the east.[27] On the whole, without having seen Scotland, I was disappointed in his *Journey to the Western Islands*. Well treated and kindly received everywhere, he can only speak ill, and seems to have travelled solely in order to have the opportunity to do so. He shows much spirit but very little good nature; and if I may judge him on the strength of what I have seen at the start of our journey, he was blinded by his antipathy and saw only what he was predisposed to see.

Anyway, whether or not he saw what was there, or what I shall see, my own actual observations are what I'm interested in.

Leaving Dunbar I saw, at a distance, a farmer sowing on to the stubble of last year's harvest. The novelty of the sight made me draw near, and I learnt from him that that was his method of sowing peas: the plough followed, burying the seed. Then harrowing, and that was it. The peas take the place of fallowing, and often it's the second crop of the year, if they sow turnips next, without waiting for next spring.[28] I repeat, I now have no doubt that in this part of Scotland, where quite

---

25   They stayed in Edinburgh four nights, leaving for Perth early on the 15th.

26   To dine at the Blue Bell, according to Alexandre, who wrote up some of his journal during the pause. It survived as a celebrated inn till 1855, with a protruding stair-well on the south side of High Street. There were great stables at the rear. (Colin McWilliam, *Lothian*, 1980, p. 241; and information from Chris Roberts at Haddington Library.)

27   It must be explained that Johnson travelled from London to Edinburgh in post-chaises: 'of which the rapid motion was one of his most favourite amusements' (Boswell, *Journal of a Tour to the Hebrides with Samuel Johnson*, Folio Society, 1990, p. 135). He had the chance to travel up with one friend to Newcastle, and with another on to Edinburgh, where he had arranged to meet Boswell and begin their joint tour to the western highlands. François de La Rochefoucauld had already noted that these post-chaises went at a spanking pace, at least 8 miles an hour for 12 or 16 miles before changing both the carriage and the two horses (*A Frenchman's Year in Suffolk, 1784*, 3rd impression, 1995, p. 5). Dr Johnson's stricture about 'no tree for either shelter or timber . . . the whole country extended in uniform nakedness, except that in the road between Kirkcaldy and Cupar I passed for a few yards between two hedges' was written when he had reached Arbroath ('Aberbrothick'), north of Dundee. Did the excitement of the post-chaises to Edinburgh, the dashing spanking pace, coupled with the possibilities of uninterrupted conversation, impair Johnson's view of Lothian, which, incidentally, Lazowski, unwittingly, had been riding through at, for instance, Haddington? The boundaries of Lothian were perhaps not marked. At least he appreciated its cultivated, well-wooded appearance, which had most probably improved distinctly in the 13 years since Johnson's journey.

28   Here M Jean Marchand seems to have skipped across nine pages of Lazowski's notes. Fortunately Alexandre, once they had dined at Haddington, noted another local use of straw, spreading it while it was still warm over the land, sowing beans after their oats, etc. Two more close pages

certainly they are their own farmers, their efforts and their industry can be held back only by this one circumstance – that they have no enclosures.

Haddington   Arriving here is most agreeable, the countryside beautiful, well peopled, numerous country houses (among which we noticed an extremely handsome one built of brick), the town itself well situated, with a cheerful, lively atmosphere.[29] It sits beside a little river, the banks of which are charming as it leaves the town.[30] It is a town of some importance, a parliamentary borough, the chief commercial centre of the neighbourhood, manufacturing broad cloths (though in small quantity), stockings and linen.[31] For several miles around, there are mines of very good coal. As I entered this town I came upon some fat bullocks driven by a peasant with whom I got into conversation. The bullocks are Scotch from a district below this, in the south, and have been fattened up with turnips. They're as fine as any I've ever seen in England: like those in Northumberland they are kept very clean.

Speaking of cattle, I'm reminded of one circumstance – the fleece of their sheep gives good wool but in small quantity; and this quantity varies from district to district and depends on the quality of the sheep-farming. It's a small breed: the sheep are short, round, with a strong head and big bones, the qualities needed to stand up to the climate.

What I've told you of the farming as far as Haddington holds good for the lands between there and Edinburgh: indeed it should be still more profitable in view of the nearness of a great town, the availability of mulch and manure, and the certainty of finding a market there at all times.

At a few miles from Haddington you reach a high vantage-point from which you enjoy a most extensive view, of rare beauty and abundant fertility.[32]

survive detailing the local arable practice, and show Alexandre as a sturdy reliable understudy in the master's absence. He also noted that all the Scots he'd seen, men and women, wore blue clothes, including their bonnets. They carried heavy loads, especially the women, with straps round their heads. They had small carts, with horses in fair condition, and always rode in the cart, whether empty or loaded, even driving 4-in-hand, 'a practice forbidden in England'.

[29] There is neither sight nor record of a handsome brick country house at the approaches to Haddington. Chris Roberts, the local studies officer at Haddington library, feels certain that Lord Wemyss's magnificent deep red sandstone house, Amisfield, was the one they saw. It was destroyed in 1928. Much of the atmosphere of this beautiful town is 18th-century, and lovingly described by Colin McWilliam in the *Lothian* volume of the Buildings of Scotland series.

[30] Tyne Water, another river Tyne, retains its charming banks on both sides of the town.

[31] It is the capital of East Lothian and in 1884 had one of the best grain markets in Scotland. John Knox was undeniably born here in 1505. *SAS*, VI, 1793, pp. 538–9, speaks of a declining woollen business and says nothing of either stockings or linen. Alexandre says they stopped for a meal at the Blue Bell Inn. It is now no. 44 on the south side of the High Street. He was impressed by the picturesque outskirts and mentioned an abandoned-looking church. St Mary's was the more impressive of the two candidates, but St Martin's chapel must be what they saw, entering from Dunbar: Chris Roberts and a colleague have helped in discussing this.

[32] Chris Roberts thinks that, after eating at the Blue Bell, they would have left by the west end of the town: they could have enjoyed 'the most extensive view of rare beauty' just west of Gladsmuir, 4 miles out of Haddington. The Garleton Hills offer fine views but are only one mile north of Haddington.

You thread round the length of Edinburgh's bay for about a mile and a half. The whole width of the inlet, which is called the Firth of Forth, is perhaps seven, nine or ten miles across; the opposite shores rise in hills, irregularly grouped. They enclose the view and, over there, there's not a dwelling in sight; in contrast with the fertility of the terrace separating you from the Firth on this side, over which you have a very grand view. All this countryside is amply peopled and built-on: good houses with their little gardens; villages multiplying; two towns, Musselburgh and Leith, which compose the port of Edinburgh,[33] spread out so that you have, so to say, at your feet half a bird's-eye view (cut off by the hills above Leith).

The estuary is perpetually covered by both an enormous fleet of fishing-boats and by the merchant ships; and this movement, interrupted by a fixed rocky isle in the middle of the inlet, gives life to this fine maritime landscape.

Musselburgh, which you pass through at about five miles from Edinburgh, is a small harbour which won't grow much, in view of its closeness to Leith. It is quite well-built,[34] has manufactures in a small way, and is flowed through by a little river which, equipped with jetties, forms the port. The approaches to Edinburgh do not suggest by their activity the edge of a great capital; but our eyes and our ideas have been conditioned by the surroundings of London and Paris.

EDINBURGH 13 April[35]

Edinburgh's situation is one of the most extraordinary you could ever set eyes on: it is entirely built on a projecting ridge of rock running from just south of west to just

---

33 Musselburgh is still physically distinct from Edinburgh, separated by a little river, the Eskwater. Leith, which had a small wharf and dry docks in 1786, expanded its docks phenomenally (indeed in 1833 ruinously) down to the middle of the twentieth century. At 'the Shore', one or two buildings would still be recognisable to someone there in 1786. The umbilical cord, Leith Walk, connecting Leith with Edinburgh, may still be walked. The first scheme to 'develop' it dated from 1785 but actual development was piecemeal.

34 Lazowski is disappointingly lukewarm: McWilliam reckons the arrival at Musselburgh's High Street from the east 'one of the most decisive entries in any town in Scotland, flanked by the Pinkie Pillars, two rusticated piers of 1770, bearing urns', and broadening into the former market place. The old bridge across the Esk is nowadays restricted to pedestrians by steps built at each end. Eskside West has an irresistible octagonal gazebo dated 1771 and initialled GS. It marks the Eskside villa built by George Stewart (1715–93), Professor of the Latin language and Roman antiquities at Edinburgh, and evidently served as study to his talented but intemperate son, Gilbert (1742–86), who wrote well on Scottish constitutional history, but persistently attacked Principal Robertson (whom Alexandre and Lazowski were on the way to meet). After ruining his own reputation, Stewart died in this house in this same year, 1786. Two miles further on, they may have noticed Newhailes (Scottish National Trust), the house built by William Adam for the Scottish judge and historian whom Boswell and Johnson visited on their tour.

35 Lazowski wrote this after their second day here. Alexandre described the arrival: 'We entered on the 11th from the north-east: we found only one road that brought us round the town and into the New Town where we were lodging at Dunn's Hotel. As we planned to do our sight-seeing over the 12th and 13th, I shan't distinguish between them.' (They stayed on till the 15th.) *SAS*, V, p. 586, noted: 'Dunn, who opened the magnificent hotels in the New Town, was the first who attempted a stage-coach to Dalkeith.' Alexandre explained: 'It's the custom here, as in London, to

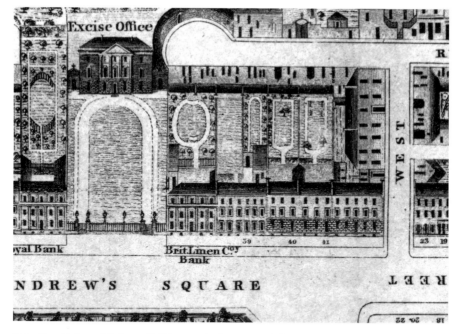

36. *Detail from Kirkwood's Plan and Elevation of the New Town, Edinburgh, 1819, showing James Dunn's Hotel, where the La Rochefoucauld party stayed for four nights, at no. 39 St Andrew's Square. It stood close to the house Sir Wm Chambers designed for Sir Laurence Dundas in 1772, and which became the Excise Office in 1795, and after 1825 belonged to the Royal Bank of Scotland. See footnote 35 in this chapter.*

north of east.[36] On the west side it ends with the castle standing up vertically above the surrounding country:[37] to the east the rock is more level, but it still involves a considerable climb to reach the town. To the north and south of the ridge lie two

stay in these houses, as the inns are very bad and dear.' He added: 'At Dunn's we had a superb *salon*, with gilded mirrors and every magnificence.' Andrew Bethune (Edinburgh Room, Edinburgh Central Library) has kindly found, in the *Directories*, that in the years 1784–90, James Dunn was described as 'hotel keeper' at 39 St Andrew Square. It was one of the most fashionable neighbourhoods, and Kirkwood's plan with elevations, 1819, shows how grandly situated no. 39 was (above): it's a pity it was rebuilt, 1847–51, for the British Linen Bank. The magnificent house marked as Excise Office in 1819 was built to Sir William Chambers' design in 1772 for Sir Laurence Dundas. It became the Excise Office in 1795 and since 1825 has been head office, Royal Bank of Scotland.

[36] Edinburgh's spectacular spinal ridge, marked by the Royal Mile running from the Castle to Holyrood Palace, is formed of a volcanic rock that was scored by glaciers moving west to east: they chunnelled out the Nor' Loch, its line now occupied by the railway, with The Meadows to the south. Lazowski got the cardinal points wrong: I've corrected, to avoid confusion.

[37] It stands about 380 feet above sea-level. In the town itself it rises with spectacular abruptness to the north, above the Grassmarket, where Joseph Farington painted a famous view in 1788 (Pl 37, over).

37. Edinburgh Castle from the Grassmarket, *1788, by Joseph Farington.*

deep narrow valleys, the northern one once a canal.[38] The one to the south and east foots the most formidable rocky hillside, dominating the south-east side of the town.[39] The site of the castle (which, especially before the development of artillery, was immeasurably strong) presumably decided them to build the town where it is: if it looks picturesque, it is extremely inconvenient, but that was formerly its great advantage.[40]

This castle, which has played such a great part in history, is built, as I've said, on an inaccessible rock. It is joined to the town by a very lofty causeway, Yet, although the causeway is raised high on a very steep ramp, the castle's outer gates stand at the

[38] John Craig's winning scheme (1766) for the New Town (in consultation with Robert Adam), proposed converting the glacial lakes of Nor' Loch into an ornamental canal with gardens. The gardens were realised, but not the canal, though in 1786 Lazowski seems to have thought there was one 'once'. The name of the present Canal Street gives the same impression.

[39] Salisbury Crags, and the even craggier Arthur's Seat, with a cliff rising over 800 feet above sea-level: with Dunsapie, they provided the three most striking of four great prehistoric forts in Holyrood Park.

[40] This is the first point made by the authors of the indispensable *Edinburgh* volume (1984) in the Buildings of Scotland series.

head of a further considerable climb.[41] Round the remaining girth of the rock no approach is possible: in several places there is a vertical drop of 200 feet.

You will understand how impossible it would be to build anything remotely regular, though they've taken advantage of terraces and spaces naturally formed, and in some places have created three stories, which adds greatly to its singular appearance. Its fortifications owe their inaccessibility solely to their position.[42] All are of stone and of no clear pattern: angles intersect in the most advantageous way for local defence. They are equipped with a small number of bronze artillery pieces.

The Parliament formerly assembled here in the Castle but the buildings, even those intended to house the King's retinue, have been converted into barrack-blocks,[43] occupied in peacetime by a garrison of four or five hundred men. There one sees an arsenal[44] full of beautifully maintained arms, enough to equip no fewer than eight thousand men; also the ancient palace built for James VI of Scotland and I of England.[45] You are shown the room, within a very small apartment, where the unfortunate Queen Mary gave birth to her infamous and contemptible son.[46]

It is said that the regalia – the crown and sceptre of Scotland – are kept here. It is difficult to discover whether these insignia, which were certainly firmly secured in this place, have been withdrawn secretly. What is clear is that no one has been informed, and nobody knows, whether the place was for a time unprotected and has in consequence now been closed and the insignia not on view; which is possible; one supposes they are still there.[47]

---

[41] This refers, I suppose, to the parade-ground known as 'The Esplanade' and built in 1753 at the approach to the Castle.

[42] Not quite. The whole of the west and south perimeter wall was rebuilt in the 1730s, and the dry ditch across the east front completed in 1742 (*Edinburgh, op cit*, p. 86).

[43] The Great Hall became a barracks as early as 1650. It was modified in 1737, and in 1708 an officers' mess was built. Lazowski would have seen the North Barracks, built in 1755; they were finally altered in the 1920s to form part of the Scottish National War Memorial (*Edinburgh, op cit*, pp. 87, 99).

[44] Probably the powder magazine built in 1747, and replaced by the Hospital.

[45] It occupies the northern half of the whole palace area, and was remodelled, c1615–17, for formalities.

[46] The room in which King James was born in 1566 is preserved: he was clearly something of a disappointment to Lazowski. Alexandre confined his comments to the smallness of the room. It isn't all that small, though the adjoining panelled cabinet is, which bears the painted inscription with James's birthdate, the Scottish royal arms, and an edifying Scottish verse.

[47] An article in the Act of Union, 1707, provided that the regalia should never be removed from the kingdom of Scotland. They were accordingly deposited, with ceremony, in an oak and iron chest, secured by many locks, and in turn placed in a strongly bolted and barred room, the Crown Room, leaving, as Walter Scott wrote (Lockhart's *Life of Scott*, ch XL) 'to nationalist pride the satisfaction of pointing to the barred window, with consciousness that there lay the regalia of Scotland'. The rumour grew, as Lazowski in 1786 testifies, that the regalia had been withdrawn to England. Scott remembered being shown, in the Jewel Office in London, a crown '*said to be* the ancient crown of Scotland'. In 1815 he took the matter up with the Prince Regent, who authorised 'an express search for the Regalia'. A commission of ten Scottish grandees, including Scott (as one of the Principal Clerks of Session) assembled on 4 February 1818 and witnessed the solemn breaking open of the chest, and the emergence of the Regalia, including the Sword of State

Otherwise, this castle is very much more famous for what it has been than for what it is today. It is a conspicuous eminence, a great spectacle, but as a castle for the defence of the town it is ineffectual: it could do nothing to prevent the town's complete destruction. You can see the proof of this in what happened when the Pretender came in 1745.[48]

I have described how the town, like the castle, is built on a rocky escarpment between two ravines. The result of building on these escarpments is very pictur-esque, for you see three tiers of houses, one above another, as if the roofs of the lowest tier serve as footings for the tier above: the third reaches a great height. I've counted several houses of six stories, and the buildings that crown the ridge, standing along the very top, are even more dominant.

In such a situation, building land must be extremely valuable: so, with the excep-tion of the roads that lead off the main road running across the Old Town from Holyrood Palace to the Castle,[49] there wasn't a single one of them (and there still are very few) with any room for carriages: they are more like narrow alleys paved with broad flat stones. So you have no carriages in Edinburgh,[50] but plenty of sedan-chairs, and this form of transport persists. When you add, to all that, that the levels are extremely uneven, so that you are perpetually climbing and descending almost vertically, you will agree that the topography of this town may, and must, be extremely beguiling to strangers, but inconvenient to its inhabitants.

So it was impossible, especially given the enterprising spirit of this nation, that Edinburgh should remain in this condition: a new town is building, and they are building it as now London is being built – that is to say on a grand plan. The streets are superb and well aligned; the large squares are superb; the houses plain but well built, and the majority are of freestone. The approaches to the main part of this new town are grand, easy and well thought out, which is essential in this hilly landscape.

The principal area of the new town lies to the north of the old one. It is joined on to it by a fine bridge[51] and an embankment levelled up between the road and the

presented by Pope Julius II to James IV. Scott himself intervened sternly to prevent one of the more frivolous grandees, on a second visit to the room, from trying out the crown on the head of one of the young ladies who had been invited: 'By God, No!' he said. Scott's full account of the proceedings appeared in his *Prose Miscellanies*, vol VII.

48 What happened was that Charles Edward, the Young Pretender, without trouble, and finding some welcome in a town disenchanted by Captain Porteous and his English taxes, slept in Holyrood Palace: there was no question of his attempting to take the Castle. He marched 9 miles east along the Firth to Prestonpans and defeated the King's army there (as readers of *Waverley* have all but experienced for themselves). Then he marched south as far as Derby before the truth sank in that there was virtually no support for him in England.

49 It is known as the Royal Mile.

50 Lazowski, perhaps thinking of the Old Town, is curiously adrift here: in 1763, *SAS*, VI, p. 592, reckoned there were 396 four-wheeled and 462 two-wheeled carriages; in 1790, 1,427 four-wheeled and 462 two-wheeled carriages. It was thought coaches and chaises were constructed as elegantly here as anywhere in Europe, and stronger and cheaper.

51 North Bridge's foundation stone was laid in 1763: Wm Mylne's triple-arched stone bridge was opened in 1772. The present 1890s bridge was made to accommodate the North British Railway's Waverley Station.

valley so that climbing and descending are evened out. This valley has been filled up at the end opposite the castle by a great causeway,[52] but the causeway is an earthwork in-fill, passing beneath the three great arches of the bridge like three great covered roads.

This new town will be truly magnificent, on the strength not only of the plan on which it is being built, but also of its elevated site, on a level with the old town which supplies its view to the south. To the north it enjoys the panorama of the bay with the daily movement of the shipping, the port of Leith, and all the fine landscape between town and sea, beyond which rise the hills.[53] The other part of the new town lies in the opposite direction, to the south of the old town. It is fine: George Square is perhaps grander even than St Andrew Square, though it is less well built.[54]

In brief, the town is not only increasing daily, but it grows daily more beautiful. New roads are driven through, arcades built and small valleys filled in that would otherwise impede communications. In a few years, Edinburgh will be a town quite as agreeable and a great deal more picturesque than any other town in Europe. But you are more curious to find out what it is like, and I will try to tell you.

As to its monuments, if some of them were not bound up with interesting historical events there would be no need to mention them; indeed, other kinds of monuments would not be worth seeking in Scotland.

The ancient palace at the eastern extremity of the town, at the foot of the rock on which it is built, is in a modern architectural form.[55] Most of it was rebuilt by

52 This 'causeway' is known as The Mound, but in 1786 Lazowski was describing it in its infancy. *Buildings of Scotland: Edinburgh* (p. 309) records its formation from some two million cartloads of 'spoil' from the building of the New Town between 1781 and 1830. Lazowski was fifty years too soon to report on the architectural consummation of The Mound, as seen now from Hanover Street. *SAS*, VI, 1793, p. 585, claimed this mound was unrivalled by any work but Alexander the Great's at Tyre.

53 Of Fife.

54 George Square and St Andrew Square were at this time 'fashionable above all others' (A. J. Youngson, *The Making of Classical Edinburgh*, 1966, p. 228). In George Square, the duchess of Gordon, the countess of Sutherland, Lord Melville and Viscount Duncan were neighbours of Walter Scott, father of the great novelist (Youngson, p. 69). Scott was a student of fifteen in 1786, and already a gifted story-teller, and friend of Adam Ferguson, the philosopher's son. In St Andrew Square, Dunn's Hotel had for grand neighbours not only Sir Lawrence Dundas, who'd made his fortune as Commissary-General in Flanders, 1748–59, and got Sir William Chambers to design the grandest house in the New Town for him, 1771, but the earl of Northesk, the dowager countess of Leven, and the trusted banker, Sir William Forbes: on the north side of the Square, nos. 23–26 were designed by Chambers for Sir John Whitefoord, 3rd Bart, and two associates. Whitefoord is said to be the original of Sir Arthur Wardour in Scott's *The Antiquary* (*Edinburgh Portraits*, 1877, no. cxcii). St Andrew Square has been much altered in detail since the 1780s, but it remains the handsome square it was when newly built, and when Alexandre and Lazowski stayed four nights in no. 39.

55 In 1528–36, the royal palace of Holyroodhouse, a large quadrangle, was given its projecting round-turreted north-west tower. At that time the palace acquired a highly picturesque appearance with elaborately glazed fenestration, the straight front interrupted by angled bay windows and bow windows. In 1650, a serious fire led to the removal of soldiery and to dilapidation. What Lazowski saw as 'modern architectural form' was the work of Sir William Bruce and Robert Mylne

Charles II: handsome, and pleasantly proportioned, but what we were most interested in was what remained of the old house. This consisted chiefly of the long gallery and the apartment of Mary, Queen of Scots. The gallery is 152 feet long, 22 feet wide and 18 feet high, and full of bad portraits of the ancestors, both fabulous and authentic, of the King of the Scots.[56]

The duke of Hamilton, by virtue of an hereditary office, occupies the ancient apartment of Mary, Queen of Scots, in which they keep, with reverence, various furnishings from her time; such as her damask bed with fringes, etc, in silk; her armchairs, and some of her embroidery.[57] We were interested to examine the small cabinet,[58] through the Queen's bedroom. There she was at supper with the duchess of Argyll,[59] and with Riccio, when he was wrenched, so to say, from her arms by Lord Darnley[60] etc (who had arrived by means of a back staircase that is still to be seen) and stabbed to death in the Bedchamber and the Ante-Chamber of the Queen. One can still see his bloodstains[61] on the floor.

under Charles II. In 1884, Murray's *Handbook to Scotland* asserted that Bruce's design was 'a copy of the Château de Chantilly'. Would that it had been! In fact, a south-west tower was constructed to balance the old north-west tower and supply a drawing-room; and the north, east and south ranges were largely rebuilt with external pilasters facing into the quad, and carefully orchestrated internal sequences of grandeur. Then, after 1676, the west front was rebuilt with its ponderous entrance, surmounted inelegantly by a crowned clock.

56 The gallery was created in 1671 (its present ceiling only in 1968). Devotees of Scott will remember his description of Edward Waverley, 'sixty years since', in the harvest-time of 1745, waiting here, unaware that he was about to be presented in the adjoining room to 'the young Chevalier – a prince to live and die under' – Charles Edward Stuart. Scott, so familiar with it, brought this house wonderfully back to life. His response to the gallery chimed with Lazowski's: 'a long, low and ill-proportioned gallery, hung with pictures affirmed to be the portraits of kings who – if they ever flourished at all – lived several years before the invention of painting in oil-colours'. In 1684, the painter Jacob de Witt (1640–97) was commissioned 'to make them like unto originals which are to be given to him'.

57 The 1st duke of Hamilton was made Hereditary Keeper of Holyroodhouse on 10 August 1646: he was beheaded 5 weeks after Charles I, 'for invading England in a hostile manner'. The 2nd duke was mortally wounded in the battle of Worcester. It was the 3rd duke who took over the apartments of Mary, Queen of Scots in the north-west tower c1682 and died there in 1694. (He was among the first Scottish magnates to desert James II and to declare the throne vacant in March 1689.) A northern extension added to the north-west tower in the 1670s as part of the 'Hamilton apartments' was removed under George IV, who romantically believed he was preserving the tower as it had been when Mary, Queen of Scots lived there. William Adam's fireplace of 1740 was put into the Queen's bedchamber for the Hamiltons.

58 In a corner turret.

59 Jean, *countess* of Argyll, was the queen's half-sister and favourite attendant. (The *dukedom*, prominent in Lazowski's day, dated from 1701.)

60 David Riccio, a mere secretary to one of the ambassadors from Italy, but very able, quickly made himself politically indispensable to the queen. It was he who organised her marriage to the earl of Darnley, a handsome, fatuous, headstrong popinjay. The leading Protestant politicians, resenting the young Riccio's influence, encouraged Darnley to think his place in the queen's bed was being usurped, and accordingly the assassins left Darnley's dagger in Riccio's body. Darnley organised the *coup* but wasn't present: he was himself inevitably murdered before long.

61 As unlikely as Thomas à Becket's in 'the Martyrdom' at Canterbury cathedral. Blood spilt violently exerts a curious attraction, even after its total transmogrification.

It's in the oldest part of the house that the Peers of Scotland assemble to elect the sixteen Representative Peers to sit in the upper house at Westminster.[62] Today this house is badly neglected: there is very little or nothing being done to keep it in repair. The ancient Parliament of Scotland was held at the other end of the town, towards the castle, in an immense, unadorned assembly room: it is now divided in two, one part serving as a Court of Justice.[63] The rest of this building is occupied by the Court of the Exchequer with its associated offices.[64]

In the New Town, they have been building – and all is not yet completely finished – a new home for the archives, and various offices.[65] It is hard to imagine a more elegant building, or one of finer taste and at the same time greater nobility. It is the work of Mr Adams, the celebrated London architect,[66] and this has been reckoned his masterpiece. It is raised up on a terrace about eight feet high, graced with a pedimented centrepiece; the sides representing the fronts of the two wings contain two magnificent Venetian windows, one at each end, and each surmounted by a sort of turret, creating a feeling of opulence.[67]

The Old College of the university is ancient, square-built, and unworthy of the

[62] Since 1716, seven-year parliaments had 26 bishops, 178 English peers and 16 representative Scottish peers elected for the term of each parliament. The present five-year terms, with already altered proportions of peers, date from the 1911 Parliament Act. The elections of the sixteen 18th-century peers took place in the gallery at Holyroodhouse.

[63] The Scottish Parliament met in the Tolbooth till the building, 1632–40, of this Parliament House. The Scottish Parliament ceased with the Union of 1707 but the Parliament House survives, rather dramatically 'adorned' by a hammerbeam roof of Danish oak devised in 1637 by the 'Master Wright to the town of Edinburgh', John Scott: the bold curves and the hammerbeams pointing downwards like the tensed arrows of avenging archers disguise the flatness of the roofspan itself. Entered from the SW corner of Parliament Square.

[64] Later reconstructed by Robert Reid, 1804–6, and fire-damaged 1824: rebuilding completed 1830.

[65] It is called the Register House and was intended solely to house Scotland's public records, but by 1815 it had run out of room for more. Designed by Robert Adam in 1771, it was begun in 1774, stood an empty shell six years after 1778, and was at last being furnished and equipped when Lazowski saw it. Gifford, McWilliam and Walker note that 'this was the first important government building in the UK since Kent's Horse Guards', and their distinguished opinion suggests that its 'cool authority is not Palladian but Neo-Classical in spirit, well attuned to the strong quadrangular form of the whole'. Before its setting was eroded by street-widening, it stood 'back on a paved platform, the "movement" of the original curved stair answering the curve of the dome'. The City Fathers had sited it just across the North Bridge, to encourage the development of the New Town.

[66] Robert Adam was a Scot, educated in Edinburgh, the friend of the leading members of the 'Scottish Enlightenment'. Although he was now Architect of the King's Works with responsibility for Scotland, his main office was truly, as Lazowski implied, in London, and his inspiration was less Palladian than Neo-Classical, based on the discoveries he had made in Rome, most notably, at Diocletian's palace at Split, in Dalmatia. Sir Howard Colvin says: 'Only the Register House remains as the nearest approach to a monumental building in the list of Adam's works' (*Biographical Dictionary of British Architects, 1600–1840*, 3rd edn, 1995, p. 53). Clearly it was already being seen in this light in 1786.

[67] Perhaps he means 'opulent by contrast with the relative austerity of the whole composition'. The turrets are crowned by small, elegant 4-sided clock-towers.

university's high reputation.[68] Dr Robertson, the historian, is the Principal.[69] Edinburgh's university is justly famous: its academic achievements are excellent, and its professors are all men of outstanding ability. You have only to recollect that Mr Hume was librarian of one of the principal libraries,[70] that Dr Robertson is at the head of studies, that Dr Black[71] is professor of chemistry and Dr Home professor of medicine,[72] and so on, and so on. You'll agree that there is not a university in Europe that merits such celebrity.

The same circumstance that engenders these famous professors also produces good scholars: poverty and the need to make one's own career arouse one to activity, promote diligence and develop all the capabilities of each of us. The salaries attached to these chairs are paltry – nothing compared to those available in the English universities. If a professor's lectures are dull, his class dwindles and his salary is reduced to nothing, for he is paid so much per pupil.[73]

---

68 There was agreement about the need for new buildings, and Robert Adam's design for replacing the Old Quad, just south of South Bridge in the Old Town, was built 1789–93. It would certainly have impressed them: the main entrance front is majestic by any standards, adding appropriate dignity to the university's high reputation. The student numbers rose from about 500 in 1763 to 1,306 in 1792.

69 William Robertson (1721–93), a son of the manse, was writing his remarkable *History of Scotland* (down to 1603) in the years 1753–58, while his young cousin Robert Adam was developing his ideas of classical architecture in Italy and the Adriatic. The *History* made Robertson's name: he was appointed Principal of the university in 1762 and moderator of the general assembly next year. In 1769, his masterpiece on the *History of Charles V* established his fame in Europe. He retired as moderator of the general assembly after 16 years, but continued as Principal 31 years, till 1792, the year before he and his young cousin died, each having added great distinction to their alma mater. (*Charles V 'me fait oublier tous mes maux*, makes me forget all my troubles' wrote Voltaire. Catherine the Great, on the strength of it, sent Robertson a gold snuffbox set with diamonds!)

70 David Hume (1711–76), a leading philosopher of the science and nature of human understanding: he also wrote a *History of Great Britain* that has gone into some 200 editions, and won the admiration of Gibbon and Voltaire. The *History* came from the five years 1752–7 when he was Keeper of the Advocates' Library. The passion for philosophy started at Edinburgh University: at 18 he had glimpses of 'a great philosophical discovery' and at 26, in France, he had written *A Treatise of Human Nature*.

71 Joseph Black (1728–99) MD and pioneer chemist: Lavoisier a disciple of his. Born at Bordeaux, the son of a Belfast wine-merchant. At Glasgow University he came under the spell of William Cullen, whom he succeeded in 1766 as Professor of Medicine and Chemistry. A friend of Hume, Adam Smith, and Adam Ferguson (1723–1816), another son of the manse, chaplain to the Black Watch at Fontenoy, 10 May 1745. Ferguson became Professor of Pneumatic [=mental] and Moral Philosophy in 1764, with a salary of £100.

72 Francis Home (pronounced Hume): 1719–1813, was Professor of *Materia Medica*, 1768–98, surgeon to the dragoons in Flanders and a student at Leyden, 1742–8. His *Principia Medicinae*, 1758, was widely used by Europe's medical profession. His gold medal essay on the principles of agriculture should have interested Lazowski, whose 'and so on' presumably included the delightful Dugald Stewart (1753–1828), popular teacher of philosophy and mathematics, who seems to have been a friend of all the Edinburgh luminaries. In 1785 he succeeded Adam Ferguson as Professor of Moral Philosophy, and when the French wars discouraged 'the grand tour', many young men were sent to Stewart in Edinburgh instead. James Mill thought him more eloquent than both Pitt and Fox, 'whose most admired efforts' he had heard.

73 See note 71 above. The chair Adam Ferguson coveted, and won in 1764, was worth £100 (he

From another aspect, the students receive their education in exchange for the principal – and sometimes for the total – sum of their patrimony. In this struggle, it is imperative that they distinguish themselves and make a reputation. To provide themselves with a career, there is little opening in Scotland, especially for the younger sons. There lies the explanation of their great industry and the excellence of the learned works they publish. One may add that – independently of the taste they have acquired in their youth for employment and for useful activities – they are resolved to continue in this way, for their income can never be very great: neither the climate nor the country itself lend themselves, as they do in so many other places, to their support.

There is no point in my giving you the details of all the different professorial chairs in this university: they are many, and those that are not occupied by celebrated scholars are occupied by very able ones. But if I want you to understand the workings of this university, I must at least give you some idea of the main faculties and departments which will enable you to judge the rest. Law is divided into three professorships: civil law, natural and international law, and Scottish law. These two last chairs would replace in France, with great advantage, the endless lessons in Roman law that, in the way they are taught, do nothing to broaden the mind, and which one has so little understood on leaving school.

Medicine is divided in this way: botany, *materia medica*, anatomy, midwifery, chemistry, *l'institution de physique* [?physics] and medicine and clinical medicine (*'pratique'*). The botany lessons are enhanced by an excellent botanic garden that has been closed for some years, and for which funds have been made available, but with such great moderation that it might be described as miserly, whatever the explanation. It is said to be very complete. The classification follows the system of Linnaeus, and there are fine hot-houses for the keeping of exotic plants.[74]

There are two public libraries: that of the College[75] and that of the advocates [ie barristers]. I haven't seen them. The second comprises 30,000 volumes, some manuscripts and a collection of medals. These libraries might be a lot more useful if the books might be lent out, naturally with rules to safeguard them.[76]

---

was able to augment it to £300). When Dugald Stewart succeeded him, Stewart almost doubled his class, from 102 in 1785–6 to 196 in 1807–8, in the thick of the Napoleonic war: this presumably produced a suitably increased stipend.

[74] Alexandre noted their quick visit to the 'Botanick' Garden on the morning of the 14th, before Adam Smith collected them at Dunn's Hotel to go and meet Dr William Robertson, Principal at the University (see note 69 above). His impression was that 'it was not yet completely planted, but beautifully laid out and maintained. In the middle of these gardens they've erected a stone urn [*vase*] in honour of Linnaeus. They have an entire library devoted to plants. This garden employs the workmen and the master.' Andrew Bethune (Edinburgh Room, Central Library) kindly informs me that the Royal Botanic Garden stood in Haddington Place until 1823. The very handsome urn was erected by the Regius Keeper, John Hope, in 1778. It was moved, with the garden, to the present beautiful position in Inverleith Row, and now stands in the Students' Collection.

[75] ie the University.

[76] This proposal might have seemed sounder if Lazowski had actually seen the two libraries in use.

Apart from the university and the college there is a high school in Edinburgh, more or less on the lines of the grammar schools of England.[77]

There are many societies established in Edinburgh that I think you would want to know about, at least in general.

The Royal Society of Edinburgh, the number of its members not, I think, limited. It is divided into two groups: sciences and literature. It combines the double functions of our French academies.[78] [Is not this the *Royal Society* founded in 1783 that was formerly the Philosophical Society of which David Hume became secretary in 1752?]

The Speculative Society occupies itself with metaphysics and all research and general and particular discussion of philosophy, without particular experience of a particular art.[79]

The Royal Society of Medicine. Its name explains its purpose. There is also a *Royal College of Surgery*.

The Antiquaries are grouped in regular academic bodies, with their officers. The researches are not limited to a single school.[80]

The Society of Judicature for the advancement of progress of the knowledge of the laws.

The Society of Natural History. The number of its members is not limited. The membership is large and devoted to writing on natural history. Their papers are read and discussed publicly.

The Highland Society. If the different objects of this society are pursued well they are very interesting. Their aim is to illuminate everything connected with the natural history of the Highlands; and as one can partition off part of that subject for the arts and sciences, a second main aim is the advancement of trade, civilisation, the arts and culture of the Highlands, to encourage there the building of bridges, villages, market-places, and in general everything that can change the face of this country; a third main aim is to maintain and reduce to principles – or, rather, to classify – the language and the music of the Highlands.

There are still other societies – for hunting, for archery, for music – but these have less public bearing.

To my great regret I've seen none of Edinburgh's hospitals, which are so

---

[77] There were 200 grammar-school boys in 1763. At a cost of £4,000, a new great hall, 5 teaching-rooms, a library and smaller apartments were built in 1777. In 1783, Edinburgh's Grammar School had 500 pupils (*SAS*, VI, p. 591).

[78] It was constituted by Royal charter in 1783, and published its first volume of transactions in 1788 (*SAS*, VI, p. 589). It was previously the Philosophical Society, of which David Hume became Secretary in 1752.

[79] It was instituted in 1764 by six university students, for improvement in composition and public speaking. It went on to build a hall in the University and furnished a Library for its Members (*ibid.*).

[80] They were constituted by Royal charter in 1783 and published their first volume of transactions in 1792 (*ibid.*).

numerous: I can only name them, making the one observation that, for cleanliness, they are very different from those in England.[81]

The Royal Infirmary,[82] large and well-built, is mainly for the treatment and dressing of those with injuries. Watson's Hospital[83] – one for girls, one for orphan boys that is still a workhouse – the Trinity Hospital,[84] and the charity workhouse which is really a poor-house; these houses are the majority of the foundations devoted to receiving boys, girls, the old and the poor. But although there isn't a poor-rate in Scotland, these houses are not only praiseworthy in intention, they are truly a small blessing in respect of expense.

Lastly, there's an institution for bringing outdoor relief to poor people in their homes, and this kind of public charity alone can prove truly useful. If you add to these establishments that of the Exchange, you will have practically everything there is to take note of in Edinburgh.

The Bank of Scotland[85] deserves special attention for it has been the chief engine for inaugurating change in the face of this kingdom, but as it is a curious aspect of politics, and one that could enable you to draw an important conclusion, I can't forbear to tell you a little about it.

The country is poor, with very little trade. More than half of it is uncultivated, and what there is of cultivation is miserably done. No enterprise is created, nor can it be. The great landowners go to London, and those who find their resources in their own natural gifts go to England to use them. Some patriotic landowners, fired by the public spirit of their neighbours, and provoked by the spirit of hereditary jealousy between the two nations, created a suitable opportunity to get together, and soon had a chance to go further. Their great project was to build up a large amount of capital in circulation, on the principle that, with this capital, improvements of all

---

[81] One wonders at the temerity of this observation from someone who'd seen none of Edinburgh's hospitals.

[82] Here, his failure to visit has let Lazowski down disastrously. The stock of the Royal Infirmary rose from £5,000 in 1750 to £36,000 in 1790. By then it was admitting over 2,000 patients a year, and boasting that on average only one patient in 25 died, a record unequalled in Europe. It was daily attended by 3 physicians. Members of the Royal College of Surgeons attended in turn, monthly. During the sitting of the College (University), October–May, two of the Professors of Medicine gave clinical lectures on the cases of selected patients. Over 300 medical students were by then attending the Infirmary (*SAS*, VI, p. 599). It was built in 1738 by William Adam, with 'an open forecourt in the Dutch Palladian manner . . . and ponderously scrolled attic' (Gifford, McWilliam and Walker, *op cit*, p. 66). It was found to be ill-ventilated and largely demolished in 1882.

[83] Watson's Hospital, or School, was founded by George Watson, a merchant, in 1727, with £12,000. It was for the sons or grandsons of decayed merchants, members of the Merchant Company, schooling 70 boys aged 8–15 in 1793, with a revenue of £2,000 a year. For girls there was a Merchant Maiden Hospital and a Trades Merchant Hospital as well as an Orphan Hospital, for boys and girls.

[84] The Trinity Hospital had an income of £1,100 for decayed burgesses, or their widows and daughters, not under 50 years old. In 1793 it looked after 14 men and 40 women.

[85] For years it had been standing in Bank Close, a narrow alley opening out to the Parliament Square. A building on a new site was ready only in 1806 (A. J. Youngson, *op cit*, p. 161).

kinds took shape by themselves, so that agriculture would improve itself, and the wasteland capable of cultivation would cease to be waste. But this capital could be realised only in a fictitious way: so they formed a bank on the security of their funds, and issued impartially bank-notes, payable to the bearer, to all who applied and who offered a mortgage.[86]

The effects of this institution have been astonishing. Not only has cultivation increased, not only have land clearances and plantations been greatly pushed forward, but Scotland has become both a manufacturer and a trader, and useful work has expanded with the capital. Farming above all – contrary to a notion all too prevalent in France that it can make no great progress without great capital – has made astonishing progress in Scotland.

But if this association had calculated well the effects of its operation, it had hardly perceived those of the general movement that was bound to result from it through its revenue; nor those effects of the jealousy of the Bank of England which, instead of offering a helping hand in these difficult circumstances, had to pursue further the landslide under which it was bound to be buried.

So, in the result, the movement grew too big for the forces of the bank; a considerable amount of capital that could be employed and poured out only successively was found to exceed the limits of work; it has been partly unused in circulation, the bank-notes they had reckoned could stay in circulation were suddenly presented for payment; and the Bank of England (which, like all commercial associations, feared its operations) may have added to the catastrophe. The Bank of Scotland fell, but the good it did over a few years remains, and has contributed to the founding of a bigger one.[87] This bank still exists, but its operations are regulated and it seems to be one of the useful commodities of this government.

Edinburgh certainly has manufactures, but none is very considerable: its manufacture of carriages is the most important. She exports them mainly to France for a pretty big sum.

But if this town doesn't manufacture very much, it is the entrepôt of a very considerable trade. Here they sell a great quantity of clothes made in Scotland. The place of sale is a hall where the manufacturers bring their cloths as we found in

---

86 This is the Royal Bank of Scotland. In 1763, its Stock sold at £160 per cent: by 1791 it had risen to £240 per cent. In 1793, William Creech contributed three letters on Edinburgh to Sir John Sinclair's *Statistical Account of Scotland*. Of this Bank he wrote: 'The capital at present is £600,000; and the liberal support it has given to the landed, commercial and manufacturing interests of Scotland has added greatly to the prosperity of the country' (*SAS*, VI, p. 596).

87 William Creech, in Sinclair's *SAS*, 1793, glosses over the temporary collapse, saying 'It would be too tedious to enter into a detail of the history and progress of this Bank – The capital at present is above £600,000 . . .' On the following page, Creech described the founding of the Bank of Douglas & Co, with stock of £150,000 subscribed. 'A few years after, this bank by mismanagement failed; it is said this failure occasioned land to be brought into market to the value of £750,000.' He added, and it may be this Bank's failure that Lazowski was confusing with the Bank of Scotland's fortunes: 'Although this loss was hurtful to many individuals, the country was highly benefited; for the money having been bestowed principally on the improvement of the soil, the gain was lasting and general.'

Leeds. There is a company for the marketing of this type of cloth, but I can tell you nothing about it. It has all the appearance of a disguised monopoly, and if anything could make this exception supportable, it is the state of Scotland which perhaps in general cannot be self-sufficient.

Edinburgh's water is excellent. It is brought five miles in lead conduits. There is a reservoir in the highest part of the town from which it is distributed to the rest of the town.

There is comedy all the year round, organised as in England by a manager.

The corporation, or rather the council, of the town has certain funds that do not cover their expenditure: they are supplemented by duties on consumption goods.

LEITH   The port of Edinburgh is one and a half miles away: it is really the port of Leith.[88]

Leith is a little town at the mouth of the little river, or stream.[89] Its harbour belongs to Edinburgh, which has spent a good deal on the construction of two fine jetties: they provide bigger and safer port facilities. On one side there is a very long quay, and on the other side are dry docks created by lock-gates for the construction and repair of ships.[90]

To judge by what I've seen and what I've been told, the place is frequented by a great number of ships, merchantmen, coasters, colliers, and I have seldom seen such great activity. They import everything needed by the consumers of Edinburgh and the whole district around. Coal plays a big part in the navigation. They export raw materials and the manufactures of the whole hinterland. The construction of this port is considerable: its builders are members of a harbour authority.[91] They have a very handsome Assembly Room which we haven't seen and which I mention only because apparently one may see there an excellent portrait of Queen Mary [of Guise].[92]

We came to the port to see ships of a particular construction, made at the charge of a particular builder who experiments on rather an expensive scale. I saw four, of which three have useful aims. The first is only a pleasure-ship.[93] The fourth is not

88 'The road which joins them is superb', added Alexandre.
89 The Water of Leith.
90 Made in 1772 and 1787: *Buildings of Scotland: Edinburgh*, p. 460.
91 In 1786, Robert Whitworth's schemes for Leith included a 7-acre wet dock up stream. It was carried out in 1788–9.
92 In 1548 she moved the seat of government here. It didn't survive the Protestant siege of 1560 (*Buildings of Scotland, Edinburgh*, p. 449). The old Assembly Room, 1783–5, in the rear wing (off Assembly Street) of the Assembly Room and Exchange was built by Thomas Brown, 1809–10, at 37–43 Constitution Street. An 'Adamesque' ceiling is now incorporated in the work-space of Messrs Feather Brooksbank Connexus Wirr Ltd. This Edinburgh architect and City Superintendent of Works is not to be confused with his Renfrew namesake (see p. 206). His ambitious church, St Mary's, Bellevue Cresent in the northern New Town, compares with St Andrew's, Glasgow (see p. 200), which was built eighty years earlier!
93 Alexandre describes it as what was, obviously, a primitive catamaran, sailing at speed but useless in rough seas. Neither describes two of the ships with 'useful aims', but Lazowski gives a

yet completed, but although the ships are not tarred and launched, they will be tried out during this summer.

This is an imitation of the warships of the island of Tahiti from the description of Captain Cook. Three boats are joined together abreast. They are about 4 feet high, and about as much in width in the middle, gradually diminishing to a point at each end. The middle boat is 65 feet 9 inches long, those either side only 60 feet. The object of this experiment is to test the possibility of sailing these boats in our northern seas; their safety and their speed. Their use would be to transport, in a short time and over a medium distance, several people with their arms or their goods, and with the possibility of landing on the coast from these boats, and of re-embarking.[94]

The navigation of this port has been reckoned for the year contained between 5 January 1777 and the same date in the following year. In ships belonging to Leith, fifty-two vessels were engaged in foreign trade, of which the tonnage amounted to 6,800 *tonnes*, manned by 428 seamen; forty-four coastal vessels moved 3,346 *tonnes*, manned by 281 seamen.

This navigation was more than a quarter of the two tonnages of the merchant shipping that frequent this port, to which you have to add that the ships that sail to London make seven trips every two years.

The navigation is greater today, and if you worked out a proportion based on the increase in trade, agriculture, the population and the consumption of Edinburgh and Leith, which would seem natural, it would have increased by well over a quarter [in the nine years up to 1786]. I don't include all the fishing vessels which are a matter of extreme national importance if you count in the whole extensive bay.[95]

The town of Leith is a mile and a quarter distant from Edinburgh, but they are building so much that in a few years the two towns will be one.

very interesting account of the fourth, based on a Tahitian idea. The rich inventor seems to have been experimenting with an early assault landing-craft.

94 Alexandre added: 'He has spent huge sums in designing and constructing different boats. And in artillery he has managed to create a cannon which, with 9 pounds of powder, can propel a shell of 132 pounds over two miles, and which six men can load and fire from a ship by means of a mounting expressly designed for it. In short he has invented all sorts of mechanical contrivances and is almost ruined by the experiments. His reward is that at least he feels he is useful to the public, even though his inventions are at present still ignored.' This ingenious and public-spirited shipbuilder now proves elusive. Andrew Bethune has kindly scanned the contemporary *Scots Magazine*, the *Edinburgh Advertiser*, and the *Evening Courant* without finding any of those experimental warships. Sue Mowat's book, *The Port of Leith*, pp. 240–1, refers to the building of a sloop of war in 1780 by John Sime, junior, but gives no hint of experiments based on Tahitian craft in 1786.

95 Lazowski's figures for 5 January 1777 applied to the port of Leith alone and need to be seen against a remarkable increase over the years 1763, when only one ship traded annually with St Petersburg, and 1783, when ships from Leith and the Firth of Forth to the Baltic 'amounted to some hundreds' (*SAS*, VI, pp. 601–2). In 1783, the increase in tonnage of shipping in the port of Leith since 1763 was 42,234 tons: in 1791 the registered tonnage was 130,000 tons and there were ambitious plans to enlarge the harbour.

BACK IN EDINBURGH   Edinburgh has three manufactures that go very well together: glass, soap and candles; but it has no other industry.

The population of Edinburgh was calculated in 1778 on very sound principles, based on the families established there. At that time, there were over 80,000 souls, but since then there has naturally been a great increase. The new town has been building, Leith has expanded, and they have built in the space between the two towns: in a word, commerce and manufactures are greatly increased, and the population has kept pace. So I doubt if we'd be far from the truth in imagining an increase of a quarter [in those eight years]. And, increasingly, it must be that the rest of Scotland approximates to the population of Edinburgh.[96]

I've told you that this university was made up of men most of whom are well-known and well-thought-of, or who are famous in letters and the sciences. We have met three of them, one of whom was formerly a member of Glasgow University, and now holds the post of Commissioner of Customs in Scotland. He is Mr Adam Smith, for whom we had a letter of introduction.[97] You will know him through two works (of which one, above all, has earned him his high reputation). But both are extremely well-known: *The Theory of Moral Sentiments* and *The Wealth of Nations*. The second is known in Europe as marking an epoch in the understanding of the principles of trade and finance.

Mr Smith has many papers in his possession, but he lacks the leisure to put them into order. He hopes nevertheless to take a break from the occupations of his employment and to be in a position to give the public a new edition of *The Theory of Moral Sentiments*, with corrections and a supplement, in which he will join the practice to the theory. This last is a new work[98] which so far has not been treated.

This Mr Smith is a man of prodigious knowledge. He has travelled much and worked much, his research is immense, and for my part my greatest desire is that he

---

[96] Well, the 1778 figures were perhaps over-generous; but *SAS*, VI, pp. 562–3, gives good reasons for thinking the population of Edinburgh and Leith in 1791 approximately 85,000.

[97] Ian Simpson Ross, *Life of Adam Smith*, Oxford 1995, has an excellent chapter 16 on Smith's appointment as one of 'the five Commissioners of Scottish Customs', and on his life in the house to which he moved in 1778: Panmure House at Little Lochend Close just behind the north side of the Canongate. In 1957 it was renovated, and opened as the Canongate Boys Club by Princess Mary, the Princess Royal. In 1999 it stands empty, hemmed in by disagreeable tenement buildings of 1966. On 1st November 1785, Adam Smith had written to the 'Enlightened' duc de La Rochefoucauld, later murdered by a mob at Gisors in 1792, regretting that he had had no more correspondence with Turgot and promising to send him an edition of his *Theory of Moral Sentiments*. The duke had earlier (6 August 1779) written to thank Smith for sending him a copy of his friend David Hume's *Dialogues Concerning Natural Religion*: '*On ne peut pas mieux plaider le*' etc. The duke had supplied his young cousin Alexandre with letters of introduction on their visit to the industrial Midlands the previous year, and no doubt did so now: ed E. C. Mossner and I. S. Ross, *Correspondence of Adam Smith*, Oxford 1977, pp. 286, 238, *Corr* no. 248, no. 199.

[98] 'I have inserted after the fifth part a compleat new sixth part containing a practical system of Morality, under the title of the Character of Virtue': I. S. Ross, *Life*, p. 383, *Corr* no. 287; and see *TMS*, 6th edn, 1790.

38. *Panmure House (top), Lochend Close, Canongate. The house where Adam Smith entertained his French visitors. At the time of this photograph (1999), it was concealed from the Canongate by deteriorating buildings of 1966.*

39. *Portrait of Adam Smith in his last year, 1789. Paste medallion, by James Tassie, in the Edinburgh National Portrait Gallery.*

40. *Caricature of Joseph Black, Professor of Chemistry, lecturing to his students. From Kay's* Old Edinburgh Portraits, *1787.*

should carry through '*une histoire philosophique*'[99] which he is in a better position than any other author to do and which he intends to write.

He took us to the home of Dr Robertson.[100] You only have to name him to realise how much we desired to meet him: and with what interest and what respect we actually met him. One of his sons was leaving for France, and that prevented him from returning to supper with us at Mr Smith's house. Our conversation turned chiefly round Voltaire and the abbé de Mably[101] who, if you remember, attacked him [Robertson] quite indecently for the opinion of Voltaire he expressed in his admirable Introduction to the *History of Charles V* (1769): he [Robertson] seemed aware of the opinion we in France had of this attack, and he told us that Voltaire seemed to have taken notice of his reference to him, and had written him a charming letter of thanks. Our conversation on Voltaire seemed rather long drawn out. Dr Robertson repeated with a sort of warmth and an air of conviction that it was evident to him that Voltaire had never written on history except after reading and making a formidable study of the best authors of the period, even though he didn't quote from them all the time; that one saw him everywhere the master of his material, and that for himself he thought it perfectly possible that Voltaire mistook a name in a genealogy or perhaps made a slip over a date, but for the great actions of history, the picture of manners, their trend, their changes and the cause of those changes – the spirit of history properly speaking – the causes of revolutions and their general effects: everything that went into the making of a great historian, Voltaire had it to a degree that no one had surpassed. he added that he [Robertson] had as many enemies in England as he had on the Continent because of what he had said of Voltaire, but that all that one had been able to say had made no difference to opinion.

He is now, without being old,[102] afflicted with a degree of deafness which sometimes is almost total.[103] Don't expect to see the sequel to his *History of America*: he

---

99 It seems very likely that among the materials left at Smith's death (17 July 1790) were some manuscript volumes on which he hoped to base a projected 'Philosophical History of all the different branches of Literature, of Philosophy, Poetry and Eloquence' (I. S. Ross, *Life*, p. 405). He clearly mentioned this to Lazowski, as he had to the duc de La Rochefoucauld.

100 Principal Robertson lived in vacation-time out at Grange House, where his orchard has given its name to the Victorian suburb of Grange, west of Edinburgh, off the Glasgow road. In term-time he would have received them in the Principal's House in the Old College, shortly before Adam transformed it with perhaps his finest public building (1789). The former Principal's House stood at the corner of the quadrangle looking east into his garden, shaded along the south side by 537 feet of the Town Wall.

101 Gabriel Bonnot de Mably (1709–85), French philosopher and historian, author of the *Droit public de l'Europe* and *Observations sur l'histoire de France*.

102 He was 65. Alexandre said he received them with many kindnesses but seemed 'rather cold, elderly and very deaf'.

103 'A small hearing-trumpet was fastened by a black ribbon to a buttonhole of his coat . . . He struck us boys, even from the side table, as being evidently fond of his dinner, at which he sat with his chin on his plate, intent upon the real business of the occasion. This appearance however must have been produced partly by his deafness, because when his eye told him that there was something interesting, it was delightful to observe the animation with which he instantly applied his trumpet . . .' (Henry Cockburn, *Memorials of his Time*, 1856).

won't be able to finish it. In place of the history of the different colonies, he will be obliged to give the history of the last war [of American Independence]; where the causes of that war, and its history, are matters too sensitive to touch on at present.

I've certainly no need to tell you of the opinion entertained in England of Dr Robertson as historian: it seems to be the same as it is in the whole of Europe. But it mightn't be a bad thing if I told you something that showed another aspect.

His *History of Scotland* was the first to appear and it made him known. When he had published his *History of Charles V,* his reputation was established, and as it is usual in London to sell one's manuscript to a printer for an edition or for ever, he at once made £4,000 sterling, or 96 thousand francs. His *History of America* was worth to him from the first £7,000 sterling. I don't know if there has ever been a manuscript sold for a comparable price in Paris, and I doubt it.

He was a very close friend of Mr Hume, of whom he speaks with a great consideration. He told us, on that subject, that he had never seen, nor heard of, any living man who had so immense a memory.

We dined at Mr Smith's with Dr Black[104] who was without question precious company for me. It's always interesting to see a great man at close quarters: but it was also very embarrassing, to be talking to the first chemist in England, and perhaps in Europe. His manners were extremely simple. But I couldn't talk chemistry, so I can't tell you anything he said on those matters, and for the rest I mustn't delude you with any idea that you will soon know of his discoveries. He loves his leisure and its enjoyment. When I touched on this subject, he told me that his lectures take up his whole time during the winter, and that in summer he loves to relax a little. Pressed further, he took cover behind the need to conduct a great number of experiments before having anything to show to the public. But he has research-material, and experiments concluded, that have no further need of testing, and one could easily detect that he is not spurred by ambition to revel in more of a reputation than he has already. He can't conceal from himself that he has created a new chemistry and he wants no more than that.

At dinner we also had a Dr Walker,[105] professor of natural history, who has twice

104 Professor Joseph Black, see caricature, Pl 40, p. 122. In term-time Black lived in Nicolson Street, near the University: vacations he spent down at Leith Links, or the Meadows. Smith's friends came uninvited to 'plain suppers' on Sundays (I. S. Ross, *op cit,* p. 309). His revered mother, who had kept house with him, had died at 89 in May 1784, but his old cousin Janet had long managed his household and tried to keep the sugar-basin from him. This was not one of Smith's open-house Sunday suppers, for it was a Friday: presumably it was a dinner-party assembled specially to mark the Frenchmen's visit. Lazowski didn't refer to his hostess; Alexandre referred to her as 'a cousin, Miss Douglas'. He observed drily: 'The interior of their house is very simple, decorated with economy', a nice comment.

105 Professor John Walker (1731–1803), born in the Canongate where his father was rector of the grammar school. At 10 he enjoyed Homer and read Sutherland's *Hortus Edinburgensis.* In 1764 he was appointed to survey the Hebrides: 3,000 miles in 7 months: *An Economical History of the Hebrides,* printed 1808. Regius Professor 1779: clear, dry formal lectures. From 1762 to 1783 he held the ministry of Moffat. He was interested in rural economy.

toured the Hebrides. I will cite him only in one observation he made. You know that the columns one meets in the Vivarais and the Auvergne (which people attribute to giants) are believed to be volcanic formations; at least that's the explanation we are given in the French philosophic transactions. The columns are in blocks, one concave and one convex. So are those one finds in Ireland and the Isle of Staffa. But he has seen some in the Hebrides that have not this last important singularity. If time allowed us to go to the far north, he would have been a great help.

I will say nothing of the customs, or the tone of Edinburgh. I will reserve my observations on the kingdom in general and on its inhabitants till I leave. I've no need to tell you that I am not finishing my letter on the day I began it.

On leaving Scotland at Portpatrick in May, Lazowski favoured his patron and friend the duke with no observations on 'the kingdom in general', though at Glasgow he did express, for a second time, the sympathies he had acquired for the inhabitants of the Highlands. We omit the repetition of what he describes so well in the Great Glen and in the inn at Fort William. We may assume that he shared Alexandre's high delight in the manufactures of Paisley and Johnston. It was Alexandre who, on leaving Scotland, made time to write his general reflections on their inquisitive five weeks.

7

From the Forth to the Moray Firth

Across the Forth with gig and horses in open boat at Queensferry. At Blair Adam, admiring the plantations, particularly the larches, without realising who the Adam family were. Rare beauty of position of Kinross House beside Loch Leven: hurry on to Perth. *Nine-arched bridge and two good streets: fast spinning, profitable textiles, a salmon fishery and great perfection in farming. Attractions of Tayside road to Dundee compensate Lazowski for his curious disappointment at missing Killiekrankie. At Dundee, they liked the Town House next-door to their hotel, and the handsome jetty and easy loading at the harbour. At Arbroath they noted the fortified harbour, an absurd innkeeper, and the ruined abbey. They experienced the difficulty of reaching Montrose in a flat-bottomed boat across the Southesk river: Town House and High Street admirable, and new 7-arched bridge over the Northesk river, 'the beginnings of the active public spirit these parts need'. Inverbervie's one inn's good food and drink. Stonehaven a jolly little port with a wheeled plough for deep ploughing. Halfway House 'more a cabin', but veal cutlets, fresh eggs and slices of grilled beef: 'no bread, only oat-cake'. Aberdeen: lively descriptions of the New and Old Aberdeens, including their menu at the New Inn. Mr Skene's farming enterprise at Fintray. Old Meldrum's sleazy inn with beautiful landlady and very pretty daughter. Fine Gordon estate at Fyvie. Sudden arrival at Moray Firth at Banff; noting Duff House (Lord Fife) and beautiful women promenading in the town, but not noticing Lord Findlater's good works in and around Cullen. Duke of Gordon's immense plantations at Fochabers: the house of a grand seigneur, and beginnings of a 'new town'. Lord Fife's improvements in Urquhart. Nairn to Fort George countryside 'underpopulated', though here they meet and describe Scotsmen in their 'indecent' Highland dress. Dine at Fort George: the officers' quarters very fine. A day's pause in Inverness, after 9 days – 216 miles – from Perth without a break.*

Perth, 16 April (Easter Sunday). Campbell's Inn[1]   I can give you several notes that occurred to me on our way here from Edinburgh yesterday, though they are not very precise. We had a terrible journey of 41 miles, including a 2-mile ferry-crossing, and

---

1 Campbell's Inn, Perth is untraceable: no *Perth Directories* survive for this period, the licensing records give only patchy coverage from 1801, and Rutherford's splendid *Plan of the Town of Perth*, published by J. Kirkwood, Watchmaker, Perth, in 1774, names everything but the inns. Jo Peattie, Perth Archives Assistant, has been very helpful; so has Robin Rodger at the Museum and Art Gallery Lazowski describes.

were held up there three hours,[2] so you see that it was difficult to gather any useful information; we had to do much of the journey after dark. We had been told that the view of the country on the way to Queensferry (8 miles) was superb, but the mist would not allow us to judge.

It is easy enough to see that the immediate surroundings of the capital would be built, embellished and better cultivated than the rest of the kingdom, accordingly there is much planting even on the crests of hills, in places that are hardly cultivable; and even in those they have tried to adorn the landscape.[3] We passed a park of very great extent which has the merit of occupying extremely little cultivable land and being greatly embellished, probably at great expense.[4]

The soil is generally good, rather inclined to be heavy and intractable; the farming is moderate. One sees some fairly good artificial meadows, but the enclosures are in poor order, and the land often riddled with couch grass, clear evidence of not very intelligent farming, not very vigorously practised: also, they have to let land lie fallow, otherwise the grain would be choked by weeds. These lands near the place where we embarked (Queensferry) were farmed at 25 shillings an acre.

The Edinburgh estuary [Firth of Forth] reaches nine miles to this place, where it narrows to 2 miles in width. A large rock projects from the channel between N and S Queensferry.[5] On it, during the last war, a stone fort was built to house batteries. The cause of this was Paul Jones, who succeeded in cruising up into these narrows, making everyone along the Forth tremble: he is a Scot, and knows the whole coast.[6]

This estuary is navigable for the most powerful warships twelve more miles above

---

2   It's odd that he doesn't refer to the turnpike on 'the great road from Queensferry to Perth', erected in 1753. *SAS*'s account of the parish of Cleish (III, 1792, p. 561) said it was let in 1756 and produced £40 15s. By 1792 it was producing £250–£260 a year.

3   The sense here of contemporary planting, or planting by the past generation or two, bears out Dr Johnson's observation at Arbroath: 'From the bank of the Tweed to St Andrews I had never seen a single tree which I did not believe to have grown up within the present century.'

4   Perhaps Neil 3rd earl of Rosebery's estate at Barnbougle, just east of Queensferry. When Taylor and Skinner surveyed the road Edinburgh–Queensferry, they suggested a large park by lines of trees, and hills by hachured circles. He lived in the old Barnbougle castle by the shore, holding out against a grandiose scheme by the Adam brothers, 1774–93. (Taylor and Skinner, 1776, pl 21: McWilliam pp. 93, 170.) Alexandre didn't fail to note that they had lunch (*déjeuner*) at Queensferry. Motor-traffic and suburban spread make it almost impossible nowadays to reach Barnbougle, and even Dalmeny, between Cramond and South Queensferry.

5   In fact it narrows to a mile in width, but at the ferry it is 2 miles wide. On Taylor and Skinner's map, pl 21, it was named Inch Garvey. In the 1880s, Inchgarvie was used as the base of the centre pier of the Forth Bridge: as a platform it proved indispensable to the whole plan of construction: Murray's Handbook, *Scotland*, 1884, p. 150.

6   John Paul Jones, famous intrepid 'naval adventurer', 1747–92, was born on the Solway Firth and from the age of twelve was involved in the transatlantic sea-trade, including slaves and smuggling. During the American War of Independence he joined their navy. In August 1779 he was given command of an ancient French East Indiaman, with rag-tag crew, stiffened by French peasants, under American flag and French orders. On 14 September, off the Firth, he planned with two other ships to attack Leith and Edinburgh, which were defenceless and truly 'trembling': one sees why Inch Garvey was fortified. A great squall of wind came to the rescue just as Jones came within firing range: he was blown back out of the Firth and into a glorious fight with *Serapis*, 44

Queensferry. If you want to travel to the north, you have either to take the ferry over the estuary here, or go right round by Stirling, where the Forth is bridged; but that adds fifteen or sixteen miles to the journey.

You can't make the ferry crossing when the wind's high: the boats are not decked and there are strong tidal currents. You will see that although the crossing is regular, it is very uncomfortable. We crossed in an open boat [*canot*] the better to enjoy the view, in all ways: it is prosperous, the whole coast peopled, with villages and small towns, all with harbours and boats, the shores on both sides rise, often steeply, and often cultivated right to the summit of the tallest heights, scattered with houses, farms and great plantations behind which the furthest hills are massed. If we had crossed earlier in the day we would have had in view the most beautiful front of all the country houses of Scotland, but at the time it was in the shade.[7]

In general, all the edges of this estuary are rocky reefs or sheer rocks, which is why the land is perched so high. The navigation is dangerous in winter, during the rough weather. All that I've seen so far of Scotland has a core of live rock. The waters have washed the land-bed and everywhere the rock is laid bare along the shores and the islands of this estuary.

After the crossing, you are at once in a land of bare hills, with a thin covering of earth: the crests of the hills are often of naked rock. The soil is beyond all description poor, sometimes little more than the rocky scree, sometimes a mixture of gravel and turf or peat: in a word it is very poor land, requiring a lot of work for any improvement. All this area, extending over ten miles, is scarcely better than desert, with farms very few, badly built, poor, cottages [bothies] rather than farms, their horses and harness wretched, with collars no better than twisted straw.

With such poverty, they are determined that everywhere must be tilled, from the

---

guns, convoying a Baltic merchant fleet. Empress Catherine made him rear-admiral in the Russian navy, but he quarelled with Potemkin. He died in Paris, 1792.

7   This was Hopetoun House, just over two miles further along the south shore of the Firth, and facing east. That morning they had had a misty drive of eight miles from Edinburgh and then been held up the three hours for the ferry. By the time they got out into the Firth, the sun had moved south and west and obscured the east front of what John Macky, in *A Journey through Scotland*, 1723, p. 205, saw being remodelled into 'much the finest seat in Scotland'. Macky is quoted in Alistair Rowan's essay, 'The Building of Hopetoun' (in *Design and Practice in British Architecture, Studies presented to Howard Colvin, Architectural History*, vol 27, 1984, pp. 183–209). Rowan makes out a good case for believing that the 1st earl of Hopetoun took the lead in the remodelling of what William Adam undertook for him from 1721: both were in their thirties but the earl had travelled in France and Italy, and wanted a more ambitious building than the west side of the house that Sir William Bruce had designed for his father. William Adam, founder (with the backing of Hopetoun) of his famous family's fortunes, was a brilliant *entrepreneur*, running timber-mills, barley-mills, and twenty other such projects as well as the design and building of half-a-dozen impressive country houses. When his friend and patron, Hopetoun, sent his own younger son, Charles, on the Grand Tour in 1754, his elder son, John, suggested that William's son, Robert Adam, the most gifted of them, should accompany him: that suggestion led to the transformation of English classical design. Among their earliest ancestors, John de Hope had a grandson who married Jacqueline de Tott. In September 1793, Alexandre's elder brother, François, married Marie-Francoise de Tott: *Innocent Espionage*, p. 254. Anyway, Hopetoun remained in the shadows.

bottoms to the very tops of the hill-sides, they take two harvests in succession of oats or barley, seed their grass with the second, to continue three or four years, after which they plough, have a year's fallow and sow their oats again. If they interrupt this rotation it's to sow peas, but in small patches. The pastures they gain in this way are miserable, feeding horned cattle of a small pitiful breed. They have no sheep, or very few, and their lands aren't enclosed. They are hard-working, but their system's no good, and they can have no other without capital. The farmers can make nothing out of these wretched lands: it's up to the landowners to advance funding. The lands are let out at between 3 and 6 shillings, but I think that's much too dear.

Amid all these miles of barren hills, I have nevertheless caught sight of a patch on a hillside, quite high up, a good clay soil well cultivated, yielding wheat at five or six quarters to the acre. This exceptional soil, a real phenomenon, is farmed at 30 and 40 shillings.

Blair Adam   I've already observed to you, many times, that whenever you come upon the home of a gentleman who lives in the country all the year round, you see a change in the cultivation of the neighbourhood. Today I've observed this yet again. [One page removed by Jean Marchand.]

A mile and a half further on, you come to an extremely agreeable village, with resident gentleman-farmer who to the merit of having created an excellent farm has added the creation, on a large scale, of planting woods in an entirely new way.[8] The whole village is planted: the banks of a stream that runs through, the hedges of the gardens and fields, the spaces between houses, and on all the hill-crests on either hand, where the plough cannot penetrate. These immense plantations come

---

8   This is the estate of Blair Adam, built up from the 1730s by William Adam, the founder of the remarkable family famous chiefly as architects. *SAS*, III, 1792, pp. 551–4, didn't even mention their architectural achievements but, just as Arthur Young would have done, recorded: 'Mr [Wm] Adam of Maryburgh and his son John Adam, Esq, MP, the present proprietor, were the first persons in this part of the country who gave an example in the improvement of land by enclosing, planting and raising artificial grasses, cabbages and turnips. By them some millions of trees have been planted, a considerable part of which are in this parish [Cleish] and in a very flourishing state. Mr Adam was the first person in the County of Kinross who planted potatoes in the fields. Not being able to obtain what he wanted for seed in this country, nor in the Edinburgh market, he brought them over land from Carlisle. Upon a particular occasion, many of the poor had scarcely anything else to subsist on for about 2 months after the old corn-crop was consumed and before the new crop was ready. Almost one half the parish is enclosed and enclosures are increasing well. Hedges thrive very well.' *SAS* also mentions coal on the estate of Blair belonging to John Adam, Esq, of Maryburgh, producing £180 a year, but not wrought for some time on account of its vicinity to the proprietor's house.
    The informal gardening and planting at Blair by John Adam was described by his son William in his book *Blair Adam*, 1834 (qv), and very well summarised by A. A. Tait, *The Landscape Garden in Scotland, 1735–1835*, Edinburgh UP, 1980, pp. 98–101. Tait thought John Adam's inspiration at Blair was the 3rd duke of Argyll's tough husbandry at Inveraray, who gave Adam the opportunity 'of taking from his nurseries the most useful and best trees for the propagation of the fir tribe: so that the most ancient larches, spruces and silver firs to be found on the estate at Blair Adam were sent by the duke of Argyll' (*Blair Adam*, pt 1, pp. 97, 98; see pl 41, over).

41. *View of Blair Adam, with larches: William Adam,* Blair Adam, *1834. Lazowski comments below on these larches*

together to form a very fine design composed of all kinds of forest trees and ever-greens, these last in very great numbers. In two or three weeks' time, the effect will be even more agreeable for the larches will be green:[9] they are mixed among the other trees, and sometimes they interrupt the woodland mass by being planted singly and, sometimes, in large numbers.

The estate[10] is encircled and bounded by woodland plantations: you would

[9] Travelling in Scotland in April, I have felt the same pleasure as the larches begin to show the pinkish-buff tinge that heralds their fine green foliage. They look particularly handsome planted against the darker greens of the other pines. (They are members of the pine family of conifers, but they grow short, fine, deciduous leaves in dense clusters: Bentham and Hooker, *Handbook of British Flora*, 6th edn, 1896, p. 416.) It seems a pity Lazowski and Alexandre knew nothing of the Adam family, and equally, that when they reached Inveraray torrential rain prevented them from visiting the 3rd duke of Argyll's plantations.

[10] John Fleming, in *Robert Adam and his Circle* (1962) showed how William Adam was investing in the Blair Adam landscape some of the fortune he created from a great diversity of successful enterprises as well as building and architecture: from, for instance, the manufacture of Dutch pantiles, and brewing based on the model of a barley-kiln from Holland, and leasing the Pinkie coalfield for which he drove an aqueduct through the hill on which Inveresk stands. Blair Crambeth was the nucleus of Blair Adam. Dowhill, with its picturesque peel tower, has views over the Fife hills to Loch Leven. His son Robert inherited Dowhill: the elder son, John, had Blair House; and his son William, Commissioner of the Jury Court of Scotland, had it after him, and

hardly believe how many of the pastures have been improved by being sheltered in this way, and how much fitter the cattle are in consequence. In the plantations, the species of evergreen that evidently does best is the spruce, and the larch is the next most successful: and the next, coming so close that the balance could go either way, is the Scots pine that I would have thought must surpass all the others. It comes only after the silver spruce [*spruce d'argent*] and, in general, after all the other evergreens.

In the village, linen is woven and bleached and you can't help feeling that these people who flourish in these plantations add much to the singularity of its appearance. It is a short distance from *Kinross*, the capital of a small county, Kinross-shire. I mention this town only to tell you of the infinitely rare beauty of its position.[11] From the south-east side of Kinross spreads a lake covering several miles – large enough to be marked on the maps with the name Loch Leven.[12] The land round the lake rises irregularly, at first in gentle slopes, then in steep heights until the picture closes in distant ranges. Beside the town the proprietor has built his house[13] facing down the greatest length of the loch, and he has planted the hills he looks across to, in the places where the beauty of the outline of the loch is a picture on its own. These plantations form grand masses, perfectly imitating the natural forest. About two hundred yards[14] from the house is an islet formed in the loch on a soil-covered rock. A pretty round tower has been built on it, and some trees planted. There is a room in the tower for taking tea after a boat-trip on the lake (the tower has a chimney). The trout in this loch are famous in Scotland.[15]

Of the route from Kinross to Perth I can say nothing: night fell too soon. I saw fields sown with flax on the lower slopes, but learnt no details.[16]

---

published *Blair Adam from 1733 to 1834* (1834). He and nine friends spent two or three days there every summer – 'the Blair Adam Club' – including from 1816 to 1831 Sir Walter Scott. One day was usually devoted to an antiquarian excursion. The story of Scott's *The Abbot* came into his mind on one of these, recreating Mary Queen of Scots' imprisonment at Loch Leven castle nearby.

[11] Alexandre mentioned it because, after 15 miles, they dined there: he says 'at the *Crown*' (not the Red Lyon Inn, marked on Taylor and Skinner's map, 1776, pl 21, just to the north of the Bruce estate: the Red Lyon has become the Green Hotel). The obvious former coaching-inn in the town is 'the Salutation' and there seems to be no record of a Crown.

[12] Now perhaps 9 miles in circumference, it was reckoned (*SAS*, VI, p. 166) about 12 miles in 1793: 1,400 acres were reclaimed by drainage in the 19th century. The area round the castle on the island has been increased: one no longer lands under the castle walls, as in Mary's day, and Scott's.

[13] The house was built c1685 for himself by none other than Sir Wm Bruce, Bart, the re-modeller of Holyrood Palace for Charles II. He died here and was succeeded by his son and then his nephew. The house here was re-modelled by Wm Adam. It is surprising that, in their hurry to get to Perth, Lazowski and Alexandre completely overlooked the romantic castle of Queen Mary's imprisonment 700 yards further out in the loch.

[14] 100 *toises*: 1 *toise* = 6 feet.

[15] The Loch Leven variety were described in Murray's *Scotland* in 1884 as 'pink trout'. In 1880, anglers in the loch caught 19,000 of them, and next year 17,000! *SAS*, in 1793 (pp. 166–7) ascribed their 'high flavour and bright red colour' to the vast quantity of small shellfish, red in colour, which abounds all over the bottom of the loch among the aquatic weeds: the trout were often caught with a belly-full of them.

[16] He might have learnt of several advantages favouring the linen-manufacture – Silesia linens: 126,803 yards (27–30 inches in breadth) woven here in 1786 (*SAS*, pp. 168–9): 200 or so looms

PERTH stands on the river Tay,[17] navigable by trading ships up to the town's port. It stands in quite a broad plain running west and south, and a little to the north and east: nearby are ranges of beautiful hills well planted and well peopled. The river is superb: about twice the width of the Seine at Rouen. It flows through a rich and admirably cultivated plain to the north, the hills terraced and dotted about with farms and forming a delightful amphitheatre. To the south is a quay, the town's harbour, separated by a beautiful avenue of sycamores – a public promenade – from a pleasant meadow[18] serving as parade ground for an Artillery Regiment.

At whatever distance the hills (except to the south), which rise in grand majestic mass and define the distant horizon, your view from here embraces everything and ranges over a rich, lively and magnificent country, three characteristics not often allied. For myself, I've been tremendously impressed by the position of the town and by its surroundings. It combines everything that's pleasant and striking in its landscape – a beautiful river with waters as clear as those of the Rhône, and a view enlivened by shipping that sails back and forth from the sea, and by the very handsome freestone bridge of nine arches over the river,[19] its banks attractive and lined with dwellings, the level plain near the town well cultivated, woods very extensive but not spoiling the views out, and lastly the hills, sometimes cultivated, sometimes covered with woods, and sometimes rising in bold shapes, weathered. If I don't covet every field before me, I think I would love to own one of those I see on a lower slope facing the river.[20]

in a population of about 1800. In addition, they made all their own shirts and bed-linen. There was plenty of coal 5 miles away, a fine stream of soft water running through the town for boiling and washing the yarn, and two extensive commons for bleaching: one beside the loch, the other to the west. Todd & Duncan, Cashmere Spinners (at Loch Leven Mills, Kinross) carry on the industry today.

[17] Lazowski called it the Ryne, confusing it perhaps with the Earn, one of the Tay's tributaries here, or with a nearby small place called Rhyne.

[18] It is known as the South Inch. Alexandre said it furnished all the inhabitants with a charming walk on Sundays in summer. (They were there on Easter Sunday: 'We didn't want to travel on that day.')

[19] It was built in 1766–71 by John Smeaton, after the previous wooden bridge had been swept away by the river in 1621: since then, civilian and military north–south travellers had no option but ferry-boats at this lowest and only crossing-point of the Tay. Smeaton had built the Eddystone lighthouse. In his 2nd *Tour in Scotland*, 1772, Pennant noticed that the piers of Smeaton's bridge were founded 10 feet under the bed of the river, on oak and beech piles, the stones laid in 'puzzalane' – the volcanic ash found near Pozzuoli, much used in the preparation of hydraulic cement. (Smeaton had also used it at Eddystone.) Pennant doesn't mention Smeaton's ingenious piercing of the masonry structure, between each pair of arches, by a round, cylindrical hole through the whole width of the bridge: this served both to reduce the weight of masonry on the cutwaters and to reduce the resistance of the river to the weight of the full flood. These holes are no higher than the arches of the bridge, so that the water can flow through them at fullest flood (Pennant's engraving shows them too high). The holes now appear closed off, but could presumably be opened when floods threaten.

[20] Alexandre was equally pleased by Perth: 'I'd love to live here if I lived in Scotland – a country I would not choose for my domicile'!

42. A View of Perth from the South, *drawn by Rutherford, engr. Picot, 1775/6. Perth Museum and Art Gallery. The town's little harbour on the Tay was 'separated by a beautiful avenue of sycamores – a public promenade – from a pleasant meadow', the South Inch, across which a coach-and-horses marks the road from Edinburgh and the south that Alexandre and Lazowski arrived by. In 1786, the South Inch served as a parade ground for an Artillery Regiment. 'The very handsome freestone bridge of 9 arches' was built by John Smeaton, 1766–71, of pink sandstone. In the engraving, 3 arches are concealed by riverside buildings.*

But I'm writing only to please myself, and I owe you more interesting information.

Perth is a town of quite considerable size and much better built than I expected for a town in Scotland, though I'm not quite sure why.[21] There are two streets that, for length, breadth and lay-out, would count as fine streets in London.[22] The houses are all built of stone, and although they certainly don't have the air of neatness and comfort of English dwellings, they are good houses. It must be a town of at least ten

---

[21] The highly profitable manufacturing, see footnote 26 below, must be one explanation.

[22] It seems clear from A Rutherford's plan of the town in 1774 that these two fine principal streets are South Street and High Street. They have survived in tolerable order in the year 2000. Knox preached a revolutionary sermon here on 11 May 1559: much evidence of the town's medieval importance was destroyed by the Protestant mob: 'After the sermon, a number of people broke down all the altars and images in the parish church, and then proceeded to the entire demolition of the monasteries: no vestige of the monasteries and chapels is now to be seen' (*SAS*, XVIII, 1796, p. 537).

or twelve thousand people.[23] There is no outstanding building except a house now serving as depot to the artillery and which now belongs to the town: after the 1745 rebellion it was confiscated from a lord and handed to the duke of Cumberland who sold it to the town.[24] It is remarkable in being built on the foundations of the house where James I (of England) is supposed to have foiled an attempt to kidnap him.[25]

This town is greatly increased by the manufacture of cloth in Scotland. Here the manufacture is carried to great perfection and on a large scale. One of the manufacturers alone has working for him 200 looms every day, from which you will see that as the looms are multiplied, the town is occupied more and more by cloth-workers and cloth-merchants.

Here they make cloth of all kinds: in cotton, linen thread, hemp and damask. This manufacture is the more precious for Scotland as it all profits the country, except the raw cotton. They spin the cotton in the new mills: one of them is established three miles from Perth and two more are being built. This invention has greatly increased the output of these linen-cloths, of which shirts are made for export to the coast of Africa, and in these islands. The people living in the north are themselves beginning to make use of them. They are now making cloths 122 inches wide, using the English shuttle. The damask is superb, and perhaps you already know that it is better – better made and better marketed – in Scotland than in any part of England. I've seen magnificent examples and they will carry out the designs one orders.[26]

When an individual wants to have a damask made to order he goes to see the workman and pays him so much a yard, and provides the thread. The craftsman provides the loom and equips it: he is paid three shillings a yard for the most beau-

23 *loc cit*, pp. 524–7. The 1755 population was reckoned at 9,000, the 1793 population just under 20,000 (by multiplying the burials by 3). I daresay Lazowski wasn't far wrong.
24 The magistrates presented it, with its gardens, to the duke of Cumberland in 1746, who at once sold it to the Board of Ordnance: they turned it into artillery barracks.
25 This was Gowrie House, built c1520 and replaced in 1808–20 by the County Buildings. On 5 August 1600, three years before James VI succeeded Elizabeth I, Alexander Ruthven lured James to the house of his brother, earl of Gowrie. They planned to keep him there in a tower and then abduct him, but the king got to a window and called for help. The brothers were killed in the rescue. Lazowski knew that there were doubts about the truth in this conspiracy.
26 *SAS*, XVIII, 1796, pp. 513–00, quotes a Report of 1794: 'The staple manufacture of Perth is linen; and of late a considerable quantity of cotton-cloth.' Damask first suggests silk, but here is presumably twilled linen. It mentions Silesias and Pulicats among Perth's considerable linen and cotton products, but not damask. From Lazowski's enthusiastic description, it sounds rather unlikely that it would have gone completely out of production in the eight years 1786–94. In any case, Lazowski's report on it is valuable. So is his recording, a paragraph further on, the prices and wages. *SAS* sticks to prices and turnover, without a word on wages. Alexandre shared Lazowski's interest in wages: 'the cloths are superb and very reasonable prices (the most beautiful about 4 shillings): it is rarely that a workman can earn a shilling a day'. *SAS* gave the turnover and value for 179: 'above 1500 looms in the town and suburbs manufacture linen and cottons annually, about £100,000 sterling, as well as £120,000 sterling more from the surrounding county'. This highly profitable manufacturing helps to explain why Perth looked 'much better built' than they expected.

tiful damask, and earns about 1 shilling and 6 pence a day. But as he has to spend so much time servicing his loom, he can't count on making more than a little over a shilling. The cost of the material plus workmanship works out at between 4 shillings and 4 shillings and 6 pence per yard for this fine damask. The fine thread required generally costs 4 shillings a pound weight.

If the damask workers earn only a little over a shilling, the others earn less: on average 11 pence seems to be the sum.

The women and girls are all employed in spinning, not only in the town, but in all the country around. They spin as I remember I told you I saw it done last year in Leicester,[27] spinning with each hand, yet with the utmost speed, on wheels of the kind I described in Leicester.[28] Passing through the villages, I have seen spinning by spindle, but seldom, and by old women, earning at most 4 pence a day. They can never lack work: those who can't afford to buy the flax or hemp to spin and sell on their own account are employed either by the manufacturers or by merchants trading in the business. Finally, there are establishments where all those who come asking for work receive it: these places are storehouses of hemp, flax and yarn where both the merchants who organise the trade and the manufacturers who are prepared to sell the finished cloths come to stock up with the raw materials. It is this spinning-business that is replacing the wool-spinning in England: there is this difference, that the poor here can only gain assistance by working: they work harder and live less well, for here there is no Poor Rate.[29]

Apart from the shipping and navigation of the river, which occupies some of the population, there are the fisheries, principally the salmon fishing. It is let out to one individual, who returns to the riparian owners, between Perth and the sea, £9,000 sterling. He has four sloops devoted solely to transporting his fresh salmon to London at the beginning of the season, and later to different parts of the Continent. The fresh salmon are packed in ice for transporting: that's the best way to preserve them and keep them fresh. They've tried transporting them alive, in water, but they arrive thin and wasted. In the summer they are pickled [*picklés*] in vinegar and salt,

---

[27] Lazowski's account of the spinning they saw in Leicester seems not to have survived, but the clear account of his young companion, François, may be read in *Innocent Espionage*, 1995, p. 28.

[28] François described them as 'simple and low down, a foot-wheel placed on a small board and bound round by a leather thong which passes over the spindle of the two little bobbins set in front of the woman, above the wheel and level with her stomach. Above the bobbins is a distaff which is no more than a little double fork on which one lays the wool, which divides in two, each half going to a bobbin. This neat arrangement is easy for the woman to work: she doesn't get tired by having to lift her hands too high. The movement of the pedal is generally slight: they spin with the greatest speed I ever saw.'

[29] *SAS*, XVIII, pp. 527–8, expanded on this: 'The great resort of the poor from all parts of the country is to Perth. Some make a shift, perhaps for three years, to maintain themselves, and then when they fall into distress, or their cart-horses die, by which they gain their daily bread, they apply to the public for relief. The inhabitants in general are charitably disposed. Besides what they give in private to distressed persons or families, they often make large voluntary contributions.' *SAS* then lists the friendly societies and charitable institutions, and contradicts Lazowski by recording that the Magistrates yearly assessed the inhabitants to the amount of about £300 'which, however, is not sufficient to maintain the begging poor'.

but they can't travel far, only for local consumption. What goes abroad is salted, for the market in Flanders, France and Spain.

If Perth's industry is considerable, so equally is the agriculture of the neighbourhood. It is practised in a way that merits describing in detail. The soil is excellent, the best in all Scotland, and it would be hard to find better in England or on the Continent. It is a mucilaginous [soft, moist, sticky] clay formed by river deposits, or rather by the sea, for on inspection . . . [here Jean Marchand cut out 10 typescript pages!].[30]

Alexandre's ten enthusiastic pages on Perth's agriculture list the growing of wheat, barley, some oats, hemp, flax, beans, peas, turnips and grass pasture. Farmlands frequently valued at 2 to 3 louis the acre of what they call loam ('lome'). 'Methods comparable with those I described around Doncaster' (pp. 42–5 above). Alexandre gives the rotations, adding 'not widely enough practised nor even regarded as being good, for their cloth-making is pushed to such perfection that the thread from their local flax isn't good enough and most has to be sent from Russia. A man who spins flax to great perfection has 2 shillings for a pound-weight, earning scarcely more than 12 sols a day. They spread their straw over the land in great quantities, asserting that if it isn't smoking like a pipe, it's worthless. They're fond of beans, and regard oats as too poor to waste their strong lands on.' He concludes his observations with a warm appreciation of the high perfection reached – 'not overnight, but with much trial and error' – by, for the most part, the gentlemen-farmers, their lands generally well enclosed, going about their business in different ways, establishing a sure route for those farmers with less money to risk, a new agriculture. He saw the obvious importance to these gentlemen-farmers themselves, as well as to their lands, that they should live on their farmlands, or at least visit them often enough to keep them in hand and in good order, and not follow the examples of some great Scottish landlords and go off and spend the revenues of their lands in London and Newmarket. He mentions, on what grounds he doesn't say, Lords Queensberry and Stormont as examples. He clearly had no premonition of the imminent tragedy in which the introduction of a new hardier version of the Cheviot sheep into the Highlands somehow led his gentlemen-farmer-improvers into the horror of removing the clansmen-crofters all over the Highlands, to replace them by the new Great Sheep. Sir John Sinclair, of Thurso Castle, promoter of the SAS, promoted these great sheep with the best intentions.

Lazowski: Dundee, 17 April   [Monday, the day after his notes on Perth!]

Gordon's Inn   I left Perth this morning with great regret, and the picturesque quality of the early part of our route made me regret leaving the neighbourhood still more. The road follows a *corniche*, the hillside[31] on your left covered in woods on its uncultivable

---

30 *SAS*, p. 510, limits itself to 2 sentences on 'Soil and Cultivation: The soil is partly loam, partly clay. The lands being in the neighbourhood of a populous town, and of a port to which great quantities of lime are conveyd, are generally so well cultivated as to yield rich crops.'

31 Kinnoul Hill: marked as Kinnoul Craigs on Taylor and Skinner's 1775 road map: their Perth–Dundee road coincides precisely with the present A90.

parts, the river Tay below on your right, dividing, half a mile from the town, to form an island[32] which, though uncultivated and not even meadowland, doesn't fail to make a good effect.

I would certainly have some observations on farming for you, but in spite of my inclination towards gathering such observations, I am in a very bad humour at having taken this route.[33] It was the most beautiful, we were told, and the most agreeable, this eastern route, bordering the sea; and it was the most populated. But apart from the impossibility of planning a good tour by always following the easiest routes, one gets to know very little of a country by going through only the best parts.

So I wanted to take the middle road through Dunkeld, going fifteen miles farther north, then turning east to join the coast-road at Montrose. What decided me that *that* was the road we should have taken was chiefly that it would enable me to see the place where Dundee fell, a man truly worthy of the ancient Greek republics and of the Cameronians. You know of the Pass of Killikrankie and – where the Pass opened out into the valley to the north – how the battle was won by Dundee, though in it he was killed. If you read the account of this in *The Memoirs of Great Britain and Ireland* by M Dalrymple, you will certainly want to see these places carefully for yourself; and you won't be surprised that, finding myself so near this justly celebrated scene, I badly wanted to go there.[34] But one must make the best of it; and I haven't arrived here empty-handed.

---

32 Surveyed by Taylor and Skinner, but nameless.

33 Alexandre had not neglected *his* observations on farming, having met a workman [*ouvrier*] who gave him cropping details almost identical with those they'd earlier been given in Perth. But he was interested in the local method of sowing beans with a working plough – ploughing and sowing together. Then clearing the beans with great care, using a very small plough drawn across the furrows by a horse. The horses were not large, but very strong. (There is now, in 2000, a disappointing Heavy Horse Centre at Kingfauns.) He described in detail how the plough differed in shape from Suffolk ones ('instead of a regular curve, rounded but slightly flat in the middle'), and how careful they were to clean (ie weed) the turnips. He managed several pages along these lines and noticed the house of Mr Graie: see footnote 35, p. 139.

34 John Graham of Claverhouse, 1st viscount Dundee (1649–89). As captain of James, duke of York's troop raised to suppress the presbyterian covenanters in the lowland south-west of Scotland, Claverhouse, an educated and experienced soldier, started the work gingerly and ineffectively in 1678: but his severity next year led the followers of Richard Cameron to disclaim allegiance to Charles II for his 'breach of the covenant'. In July 1680, Cameron was killed by Claverhouse's dragoons in a fierce skirmish at Airds Moss, after which the covenanters acquired the name of Cameronians. A kind of guerilla war developed into 'the killing time' (October 1684) and worsened with James II's accession in 1685. James's Letters of Indulgence in 1687 were accepted by most presbyterians reluctantly, and the persecution of Cameronians went on. When William and Mary succeeded (February 1689), all presbyterians were safe, but their subjugator, Claverhouse, lately made earl of Dundee by James, was not. He gathered what Jacobite forces he could in the Highlands and was able to choose the field of battle against William and Mary's general, M'Kay. On 16 July 1689, M'Kay's men had filed north through the gorge of Killiecrankie and out into the valley above, at the top of which Dundee and his Highlanders appeared with a shout, just before sundown; pouring down the slope and routing all but one English regiment. At the head of his Highlanders Dundee was killed by a bullet in the armpit. M'Kay's superior numbers managed their retreat with fewer casualties than the victors. Sir John Dalrymple's account of the engagement – the source of Lazowski's devotion to Dundee – is written with an eloquence comparable

From some miles on from Perth the soil is light, a sandy loam. They are working on the turnips, which they feed to their cattle as they were doing back in Perth. Most of the farms have a number of cottages, each with a couple of acres let at £5 but without security of tenure. The cottager fills his plot with potatoes, wheat, barley and a patch of grass for a cow and two pigs . . . [*Here 7 more pages have been cut by M Marchand. However, SAS contains more than adequate descriptions of the parishes of Kinnoul, Kinfauns and Longforgan, largely covering their road Perth–Dundee.*]

Kinnoul (SAS XVIII, 1796, 540–62) experienced rapid progress in 20–30 years, raising the land value amazingly, and were leases to expire, the rent would be doubled. The hilltops were now covered with thriving plantations. Near Perth no strict rotation of crops is observed, as easy carriage from Perth brings lime and manure to keep their ground in good heart. However, the Rev Lewis Dunbar thought rotation would prove a better economy. He reports a considerable part of his parish hedged with hawthorn or beech. 'The English plough is generally used, drawn by a pair of horses and managed by one man.' Since 1767, Dickson & Brown's nursery, 30–40 acres on the east bank of the Tay, opposite Perth, had flourished with 'all kinds of fruit and forest trees, evergreen and flowering shrubs, flower roots and plants, naturalized to the climate'; also a large greenhouse full of exotic plants and a shop in Perth. 'An example of so much ornament and utility is every year finding many imitators.' Just across the river, Lazowski and Alexandre might have gone out their way if they'd had word of it.

The Rev George Chapman (SAS XIV, 1795, 212–23) described the parish of Kinfauns in clear detail; its landscape, the trout and salmon fishing of the Tay, the relatively few enclosed farm fields, though it was corn country, and the regrettable neglect of a proper rotation of crops, the best of which was reckoned 1) fallow dressed with lime or dung 2) wheat 3) pease and green crops to prepare for 4) barley, sown with grass seeds 5) hay 6) oats. A great deal of the grain is marketed outside the parish and is generally excellent. Prices and wages regulated by Perth market. Remarkable change in dress, manners and cleanliness of the people: great rise of wages: in memory of oldest inhabitant, no person has been tried for any crime. Great advantages from turnpike recently made, Perth–Dundee.

Alexandre added some details of crop rotation he had acquired from conversations with a workman, un ouvrier. 'A short while after our conversation we passed the house of Mr Graie which is simple but pretty. The park and farm seemed, as one passed, to be beautifully kept. In Perth he was named as one of the best farmers. We wished we could

---

with that of Sir William Napier's *History of the War in the Peninsula and in the South of France*, 1807–14, and that of Lord Macaulay, not least in *his* description of Killiecrankie: Dalrymple's title is *Memoirs of Great Britain and Ireland, from the Dissolution of the last Parliament of Charles II*, 3 vols, 1771, reprinted 1790. In the reprint, this episode follows a romantic account of the dress and the fighting qualities of the clansmen. One sees how Lazowski was moved to want to visit Killiecrankie; and one wonders how he came to the strange conclusion that Dundee was 'worthy' not only of the Greek republicans but of the Cameronians he had hounded and slain for their presbyterian nonconformity. 'Bonnie Dundee' is emphatically a reference to the place, not the soldier: Scott's refrain goes: 'It's up with the bonnets of Bonnie Dundee'. Meanwhile the government had formed a regiment of Cameronians which served, it was said, 'with all their unequalled determination'.

have met him. He would have given us useful information and advice. This journal of mine would have been so much more complete and less humdrum. The road went on agreeably between hills and river.'[35]

To the Statistical Account *'a Friend to Statistical Enquiries' contributed no fewer than 103 excellent pages on Longforgan (XIX, 1797, 459–562). One of its more unexpected ingredients is its account of a steam melon-pit for producing melons thinner-skinned and better flavoured than those 'produced in the common way': and a diagram assisted the description of a steam-heated vinery. This is part of a very full picture of the two chief estates – Castle Huntley and Mylnefield; the former (now part of the Scottish Prison Service) with battlements rising 116 feet, with a glorious view across the Tay; the latter at the east end of the 7-mile-long narrow parish towards Dundee: Mr Mylne's grounds laid out 'in great taste by Mr White', with fine grass parks supplying excellent mutton. Farmhouses are described, the occupations of the inhabitants enumerated, starting with Minister 1, Schoolmaster 1, and continuing through male-servants 136, female-servants 80, farmers paying £100 a year upwards 15, ditto paying from £5 to £10, 28, families, 307. Mr Mylne kept about 400 sheep of the Bakewell breed; thinks they fatten much sooner than the black-faced wedders brought from the Highlands at 4 years old if they can be had. The reclamation of 5 or 600 acres of uncultivated moor spread from east to west ends of the parish was an enormous improvement of the early 1760s. Levelling and draining is discussed is these SAS pages at a length that would have delighted Lazowski, but Sir John Sinclair's great volumes of 'statistical account' were not even an idea in his vigorous Highland mind in 1786. Lazowski would have been vexed to know that here, still in 1796, 'fallow was generally thought to be the best preparation for wheat upon clay'. It is surprising that neither he nor Alexandre seems to have noticed, on the Mylnefield estate, Longforgan's principal stone quarry, at Kingoody, thought by the SAS to be 'perhaps one of the best in Great Britain'. Its grey 'grain stone' furnished the material for the making of the Gipping Navigation between Ipswich and Stowmarket in Suffolk (SAS, p. 464n). (Wedder is dialect for wether, a castrated ram.)*

Lazowski resumes, his ill-humour at missing Killiecrankie forgotten:

This road is delightful, overlooking the river or estuary [Firth of Tay] almost all the way. It's over 4 miles wide, and alive with ships.

---

[35] I suppose his 'Mr Graie' was Charles, lord Gray (1752 – December 1786), whose mother inherited the Kinfauns Castle estate, where both his parents had died (GEC *Peerage*). Taylor and Skinner's map (pl 51) has a 'Gray Esq' with a house at Kinfauns and another at Ballegarry, 14 miles from Perth, 8 from Dundee. Alexandre's 'Mr Graie' seems likely to have been based at Kinfauns, and well known in Perth. Kinfauns Castle is now a handsome hotel set in the heights of a steeply climbing park, with the top of the ridge above the Tay signalled by a castellated turret on a romantic Rhineland model. The present A90 dual carriageway cuts straight over the Carse of Gowrie, sparing the Frenchmen's 1786 road which keeps blissfully to the foot of the Braes of the Carse; winding along between well-wooded hedges from Glendoick through Myreside, Kilspindie and Ballindean. Regrettably, it now joins the line of the hectic A90 at Longforgan, entering Dundee along the Tay-side but missing the once active stone quarry at Kingoodie.

Dundee   is bigger than Perth, and altogether contains, at a guess, 12 to 15 thousand people.[36] Its harbour is artificial, formed by two jetties, one from the shore, the other in the Firth, so that you can enter and leave at two places. One of the two openings leads out to the south, the other to the east.[37] It's clear from the number of ships in the harbour that the river navigation is considerable, suggesting an extensive trade. This town manufactures textiles of various kinds, and ropes, from the hemp left over in the spinning mills. It serves as a depot for the cloth made in the surrounding neighbourhood. It also manufactures cloths and light woollen material, but all for local consumption, not for a wide market.[38]

Alexandre   The town is not badly built, the main square large, the Town House (I think) is fine but very heavy.[39] The large harbour makes use of a quayside all round it, and a beautiful, though not very long, jetty where the ships can load and unload very easily.[40]

On the 18th, we left Dundee   for Arbroath, and on to sleep at Montrose, 30 miles, always following the sea-coast. At first the road was flat, but later hilly. Much cultivated land, some of it poor, unenclosed and sheepless. Some gentlemen's houses, sometimes in rather lonely places,[41] and some of the least cultivated lands I've found on our route.

36 By 'actual enumeration', in 1781, 15,700; and in 1788, 19,329: *SAS*, VIII, 1793, p. 208. The *SAS* description of Dundee (pp. 192–250) is superb.
37 Crawford's plan of Dundee in the 1790s shows a longish pier running south and framing the east side of the harbour. (There was also a short jetty marking the west side.) Lazowski's jetty 'in the Firth' was a mole, or breakwater (in fact two, labelled West Head and East Head, one long and one short), shielding the wide mouth of the harbour.
38 After their enthusiasm for Perth, neither Lazowski nor Alexandre is 'on form' at Dundee. That is amended by *SAS*, pp. 216–19: 'The staple manufacture is linen of various kinds: coarse fabrics for exportation in the year from Nov 1788 amounted to 4¼ million yards valued at £108,782, a quarter of which came from the six surrounding parishes. Different sorts of canvas for shipping, 704,000 yards, worth £32,000. In 1793, cotton manufacture was gaining in importance and an English company was establishing itself here in woollens. Two cordage and rope companies employed 30 persons. A century later, the Dundee linen export was worth nearly £3m. By then 100,000 tons of jute was being imported from Calcutta, worth about £700,000, and made into sacking worth £2m.
39 Designed by William Adam, 1732, and demolished 1932 to celebrate its bi-centenary. (See *Vitruvius Scoticus*, ed James Simpson, Edinburgh 1980, pl 104.) Gordon's Inn, where they stayed, stood next door to it. (Information kindly supplied by Mr Iain Flett, Dundee Record Office.)
40 By January 1792, 116 vessels belonged to the port; 34 trading abroad, 78 coasting and 4 whaling.
41 If they were using Taylor and Skinner's road maps (1775–6) they would have seen these squires' names – Johnston Esqr, Graham Esqr, etc, including a park noticed by Lazowski, about halfway to Arbroath. It was among the earl of Panmure's estates (Taylor and Skinner, pl 33). He was the son of a Jacobite, but by fighting at Dettingen and Fontenoy, and helping to pursue the Pretender from Derby to Carlisle in 1745, he recovered the family estates, only to die unmarried in 1782. In 1786 they were in the hands of the earl of Dalhousie (GEC *Peerage*, X, p. 307, footnote c) which may excuse Lazowski for being unable to remember his name. He or his predecessor had set 'two excellent examples, building two farms that would be excellent in any country, and dividing

43. Arbroath Abbey, *drawn from* Pennant's Tour, *1772 (pt II, pl XIV). 'Its very ruins give some idea of its former magnificence: most deliciously situated.'* P. Mazell *after* Moses Griffiths.

Arbroath itself is surrounded by what seemed good farmlands, worth perhaps 20 or 25, some even 30, shillings.[42] Beside the sea, the town rises to a slight elevation, commanding extensive views. You can make out the hills of Northumberland in winter when they are snow-covered, or even on a very fine day when the horizon's clear and cloudless.[43]

Lazowski It's a little town which once had an abbey: you see the ruins from a distance and they raise false hopes.[44] It's a small market-town, with no very great

and enclosing their lands with good hedges. His farmers' prosperity was easily seen from the condition of the horses' trappings and their farming equipment, let alone the improved farming itself.'

[42] Confirmed by the brief report in *SAS*, VII, 1793, pp. 340–52: 'produces excellent crops of wheat, oats, barley, pease, rye-grass, turnip, potatoes, &c. About 1766, the magistrates planted 110 acres of muir with Scotch firs, which are thriving well and will soon be adding to the town's revenue.'

[43] I daresay the Cheviots are, as Alexandre says, visible occasionally from here. *SAS, loc cit*, claims only 'a fair and extensive prospect of the Lothian hills, the coast of Fife . . . and to the north the Grampian hills'.

[44] Lazowski meant that the ruins looked even more substantial at a distance than close to. Alexandre noticed that the ruins occupied a site of 16 acres altogether, and was amazed to hear that its rents, in its heyday, were worth 20,000 *louis*; innocently thinking, I suppose, that the abbey's endowments were limited to those 16 acres. Dr Johnson's response to these ruins was more decid-

business: the spinning and weaving of flax and hemp into cloth.[45] There is a small harbour, defended by a battery of seven cannon.[46] As we lunched, I couldn't help thinking that our host could well have been mistaken for one of the characters described by Lesage in *Gil Blas*: until then, I had never encountered in England so pretentious and bogus an innkeeper, one whose portentous manner made it hard to preserve a seemly gravity.[47] From here to Montrose the farming is without any enclosures, properly speaking: there are many great fields surrounded by dry-walling, but with different crops growing on the same field: I cannot call that 'enclosed farming'.

Montrose, The Ship   Alexandre   In the evening, when we were in Montrose, we found the lands much better farmed. They raise many cattle and send them to the north of England for fattening, though some they fatten at home with turnips or a very good kale. They manure the land for barley. Turnips they sometimes sow between two grain-harvests, and put the sheep in to feed on them. The land's worth 15 to 20 shillings, and sometimes gives good wheat harvests.[48]

edly romantic: 'I should scarcely have regretted my journey had it afforded nothing more.' Francis Grose's engraving of these ruins, of May 1789, in his *Antiquities of Scotland*, II, 1791, makes Johnson's response incomprehensible. But Griffiths and Mazell's illustration to Pennant's 1772 *Tour* (see previous page), makes Johnson's enthusiasm easier to share.

45 This sounds like an underestimate: in the year from 1790, 'the principal manufactures are sail-cloth, Osnaburghs and other Gown linens and a million and 55,000 yards of the last two in the town and immediate neighbourhood, equal in value to just under £40,000: sail-cloth to the same amount, and nearly 500 looms employed'. As at Dundee, the chief imports were flax and hemp from Russia.

46 The harbour is famous for its landing of haddock, smoked near the quay, and widely relished as 'Arbroath Smokies'. *SAS*, pp. 344–6, explains how it was strongly built of stone in 1725, small but very commodious, and with wooden gates capable of breaking the force of the sea. It also explains the occasion of the mounting of the battery of six 12-pounders. During the recent war against the French and Americans, a French privateer, the *Fearnought*, came to anchor in the bay on 23 May 1781, fired a few shots into the town, proposed a ransom of £30,000 sterling, was enraged and disappointed when they declined the deal, and began a heavy bombardment but only knocked off a few chimney-tops. After another day's bluster, the ship weighed anchor. The battery was installed 'to prevent all future insults of this kind from so mean an enemy'.

47 Early in Lesage's delightful story of *Gil Blas* (book 1, 1715, chapter 2), Gil Blas, aged 17 (one sees why Lazowski might have been thinking of him), had just set out on his mule from Oviedo, near the north coast of Spain, on his way to the university of Salamanca. He arrived at Peñaflor, stopped at the door of a decent-looking inn, and was immediately exposed to the garrulity of 'the biggest babbler in the Asturias', the innkeeper, André Corcuelo. Lazowski may have been reminded of Corcuelo at Thrapston, in Northamptonshire, at the outset of their 1785 expedition. There the innkeeper amused François 'because he irritated M de Lazowski so much: he is a prattler of the most incorrigible kind' (*Innocent Espionage*, p. 18). At Arbroath, neither Lazowski nor Alexandre names the inn where they stopped to eat. There is no longer an obvious one.

48 They may have skipped some excellent farming just before Montrose. At Inverkeillor, the minister reckoned that 'in every branch it is little inferior to the Lothians', and his neighbour, at Lunan, gave good details of all aspects of the farming, including prices of provisions, labour, etc.

Lazowski Montrose is a seaport with no defences. The town and port have one very remarkable feature. The harbour stands where the little Southesk river pours into the sea after flowing through a lake almost circular in shape and about ten miles in circumference [it is known as the Basin: Alexandre scrawled a pitiful sketch of it]. You have a quarter-mile crossing of the river by ferry to reach Montrose: a flat-bottomed boat, very difficult for the horses; it is very near the sea, and in bad weather you can't cross. This is a great nuisance for the country people south of the river who are then obliged to make a long detour to arrive at the market.[49] Montrose is inhabited by perhaps 10,000 souls. Its imports by sea consist chiefly of coal to supply the surrounding area: everything needed to supply its manufactures seems to be carted. The manufactures are chiefly all kinds of cloth, distilleries and tanneries, much like Dundee, but not so active.[50]

The Town House[51] is a fine building, in freestone: the houses are mostly stone-built, and there is one beautiful street. [*There he concludes his letter to Liancourt: Je, etc.*] *Alexandre continues*: The town is rather fine and large, with one street over a mile long: not straight, but nevertheless beautiful. The other streets are narrow, but still one would rate the town passable by English standards, and handsome by Scottish. This street leads to a point where the quay has been made for unloading the ships that, for the most part, are only single-masted. Fishing is one of the trades the men here are most involved in: the sea is full of all kinds of fish and provides them with a good living.[52]

On 19th they left Montrose   *Lazowski provided a description of the road on to Inverbervie (sometimes called Bervie), written at the inn there, which we wait for Alexandre to name:*

[49] The Southesk river bridge was built soon after their visit (1793–6, in timber, by Alexander Stevens) and replaced in 1828 (Colvin, p. 923).
[50] *SAS* (V, p. 32) gives a population of only 5,816 in 1784, and 6,194 in 1790, for the town; an extra 950 and 1,000 respectively, for the country around. The *SAS* writer considered that the population had increased more than was expected in view of the falling-off of the canvas trade when the American War ended in 1783.
[51] John Hutcheson, a Montrose surveyor and architect, was responsible for the Palladian design (Colvin, p. 524): it projects boldly into the south end of Murray Street. An upper storey was added by Wm Smith of Montrose in 1818 (Colvin, p. 903). A house was designed in Montrose High Street for Lieutenant Strachan in 1778, by Andrew Barrie, who with help from Smeaton and John Adam, designed and built in 1775 the 7-arched bridge over the Northesk river on the post-road north from Montrose. Till then it was forded, and the ford often proved fatal. The 1775 inscription near the bridge begins: 'TRAVELLERS: Pass safe and free along this Bridge . . .'
[52] *SAS* (p. 38) lists haddocks 'just now remarkably rare', mussels 'excellent', 'incredible numbers of lobsters some years ago, but no longer advantageous. Quantities of white fish, as cod, turbot &c, might be taken on the great sand banks off this coast . . . swarming with fish, but nevertheless neglected.' 'At the harbour there is a good wet dock where ships are built and repaired, not only for this but for other ports. In 1783 a plan was adopted by several gentlemen and merchants of Montrose for insuring ships and goods at sea.' In 1789, Montrose and Ferryden (beside the Southesk Ferry) had 53 ships with a tonnage of 3,543: the two Frenchmen seriously underestimated.

Lazowski The coast at Montrose is easily accessible from the sea: the beach is sandy, washed ashore here by the sea, and deposited in the form of dunes. These are just like those at Calais, and produce the same flora, though I don't see here the shrubs that contribute such useful stability to our dunes. As far as my eyes could make out, it was the coasts further down south that were more dangerous: here the rock is covered with sand and smooth pebbles. The rock lies at some depth and is completely covered.

The hills don't extend to Montrose. But when we started out from there today, immense boulders of rock were standing, mostly upright, like those we've passed; smoothed by the action of earth and water and left stripped bald, especially on top. It seems like a conglomerate[53] of sand, grit and fossil mud, and pebbles in great numbers. For a mile or two as we left, the land is flat, a great bay with a raised isle on which Montrose is built. And the soil enjoys the fertility of lands once conquered by the sea. After a few miles you descend into a narrow valley and cross over the river on a bridge built in 1775, and at least 500 feet long, with only 7 arches but very long abutments. It cost £6,500, raised by public subscription. Here are the beginnings of the public spirit that these parts need.[54]

Beyond the bridge, the farms look poor. They are spread all across the country and, so multiplied they are naturally of no great acreage. The soil is a kind of loam which, on the hillsides, becomes light and sandy. Although in southern Scotland I saw very welcome plantations of spruce and pine, I see small evidence of comparable developments up here, indeed no attempts. The further we go north, the fewer the signs of comfort; or, to be blunt, the more signs of poverty. Several cottages supply good proof. They are built of turf, the walls of thin crusts of turf laid in herringbone fashion: they are covered by wretched roofs of thatch, and a chimney made up of rotten planks bound with cords of straw, its opening crowned by a cap fixed on two hinges, so as to shut it off and keep out the wind when the fire wasn't alight.

The people live miserably, yet on this part of the coast there are fish for the taking, which is their staple food, with potatoes and oat-cake. We're here for the night in the one inn in the place. Compared with the English inns this is pitiful, but it's very much better than the great majority of those on the Continent that are away from the main roads. Here we have good bread, game, good beer, wine, and even a sweet course, like having redcurrant jelly with our tea; but this is a Scottish usage with which one mustn't argue. For breakfast we are given various kinds of dry cakes

53 At Kinneff, just beyond Inverbervie. The *SAS* author described this conglomerate as 'rock of the plum-pudding kind'.
54 This is the bridge by Andrew Barrie, referred to in footnote 51. It marked the north boundary of Montrose parish, also Angus's shire boundary with Kincardine. At the south end of the bridge, an inscription in marble, framed in freestone with a curved coping that in 1999 needed urgent repair, refers to the 'active public spirit' of the promoters, and the cost: £6,500. Lazowski clearly stopped to read it. There were two 'mason-undertakers' – Barrie of Montrose and Patrick Brown of Dryburgh. Modern traffic deters this reading.

[scones], with butter and jam, usually orange [marmalade], which is what we are given with tea in the evening.

An indication of the poverty here is the lack of commerce, and how often there seem to be few people about: it is not just the emptiness of the roads but the fact that there are no turnpikes. Bervie is what we would call a good village, but it is dignified with the name of town.[55]

Inverbervie, The Ship   Alexandre   The town's so small that, in France, we would call it a village. A little stream runs in a narrow valley, valuable for the very fine trout swimming in it, and also for two or three mills: a bleaching-place for cloth and two fulling-mills.[56] I'll give some details of these for I was taken with them. We're looking at the making of three different cloths: those made from hemp, coarse, such as ships' sails, dish-cloths, &c; those made of fine hemp or ordinary flax, such as are made into clothes for servants; and then all the finer table-linen that they reckon they make here better than anywhere. These three different types of cloth involve three quite different preparations.

The most common don't go to the fuller at all and are bleached only twice – in great bleaching-pans of which the first is of copper, the second of wood. These serve to remove any remaining dirt and give it the degree of clean-ness required before drying. They are passed twice through this simple process. The second type of cloth goes once through the fulling-mill and then to the bleaching-house. There it goes through three processes, mixing in with the usual ashes [*cendre*] a yellowish powder I didn't recognise. The same operation is repeated three times. Then it's dried, and when it's half-dried, it's taken to be washed, with soap, then dried again.

[55] Bervie is the only royal burgh in the county of the Mearns (Kincardine). Its charter was granted by King David II in 1342: *SAS* XIII, 1794, p. 2, which adds: 'the burgh consists of three streets, which form nearly 3 sides of a square'. This describes the present, rather forlorn, market-place.

[56] *SAS*, XIII, p. 4, mentioned a new lint(flax)-mill, two mills for cutting barley, and an ancient corn-mill, but no fulling-mill: also 'a regular bleachfield'. Further on, Alexandre cancels one of his two fulling-mills. *SAS*, XIII, p. 3, mentioned a firm of sailcloth makers from Montrose setting up here in 1750, but closing down c1782. However, the weavers themselves continued the purchase, spinning, weaving and bleaching of flax on their own account (*ibid*) and they are presumably some of the people Alexandre describes making his second type of cloth. *SAS* (*ibid*) also mentioned a manufacture of coloured threads, established in 1779 and 'still carried on' and developing ambitiously in 1794. This was missed by both Alexandre and Lazowski, but Alexandre contributes valuably to our knowledge of cloth-making in the little town in 1786. He also named the inn, where Lazowski gave such rare details of the simple hospitality. *SAS*, XIII, p. 5, recorded five alehouses 'besides the tavern, which is intended for the accommodation of travellers, and the genteeler sort of company in the town and neighbourhood'. That tallies with Alexandre's *Ship*. But the only feasible 'tavern' going back to the 18th century that survives today is the modest 'Salutation Hotel'.

The mills are now represented by a collection of sorry-looking industrial buildings clustered 30 feet beneath the road bridge of 1935. In 1786, travellers crossed the steep ravine by a 2-arched bridge of 1696, the central pier of which is embodied in its successor of 1799: *SAS*, XIII, p. 12, noted five years earlier that His Majesty has been pleased to give £1,000 towards the intended new bridge, and that committees were considering 'the propriety of establishing turnpikes in the county'.

In order to achieve the third, finest, cloth they pass it twice through the fulling process and through the bleaching-field as often as six times. They throw fresh water on it all the time they are drying it in the sun: this is to prevent the cloth from expanding, and to make it form one single consistency, as far as possible. This cloth was the dearest and the most highly thought of.

Each independent weaver brings his cloth and has it washed and bleached and from there takes it to market at Montrose[57] where often it is exported to London or abroad. For bleaching and preparing one piece of the first cloth, one charges 4 sols; the second, 7 sols; and often, for the finest, when it's superb, 18 sols; and less, according to quality. The fulling-mill is the only one for 15 miles around here; it serves the individual weavers and it costs a lot to maintain the water power. The Bervie stream becomes torrential with the melting of the snows. A man told me his master would have given up a long time ago if it hadn't been for the quantity of cloth arriving steadily all the time, and always having more business than he could take. In a good year they hope to make enough to recoup all their losses. They showed me the warehouse in which I saw some superb cloth. The one fault I could see was that it turns out, in general, too loose-woven. I suppose that comes from their stretching too much on squares of wood as part of the drying process.

On 20th April they left Inverbervie for Aberdeen   *It is hard to reconcile Lazowski's account of the start of the day's journey (written that evening in Aberdeen) with the* SAS *description of the parish of Kinneff, its church 2 miles north-east of the burgh of Bervie (VI, 1793, pp. 197–211). The parish ran 5 miles along the coast from the river Bervie. The Rev Mr Stewart in the* SAS *recorded: 'There are only 2 or 3 small rivulets in the parish, which, by means of dams, make shift to turn water-mills, principally in the winter season . . . There are about 20 weavers, chiefly employed in manufacturing sacking and ticking, which are the ordinary cloth[e]s made for sale in this parish.' This hardly tallies with Lazowski's:*

As you leave Bervie you climb a fairly steep hill and drop into a very narrow valley where the stream supplies the water-power for a fulling-mill, a bleaching-house and a mill. [*But Lazowski then wondered if he wasn't mistaken and had, perhaps, seen the bleaching-house the previous evening. It was presumably the one carefully looked at by Alexandre. One guesses that Lazowski may have been regretting his failure to describe it, for he blusters:*] To tell the truth, you could study the business most comprehensively in the standard treatise on it written by Dr Home.[58]

Here the depopulated lands begin;[59] already they interrupt the cultivated farm-

57 This bears out *SAS*'s account of a weekly market being attempted at Bervie c1764 and not succeeding.

58 Dr Francis Home (1719–1813), a fellow of the Edinburgh College of Physicians, won a gold medal in 1757 for an essay on the principles of agriculture. The previous year, he had won a gold medal from the trustees for the improvement of agriculture in North Britain, for his essay *Experiments in Bleaching*, which was translated into French and German. The point of Lazowski's tour was its first-hand observations!

59 It's the beginning of the grim saga of the depopulation of the Highlands. Stonehaven is the town and harbour at the north-east corner of the parish of Dunottar which suffered by being sold

lands, becoming difficult to clean and get back into good order; already they convey an air of poverty, though the lands are perfectly cultivable. A few houses are better kept and planted and around them the farming is rather better, breaking a sad uniformity. After nine miles you arrive at Stonehaven.

Stonehaven   is a little town with what is more of a creek than a harbour.[60] It is frequented by sloops bringing coal and loading up with grain and fabrics from these parts. It is a very jolly little place, better built than its size would lead you to expect. Cloth-making is established on a good footing: they have put up large wooden sheds, well lit by glass, to display their goods. The lower floor is divided into small rooms where the craftspeople work. In Stonehaven I was surprised to find a good wheeled plough in use. They've adopted it chiefly to enable them to plough more deeply, which they are able to do much more regularly than is usual in Scotland. They usually plough to a depth of ten inches, and one reason is that if the wheat seed, for example, isn't planted to that depth, it will suffer badly from the frosts; and this way their oats and barley suffer much less from the winds that batter the coast; finally, of course, they loosen up a thicker bed.

From Stonehaven to Aberdeen, 17 miles,[61] there is only one house where one can break the journey: less a house than a cabin. However, we found there a stable with stalls, a servant, and good hay and oats. But it's a poor inn, unsupplied with bread, so that we had to make do with oat-cake. And yet there wasn't too much to complain of: one can dine well enough, with veal cutlets, fresh eggs and slices of grilled beef.[62] The circumstance of this solitary inn gives you a clear idea of this stretch of country:

to the York Building Company as part of the Highland forfeitures after the 1715 Jacobite rising. The Company's affairs fell into disorder about 1740, and with the sales of their lands the cottagers were evicted and moved into the town. To begin with, the process looked promising in economic, if not humane, terms: enclosure and planting was reported in Dunottar in the *SAS* (XI, p. 223). 'The culture of turnips has been greatly extended, which here succeed remarkably well.' That was in 1794. Already the Great Cheviot sheep had been established in the Highlands, and stood ready to replace the Highlanders.

[60] *SAS* describes it as having 'the best natural situation – a basin sheltered from the SE by a very high rock standing out into the sea: on the NE there is a quay, which in some measure defends it from that quarter. If the present quay were extended and another built opposite, vessels could lie in perfect safety . . . There is not a harbour betwixt Forth and Cromarty that vessels in distress can so easily get into.' A mile south of the harbour stood the ruins of Dunottar castle on a large flat-topped rock jutting into the sea, divided from the land by a deep chasm. In *SAS*, the minister, Mr Walker, described it as 'one of the most majestic ruins in Scotland', and noted its 17th-century history as safe shelter of the regalia of Scotland against the Roundheads in 1651, and barbarous prison of 167 Presbyterians in 1685. He ended with an eloquent plea to preserve 'the temperate and healthy family of the country labourer or tradesman . . . to cultivate our fields or defend our property in the time of danger'.

[61] Only 14 miles on Taylor and Skinner's map.

[62] Alexandre's account differs: 'Dined at an inn in the middle of the fields and called "The Halfway House": it was only a cottage. We were scarcely able to dine, for we had no bread, and wretched meat. Only the beer was passably good.' I think this may be what appeared on pl 31 of Taylor and Skinner's road maps in 1776 as Jeally Brans Inn (it was 5½ miles from Stonehaven, 8½ from Aberdeen).

it's very hilly, often with bog at the foot of the slopes, and often nothing but peat the only fuel available.

Everywhere, from the hilltops to the lowest places, the surface is covered by great numbers of rounded stones: much more than I mentioned earlier. They are mostly of large sizes, sometimes enormous smoothed boulders. Their material is very varied, from granite to composite, and all colours: I'd bring you a collection if we had room. Of course they are used – in road-making, houses, field-enclosures, and one could build whole towns with them.

I've said nothing to you about plantations. I've already seen some that are immense, and well fenced and well maintained. These afforestations are the potential cause of retarding great agricultural advances. This is a question hard to resolve, and I don't lose sight of it.

Two miles from Aberdeen, you cross the river Dee on an ancient bridge of seven great arches: it would do honour to modern architecture for its grace and remarkable lightness: and it is perfectly flat, like those we build today.[63]

ABERDEEN   Aberdeen is generally reckoned one of the principal towns of Scotland: some would rank it second. It has a university and sea-port. It is the seat of a bishop; but you know the Scottish hatred of bishops, so that doesn't count in its favour.

It's a long time since our eyes have been delighted by a place that's active and lively: here I find myself in a new country. There are two Aberdeens, the old town and the new, and they are about a mile apart. Has the river changed its course? It seems impossible. Has a new site been chosen for convenience of navigation and the possession of a port? That seems very likely. But it is what one sees that naturally takes over.[64]

---

63 The bridge was begun and endowed by the admirable William Elphinstone, bishop of Dundee 1488–1514: he also added a great steeple at the east end of his cathedral and furnished it with 14 bells; and he was founder of King's College at Aberdeen, 1498, modelling it on Paris and Bologna, but with stipends for teachers of theology, canon and civil law, medicine, language and philosophy. He was largely responsible for the introduction of printing in Edinburgh. The bridge was completed by his successor, Bishop Gavin Dunbar (1518–32) to whom it has often been attributed. Dunbar, too, embellished St Machar's cathedral and endowed a hospital for 12 poor old men.

64 The explanation of the distance between the two Aberdeens seems simple enough: Old Aberdeen grew at the mouth of the Don, which reached the sea 3 miles north of the Dee (according to Taylor and Skinner: 1¼ miles according to *SAS*, XIX, 1797, p. 144). Beside the Dee, the new Aberdeen grew. The Don had smaller potential for a harbour. The names Old and New Aberdeen were in familiar use in 1786, but Old Aberdeen still featured in *SAS* as Old Machar, after St Machar who, in the 6th century, came to Iona with Columba, and then came to evangelise the Picts around Aberdeen. Water from his well was used for baptism in Aberdeen cathedral in Old Machar (Farmer, *Oxford Dictionary of Saints*). In New Aberdeen, or 'the city', the ancient church of St Nicholas was pulled down and rebuilt in 1751 from designs given gratis in 1741 by the celebrated architect James Gibbs, son of an Aberdeen merchant and educated at Marischal College in the 1690s (Colvin's great *Dictionary of British Architects*, 1995 edn, p. 399). It is now St Nicholas West Church. (St Nicholas East Church was built in 1835, rebuilt to same design 1874.)

44. *Castlegate, Aberdeen, 1812. The New Inn, 1755, adjoins the Tolbooth (tower and spire): shaped gable facing this way marked by Venetian window in upper floor.*

Alexandre's arrival in Aberdeen was less rhetorical and much more matter-of-fact.

Alexandre In the evening we were in Aberdeen. The route very hilly and stony and bad for our gig. Four miles out you descend a very long hill, with the right-hand side[65] all planted with evergreen trees, and on the other side it's uncultivated, a land that's not been farmed, but someone is building a wall round fields with the stones removed from them. In the bottom of the valley runs the river Dee, very wide and beautiful: crossed by a fine paved bridge, by which you arrive. I imagine the river's teeming with fish, judging by the number of little boats and nets on the water, and men fishing. The current is rapid and I should think it's dangerous at high water. The bridge is a mile out of town.[66]

Aberdeen, New Inn. 20 April Aberdeen occupies an amphitheatre above the river (Dee) and facing south. One discovers beautiful streets and a very large market-place.[67] It is all well-built, especially the new town, which is very considerable, and expanding every day.

[65] Taylor and Skinner suggest that he may, in the excitement of arrival, have confused left with right!
[66] Taylor and Skinner put two miles between Dee bridge and the town in 1776. Alexandre was looking at Aberdeen, not the map.
[67] Its polygonal market-cross was designed and built in 1686 by John Montgomery, an Aberdeenshire stonemason. They had a good view of it from their hotel in Castlegate, which is a continuation of the great open space of the market-place.

149

Lazowski   The whole space between the town and the river Dee is now well-built, and a very beautiful road leads to the harbour. This is on the N side of the mouth of the river, and furnished with a fine long quay alongside which the boats come to moor for loading and unloading.[68] They have all the facilities for speeding up the work. The quay is largely built-up, but they have left plenty of space: there's a sugar refinery, and large storehouses for grain and fish. Large numbers of ships use the port, in which there are many colliers [*sloops charbonniers*].[69] It's an ordinary sight, but what you'd never guess is that the coal they're importing comes from Newcastle, and not Scotland, for it's worth much more. It's at a premium so high that we in France are far from understanding, in terms of its importance for England. Nevertheless this coal has to pay 3 shillings and threepence a ton once it passes north of the Red Head [between Arbroath and Montrose]: this is intended to discourage export and preserve to English manufacturers the advantage of this superior coal. Yet Scotland has a coal-bed 69 miles wide by about 170 miles running west, and, as far as one can judge, it's been reckoned there's enough to last 1000 years. It runs at such a depth that there's no fear of the supply ending. Scottish coal seems to be, in general, less hard than the English stuff, but it burns with a clear flame and a good light. Some specimens of Scottish coal are smooth and polished like jade: they come from a different seam and a different area, and sell chiefly as luxury objects in London. It's confidently said that certain Scottish coals keep away rats, which are allegedly not to be found in colliers carrying it: I do not guarantee the truth of this. I can't think how I deviated into coal, and return at once to Aberdeen.

The town is certainly distinguished among its neighbours in Scotland; although it's extensive and composed of houses of the local stone,[70] it makes only a modest

---

68 The harbour-mouth had been dangerously subject to shifting in rough weather. A new pier was designed by the able engineer John Smeaton (1724–92) in 1775 and finished in 1780. 'It extended 1200 feet along the N side of the river and a considerable way into the sea, and a jetty was added to shelter the shipping within the harbour from the violent inrun of the sea in strong easterly winds' (*SAS*, XIX, p. 154). The Harbour Plan, 1773, exhibited in Aberdeen's excellent Maritime Museum, shows Smeaton's design for the N pier, built 1775–81, 'to scour the sandbar and provide a deeper channel'. A Harbour Plan of 1810 reveals 'the new quay for loading and unloading'. A Prospective View of New Aberdeen, engraved c1790 for *The Complete English Traveller*, makes very clear the daunting complexity of approaching the harbour through islands at the mouths of the river, while imperturbable men stood fishing on the banks with rod-and-line, and a net.

69 It is something of a relief to be able to record that neither of the Frenchmen noticed, or at least didn't bother to report, the batteries erected by the town in 1781–2, for defence of the shipping and harbour: ten new iron cannon, 12 pounders. Also two 3 pounders; and 400 stand of small arms in the town's armoury. All proudly announced in *SAS*, XIX, 1797, p. 164.

70 Alexandre notes, briefly, that 'all the hills round here are of a kind of granite', but neither of them refers to the effects of this on the appearance of the town, nor on its economy. *SAS*, XIX, pp. 157–8, admirably makes good: 'Granite abounds in this parish. There are excellent quarries of it at . . . besides plenty of outliers in the hill of Grandhome. The annual rent of these amounts to about £80 sterling and about 100 men are constantly employed . . . Our granite is much harder to work than freestone, and is capable by much labour of receiving a very fine polish. It is generally of a grey colour, and is mixed with shining talcky particles which give it, when well dressed, a considerable degree of lustre. About 12,000 tons of stone are annually exported from Aberdeen and are valued at 14s a ton, amounting to £8,400.' Dr Johnson noted its use in 'the new pavement of

comparison with England. It manufactures coarse draperies for local consumption, and also makes very much cloth. They double the threads precisely as silk-weavers do, and by the same means: proof that this manufacture is of some importance.[71]

The University consists of two colleges: one in the New Aberdeen, its building less than mediocre; the other is the old university college founded in 1477, its building properly designed but of great simplicity. The library is kept in an ancient chapel, with the room for the hearing of theses and awarding of degrees: it's there that the scholars of the other college come for their degrees. The library is well-arranged, with perhaps 20,000 volumes, mostly classics though everything modern is here since a library law was passed under, I think, Queen Anne. The student members of the university borrow books from this library in return for entering their names and the book-titles in a register. This college admits young men as boarders for £5 sterling per quarter. The studies are highly respected, and foreigners come to work here.

There is also the charitable educational establishment founded by a Gordon, which takes in the sons of freemen of the town without payment. They are taught to write, read and count. Certainly this instruction would have been excellent in an age of illiteracy, but today this looks like a bad use of funds. It's a fine building.[72]

London'. Here, 'they shape it easily. It is beautiful and it must be very lasting.' *Journey to the Western Isles*, 1990 edn, p. 11.

[71] *SAS* amplifies (pp. 178–9): 'Many of our manufactures, especially the bleaching and thread-making businesses, employ a much greater number of women than of men; and the great manufacture of the place, the knitting of stockings, is carried on almost entirely by females.' Why had the Frenchmen missed 'the great manufacture of the place'? They certainly didn't miss it in Leicester, the previous year. I suppose they were deliberately trying to concentrate on agriculture, Mr Lazowski's mission. *SAS* went on to explain how the cheapness and commodiousness of the houses, and the high chance of finding employment 'induced many old women, and many widows and daughters of farmers and tradesmen, to come in from the country and reside in this parish, while their sons have either settled as farmers or gone abroad, or entered into the army or navy'. Alexandre's only observation on the (predominantly) womenfolk was that they were no longer all barefooted, and that, instead of the plaid they'd worn on their backs, they were wearing a lightweight brown cloth made into a cloak and hood exactly like the Carmelite habit.

[72] He seems not to have stepped inside. In 1730, Robert Gordon, merchant in Aberdeen, founded and endowed 'an Hospital for the maintenance of indigent boys in Aberdeen', being the sons and grandsons of tradesmen, freemen, burgesses etc. In 1732 the Governors obtained a charter of incorporation as President and Governors of the 'Hospital'. It bears that date over the front door, beneath a fine full-length sculpture of the founder. The Governors of the Hospital decided in 1753 to erect a statue of their founder, and applied for a design from John Cheere, head of the Hyde Park Corner business associated with his better-known brother, Sir Henry. In December 1930, Mrs Esdaile wrote, in *The Gordonian*, 'The scheme so closely recalls the statue of Sir Thomas Molyneux at Armagh of the previous year, 1752, that I had no hesitation in saying that it was designed and I thought carved by Roubiliac.' Rupert Gunnis included Thomas Molyneux, but omitted this work from his *Dictionary*, presumably because he hadn't managed to inspect it and find it signed. Two years later, Roubiliac carved his great statue of Newton for Trinity College, Cambridge. *SAS*, XIX, pp. 186–7, reported: 'There are at present maintained, clothed and educated in it 60 boys, at an expense of upwards £1,000 sterling.' The branches of education taught in the hospital were very remarkable: 'reading English, English grammar, writing, arithmetic, book-keeping, the elements of geometry, navigation, geography, French,

To give you a more complete idea of this country, I must give you the general prices of provisions in this capital town, sea-port and university town:

	s	d
1lb loaf of wheat-bread sells @		2
1lb beef		4
1lb mutton		4½ and 5
1lb veal		4 and 4½
1lb butter		7½ and 10
1 bottle of milk		1
1 stone of hay		6
1 stone of straw, between		6 – 12
1 boll[73] of wheat	20	
1 boll of barley	15 – 16	
1 boll of oats	10 – 12	
1 boll of oat-flour, variable quality	13, 14, 16	

House-rents in Aberdeen vary between £10 and £60: a good house averages £15 to £20.[74]

I must explain these measures. The *livre* [1lb weight] here is what they call the Dutch pound: 19 ounces plus something: not quite 20. The stone here, instead of 14 pounds, as in England, is 32 pounds. The boll is more than 5 bushels, or one and a quarter *sétiers*: it weighs at least 350 lbs. This is the actual dearest price of the year. Straw's regarded as exorbitant, and hay is dearer than in other years.

But if provisions are very cheap, the cost of living is even more below the lowest cost in England: so that with £100 sterling one can live in this country in the same style as you could in England with £400 – indeed even better. And I'm not thinking of London, but of general costs in England.

I judge this with some assurance: the cost of travel is a good touch-stone, and travelling here works out in general at a shilling a head for what would cost us at least 3 shillings in England. As you know, apart from the cost of necessities, this *difference* in the general costs is fundamental. *Je . . . etc.*

---

church-music; and such of the boys as discover a genius for it are instructed in drawing also'. It is disappointing that such a school should have been so offensively dismissed in a letter to Alexandre's father, who himself was the founder in France of *l'Ecole nationale des arts et métiers*. One can only suppose that he was trying to see and report too much in too short a time. Such an example of his misrepresentation is worrying, but is fortunately unusual.

73 A boll is 'a measure of capacity for grain &c, containing in Scotland 6 imperial bushels' (*OED*). But see Lazowski's equivalents below.

74 Alexandre also reproduced these costs, and added agreeable details of Aberdeen's New Inn: 'We have had, Mr de Lazowski and I, at supper, a roast chicken, a lobster, veal cutlets, potatoes and carrots for, between the 2 of us, 36 *sols*' (roughly 36 pence).

45. *Bridge of Don or Brig o' Balgownie, built by Bishop Henry de Cheyn over the Don, north of Aberdeen. Arch 60 feet high, span 70 feet. Engraving by H Wallis from a drawing by W. Purser, c1810: see title-page.*

Alexandre: On the 21st we left Aberdeen   and slept at Old Meldrum, 17 miles on. You leave by a very long suburb, and then after a mile Old Aberdeen, a little town, its paving very bad and its streets very narrow. When you've left the Old Town, you see on the left a gentleman's house, down low, looking very handsome.[75] Farther on, you cross the river Don by a very fine bridge.[76] It flows through a valley full of rocks, a picturesque sight, and serves this place, where it flows into the sea, as a port full of 3 little ships. Further on, you leave the coast road we've followed for so long, and take the road leading off slightly to the left for *Old Meldrum*. You enter a stony, hilly country. The roads here are deplorable: too many great stones are capable of capsizing our poor gig, which is so light without any of us in it.

   Three miles from Aberdeen you find a really handsome plantation, about 20 years old. Beside our road we found a workman making a wall to enclose part of a

[75] On Taylor and Skinner's map, pl 31, this seems to be a reference to the valley of the Don, with a house called Seaton, in a park; owned or occupied in 1776 by Lady Diana Middleton.
[76] It survives, though its old stone roadway is barely one carriage wide: a very striking single-arched bridge of c1320, the arch sharply pointed about 60 ft above the dark river, the span some 72 ft. According to tradition, it was built with revenues accumulated in the Aberdeen bishopric of Henry de Cheyn (1282–1328), exiled during the displeasure of the king, Robert Bruce, who restored him to favour in December 1318. The river is now effectively overshadowed here by trees, in contrast to its rather naked appearance at the time of Pennant's 1769 *Tour* (Pl XX).

common that seemed entirely covered in stones. We got into conversation. It's important to notice that what I'm describing is only 3 or 4 miles out of Aberdeen. It's only about 20 years ago that someone made the serious decision to take these lands in hand.[77] They were, as so often, commons all covered with rocks. Cultivation was steadily increased, with more clearance every day: in 30 or 40 years the whole countryside may be cleared.

Before you can start, you have to remove the stones, and make a wall to serve as field-enclosure. Luckily the rocks lie only on the surface: they're easily removed. You then apply manure: no burning, as in other places when the stubble and muck are spread. Then ploughing, and the sowing of either turnips or potatoes. The work of clearance costs about 12 or 13 *louis* an acre. Once the wall is up and the ground prepared, a rent of 2 *louis* soon repays capital outlay. The turnips feed the cattle and the potatoes go to market. Some person, or gentleman, may give an acre or so to pigs, but this isn't a general practice.

They enlarge all the time, and the land finds itself better occupied than with the plough. (Alternative rotations are given.) You can get a workman for 6 pence, and in summer a shilling. I don't understand how the lands are all so dear when the peasants, and even farmers, are so poor, and look it.

For the rest of the day's journey the land was hardly cultivated at all – most of it deserted and covered with wretched grass: houses infrequent, country hilly, large plantations – but they seem even rarer. The landscape is cut across by a great many streams (*torrents*), often considerable, but the whole aspect of the country is so awful that the pleasure of travelling is nil. Even the animals are hardly to be seen, and the ones that are are mangy-looking. However, I can tell you that the women up here seem to have become extremely pretty, and much more 'my type'. They're not like the dirty and ugly creatures we found in the Edinburgh neighbourhood.

Old Meldrum, The Ship[78]   The town of Old Meldrum is tiny[79] and shouldn't be called a town. There are only two streets, very ill-favoured. It stands on the slope of a hill and looks over a valley: dry and arid, and everything here seems ugly.

We're in a dreadful inn. However, our hostess is beautiful, with a very pretty daughter who waits on us, very good-natured. So although we are extremely ill-accommodated, we pass the time very pleasantly. We had no bread, only oats, the appearance of which alarmed us: we make the best of it [*nous sommes des bonnes*].

---

77 From Taylor and Skinner's map this is evidently the enterprise of Mr Skene at Park Hill and Rosehall. He emerges in the *SAS* account of this parish, Fintray (III, 1792, p. 238) as Mr Skene of Skene and owner ('heritor') of nearly one-third of the parish's 10,000 acres. Park Hill is still (1999) notably well-planted, in strong contrast with the neighbouring countryside.
78 Old Meldrum now has no Ship Inn. The Meldrum Arms presents a cheerful face to visitors arriving from Aberdeen (with, by coincidence, a small early-20th-century statue of a French sailor). Morris's Hotel ('founded 1673') stands, less cheerful, at the other end of the little town.
79 *SAS*, XIII, 1794, pp. 154–5, says the population in 1785 was 775. It became a 'burgh of barony' in 1672. *SAS* recorded 'a very good weekly market, for all kinds of provisions, the best in the county N of Aberdeen'.

On the 22nd   we left our charming lodgings in Old Meldrum and dined at *Chapel Seggatt*[80] on the road to Banff: journey 27 miles. The road is much better: we've left all those stones, and although the country's pretty uncultivated, having a black soil (?peat) above the deep rock-foundation, for this part of our road I find myself in Paradise[81] after the dreariness of the last 3 or 4 days. The views over the landscape are very melancholy, almost wholly uncultivated and extremely hilly, but after nine miles you find a little village[82] very nicely built, and from there, on your left hand, two hills and the valley that separates them all in a plantation of Lord Gordon;[83] in trees, very fine, and surrounded by a good wall, which gives you a splendid glimpse. On the right you see the owner's house which is simple, old, but very beautiful.[84] And his lands you see as far as Chapel,[85] which is only an assemblage of 7 or 8 houses. His farm lands are not very good here. They are worth 2 to 20 shillings.[86] They have very little wheat: the lands wouldn't support it. It is still astonishing that one finds an inch of cultivation in all this countryside, and this points to the large number of young plantations along our route. My opinion is that in a very little while all this country will be cultivated and notably, recognisably, but much more in plantations than in the other forms.[87]

On the road to Banff we passed through *Turriff*, a little town, unremarkable. From there to Banff is hilly, the road good, but the hills very vertical and steep: the land is cut into by many streams and occupied by woods.

As you approach Banff you see the sea ahead, suddenly. The town, well-built, stands on a rock; and nearby stands the house of Lord Fife, half a mile below the town, beside the Deveron river. It's a small square building set within four narrow

[80] The Chapel of Seggat is marked on Taylor and Skinner, 11 miles north of Old Meldrum, in the valley of the little river Ythan; 3 miles north of Fyvie. Banff lay a further 15 miles north.
[81] Spelt, teasingly, 'la perrad is': induced perhaps by his thoughts of Old Meldrum *Ship*.
[82] The little village, Fyvie, stood in a parish 13 miles by 8: 20 or 22,000 acres, 8,000 possibly being farmed, 1,200 in plantations and natural woods (*SAS*, IX, 1793, p. 459).
[83] 'Lord Gordon' is only the Hon Colonel (William) Gordon on Taylor and Skinner's 1776 map. he had become the Hon General Gordon by 1793 (*SAS*, p. 461), and as one of the Gentlemen of George III's Bedchamber he was then residing 'only occasionally at Fyvie Castle, which stands in a fertile and pleasant plain on the banks of the Ithan; the surrounding eminences being covered with firs and other forest trees. When the addition at present making to the house is finished, it will be one of the largest and most commodious houses in the county' (Aberdeenshire). *SAS* adds (p. 463) 'the church is one of the best and most commodious old churches in the county. The manse was built in 1762. Near the church are the ruins of a priory, said to have been founded in 1172.'
[84] It was being furnished with two new chimney-pieces in 1773 by James Byres, son of a local Jacobite laird; and again refurbished in 1793 (*SAS*).
[85] ? Chapel of Seggat.
[86] The Rev William Moir, compiler of the *SAS* entry, was a man after the Frenchmen's hearts: a meeting with him would seriously have delayed them. He said (p. 460) 'The soil is various, but in general kindly and yields pretty good early crops of bear [barley] and oats, especially near the church and Fyvie castle. The remote parts, near the mosses and moors, are of a colder nature, but capable of improvement, and a great part has of late been considerably improved, there being few or none of the farmers who have not a part of their fields in turnips or potatoes and afterwards laid down in clover and rye grass. The writer of this was among the first who set them the example.'
[87] Ten years later, Mr Moir (see footnote 86) more than justified Alexandre's optimism.

square towers that rise a little above the rest of the house.[88] It is said to be beautiful but I'm not sure. The garden and park are simple and extensive, occupying the bottom of the valley and the banks of the river over which Lord Fife has built a very handsome bridge leading to the town.[89]

Banff, The Cross Keys[90]   Banff is small but pretty, built on a rock on a slight rise above the sea. Its harbour is extraordinary, made up of three different basins, all open: not very big.[91] It had only five ships in it when I was there. All the town's streets are straight, beautifully built and broad. I'm told it's a fashionable place to reside in, and I saw a lot of beautiful women promenading in the streets, which is perhaps the best indicator.

It has a large cotton manufacture, but nothing else.[92] As in all these parts, the cloth is beautifully finished, yet nothing out of the ordinary.

88 'small square building' reads oddly until you remember the size and grandeur of Alexandre's home at Liancourt (see Pl 1). John Clerk of Eldin's beautiful hand-coloured engraving of Banff, c1805, hangs (1999) in the study off the Outer Library in Duff House and shows the house before the present mature frame of trees had even been planted. It did look naked and *comparatively* small, and was of course designed to stand between two substantial wings. At the outside of the two front towers, you can see where a dispute over costs cut off the wings just as they were sprouting. In 1798, *SAS* (XX, p. 324) described it as the earl of Fife's principal seat, 'well-known, with the beautiful scenery of the park, to the tourist', and adds a brief account of the interior and pictures. The design was by the elder Adam, William (1689–1748): a lawsuit about his payment showed that he also designed a temple and a triumphal arch for the grounds. Without its wings, Duff House is a strikingly dramatic vertical building, with an echo of Castle Howard. If Adam's wings *had* sprouted, his drawings show how little they would have had of Vanbrugh's sense of proportion and instinctive grace. The formidable work of rescuing and restoring the building was undertaken by Historic Scotland, with regional and district councils helping with the running costs. The National Galleries of Scotland organise the pictures and furnishing, so that the house has been open since 1995 with the hospitable atmosphere of one in which the original family is still involved: quite a co-operative achievement for national and local institutions.

89 It's a 7-arched bridge by John Smeaton, a smaller version of the one they'd seen at Perth. Its position near Duff House made it look like a Fife garden-ornament, but it saw the main post-road over a previously troublesome river, and was properly paid for from government funds. The park measured 14 miles in circumference: 'extensive' was not an exaggeration.

90 No trace of the Cross Keys in Directories etc. Boswell and Johnson found the Black Bull 'indifferent'. Cross Keys may have gone out of fashion; Alexandre didn't often misremember.

91 The coast from the harbour westwards is bold and rocky. The three basins set firmly in the rock are now sheltered by pier breakwaters.

92 I suppose they were covering too much ground and missing things. *SAS*, twelve years later, recorded quietly: 'The thread and linen manufactures were carried on here a few years ago to a very great extent, the threads when sent to Nottingham or Leicester were valued at £30,000 sterling. This production has given way to stocking manufacture, weaving on 150 highly improved frames to make silk, cotton and worstead stockings.' They missed the late Lord Findlater's experimental farms here, notably Colleonard, 'it bears a striking resemblance to a fine English farm' (*SAS*, p. 328; also Souter, *General View of Agriculture of Banffshire*, 1812, pp. 72–3): just what Lazowski was looking out for. At Colleonard too, half a mile south-west of the town, Mr Reid had begun a remarkable nursery, c1768: from that nursery, a Mr Garden alone had planted almost 2 million trees by 1798. (Colleonard now has a sculpture garden.) Another sign of the Frenchmen's too great haste is that what they were careful to record in Arbroath, they very uncharacteristically failed to notice in Banff: a small battery mounted on high ground immediately inland behind the harbour:

On the 23rd we left very early   Our plan was to go for lunch at *Cullen*, 12 miles, and then on to dine at *Fochabers*, and on again to sleep at *Elgin*, a journey of 32 miles. But as we got lost[93] we were obliged to dine at Cullen and stay at Fochabers, only 25 miles. At the outset, you cross the park and farm of Lord Fife, in very good order. But from there you fall into a land that's nothing but commons to within 4 miles of Cullen. The sea's on our right, and on our left the land, generally well farmed, the houses better built. [*Just before Cullen, Lazowski noted in Portsoy an entire newly-built street.*[94]]

Cullen is a pleasant small town in a little valley, with nothing memorable. The surrounding landscape is beautiful, the land worth 30 shillings an acre, and elsewhere 15. The farms are biggish, 100–200 acres. On a farm of 150 acres, they have as many as 30 bullocks or cows, trained to draw the plough up to 6 or 7 years: after that, they fatten them up on turnips. They have no, or at least few, sheep, and those small and pitiful. They've raised a breed of cattle for Lord Fife's herd. Lord Findlater, whose seat is here,[95] helps with the speading of a better breed *gratis*. The last had 2 bullocks that sold at 105 *louis* the pair.

Along the road to *Fochabers*, you follow the plantations of Lord Findlater, pass some land only a part of which is cultivated, and then you fall into the immense plantations of the duke of Gordon, who only began them 23 years ago: they are superb, truly measureless, covering the hills and valleys. He has also done much clearing, but he rents his lands so high that they become little pieces of 15 or 20 *arpents*, so that in spite of the apparent good he has done the district he is far from being popular. I suppose he makes great revenues with all his plantations which, they say, bring in 20,000 *louis* in rents. One sees here that if you expand your wealth at the expense of your tenants, you are not well recompensed, losing their goodwill.

two 18-pounders, four 12-pounders and two field pieces. It had been mounted in 1781 during the War of American Independence, and still had an extensive command of the bay in 1798 (*SAS*, p. 359), 'though whether it would prove of substantial service in the event of invasion is a point somewhat problematical'. The guns were removed in 1815, and the buildings leased as a coast-guard and preventive station.

[93] How *could* they get lost? Between Banff and Cullen they only had to keep the coastline in view.
[94] It is no longer clear which this was.
[95] Another of his seats was Banff castle, 'a plain modern building' of c1750 set agreeably in the town within part of the castle's ancient wall. Lord Findlater's benefactions were legendary. *SAS* XII, 1794, p. 145, remembered this: 'Before 1748, the inhabitants of *Cullen* were as poor and idle as any set of people in the north. There was no industry, trade, nor manufacture. The late Earl of Findlater, that true patriot, pitying the situation of the people, resolved to introduce the linen manufacture. He brought 2 or 3 gentlemen's sons from Edinburgh, who had been regularly bred there to the business, and also had some patrimony of their own; but for their encouragement, he gave to each £600 free of interest for seven years . . . He built excellent weaving shops, got premiums on looms, spinning wheels &c, and a small salary for a spinning mistress . . . There are in this small place 65 looms constantly employed in weaving linen, some in weaving damask; also 7 stocking looms. Despite variable markets the manufacture continues in a comfortable state.' He not only improved Banff Castle, but at Cullen House got James Adam to design the Ionic entrance gateway. He died by his own hand in 1770, but in 1794 was still widely remembered for his good works. Banff Castle was John Adam's work (Colvin, p. 50).

46. *Rev Charles Cordiner's drawing of* Gordon Castle, Fochabers, *in 1776, halfway through its great remodelling by John Baxter (1769–82). Alexandre in 1786 noted 'handsome and nearly finished, the house of a grand seigneur'. Cordiner wrote, 'still in the character of a castle, it is at once an elegant and majestic edifice'. Frontage over 550 feet and 'the higher parts of the building tower amidst the lofty trees in the park'.*

Fochabers, Gordon's Arms[96] is a village of well-built houses. The duke of Gordon's house is close by, handsome and nearly finished. His gardens seem to me very well kept. I haven't seen the house inside, but the outside has all the appearance of the house of a great seigneur.[97] He lives here almost the year, but in winter either in Edinburgh or in London. He loves planting, every day, and all his worst lands serve best as wood. Those at present under pines are in white, moving sand.

On the 24th we left Fochabers lunched at *Elgin*, dined at *Forres* and slept at *Nairn*: 33 miles. There is no point in my detailing the route for it is all disagreeable, the country uncultivated almost everywhere. The land, itself mere white sand, is often covered

96 *SAS*, XIV, 1795, p. 266n, reports firmly: 'There are two good inns, well frequented.' From its Doric portico, the present Gordon Arms may be a rebuilding for the 'new town' – see footnote 97.
97 See above: Charles Cordiner's drawing, engraved Mazell, 1780. The architect John Baxter, who died in 1798, and had some experience of Rome, remodelled Gordon Castle between 1769 and 1784, though Alexandre clearly thought it unfinished. It was quite properly castellated, but demolished 1961. Lazowski described the castle in 4 storeys, etc. In the 1790s, Baxter redesigned the nearby parish church (Bellie) as focus for a handsome new town: Colvin, *Dictionary*, pp. 112–13.

with rocks. It is the most God-forsaken land you could ever find. There are however many plantations and even some handsome ones.[98] But without agriculture or trade, everything seems impoverished. One often has sight of the sea, but very few ships.[99] The little agriculture I found was despicable and I would not be astonished if the lands produced nothing. The rotation is: 1 oats   2 barley   3 oats   4 potatoes . . .

Lazowski   About 3 miles from Elgin, the sand gives way to loam, all greatly improved by Lord Fife. The farms have multiplied with flourishing hedgerows. This is all new, and can't fail to prompt a revolution in local farming. Turnips and clover in the best fields, but also Scotch beans, and wheat after fallowing. The farms have major extensions for pigs and poultry. The best farms are stone-built but others are walled with stones and mud, turf-clad, and roofed in a poor mix-up of turf and thatch. Stables and outhouses of turf. The farms have a market with business in Elgin, a good town, with ruins of an old abbey. Rents, 20s an acre.

Lord Fife owned most of the parish or Urquhart, between Fochabers and Elgin. SAS (XV, 1795, 96–9) has an admirably detailed account of the earl's plantations, as they'd developed 9 years later.

Alexandre   Elgin is the capital of a shire, a fairly large town with one beautiful street. From Elgin to Forres you follow the sea, the line of the great inlet known as the *Moray Firth*.[100] Around Forres the land is good – up to 50 shillings an arpent, which is astonishing. The soil isn't so exceptionally good, but the pasture's improved by imported grasses. Soon after Forres, you cross a large ford through the river Findhorn,[101] and arrive at Nairn. The route is slightly more agreeable, but not very

---

98   Now, most of the land north of the Fochabers–Elgin road is very well-wooded. Lazowski added: 'Half a mile from Fochabers, a flat-bottomed boat ferries you across the river Spey, which here runs extremely rapidly: in some seasons, it's impassable. It's a fine river for salmon, but the people here are so poor and backward that it's farmed out to Perth merchants who furnish the London market and export abroad.' This was ingenuous of Lazowski. *SAS*, XIV, 1795, p. 267, explained: 'There is a capital salmon fishery here upon the Spey, chiefly the property of the Duke of Gordon, from which his grace derives a rent of £1,500 a year from Messrs Gordon & Richardson.' After describing the buildings for overseers, coopers, the ice-house etc, *SAS* noted 'an hundred and thirty men, or more, are employed in this fishery . . . some thousands of salmon are sent to London early in the season, covered with ice. Afterwards they are exported in kits steeped in vinegar.' The effect was a dearth of salmon, and a considerable increase in the cost of living in almost every article 'these 20 years'.
99   Hurrying into Forres, past the turning to Findhorn, they missed one of the most impressive and puzzling antiquities in Scotland, a 20 ft high sharply carved stone, leaning, probably 9th-century, but in amazingly good order, one side carved with armed warriors, headless corpses etc: a wheel cross on another side. On the 1775 Taylor and Skinner map it is marked merely 'Stone Pillar'. On William Daniell's beautiful acquatint, 1813, publ 1825, it was captioned 'King Duncan's Monument'. It is now known as Sueno's Stone: Scotland's version of Trajan's Column.
100 This is Morayshire. The seaward side of the road to Forres is now grown up with fine beechwoods, with no glimpse of the Moray Firth.
101 Precisely where they forded the Findhorn may easily be seen by leaving the A96 just before it crosses on the 1930s steel-braced bridge: you slip south on to a minor road and immediately see

47. *Culloden, Leanach. Edwin Smith photographed this cottage in 1954, and met there an old man who remembered Bell Macdonald who had lived in it from 1829, 42 years after the La Rochefoucauld tour, until 1912.*

eventful. However, there are plantations, especially beyond the Findhorn: all conifers. The land's well tended.

Nairn, One inn[102]   Nairn, a very small town, capital of Nairnshire, stands beside the Firth. It seems a poor sort of capital. In the middle of the town, the houses are fairly well built: I noticed one or two fine ones, but the rest not up to much. There's one

the line of the rough old main road undulating down to the stony edge of the swift river (not deep in summer). Someone with a sense of history has rescued and laid out like railway sleepers three handsomely lettered stones from the 1830s bridge, 'Erected under Act of Parliament by subscription of the Inhabitants of Forres . . . Samuel Brown, Engineer, March 1832'. Lazowski, too, noted how well the land was tended beyond the Findhorn.

102   The author of the *SAS* account of Nairn (XII, 1794, p. 383) admitted: 'Improvements in husbandry are as yet very little known', but claimed: 'In the town there are two very good inns, commodiously fitted up and well kept. The one is of longstanding, and the other, a very large house, was lately built at his own expense by Mr Davidson of Cantray [Cantray House is 6 miles up the Nairn river], so that persons travelling through this country may, at this stage, expect to be accommodated.' He deplores 'the almost incredible number of alehouses and whiskey shops' and adds: 'Nairn is remarkably well calculated for sea-bathing. For persons who require the benefit of the salt-bath, Mr James Brander, one of the inn-keepers, has a bathing machine.' The Frenchmen were a year or two early to see the development of this delightful, northerly and rather larger, version of Southwold in Suffolk.

street, not very long. There's neither port nor trade, and not very much farming. Nearly all the surrounding farmlands seem to be some kind of common, and generally of white sand, often covered with stones of some kind of granite, also a lot of rounded stones rolled smooth by the sea.

On the 25th   we left *Nairn*, dined at *Fort George*, and slept at *Inverness*: 23 miles. To get to Fort George, you leave the Inverness road and take one closer to the Firth. None of the land beside these roads is cultivated, all of it underpopulated.[103] The dwellings are made of earth, with clods of turf for roofing; the bleakest picture of poverty, these hovels are falling into ruin, and so low that one can scarcely scramble in through the entrance. I can think of nothing more awful than this countryside.[104]

The Scots people dress in little petticoats, barely covering their thighs, usually in a material made in red and blue stripes. Their stockings are in the same colours, but in squares, coming up over the calf, so that the knees and part of the thigh are bare, which seems very indecent to us.[105] Their only other clothes are sleeved coats, generally blue, and a blue cloth bonnet this shape,[106] the lower part firm and red, but the bobble seen in the example is

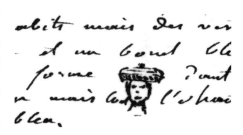

48. *'A blue cloth bonnet this shape'* *(Alexandre's sketch).*

---

[103] The native underpopulation would have been actively brought about by the neighbouring troops in Fort George.

[104] Lazowski, equally appalled by these houses, concluded: 'Read a description of Kamchatka, and you will understand the horrible misery of this small district.' Dr Johnson said: 'At Nairn we may fix the verge of the Highlands; for here I first saw peat fires, and first heard the Erse language' (*Journey to the Western Isles*, p. 19).

[105] The National Galleries of Scotland's *Highland Wedding at Blair Atholl*, painted in 1780 by David Allan, is at present hung in Duff House: see Pl 53, p. 175. The kilt of one of the more spirited dancers has parted up the side, revealing bare thigh and buttock, up to the waist, which perhaps explains Alexandre's primness, and suggests that John Prebble's conclusion may not be true, that 'the old attachment to the Highland dress had died in a generation, the old patterns forgotten' (*Culloden*, 1996, p. 313). The tartan had been proscribed since August 1747, and the proscription repealed in 1782. Prebble believes the emotive power of the plaid died in the Highlanders in those 35 years. There is evidence in Pennant's *Tours* and these Frenchmen's observations, and David Allan's 1780 picture, that the proscription was imperfectly effective. It's odd that Alexandre hadn't remembered the kilt from seeing Scots harvesters in Norfolk two years earlier, come south for better food and pay. In 1784, Mr Glover at South Creake took on 100 labourers for the 5 weeks of harvest, giving them about 2 guineas, and substantial food and lodging. Alexandre's brother, François, noted: 'They are easy to recognise by their clothes; they always wear jackets but no trousers, only a little cloth skirt down to the knees: their bonnets are well made' (*A Frenchman's Year in Suffolk, 1784*, 1988, p. 178).

[106] Alexandre sketched, just passably, a Highland bonnet, higher in front than behind, and, by 1857, named Glengarry, presumably after that glen in Inverness-shire.

49. *Fort George, built on a promontory in the Moray Firth, east of Inverness. The Main Gate was protected from the east, the landward side, by a wide ditch and drawbridge. Assuming a Jacobite enemy, the defences from the Firth were limited to these ramparts. In time of landward attack, the garrison would be supplied by the Navy. Engraving by W Watts in Cordiner,* Letters to Pennant, *1780.*

blue. The women work very hard and dress like the others, as I've said earlier: at least, I've seen no differences.

I forgot to say that when they go from one place to another the men always wear a cloak of the same material as the kilt; this is just a very big piece of light material that they wear in cold weather. In fine weather they wear, crossing the body from one shoulder, a sort of pleated bandolier. The cloaks are of different colours.

So it is an uncultivated country, and you pass through much poverty on the way to Fort George.[107]

---

107 Begun with the 1745 Jacobite rebellion in mind, its modernisation was prompted by a French invasion alarm in 1759, which caused a hurried re-arming. William Skinner, as chief engineer of North Britain, started surveying and planning in 1747; started building to own designs in 1749. John Gifford, *Highlands and Islands* (1992, p. 174), calls it 'this massive demonstration of Hanoverian military power, the largest and last of the 17th and 18th century forts built in Scotland to house what was virtually an army of occupation'; he gives an admirable account of the whole fort and its planned small town: 'a vast barracks complex to hold 1,600 men plus resident artillery'. Main walls defended, as at Berwick, by projecting polygonal bastions.

Fort George   is new. It was begun in 1746 and finished in 1767. It is extremely large, in the form of an oblong, running from east to west. It is contained within six bastions, and a demi-bastion to the east. Across the river is a hill, but too far off for any enemy who might occupy it to be a serious threat. All these fortifications are in brick[108] backed by turf. All the ramparts and vaults could, if need be, provide barrack-rooms for the soldiers. In fact it is completely self-contained.

The buildings within the fort are large and solidly built in red stone and brick, very simply designed. The parade grounds are broad and spacious. No expense has been spared. The ditch which is between the cutting edge of the place and the half-moon holds 6 feet of water at high tide. The officers' quarters are very fine.[109] The greatest care has been taken and it is wonderfully well done. At present it is guarded by a garrison of Invalids [unfit for active service], and ordinarily in time of peace by the third of a regiment of infantry divided between this and Forts Augustus and William. This is the general headquarters and in time of war is ready to house a great many soldiers, but I don't know precisely how many.

From Fort George to Inverness the road is partly along the coast and partly through the fields. The land is still very little cultivated but the houses are a bit better. We also came across two or three mills and those show a little wealth. And the nearer you get to the town, the more you find everything flourishing and the signs of poverty banished. The fields are cultivated. I've seen a very good farm. I will leave till tomorrow the description of Inverness, one of the only market towns in all these parts, and the only one since Perth. By direct route it is about 200 miles which is a good indication of the poverty of the country between.

The 26th we stayed all day in *Inverness*. We needed a break. We had travelled 9 days without resting and covered 216 miles (from Perth) which is hard going.

108 A curious mistake, though perhaps the local red Munlochy sandstone-facing of the defences is nearly the colour of a local brick. But fortifications and barracks alike are essentially of the local sandstone – a pinkish red with, for the main buildings, quoins of a yellowish sandstone. The vaulting of the long tunnel through the ravelin (before you come to the guard-room and main gate), and through the main gate itself, is of brick. It was perhaps there that the brickwork took Alexandre's notice.

109 They face you as you emerge through the main gate: the Governor's House at the left-end of the front block – the Lieutenant-Governor's and Fort-Major's houses at the other end. The Governor's House (designed by Skinner 1762–6) is a good example of the local sandstone with cherry-caulk pointing of the vertical spaces between the roughly-squared stone. Square stairwell, lit by Venetian window, leads up to Governor's dining-room: its delicate mantelpiece the work of the Adam family. In this room Sir Eyre Coote entertained Boswell and Johnson in 1773. Alexandre says merely: 'left Nairn, dined at Fort George, slept Inverness'. But he found the officers' quarters 'very fine', which may suggest that he and Lazowski were dined by Coote's successor, the Officer Commanding the Invalids stationed there in 1786. Lazowski said nothing of their dinner, but noted that all these defences were now pointless: 'the Highlanders were very far from thoughts of rebellion'. One sees why Frenchmen might not have been given a great welcome by the Invalids' colonel. The present writer of these notes devoured his wartime rations in this elegant mess in the intervals of amphibious exercises in the four months over Christmas and Hogmanay 1943–44. It is good to see the Highlanders' Regimental silver in use still in that friendly mess.

Lazowski   'C'est à Inverness commence les HIGLANDS' [sic]. Back to Alexandre:

Inverness, Masons' Inn   Inverness is the place where we halt our northward course. Our plan is to descend into the Islands and then to the town of Glasgow.

The town is large, well-enough built and a considerable port. Its two manufactures are, one, making thread, and the other, common cloth-making: they are only for the internal market.[110] However, the town grows and flourishes every day; and becomes daily more commercial. What promises well is the general district grows richer.

The lands round the town are good, and rented at from twenty shillings to 3.5 *louis*. I don't know the details of the farming, but it surrounds the town very closely and seems to be regarded as an equal partner. The town itself stands on a river that joins Loch Ness to the Moray Firth: it's large and navigable and must favour the trade of the town. Inverness is set within sight of great hills and mountains and pleasantly situated in its little valley.

110 The very helpful archivists in the Inverness Public Library quickly showed me that the Masons' Arms became the Caledonian Hotel, which provided so welcome a break from tank-landing-craft exercises between Wick and Burghead on wintry seas. It has been rebuilt since World War II. *SAS*, IX, 1793, p. 630, recorded 'The principal inns were indifferent till of late: they are now commodious and comfortable; in attendance, entertainment and beds, they emulate the best inns in the southern parts of the kingdom. There are subscription assemblies, occasional balls and concerts of music.' How grateful we were, in that wartime winter, for occasional gramophone concerts of classical music in the basement of the Caledonian. *SAS* shows great developments in the textile industry in the ten years to 1793: 10,000 persons employed in spinning, twisting, bleaching and dyeing; another 1,000 employed in the hemp for bags, sacking and tarpaulin.

8

The Highlands

The military roads, Loch Ness, Fort William, Portnacroish, Bonawe

At last they were entering the Highlands, by Loch Ness and the Great Glen, along General Wade's evocative narrow road carved out along the edge of the loch; pleased by the hazel and birch woods and the glimpses through them of that majestic stretch of water; and not even put off by the grisly squalor and nauseating oatcake of 'the General's Hut', where they managed to eat some fresh eggs and reflect: 'Good travellers feel challenged rather than discouraged when they are exploring, enthralled', a strange new country. A mile or two later they felt more than rewarded by the power and beauty of the 50-ft waterfall at Foyers.

Soon they crossed, without comment, the tall stone 'White Bridge'. Built by Wade's soldiers, it strides high over the rocky stream of the Fechlin; and by-passed now, its unused grassy surface looks much as it did when they rode over it. Alexandre sketched the kind of primitive farm-cart that, till relatively recent times, seemed preferable to wheeled carts here in the Highlands on account of the steepness of the slopes, as he explained. Before reaching Fort William, he describes very sympathetically the Highland people living in these glens. Forced to wear breeches, trous, *in place of the kilt etc, 'all their customs were at stake: they faced being a former people'. Both Alexandre and Lazowski give very interesting accounts of the way the surviving highlanders were living, forty years after the retribution for the '45 Rebellion.*

Beside Loch Lochy, at the Letter Findlay Inn, the two Frenchmen lunched with its marvellous view across the loch, their squeamishness at the General's Hut forgotten. Later, at Fort William, 'we're staying in rather a good hotel'. It was run by an admirable highlander, who'd fought at Culloden and lost two sons in one of the ten Highland Regiments which distinguished themselves against the Americans in their War of Independence. Taylor and Skinner's General Map of Scotland, *1775, showed only one road beyond Fort William, the military road heading due south to Kinlochleven. The good innkeeper and his third son persuaded them that that road was impassable for any gig: it proved alarming enough for Alexandre and his servant on horseback.*

Lazowski wisely took the gig round by boat to Bonawe, coming ashore for the night at Portnacroish, where the little inn offered an excellent menu. But Lazowski's boatmen knew nothing of the treacheries of the entrance to Loch Etive, which nearly drowned them. When he rejoined Alexandre at Bonawe, he was in no condition to visit the remarkable furnace that must have attracted them to this route: they didn't even mention it as they set off through the Pass of Brander for Inveraray. Alexandre begins:

On the 27th, we left Inverness   and slept at Fort Augustus: 32 miles. Now you leave the low landscapes and enter what they call the Highlands – high ranges of Mountains inhabited by these people who don't wear breeches and have new ways, or at least aren't as civilised as we are, yet have manners that are good to get to know, as I shall show in different parts of my journal when the occasion arises.

We have stopped for a meal at a place called *the General's Hut*. The road has been generally good, and agreeable, sticking close to *Loch Ness*, sometimes very close, but often losing sight of it. The mountains rise steeply and are mostly wooded. The rocks are big and frequent but not of a particularly hard stone – more a sort of conglomerate or pudding-stone. Often they roll down the hillsides and into the water, making the road very dangerous during heavy rains. This road is often cut through the rock: it was made for the army. Although it's too narrow, it's pretty good. Leaving the rocks, you enter very well-planted woods – mostly hazel and birch; few conifers. This is very pleasant. You catch sight of the water between the branches, and sometimes you see a house: however dilapidated, it can't help being picturesque. This is where the highlanders live. They usually have a little field to grow things near their houses, and are allowed to graze sheep or cattle on the mountainside, and so scrape a living.[1] In the middle of these woods, on the south side of the loch you find our inn.[2] Nothing would give you more of an idea of poverty, dirt and squalor than this place offers. The house was well enough built, but the kitchen, which is separate from the main part of the building, is at the same time the family's

---

[1] In 1726, General George Wade had begun his famous work of road-engineering straight down through the Great Glen here: he went on through the 1730s, beginning the judicious disarming of the highland clans. Unluckily he hadn't got far enough with this when the Pretender launched the '45 Rebellion. In the month after Culloden, young Cumberland sent his advance battalions along this road to establish bases at Fort Augustus and Fort William, from which the Jacobite highlanders were bludgeoned into submission or extinction. It was forty years later, to the month, that Alexandre and Lazowski ventured along this narrow road, appreciating the beauty of the loch itself ('you catch sight of the water between the branches'), but becoming aware of the poverty the highlanders had been reduced to. At Dores, 8 miles from Inverness, where, according to John Prebble, some of Cumberland's men were daunted by the 'high and frightful' mountains as they lit their bivouac fires beside the loch, Alexandre and Lazowski were too excited to be thinking much about improved farming. *SAS*, in 1792 (III, pp. 480) anyway confirmed that 'the new mode of farming can hardly be said to be introduced here except at Gortuleg, a property of James Fraser, Esq, writer to the signet, who spares no pains nor expense to improve it: his tenants have also got good leases'. Briefly at Gortuleg in retreat after Culloden, Simon Fraser, Lord Lovat, was soon caught, tried, and in 1747 beheaded as a traitor on Tower Hill. Here they were back in an improving mood.

[2] 'Our inn', the General's Hut, had already been stayed in by Boswell and Johnson who had found it 'not ill-stocked with provisions', but it had since declined. It was clearly marked on Taylor and Skinner's 1775 *General Map of the Roads of Scotland*, which I believe Alexandre and Lazowski used. It was a timber-framed building, according to Robert Southey, the square panels filled with mud and straw. Loch Ness reminded him of Buttermere and Wasdale. (*Journal of a Tour in Scotland in 1819*, 1929, p. 176.) It was originally a base from which General Wade had supervised the road-engineering. Its actual site is now disputed, though a bar in the Foyers Hotel bears its name. Anyone looking for it should consult Taylor and Skinner's road map of 1776 (pl 60). Any surviving trace would be found, beside the B862, just south of the ruined kirk of Boleskine (pronounced Blesskin), and exactly 17¾ miles from Inverness.

parlour and bedroom. The hearth is in the middle of the room and made with three or four stones without mortar. The whole family warms itself round a turf-fire; the smoke finds its way out through the door. The beds are only rough bits of wood nailed together, with straw for warmth. Chairs are tree-stumps. The light gets in only through a door which serves as door, chimney and window. The straw roof-thatch is full of holes and used as a hen-roost.

But this isn't all: our great horror was to find that the whole family has scabies. However, one has to eat; but we couldn't face the oatcake; after putting on a pair of gloves, I was ready to eat fresh eggs, which enabled me to feel rather less impatient for supper.[3]

I daresay this description may make you feel sorry for us, but good travellers feel challenged rather than discouraged when they are exploring enthralled.

After eating, we left our palace and made for Fort Augustus for the night, 32 miles from Inverness.[4] After the General's Hut, the road leaves the side of the loch and climbs into the hills. A mile or two on from the Hut, in the most romantic scenery, you hear the great splashing roar of a waterfall: we stopped, and couldn't resist following it down into a rather alarming place, bare rock, from which we could see this superb fall.[5] A broad river is constricted into a very narrow gully in the rock, having scooped out a bed at least 200 feet long at ground level, all cut through rock and forming, at the point where it is first constricted, a cascade of at least 50 feet, very fast flowing, such an abundance of water that it falls as a continuous sheet, giving no glimpse of the rock behind. This water finally disappears among rocks up to half a mile away. Further on, it enters the loch we've just left.

This waterfall is much more beautiful than I have been able to describe: it is a

---

3   Lazowski, too, 'made the mistake' of entering the family's quarters and seeing them with scabies. It put him off eating the oatcake, kneaded by their hands. But with tea and milk, he said philosophically, and fresh eggs and cheese and some very good rum, 'I thought you can perfectly well set your mind on the supper or dinner you hope for later, elsewhere'. They clearly had good appetites.

4   The General's Hut is in the parish of Boleskine, which has for centuries been united with that of Abertarf, including Fort Augustus. This enormous joint parish runs about 24 miles alongside Loch Ness and extends up to ten miles in width. These were all Lovat lands and, before them, apparently knew the ancient warlike clan of Comyns, and clan Grant. The extent of these lands explains their occupation (described in *SAS*, XX, 1798, pp. 20–5) by so many tribes of Lovat followers, Mactavishes, Macgruers etc, many of whom had perished near Loch Lochy in 1545 in a battle with clan Macdonald. It's as well Alexandre and Lazowski arrived a decade too soon to read the *Statistical Account*: the warlike activities of the late-medieval highlanders would, I hope, have disenchanted them. This *SAS* account reckons that even the considerable tenant families here were living, till the beginning of the 18th century, in houses built of 'sod and divot'; but all contained 'a spacious hall, with a large table where the "wadsetter" and his family and dependants eat their two meals a day' – the family at one end of the table, dependants at the other. It was 'no disparagement for the gentlemen to sit with commoners in the inns', where a single glass went round the whole company. Living on the produce of their farms, they were hospitable to strangers, but it was thought 'disgraceful for any of the younger sons to follow any profession other than arms and agriculture'. In time 'these prejudices gave way'.

5   It *is* an alarming descent, down some very slippery rocks, but worth it: see over.

50. *'A mile or two from the General's Hut . . . you hear the great noise of a waterfall.' This is the Fall of Foyers. Boswell and Johnson came here in August, 'an unseasonable time, and found it divested of its dignity and terror'. Photographed in April, the same month as the French visit.*

51. *General Wade's tall, narrow 'White Bridge', 1732, over the Fechlin burn, near Loch Knockie.*

combination of wilderness, a beauty rarely found, the fall itself, and the abundance of its water, which is remarkably clear.[6] Further on, you descend into a pretty little valley: the hills all round it are well tree'd, and at the bottom of the valley attractive meadows are divided by the river that feeds the waterfall.

For the rest of our route you find very mountainous country, in which you come upon delightful view-points. The hills are less wooden and in general there is little cultivated land. You pass two or three little lakes, one of which is particularly famous for its excellent fish.[7] You also find two or three gentlemen's houses which are extremely simple,[8] with a few cultivated acres round them.

---

6   They had found the Fall of Foyers, what Dr Johnson described as the Fall of Fiers. Here Alexandre and Lazowski got even with Boswell and Johnson for themselves enduring so much more horrible a meal at the General's Hut than Boswell and Johnson had had. At this Fall Dr Johnson recognised that, in *August* 'we visited the place at an unseasonable time and found it divested of its dignity and terror'. Alexandre appreciated its great power and beauty and felt alarm, if not terror.

7   The friendly Whitebridge Hotel near Loch Knockie says 'especially prime trout'. The delightful hump-back White bridge nearby, built over the Fechlin by General Wade in 1732, has been preserved by building a new little bridge, leaving the old one agreeably much as it was in 1786 when the French rode over it (see above). The work of Wade's 'highwaymen', as he called them. included the building of forty stone bridges – the most famous and handsome his Bridge of Tay at Aberfeldy.

8   The little lochs survive but not those simple houses: their owners preferred to be in Inverness.

In short, the barrenness of great areas of these mountains towards the end of our route is a sad and wretched story.[9] Just before you reach the fort you get a beautiful view: it is the far end of the loch and here the land is reasonably well farmed, and there are views all round of very tall mountains, almost all of them noble.[10]

Before leaving Loch Ness, perhaps I should try to give you a more general idea of it. It is 24 miles long and about two miles wide. It occupies the whole depth of the valley and its shores are in general very high hills and rocks of which the height and the colour – varying between reds[11] and grey – never fail to give a very noble impression. Its hills are generally wooded and one even finds some beautiful trees.

This loch is navigable for fairly large ships, and it abounds in all kinds of fish. So it's a useful resource for all the people of the area who are generally very poor and rely on it almost entirely for their sustenance.[12]

Fort Augustus, the Only one[13] [inn]   The Fort was built to secure the respect of the local highlanders. It is a small quadrangle strengthened by four corner bastions: the interior is a barrack square, the same shape, and well built. It fulfils its object in being unable to be taken except by cannon, but wouldn't hold out long if it were dominated on all sides by very high hills. It's at the end of the loch and is provisioned by boat.[14] The town around it is a mere 12 or 15 houses, mostly ill-built.

[9] *SAS* XX, in 1798, pp. 25–6, already observed the 'advantage' to lower tenantry here of being reduced to settling 'in the town of Inverness and working in the two manufactures there, so improving their living and enabling them to give education and trades to their children, some of whom are now sending grateful remittances from distant climes'. This long Boleskine and Abertarf entry was contributed anonymously to the *SAS* by 'an Heritor [landlord], a friend to Statistical Inquiries'.

[10] From here Boswell and Johnson headed due west, heading for Loch Alsh through Glen Shiel, where the mountains rise above 1000 metres, and one of them Boswell ventured to call 'immense'. Johnson, pedantic: 'No; it is no more than a considerable protuberance.' After their adventurous circuit of Skye and Mull, their route coincided with Alexandre and Lazowski's from Loch Awe to Glasgow.

[11] I think the end of April's two or three weeks early for the heather to be purpling the hills.

[12] Alexandre doesn't distinguish between the river Ness, which runs 6 miles from Loch Ness past Inverness to the sea, and the Loch itself. *SAS* (IX, 1793, p. 609) says 'In the river Ness are salmon, bull trouts and flounders. The salmon-fishing begins 30 November and ends 18 September. The Berwick Fishing Company have fished this river near 40 years. They pay £230 a year to the proprietors of the lower division of the river and about £100 to those of the upper division.' This difference of fee is to compensate the proprietors of the upper division for the opening of the breach from sunset on Saturday till sunrise on Monday to allow the salmon to pass upstream (into the loch). The catch in the river was about 300–350 barrels a year. 'There is but little of the salmon sold here. The bull trouts were sold here. The flounders were not good; soft, and of indifferent flavour.' It may be that the flounders were what the poor mainly got for their sustenance.

[13] In Murray's *Guide*, 1884, there was still only one: the Lovat Arms Hotel. In 2000, a Lovat Arms Hotel, rebuilt between the two World Wars, commands good views.

[14] A King's galley (*SAS*, IX, p. 608). The 15th lord Lovat gave the fort to the English congregation of Benedictines, from Germany, but its main outlines survive, 'disguised in monkish vesture' (Gifford, *Highlands and Islands*, 1992, p. 169). In April 2000 it was firmly closed to visitors.

On the 28th we were off to *Fort William*, the journey 29 miles, the road a continuation of the one made by the army. It's very good to see that, in its construction, great attention has been paid to economy, which often means that the going is quite difficult, the hills very steep and the rock seldom cut more than the width of a single cart.[15]

The landscape is generally wild, with very little wood. It is quite well peopled and poor, having small holdings; the people living in awful houses, yet with their pitiful plots cleared all round them. On the next page I've drawn the ordinary tools they make use of. The cart, a sort of sledge, as you see, is merely two wooden poles, touching the ground and without wheels, on which they have fixed a large basket (A). The tool (B) is for clearing the ground or cutting turf. This (C) is their spade. The fork (E) is very large, as in my sketch. (F) is the mattock and (D) is the bridle [and bit] that they harness their horses with. All the farm-tools are half-wood and half-iron. The reason for these carts is the steepness of the slopes so that they are obliged to put post-nails (*crampons*) at least an inch long in the horses' front shoes, and not to shoe their back feet, so that they don't slide.[16]

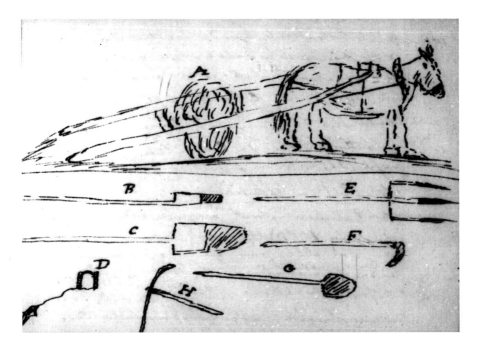

52. *'The ordinary tools they make use of' (Alexandre's sketch).*

[15] For 5 or 6 miles, between Aberchalder and Laggan, the military road they used was occupied by a railway for an aluminium works, itself now dismantled, but those few miles of narrow military road survived then by being by-passed.

[16] The excellent Louis Simond (*Journal of a Tour and Residence in Great Britain, 1810 and 1811*, 1817, I, p. 300) wrote: 'A continuation of fine mountain scenery, with bold outlines, and all black with shade from the same cause, clouds round their summits, carried us to Dalmally, the northern-

These people eat a great many potatoes, which makes up a large part of the crop. They sow them after the oats, and the women plant them by hand. In general, their family life is very good, and it's that which makes them so poor: it's very difficult for them to provide for themselves. Even in manual work, and above all in service, they are reduced to dependence on someone else. So they have, as a rule, each their own dwelling, prefering to live poor and free rather than rich (or more comfortably) but in subjection. So they live in these primitive houses which are all unspeakable, the picture of poverty, inside as well as out. Outside the houses is a small patch of land on which they are able to scrape a living. I was told that for this scrap of land, and the house, they pay 2 or 3 *louis*, which is immense. Their lands let at 2 *livres* the *arpent* of cultivable land.[17] One must admit there are many places that, from their situation, could not fetch so much and others from which a much bigger profit could be derived by planting.

The usual sustenance of these people is oatcake, instead of bread, and potatoes during the summer. To this they add milk and butter. Their drink is only gruel, which they make by putting oatmeal in hot water like a kind of tea: it purifies the water and rids it of its natural hardness, making it wholesome.

This Highland race of men is mostly handsome and tall, above all very strong and well-built. The women are strongly built and work well, usually in rather dirty work, and they are badly dressed. One of their jobs is spreading manure on the land with their hands, often having to load it on to the cart without even the aid of a shovel.

The build of the men makes them very fine warriors, and all the men round here would choose to work in no other service than soldiering. Their pleasures are fishing and hunting, at which they're very successful. But since last year, the English have imposed a tax of 2 *louis*[18] on all those who go hunting: it was such a pleasure, and now all they are left with is fishing. It's harsh to have deprived these poor people of their greatest pleasure: they should, I think, have been exempted from this general profitable tax.

They don't much like the hard work of road-building; and farming is still in its infancy. In all these parts of the country, their pleasures and their business is fishing, at which they shine, and which keeps the whole area alive.

Those who have a kind of trade raise bullocks and cows, and drive them to pastures in England. These cattle, and even sheep (of which the breed is small and wretched) are never sheltered, and roam the hills winter and summer. Only to the young animals, during periods when the ground is covered with snow, do they take some hay.

most point of our intended tour. The people were making hay, and the simplicity of their mode of transporting it attracted our attention. Two long pliable poles were fastened like shafts to a very small horse and, dragging on the ground, slid with tolerable facility with their load on. This may be considered as the first elements of carts.' Alexandre was 25 years ahead of Simond, not only noticing but drawing, and describing accurately, these primitive mountain carts. Were comparable models developed in other steeply-sloping pastoral regions?

[17] 2 *livres* = 1s 8d (or 8 new pence). 2 or 3 *louis* = 10 or 15 shillings (or 50 or 75 new pence) in 1780s equivalent.

[18] Ten shillings, or 50 new pence: a deterrent sum, in 1785, to huntsmen!

The breed of animals here is very small, from the horses down to the dogs. The cows are small too, yielding little milk, which astonished me. At present the new grass isn't ready. How the cows get into such good condition depends on the quality of this grazing, which results in their being prefered, in many places, to the fine English cows. One can distinguish two kinds of these cows: the small ones, and another, slightly larger, breed. The first fetch in England 2 or 2.5 *louis* each, and the second fetch as much as 3.5 *louis*.[19] These are all mountain cattle that they drive to England, and it's a trade quite separate from the others and which is attractive enough for them, or at least a little less disagreeable than the others.

When they drive these cattle through their hills which are, as one must see, divided by a great many lochs, they never let even the more valuable cattle go by boat, but make them swim across all the waters they come to on their drove roads; and they have told me they very seldom lose one. These cows are almost always black, and often well-formed and good looking.

They have had, especially some time ago, a great many herds of goats; but several individual landholders found that their woods were suffering very badly in consequence. As the sheep became more common, the goats became more rare. But I've eaten some delicious goats' cheese.

So now you see how things stand with these lands in the *Highlands*. All that I say now is only what is done in these mountain landscapes. Although Scotland has a quite separate régime, these Highlands are a country entirely different from the rest. The great landowners, or seigneurs, are here known as *Lairds*. They own great estates (of varying sizes). These Lairds lease their lands to a sort of tenant-in-chief, called a *tacksman*,[20] usually rich, who sub-lets the lands to the farmers. This tacksman is the man 'on the ground', between laird and peasant, who was being over-charged. The majority of these little dwellings that one sees are theirs, and they are in general men of some substance [*gens de biens*].

These simple inhabitants maintain steadfastly the same fidelity and warmth for

---

[19] Ten shillings, or 12s 6d: 17s 6d.

[20] *OED*: 'one who holds a tack or lease of land, especially in the Highlands . . . He leases from the proprietor a large piece of land which he sublets in small farms.' John Prebble (*The Highland Clearances*, 1963, pp. 20–7) has a full and disturbing account of the part played by tacksmen: 'These tacksmen took titles from the land they leased, were Mac-This of That or The Other . . . In many cases they may have held written leases, although after Culloden [fought in 1746 near Inverness] when a black-cattle economy replaced a military order and the clan needed no majors and captains, the chief began to show an understandable reluctance to name anything that gave something for nothing. Having ceased to be a King in his own glens, he slowly realised that he was now a landlord, not a warlord . . . The sub-tenants formed small communities or townships. Six or eight men might hold a farm in common . . . a portion of the glen and a tract of mountain pasture for 30 or 40 black cattle, a small herd of thin and fleshless sheep. The best of the arable was farmed in runrig, strips for which the sub-tenants periodically drew lots. Payment in kind or service for this land could, and frequently did, turn a sub-tenant into the servant of his tacksman and hold him in perpetual debt.' This transition from fighting clansmen, the essential clan system, to small farming communities in a grudging landscape, is what Alexandre and Lazowski were scanning for signs of improved farming. They were watching elements of a revolution as violent and tragic in its way as the one they were returning to in France.

their ancient chiefs. They speak of the present king of England only with contempt, and will never call him king, referring to him merely as *George*, or even *The Governor*. When they spoke of the Old Pretender, it was only as 'King James'. And if we recall with them their ancient kingdom, so dear to them and so respected, they get carried away so far as to show you the wounds they received in his service; and they recite with great enthusiasm the names of the places he passed through – especially the places that received and sheltered him during his last flight. Their reverence for him, and for these places, means that they are always on everyone's lips whenever one of his legendary actions is mentioned. They can't speak of Culloden without getting heated, and the thought that they are subjected to the English is one that grieves and torments them in such a terrible way that I'm sure that all these clansmen loyal to the flag of the Pretender would even now be ready to risk trying conclusions yet again.[21]

Everything has been done to make them give up their attachment to their *patrie*, so that their highland dress, entirely peculiar to them, was forbidden.[22] They weren't allowed to go into towns unless they wore trousers. So the markets became meagre and ill-attended. They preferred not to live well and to remain a people utterly apart; not to abandon the smallest of their ways, so much respected in the country, and distinguishing them from all other people.

They are so attached to their dress that all the gentlemen living in the country dressed the same way as the peasants: that is to say, without breeches. However, those who have lived a long time in London have lost the habit of wearing these clothes.

The general language spoken in Scotland is English in which many foreign words are mixed. That makes it difficult to understand. But their pronunciation is slower and more distinct, and very easy to follow. The highlanders however speak an

21 In his account of his and Johnson's stay with Flora Macdonald on Skye (13 September 1773), Boswell recites the travels of Prince Charles Edward after Culloden. His assertion: 'I must do the highlanders the justice to attest that I found everywhere amongst them a high opinion of the virtues of the King now upon the throne, and an honest disposition to be faithful subjects to his majesty', does not suggest great enthusiasm. Alexandre's report of their coolness clearly needs to be read with caution, yet it is specific and is supported by Lazowski. Indeed, this last paragraph looks as if it may have been inserted after Lazowski's conversation with the boatman between Fort William and Portnacroish.

22 The proscription of highland dress, imposed in 1747 after the Rising of '45, had been repealed in 1782, but it had been so drastically imposed that 'the old attachment to the Highland dress had died in a generation' (John Prebble). David Allan's delightful picture of a highland wedding at Blair Atholl was painted there in 1780, which shows that *there*, at any rate, it hadn't died, and that it was the proscription that had broken down. See opposite, and Alexandre's detailed account of the dress in his journal of 25 April, between Nairn and Fort George. Dr Johnson in 1773 recorded: 'The law by which the highlanders have been obliged to change the form of their dress has, in all the places that we have visited, been universally obeyed. I have seen only one gentleman completely clothed in the ancient habit, and by him it was worn only occasionally and wantonly.' His recent editor notes that 'many highlanders were too poor to change' in 1747, and that an inn by the bridge that joins Seil (in Argyll) to the mainland used to hire out breeches to islanders as they left the islands (Folio Society edn, 1990, p. 397).

53. *David Allan (1755–96),* A Highland Wedding at Blair Atholl in 1780. *Highland dress was rigorously proscribed from 1747 to 1782, four decades in which the memory and devotion faded: though at Blair Atholl, and in the course of the Frenchmen's tour, Highlanders still proudly wore the kilt. The dancer on the right, with his back to us, shows why Alexandre was shocked by it: see p. 161, footnote 105. Courtesy of the National Gallery of Scotland, Dunimarle Loan.*

entirely different language of which neither the English nor the French can understand a single word. They are very proud of their language, and the king of England, seeking gradually to reduce their ideas of separate nationality, has established free schools across the Highlands for teaching English, and there they send their children. I don't doubt that in a very short time they will lose this language, which will be a pity. For one can see, without going far, civilised nations one of which isn't up to the rest and which is, because of that, more interesting. I've been told something that has also troubled me: that since English was introduced, they have begun to lose their ancient customs – their music for instance, and what they talk much more about, having been made to wear breeches.

It is important to grasp how important this question of *breeches* is: everything was bound up with their having had their traditional clothes removed [Pl 53]. With their distinctive dress, all their ancient customs were at stake. They faced becoming a former people.

All the highlanders are very polite. The grandees and gentlemen are even flattered if you call to see them at home, and they won't let you go without having drunk your health with you – another of their customs. They all seem to drink, and their drinks are rum, brandy and what they call *whisky*. It is distilled from grain and they drink truly unbelievable quantities of it.

Their politeness derives from what they know of themselves and how presentable they are: they all remove their hats – or, rather, their bonnets – and speak to you very openly in giving you all the information that you could need, and even quite often coming out to show you the right road when you've gone astray.

Their horses are very small and are used only in harness, never ridden – at least, very seldom. It's true that there are many places in the Highlands where the horses, although specially shod, can't go, find impassable. Yet I've seen them in places where one supposed goats alone could go. It seems to be all a matter of familiarity and usage, which isn't astonishing. Living in a countryside as basic as this, you become accustomed to it, and as comfortable in it as you are in the most beautiful places.

It's the same with the other animals: I've seen cows, that are really creatures of the plain, surviving in places where they can scarcely get their four legs, and where to go is to be lost for ever. Yet with the cows, and with the horse, it's all a matter of custom and use.

They seem to be generally fit and healthy. The English government does send out into into the Highlands surgeons with allowances for curing the sick, but they have little need of them. These surgeons often give their services for nothing.

There are still living in the Highlands gentlemen of the Stuart clan, even bearing the name. Many of their possessions have been confiscated, but a part of them have been returned to whoever is chief. They seem to have paid very dear in order to see again the goods the English seized.

Getting back to our journey, on the 28th we reached *Fort William*, having dined at an inn beside *Loch Lochy*.[23] The road to Fort William crosses wild country, but more peopled where the farming is brought to high perfection. Potatoes play a big part in the produce, and this is how they are grown. After a year of oats, the land's dug over by spade, to sow the potatoes one by one. They generally thrive well, and it's a disaster for the whole countryside if the crop fails one year.

The whole route was on the slopes of different mountains and the lengths of Loch Lochy and Oich,[24] which are mostly set among low mountains well planted with trees. The first loch cuts through the whole bottom of the glen, but the second occupies a sort of plain and is a small affair: it's very famous for its fishing. The first is very large and very much finer. The rest of the road was all along the slopes of hills, climbing and descending, the slopes very steep and the number of torrents pouring down the slopes and cutting through the road at every moment made it a nightmare for a gig like ours, and often dangerous. You see Fort William when you're two miles

---

23 Where there is still a hotel, charmingly situated beside Loch Lochy, and called Letterfinlay Lodge. It appeared already on Taylor and Skinner's 1775 road map, as Letter Findlay Inn, nearly half-way between Fort Augustus and Fort William. In 1819, Robert Southey found it dirty and uncomfortable; 'however, we made a good fire, and got biscuits, cheese, milk and whiskey' (*op cit*, p. 201).

24 Loch Oich is a very small loch about 4 miles south-west of Fort Augustus. Loch Lochy occupies about nine miles of the Great Glen: both ravishingly beautiful in April sunshine, 2000.

54. *Beside Loch Lochy, where at Letterfinlay Lodge (represented by the white wall on the right) Alexandre and Lazowski dined on the way to Fort William from Fort Augustus. It is now an attractive hotel.*

off, and the road in becomes flatter and much better. Just before arriving, you cross a handsome bridge built over a fairly powerful torrent which pours into the loch.[25]

FORT WILLIAM. At the Golden Lion   Fort William is built on *Loch Eil* which enters *Loch Linnhe* here, which in turn goes on into the sea. This is a salt-water loch and all sorts of ships can enter. You see a great many of them, even quite small ones going as far as Glasgow in search of goods with which to furnish a market and all the houses set in the depths of these high ranges of hills.

This fortress is old,[26] and one part of it has even collapsed in ruin. It was created, like the other two[27] to keep the highlanders[28] quiet; and although it's of no great size, it was strong enough in the '45 Rebellion, despite great numbers of rebels besieging it for fifteen days, to convince them that they had no chance of taking it. There's a small town around this fort, which is something like Fort Augustus, a

25 The present bridge over the Nevis is a rebuilding of 1932.
26 Rebuilt under William III, hence the name: and again, partially, in 1746, although it had withstood the Jacobite siege.
27 George and Augustus.
28 Chiefly the restive clan Cameron.

square with 4 bastions of which two are surrounded by the loch and two are below ground.[29] The garrison is bigger than that at Fort Augustus, and the buildings more in proportion, yet I don't think that, in wartime, that is to say when the fort has to maintain all its troops, you could garrison in it more than 300 men.

The fort is guarded in peacetime by Invalids or by an Infantry Regiment. The garrison is changed every year. For the officers it must be very boring in winter. Then town is small, as I said, but also really pretty, as much for its situation on the loch as for its houses, which look well and are well-built, better than you usually find in this part of the world.[30]

We're staying in rather a good hotel – better than the recent ones. It's run by one of the highlanders, a very pleasant man. From the way he behaved, we saw at once that he had been well-to-do but had lost everything. [*Here Lazowski takes over the narrative with vigour and conviction:*]

Lazowski   We lodged at Fort William with a highlander of a good family, as I saw at once from his manner, polite and unaffected. I had an hour and a half's conversation with him yesterday, which fully confirmed me in my good opinion of him. He is well-informed, without having received any distinguished education:[31] above all he has in abundance sound judgment, a habit of reflection, and strength of character. His distinction he conveyed in his behaviour: it is often so difficult to be civil and engaging without seeming a shade servile. Although an innkeeper (?proprietor), he had been reduced to that by fortune. He has an impressive knowledge of his country's history which he loves, speaking of its records and antiquity with a warmth that's very engaging. He regards the English Revolution of 1688 as a tyranny in relation to the Scots. The present government he accepts as the government *de facto*, but he served under the flag of Prince Charles Edward, and was at the battle of Culloden. I felt I had to give you a good account of this man for whom I have so much respect, and to suggest to you that there may be other men of the same type in these hills, and whom he meets. And I'm glad to have been able to talk of my respect for him. He had three sons: two died, officers in the British Army in America. The

---

29   The town now lies east and south of the fort, whose natural defence on the east seems to be a tributary of the river Lochy, and from the west Loch Linnhe. John Gifford summarises the fort's physical structure as 'an irregular pentagon, with a 3-pointed bastion at the SE and demi-bastions at the other four corners' (*Highlands and Islands*, 1992, p. 241). It is now a rather unkempt ruin.

30   Lazowski agrees that this town is '*quelquechose*', something, thanks to its trade, and above all its fisheries, in particular the herring-fishery.

31   Alexandre noted that he had put some of his income into the education of his children, sparing nothing. His surviving son was learning navigation, in order to go to sea. He not only spoke very good English but, more extraordinary, could speak Latin. 'Although these Scots speak English, they pronounce Latin as we do in France.' Alexandre had been charmed to find here a real highlander, devoted to his sons: 'this picture of true nature must give pleasure'. It is extremely frustrating that a fire in the 1960s seems to have destroyed the bulk of Fort William's borough archives. I can discover nothing even confirming the existence of 'the Golden Lion' in 1786, let alone anything leading to the innkeeper's identity. Fiona Marwick has kindly searched what 18th-century papers she has at the West Highland Museum in Fort William.

third, whom I've met here and talked with, is intended for the sea. He's just completed a course in navigation, and is off to put his lessons into practice. Like his father, he speaks good English and Latin.[32] I've rarely met a young man kinder or more obliging.

I had got up very early as usual, and had gone out to walk beside the loch in the hope of a conversation, when I met this young man near our stables and discussed with him the route we had to take and which, of course, I didn't really know. He told me that we had to cover 42 miles in very high mountains, seriously difficult. At 34 miles we would find a house where we could shelter, but where it was impossible to get a bed. Perhaps it would be prudent to take with us some hay to sleep on, and at least we would still be on a military road. However, in the highest part of the mountain, no one had ever taken a gig, for the climbs and descents were too precipitous; he thought he had better consult his father and went off to wake him.[33]

His father confirmed precisely what I've just told you, and added that he advised me to take the lower road with the horses, for the upper route was impracticable for carriages; and he thought we should send down, with one of us, the gig and the baggage as far as *Bonawe*[34] by boat; and that it was necessary to sleep en route at *Portnacroish*, where the boat could perfectly well find a mooring. He thought the journey of 27 miles was a good one, because it involved two arms of the sea (which they call lochs) that could be easily crossed by ferry.[35] You will see on the map how the coast is, so to say, cut into long strips by the sea, which inevitably makes communications longer and more difficult.

If I'd been on my own I might have risked the high track over the hills, living on

---

32 See previous footnote. The sons who died were presumably officers in one of the ten Highland Regiments of the line serving against the Americans. The highlanders were congratulated in 1784: 'no subjects . . . are more loyal and dutiful or better affected . . . Many of all ranks have performed signal services to their country in the late wars.'

33 Our clues to the route they planned to take are '42 miles in very high mountains'; 'we would still be on a military road'; and 'the climbs and descents were precipitous'. As we see later, Alexandre and his servant and their two horses took this route 'not just bad, but often dangerous for a man on horseback'. This can only mean that their plan had been to take the military road over the mountains heading due south from Fort William to Loch Leven and the Devil's Staircase. They were using Taylor and Skinner's *General Map of Scotland*, 1775, which showed only one road beyond Fort William. That military road leads to Loch Leven Head, which the good innkeeper ruled out as quite unfit for the gig. My guess is that Lazowski decided that they should meet him at Portnacroish where he would arrive by boat with the gig. With that deflection, their ride would be nearer 49 strenuous miles than 42. Christopher Fleet, of Scotland's National Map Library, very kindly sent me a photocopy of the hair-raising 1750 Survey, by I Archer, showing this road still being carved out by detachments of Colonel Rich's and General Guise's Regiments. It was only three-quarters complete by 1750. The mountains varied from 1600 to 2900 feet: the military road rose only to 700 and 900 feet but with some very steep inclines. It didn't look too bad from Fort William (see Pl 55, over). Whether they stayed on the road to the Devil's Staircase and doubled back from there to Ballachulish, or got as far as the gully at Lairigmore (OS 122640) and doubled back from there to Callert, on Loch Leven, and Ballachulish, we have no means of knowing: it would have saved them a dozen miles, but was a steeper and much more dangerous track.

34 They spelt it Bunawe, which is how it is still pronounced.

35 At North Ballachulish and Connel.

55. *The military road that was impassable to the gig: this was the start of Alexandre and Nelson's very rough ride south from Fort William and, somehow, to Ballachulish and on to Portnacroish.*

eggs and oatcake and rum and sleeping on straw, or more probably on bracken, which isn't difficult. The longing to get to know these remarkable people better would I think have lured me on, perhaps rashly. But on my own I wouldn't have had to consider a journey of 42 miles on a road that threatened our horse-and-gig. So I hired a boat and arranged to journey this way, myself embarking with the gig and baggage, taking with me my servant who is French. He is very young and neither speaks nor understands English. My companion[36] couldn't embark with me and the gig as I only had an open boat and two boatmen, with an inadequate-looking sail. The navigation was so uncertain that I was advised to get ashore if the wind freshened. At the same time, I've taken the precaution of insisting that, if he met with any difficulty in getting past these lochs, he should himself take a small boat. With these precautions I went aboard cheerfully, though the weather was windy and cold. But we should meet again that evening, and a day passes quickly.[37]

[36] A rather distant way of refering to Alexandre in a journal addressed to Alexandre's father.

[37] The day was 29 April. Alexandre, as usual, noted it, and the fact that 'Nelson and I took the horses overland . . . The road was not just bad but often dangerous for a man on horseback: judge what it would be like for a gig!' The road he took, after discussion with the good innkeeper and his son in Fort William, involved heading left (south) off the lochside road at the edge of the town (at Upper Achintor, where the Fort William Mountain Rescue Post is situated: see OS Landranger 41, 098737) and riding due south along the Old Military Road that has now become the north end of the Long-distance National Trail, the 'West Highland Way': see footnote 33, on previous page, for a discussion of the route they chose. (Pl 55 shows the easy early stages of their ride: Ben Nevis rises 4 or 5 miles away to the left.)

I would advise summertime and fine weather for seeing the Highlands, particularly this part of them; and travel by land and water. You have the choice of two shores, and the enjoyment of great landscapes as well as the beauties of detail. The views are large and often very imposing. Not only are you sailing between two banks of hills cut in a thousand different ways by torrents and ravines, the hills often with their heads lost in the clouds. At present the deciduous trees are not yet in leaf, and the tallest mountains are still covered by snow. All the slopes are covered by flocks of sheep and cattle, and on the plateaux you can make out the crofters' cottages and little fields supplying hay and pasture for their horses. Your eyes are caught by various gentlemen's houses, carefully sited beside the water and backed by plantations of conifers and forest trees, often very extensive, forming charming landscapes, the more agreeable the closer you get. Those higher up the slopes look like cardboard castles, 2-dimensional in their splendid settings.

I landed at one of these houses, curious to see how they maintained their farms and managed to live in a style well above that of the settlements in the little townships in the glens. But these aren't the reasons for my going ashore at this house. To explain them involves a digression which I hope you'll pardon. My two boatmen were highlanders, clansmen, one neither speaks nor understands a word of English, the other understands and speaks a little, but often you have to rephrase your questions five times before he cottons on. Our conversation tended to revert to the landing of the Pretender in 1745, to the battle of Culloden and his long flight and evasion in the mountains.[38] I'd taken care to find out earlier the name of the clan my boatman belonged to, and sure that he had said he was a Macdonald, I concluded that he was a Jacobite, and on that foundation I built my questions. To me it seems impossible not to be interested in the fate of that unhappy family, and particularly in the fate of the last of them. So I asked him about the prince, and after that our conversation became really interesting.

His first response was to raise the sleeve of his jacket and show me a long scar on his wrist: 'My memento of Culloden', he said; 'and if King Charles had need of 20,000 lives, they are here at his disposition'. Thereupon, without waiting for other questions, he asked, with an urgency hard to describe, whether the king was still alive and whether he had any children.[39] 'What a misfortune – *Quel malheur*' – he

---

[38] In August 1745, aged 25, he landed on a small island in the Hebrides, in Macdonald country. One branch of the Macdonalds, with the Macleods, did not hurry to his support. With the aid of Lord George Murray, they defeated the government troops under the misnamed General, Cope, at Prestonpans, they wrong-footed Wade and the newly arrived duke of Cumberland, and reached Derby. There, Murray saw they had no hope of support either from the English or the French; they pulled back and were virtually massacred at Culloden, on 16 April 1746. Despite the enormous ransom on Charles Edward's head, he evaded his hunters in the Hebrides and the western fastnesses from April to September, when he reached France. After the Treaty of 1748, he was requested to leave France. He died in Rome only in 1788.

[39] By his mistress, Miss Walkenshaw, he had his only child, a daughter, who went to live with him in the 1780s, in Florence and in Rome. He became very fond of her and 'created' her 'Duchess of Albany'. He was by then a fairly far advanced alcoholic and the Jacobite cause was long dead, except in the hearts of such romantic dreamers as Lazowski's boatman; it's odd to find such prac-

exclaimed when I replied that the line was virtually extinct. 'All our hopes are finished. Ah, if only we'd had the 6,000 French we were waiting for in Scotland, George would have been chased back to Hanover!' You notice that the highland clans who took part in the rebellion, or who wanted to but were restrained by their chiefs, never speak of the Pretender except by the name of King Charles: nor do they ever refer to the actual king except by the bare name 'George' or 'the governor'. The boatman told me that they were never more than 10,000 altogether, but that a very much greater number were demanding to be there. He said that the 'King' (by his terminology) was saved by a woman of the Macdonald clan (as I know) and he was most emphatic that she was still alive;[40] and furthermore that all the highlanders knew, fairly well, where he was, but not one of them was tempted by the £30,000 promised for information leading to his capture.

Then he said 'over there is the house of a member of the Stuart[41] family, and the King stayed there briefly on his way west. Would you like to go there? We'll take you.' And he explained in Gaelic to his friend what we'd been saying. I said I was afraid it was putting them to a lot of trouble. 'Oh come on; I'll go with you', he insisted: so off we go. The house is called *Orchyle*. It stands on the hillside on a gentle platform which is islanded by a moat. The former fortified house has been replaced. There are many old trees, and some bothies for the farm-labourers. The farm is no more than 100 acres, some of it meadow.

The farmer, a gentleman in highland dress of fine material, came over to me and very agreeably invited me into the house. The interior's simple but clean and comfortable. He offered me refreshment, and as I could see he would be wounded if I refused, I said I'd gladly drink his health. A maid brought a glass and poured out a glass of *vin d'Arbois* which he drank to my health. She then poured a second glass and handed it to me. He told me very charmingly that he had chosen this bottle in the hope that the wine of my country would be specially welcome.[42]

He insisted on accompanying me to my boat, and on the way showed me his

tical men as Lazowski and his pupil-companion so moved by the Prince's lost cause. Alexandre's brother François showed a devotion to Louis XVI, but gave up on 10 August 1792. And Alexandre's service with Napoleon suggests some degree of realism. There's no doubt that the romantic melancholy of the Jacobite cause affected Boswell and Johnson when they were in the Hebrides in 1773, neither of them precisely irrational.

[40] Flora Macdonald (1722–90) was daughter of a tacksman in South Uist in the Hebrides. She lost both parents when she was a child and was brought up in the cultivated Clanranald household. She was on a visit to Benbecula when the Pretender arrived there soon after Culloden. She agreed (apparently with reluctance) to help him escape to Skye, disguised as her Irish spinning maid. It was a dangerous mission, but she got him safely to Portree, and was arrested and imprisoned briefly in the Tower of London. She evidently told Frederick, Prince of Wales, she would have done the same for him! She married in 1750. Dr Johnson visited her in 1773 at Kingsburgh, where she was living in 1786.

[41] Presumably a Stewart of Appin.

[42] Arbois, in the Jura (the north-west fringe of the Alps) produces a yellow wine, and is famous for its *vin fou*; pleasant, cheap sparkling wine. The glass of *Arbois* seems to have put the question of the Pretender's alleged visit out of Lazowski's mind. He refers to it no more, nor to his boatman. It seems an unlikely route for the Pretender to have taken.

farm, stables and barns, away from the house. The cow-byres for the winter are also away from the house. All built very economically, like everything I've seen so far in Scotland. It may cost the same as the equivalent in England, but has a more spare, utilitarian look.

They take the greatest care to manure and enrich their pasture: if, with good soil and a mild climate that's the key to good farming, how much more must it be the principle in these Highlands, where the soil lacks substance and where one strains to bring forward the harvest to avoid the rains. Not that they squander their farmyard manure; and here they do a valuable supplement in the seaweed left behind at high tide, which they gather up carefully: they also go and gather it from the rocks at low tide.

I rejoined my boat and – after a pretty disagreeable sail through drizzle and cold wind – arrived at *Portnacroish* ahead of the horses I'd been hoping to find there.[43] I've been hastening through this country all agitation and anxiety, not less from impatience than from curiosity. From my boat I could see everything I could possibly have seen from the road that follows the shore.

Portnacroish   is a village of the clansmen[44] in the depth of a large inlet which extends into a long valley, very well cultivated. The proof of this is probably demonstrated in the two good houses on adjoining lands on either side of the inlet.[45] Both houses are situated on the edge of Loch Linnhe, an arm of the sea, and are handsomely fronted by lawns and framed by fine meadows and plantations. One of them is infinitely desirable, in the middle of an isthmus, with a gentle slope and very beautiful lawns on both sides to give a 'sea view' out over the Loch.[46] The rest of the isthmus is planted carefully with all kinds of conifers and forest trees. The shore of this isthmus is planted in

43 Lazowski, disappointed not to find the *horses*, doesn't mention Alexandre (who'd gone quite a long way round).

44 The clansmen were the Stewarts of Appin. Alexandre noted that the inn was 'the only one'. In its back garden stood the remains of a cave [*cave*] that 'they say' was built by the druids. 'It isn't very long nor very deep. It wouldn't surprise me if it was built by the people who left those strange remains I forgot to mention on the moors just before Inverness, with a large number of very large squared stones like those I mentioned near Salisbury last year.' There is now no sign of any such cave. In the next paragraph but one, Lazowski describes the excellent food they were given at this inn. The Old Inn survives (Pl 56, over), turned into a dwelling in 1984 (Walker, *Argyll & Bute*, Buildings of Scotland, 2000, p. 433): unoccupied in April 2000. The large inlet is Loch Laich. In my photograph, the inn surprisingly hides the 3-storey, 16th-century Castle Stalker.

45 What seems to have been one of them is Kinlochlaich House, in Appin. It is three unpretending bays wide, but enlarged and Gothicised c1820 and well described by Walker, *op cit*, pp. 105–6. The other was presumably Appin House in Portnacroish, built by the Stewarts of Appin in the early 18th century: demolished in the 1960s. The clan members who fell at Culloden are now commemorated on a headstone outside the ruined old parish church at Appin.

46 The view must have included the northern tip of the island of Lismore, and presumably Castle Stalker on its own small island. Alexandre, on horseback, saw more of the attractive house 2 miles from the town. Around the house, the owner had cleared the peat to a depth of 7 feet, dried it out, ploughed it and made excellent soil before sowing it: 'it will produce wheat and very good quality oats. I hope other proprietors will follow him. His house is beautifully maintained.'

56. *The Old Inn at Portnacroish in Appin, the territory of the Stewarts of Appin. The former inn completely hides their very striking three-storey Castle Stalker, of c1540, on a small island just behind the inn; in 1786, this inn's menu was amazing.*

the intervals between rocky crags, in a picturesque way that delighted me. We didn't get a good view of it today as we sailed out into the loch [Linnhe].

There's no choice of inns here in the Highlands. There's usually one at the end of a stage, a day's journey. Obviously they aren't very sophisticated, but it's impossible to find them wretched or inadequate. You always seem to be able to find tea, sugar, rum and wine; and, to eat, as we did here, fresh eggs, calf's head ragoût, boiled chicken, and an excellent bullock's tongue, with a potato cake. You may find these details trivial, but I give them with good reason.

From *Portnacroish* you re-enter Loch Linnhe until you've passed the isle of Lismore, with its excellent pasture-land. Loch Linnhe now becomes Loch Lorne and widens to about 7 or 8 miles below the isle of Mull.

I have never been so tempted as I was by my two sailors. Today they offered to sail me out to the isle of Staffa, which all lovers of natural history in England, especially Sir Joseph Banks,[47] have been to visit as a sight greatly superior to *The Giant's*

---

[47] Banks visited Staffa on his Iceland voyage in 1772, the year of Pennant's journey to the Hebrides; Pennant failed to reach Staffa but Banks, with characteristic generosity, allowed Pennant to publish his Staffa material, including copies of the drawings he'd had made. Pennant published five astonishing drawings of the basalt columns of Staffa in 1774, including Fingal's Cave. Lazowski is much more likely to have read of Staffa in Banks's account of it, in *Pennant's Tour in*

Causeway in County Antrim in Ireland. The columns of basalt are more complete, more regular and generally perfect than anything of its kind, anywhere. If I'd been on my own, I wouldn't have hesitated half a minute, for at the same time I'd have been seeing one of the Western Isles – something I'll probably never have another chance of doing. However, this temptation gave me no serious regrets, for the idea of leaving my companion two whole days without me was not to be thought of. All these little details, are interesting in retrospect. I must continue my narrative of the tour.

Once you've passed the long island of Lismore, you enter on the left another loch which you will find on the maps as Loch Etive.[48] We're always in the bottoms of deep valleys: this time, between eminences rather than mountains, and the only thing against our sailing is the current of the tides, which is violent, and makes progress difficult, even with a following wind.

All this coast is rocky, and covered, to a great depth, in sea-weed of different species, with notably long, broad and thick leaves, almost like palm-leaves, that I've never noticed on our shores. Some have a fruit not unlike an acorn. The further west we go, the greater the quantity. It's a source of business and wealth for the inhabitants, who dry it and burn it as we do in France, though here the abundance is greater than I've seen anywhere. How they turn it into Kali[49] I haven't discovered.

After sailing for six mortal hours in cold, miserable, wet weather, we had to wait for the rise of the tide, our only way of making progress up into the loch. I had hurried to get here, and now was held up by a ridge of rock on which rests a stratum of pudding-astone or of lava. I will bring a specimen for you to examine. The countryside is beginning to show signs of spring. Bear's ears [auriculas] are in flower but so far have no scent. It's impossible for these hills to be covered with aromatic plants like those in our southern provinces. However, I'm a total ignoramus about botany: I've seen so much, yet seen nothing.

After waiting an hour and a half, I became impatient and insisted that my boatmen make another attempt. These good fellows agreed, and when we arrived again at the bar, which I'll describe later, we made another attempt to cross it. It was still impassable, and they asked for another half-hour. The wind had risen power-

---

Scotland and Voyage to the Hebrides, 2nd edn, 1776, than in Van Troil's *Letters on Iceland*, London, 1781, where it also appeared.

48 Alexandre, on horseback, and having relieved Lazowski of the gig (though it was Lazowski's chief reason for travelling by water) comes to Loch Creran before reaching the alarming Loch Etive. Soon after praising the handsome farmhouse near Portnacroish he was confronted by 'another beautiful view, of *Loch Creran* near its entry into Loch Linnhe, a marvellous spread of water: first the loch, and beyond it a fine mountain . . . We cross Loch Creran on another ferry, which is terrible. The boats are so awful, and after having waited for so long we continued our route till we came to another ferry; which didn't frighten the horses badly – at least, not the boarding-ceremony, but the loading of the gig on the ferry caused the greatest difficulties. We were obliged to use force to get the gig aboard, using ropes, which was very tricky for the horses. The road between the two ferries, only 2 miles, crosses very agreeable farmland, and houses of stone and mortar, which counts as magnificence round here.'

49 Kali = vegetable alkali = potash.

fully, and I could see that my excellent captain agreed that we must make a new attempt, but his mate was reluctant. They spoke Gaelic and I couldn't understand what they said. With the help of a strong breeze we cleared the bar and were crossing, or trying to cross, the current which, as I judged very inadequately, was terrible. We wanted to cut across it. It struck the boat amidships, and despite the sail and the rudder it spun us round; the sail, becoming very dangerous, could only fall about our ears, but at the same time we needed it to hold us to the edges of the current, closely enough to avoid being smashed to pieces on the banks of rock towards which the current was forcing us. But the second boatman had lost his head, and far from being able to manage the sail; he was incapable of detaching the cord and drawing it in. He and the captain were as white as my shirt. I could only look at them, for you know that it's on the professionals that you depend, and from them you learn to hope or despair.

At that moment, four or five fishermen came dashing towards the shore. We thought we were sunk, finished. They cried out to us not to attempt to double round a rocky point ahead of us, which would infallibly finish us, for we knew we had to come gently to the shore. After a few more minutes of distress, we at last reached the shore, where we were greeted by the fishermen who told us it was crazy to attempt the bar, even with the tide falling: the contrary currents, meeting, form funnels [*entonnoirs*] and carry you ashore: they're so violent that heavily-laden sloops never pass here without fear. One they saw at the entrance of the loch turned round twice on itself although laden with a cargo of lead and having crowded on all sail. Above all, they said how lucky it was we hadn't gone on any further, because we should undoubtedly have been lost: we shouldn't even think of re-embarking for at least an hour, at the very earliest, when the tide should be strong enough to break the force of the current.

I need to confess that yesterday, at Portnacroish, we had met a Mr Stewart, a gentleman of these parts who, seeing that we were strangers in the inn, introduced himself and obligingly offered his services after we'd told him the route we'd planned. He advised us to take a different one, warned us that the passage I'd planned to take was dangerous at all times, that that tide was extraordinary and the most curious one to watch in the whole of Scotland.[50] He said we could dispense with going to Bonawe and reach Dalmally the same day. I hadn't really believed Mr Stewart, but believed in the boatmen who promised me I could be at Bonawe in time to reach Inverary: that, in a word, proved quite impossible.

That tide is truly extraordinary, and I'd better say more of it. From Bonawe at the

---

[50] He is describing the narrow crossing at the mouth of Loch Etive, at what is now called Connell Ferry, but crossed by the largest cantilevered steel bridge in Britain after the Forth Bridge. At the old ferry crossing you still see the 'Falls of Lora', the phenomenon Alexandre describes so vividly. They are a combination of rapids and whirlpools, and are seen at their most violent one or two days after a full or a new moon. On 2 September 1803, Dorothy and William Wordsworth made this crossing in complete ignorance of its dangers. The noise and foam of the waves terrified their poor horse, who plunged about desperately so that they feared his feet would go through the bottom of the ferryboat: E. de Selincourt, ed, *Journals of Dorothy Wordsworth*, I, 1959, p. 316.

57. *On both sides of the entrance-bar to Loch Etive, whirlpools are formed by rapids, 'the Falls of Lora'; most dangerous at new and full moons. Lazowski's boat was spun round and narrowly missed being smashed against the rocks.*

far corner of the loch, about eight miles away, the slope is very rapid, which is why the tide falls with such impetuosity, so much greater than the violence of the current of the river Awe as it enters Loch Etive from Loch Awe. But, as the tide can broaden across the whole width of the loch, you can sail round its edges and avoid the battering of the current which drives down the middle. The loch is barred across two-thirds of its width by a ridge of rock at water-level, shaped like a shelf, where the water flows quietly. This bank, as I say, stretches only across two-thirds of the loch: all the violence of the water is carried to this side and all the mass of water in the loch forces itself into this narrowing current: it's so violent that it forms a great swirl with the middle raised high above the edges but at the same time the whole mass of water can't get through the narrow opening and hurls itself against the rock which hurls it back. Then it forms these terrible rapids, whirlpools and contrary currents in which boats that have the misfortune to be trapped perish against the rocks.

It was with a mixture of terror and pleasure that I later watched this fearful spectacle from the security of the rocks above, and I was acutely aware that, if I'd had the fortune to get through against the current, and get round the point, I'd have avoided a great danger only to perish unavoidably just as the fishermen assured me. In the end, I waited the hour and a quarter for the tide to reach level, and embarked with four of these fishermen who wanted to go to Bonawe and who for us offered the great convenience that they would row us, and so we left by these reliable means. The wind seemed favourable and I hoped we might cover the 8 miles in *an hour*. But in these mountains it's impossible to depend for half an hour on a steady wind: these deep gorges often cause it to change direction. It was *six hours* before I arrived: cold and hunger made it seem longer. Although I'd been up since 5.30 in the morning, I'd eaten only a bit of oatcake and drunk one glass of brandy.

The misery increased the pleasure of coming ashore from the boat and finding myself beside a good fire with my companion, and eating our supper. Life's truly a dream only when you're a traveller, or in passionate pursuit of some serious enquiry. Judging by my own case today, I've endured 3 days of a fever and they've been painful: yet I'm well enough to write to you, and at length; and I must admit to having some pleasure and having put to the test all my courage.

Alexandre and Nelson arrived at Loch Etive with the horses and gig:[51] *Alexandre saw it thus:*

The view of the second loch as we crossed by ferry near its mouth is beautiful, but in a different way, and not for its breadth but for its velocity, its speed of movement. It's called *Loch Etive*. It isn't very broad at the point where you cross; but further off it broadens out, and, after about a mile, squeezed between two points of rock, it presses against them with such strength that the water creates a cataract, very difficult to sail through. When we passed the place with our horses, the water was of such rapidity that, as we later heard, Mr Lazowski's boat had spun round twice on itself. We had a lot of trouble and performance with our horses, which were badly frightened by the noise and racing of the water. But there's no point in my describing the danger for boats here: Mr Lazowski almost perished aboard his. I imagine he will tell you *all* about it in *great* detail at the end of the 11th volume of his journal of this year.[52]

You follow the loch along the agreeable way beside it which widens into a handsome surface and passes, along the shore, several pretty country houses; the aridity of the mountains allows them no cultivation. There's a fine wood that has been allowed to grow to maturity. Then a plain leads to Bonawe. Before entering, you cross a ford[53] that is wide and deep, so that I got thoroughly wet.

---

[51] Lazowski presumably brought the gig ashore at Portnacroish, which was fortunate. 'The second loch' was Etive; the first was Creran.
[52] We have just heard Lazowski's story, not too dramatised! His journal seems to have taken the form of letters to Alexandre's father, as we've seen. I wish I could trace it, and not be dependent on the late M Marchand's typescript copy, which he occasionally cut when there was more agricultural description than he had time for. But we're lucky to have what we have got.
[53] Through the river Awe.

Bonawe. The only one[54]   Bonawe is a very small place with only 12 or 13 houses, though it has a church. We have a very good little inn, where we arrived at midday,[55] but Mr Lazowski was delayed by their terrible boat-trip and didn't arrive till 6, which prevented us from moving on: he was in a very poor way. We've done our best. We're lodging with a lady very different from most Englishwomen who, although as licentious as ours, are certainly less open about it. Our innkeeper, without more ado, while I was chatting with her, told me that she'd been in Britain only 12 years, and then went on to tell me, with all frankness, the entire story of her life. I think it's one of the most breathtaking pieces of impudence you're likely to find. But we can overlook it in view of the very good dinner: an entire pig she served up, and the best port wine I've ever drunk. These two items, especially the last, easily make up for the little lapses of gallantry.

On the 1st of May we left Bonawe   and slept at *Inveraray*. On the way, we dined at *Dalmally,*[56] 14 miles from Bonawe.

Lazowski takes over:

To get to Dalmally you first follow a very narrow pass, the Pass of Brander, which contains the river Awe. The mountains close in abruptly, the giant Ben Cruachan [3,689 feet] forming the north wall of the pass. *Here, Murray's* Guide *in the 1880s recorded: 'The most wonderful effects are produced after rain, when hundreds of cataracts dash down on either side and, reflected in the water, look like an inverted arch of waterfall.' Lazowski resumes:* These steep slopes are covered from base to peak with sheep

54 Bonawe, Bridge of Awe and Brochroy are all now regarded as part of the widespread village of Taynuilt. The original 18th-century inn is identified at the centre of the present *Taynuilt Hotel* a good 2 miles further along the Dalmally road from the jetty and the furnace at Bonawe: it may easily be Alexandre's need to get dry and warm, and Lazowski's need to recover from his alarming boat-trip, that made them reluctant to retrace their steps to the very interesting furnace. The landlady's licentious conversation with Alexandre may have put thoughts of the iron-furnace completely out of his mind. And he was perhaps genuinely worried as he waited six hours for Lazowski to appear.
55 Alexandre had six hours to spare between his arrival at the inn and Lazowski's. The iron furnace was established here in 1753 for the smelting by charcoal of iron-ore from England. There is an excellent, fully-illustrated account of these ironworks by Frank Walker in his Buildings of Scotland vol: *Argyll & Bute*, 2000, pp. 484–7. Odder than Alexandre's loss of curiosity was Lazowski's statement that Bonawe was 'important only for its *lead*-furnaces, finding work and keeping a small navigation going, as much for carrying salmon as for bringing provisions for the workmen and charcoal for the furnaces. This one foundry has brought much life to the district. The harbour consists of one little jetty, along which ships range at high tide and get stranded at low water. We left the day after our arrival, despite the lassitude caused by my fever and a painful bowel complaint.' Neither of them noticed the quarries immediately opposite Bonawe across Loch Etive. Today, the various buildings of the ironworks, including the furnace-house, are beautifully repaired and shown (April 2000).
56 Frank Walker, *Argyll & Bute*, p. 219, says the present Dalmally Hotel contains the original 3-bay, 3-storey inn, built 1781–2: this can just be made out from the outside.

58. Inveraray Castle, *from William Daniell's* Voyage Round Great Britain in 1813 *(1825). Inveraray had been the seat of the Campbells since 1474. Lazowski: 'The duke's house is in an exceptionally fine situation. To the east and south, the loch is like a lawn of water.' Alexandre: 'He has built an extraordinary house: a square block wrapped in four round towers, and with another rising out of the middle. It has a pretty park and, above all, really superb plantations . . .'*

all the year round. You have to climb high on the mountainside, on a road cut obliquely, but very steeply, just as the river reaches its source in Loch Awe. From the top, and along the rest of the road, you enjoy a really magnificent view. Dalmally, 2 miles beyond the northern tip of Loch Awe, will not detain you.[57] We headed south for Inveraray, which stands on the west shore of Loch Fyne, not far from *its* northern tip.[58]

---

[57] Alexandre thought it a pretty little place, and well farmed.

[58] Alexandre didn't omit to record, as Lazowski (perhaps not recovered from Loch Etive) failed to do, that 'Loch Fyne is famous for its herring-fishery'. *SAS* (V, 1793, p. 291) goes further: 'That part of Lochfyne by which this parish is bounded on the east and southeast, has been from time immemorial noted for its herrings, which are superior in quality to any found in the western seas.' That judgment may have been disputed, but the town's shield of arms bears a net with a herring. The *SAS* author believed 'there have been caught and cured in some seasons 20,000 barrels, valued @ 15s a barrel, and at least 500 boats employed, each crewed by 4 men'.

Inveraray. The New Inn[59]   This town is a new kind of creation, built almost entirely anew, and on a new site,[60] by the duke of Argyll who has peopled it with artisans to whom he gives so much a year to live here. He has some hand-looms and has taken every means of introducing into this part of the Highlands the leading craft technology and the work.[61] At the end of the town he has put up a building that looks like the body of a barracks. The main block forms the barns and farm-buildings, and the two wings serve as lodgings to the men attached to the farm and to fifty activities all the year round, both in forestry and in other jobs in the park.

The duke's house is in an exceptionally fine situation. To the east and south, the loch is like a lawn of water: across the loch, the little town and the hills, all farmed and forested; to the north and west is a plain leading to the hills. These hills – one of them a sort of irregular cone[62] – are tree'd to the summit. They are made up out of little valleys that are partly meadows, and in one of which the bed of a river has been re-fashioned: the idea of the pleasure-ground is everywhere.[63]

The house stands on a small eminence framed by superb lawns; it is newly built, with a fondness for a gothic style hard to accept or find agreeable.

Alexandre was especially enthusiastic about the duke's tree-plantations, but simple-minded about his family's leading part in smoothing the Hanoverian succession in Scotland. (Alexandre had no scruples, later, in deserting the Bourbon cause in favour of Napoleon.) The key figure in all this was Archibald Campbell, 3rd duke of Argyll. He served under Marlborough against Louis XIV. With his elder brother, the 2nd duke, he took part in the battle of Sheriffmuir against the Old Pretender in 1715. Walpole entrusted him with the chief management of Scottish affairs. He succeeded his brother as duke in 1743, and after 'the 1745' he put forward the effective policy of creating the highland regiments as part of the British Army, channelling the warlike gifts of the

---

59 Built 1751–5 by John Adam (Colvin, *Dictionary*, p. 50) and now known as the Great Inn.
60 The *SAS* (1793, p. 294) recorded: 'About 15 years ago [c1778], the old town, which was situated at the N end of the bay, was removed, and a new town was built on the S end of it; and if the streets were completed, no town in the kingdom of its dimensions would make a better appearance . . . there is not one thatched house in the whole of it . . . At what period it was considered as the county town is uncertain.' Robert Mylne was the duke's architect, in the new town, of two rows of tenements, Arkland and Relief Land, 1774–6, and in 1787, an arched screen-wall facade to Loch Fyne (Colvin, *Dictionary*, p. 684). Robert Southey, in 1819, said it reminded him of 'those little German towns, which in like manner have been created by small potentates, in the plenitude of their power. They have built a huge prison. Both Scotch and English have an unaccountable liking for jails-ornées.' He was reminded of Lake Como, and said that, on the whole, it exceeded anything he'd seen in Great Britain: *op cit*, pp. 241–2.
61 *SAS* (p. 297) says the 3rd duke introduced the linen manufacture here in 1748; the 5th duke introduced c1776 'an woollen manufacture, having, at very considerable expense, built houses, erected machinery and provided every material necessity for carrying it on successfully at the Water of Douglas' (about 4 miles south-west of the town). In 1793, *SAS* shows it struggling for want of spinners and an adequate supply of fuel.
62 Duniquoich.
63 *SAS* (V, 1793, p. 290) agreed. 'In regard to extent of pleasure ground, and of fine plantations, hardly any place can vie with Inveraray.'

*clansmen into famous imperial purposes. In 1745 he set about the building of his castle
here, on a new site.*[64] *According to the SAS (1793, pp. 296–7), 'the sums laid out at
Inveraray, since the 1745, do now amount to £250,000 and that the present duke, the
5th, since his accession in 1770, has expended at the rate of at least £3,000 a year.
Happily for his family and his country, Newmarket has not engrossed his attention; a
considerable part of his great revenue was employed in promoting the general improvement of his estates, in giving employment to the poor, and in extending industry and
manufactures. He was enabled to give his land to his tenants on reasonable terms: if they
are sober and industrious, none in their station of life need live more comfortably . . .
This great proprietor, even in these peaceable times, refuses to listen to any proposals of an
augmentation in rent from shepherds or store-masters which might have a tendency to
dispossess the natives and dispeople the country.'*

*In the light of the Statistical Account, one sees that Alexandre is (curiously) unable to
distinguish between the 3rd and the 5th (the current) duke, and capable of fantasy about
the feelings of the local clansmen for their chief (the duke) and about his 'loyalties' to the
absent Pretender and the present king. Alexandre wrote:*

He has built an extraordinary house: a square block wrapped in four round
towers, and with another rising out of the middle and all in the ancient style. At first
sight I'd have taken it for an old house. It has a pretty park and, above all, really
superb plantations. The prospect of the house is most beautiful.[65] It's built at the
heart of his plantations and has views of the whole landscape including the town and
the loch: nothing could be more magnificent. The duke spends much of his time
here every summer. In winter he goes to London. His friends when he's here are
mostly English, and that, combined with the way he sided with the English against
the Scots in the recent battles [the 1715 and 1745 rebellions], has made his people
regard him with a sort of mistrust, and even indignation.[66]

---

[64] Wm Adam supervised the construction of the castle to the 'Gothick' design of Roger Morris for
the 3rd duke, 1745–8. John Fleming, *Robert Adam and his Circle*, 1962, pl 20, reproduced James
Adam's drawing of the building, c1754. It does show how, as he puts it, 'William Adam, as a friend
of Sir John Clerk and Lord Hopetoun, found Morris's Gothick embarrassing', and wrote to him
for precise, detailed instructions for building those windows.

[65] Well shown in A A Tait, *The Landscape Garden in Scotland, 1735–1835*, Edinburgh UP, 1980,
p. 48; and see Pl 58, p. 190.

[66] Alexandre seems to see the 'present' 5th duke as instrumental in putting down the rebellions
(!), and seems somehow to have betrayed his own sentimental Jacobite sympathies, presumably in
the inn or the town, to someone willing to encourage him in the unlikely belief that they regarded
their principal benefactor with mistrust and indignation. The builder of the house, the 3rd duke,
had an English mother, after all (a Tollemache of Helmingham and Ham), and was born at Ham
House in Middlesex. The 5th duke's wife was born at Hemingford Grey, in Huntingdonshire, and
was Lady of the Bedchamber to Queen Charlotte, 1761–84. It can hardly have been surprising
that in 1786 Alexandre should have found that the Argylls had 'English friends'. What he might
have discovered if he had been able to visit the house himself, even in the duke's absence, was that
the duke was the (1st) President of the Highland and Agricultural Society of Scotland. He held
that useful Presidency from 1785 until he died – Alexandre would have been relieved to know – in
Inveraray Castle, twenty years to the month after their visit.

On the 2nd of May   we stayed on in Inveraray. The weather was so terrible that I wasn't even able to set foot outside. I had, for sole consolation, going over to the window to peer out through the rain at that beautiful view across the loch. There was no way of enjoying it more fully. Another consolation in my captivity was writing a lot, and reading it over carefully. All day I really wanted to go out and see the castle, to get to know the arrangement of a Scottish house, and to see in detail these great plantations.

9

Back in the Lowlands

Loch Lomond, Glasgow, Paisley, Portpatrick

At Inveraray, it rained so hard that they couldn't even set foot outside the New Inn (new in 1750, part of the duke of Argyll's 'new town'). They noticed the new buildings to house the duke's farm workers in the town, but seem to have been discouraged, by the weather and the duke's absence, from trying to visit the castle: a great pity, not least because the duke was the first President of the Highland and Agricultural Society of Scotland. They were 'infatuated' by the wild scenery all the way to Loch Lomond, the beauties of which they explored by boat, and found magnificent, despite the weather. Riding alongside the river Leven to Dumbarton, they noted the good soil, gentlemen farmers' houses, printfields and bleachfields, 'a richness I haven't seen since Dundee; and on a most beautiful day. We have left the Highlands and the aboriginal people, whom I truly love' (Alexandre).

    Their love for Glasgow was of a quite different order. Adam Smith gave them a letter of introduction to John Millar, famous as a teacher of the nature of social change, and of the relationship between law and philosophy, but also the kindest of men: he had them to dinner, once with his large family, and once with a large number of his colleagues, who told them everything they wanted to know about Glasgow's commercial strength: how the loss of their huge tobacco trade, following the loss of the American colonies, had instantly put Glasgow's merchants on their mettle, calling out all their energies and ingenuity in manufacturing and exporting, making it 'Scotland's most commercial town'. They admired the regularity of its plan, its stone-built houses with gables, urns and cornices, its handsome churches and a distinguished coffee-house, with colonnade, conveniently close by the Exchange.

    If possible, Paisley pleased them even more. They stayed in Lord Abercorn's 'beautiful' new inn: 'the merchants have established manufactures here on a very large scale, and have more or less achieved perfection'. If that were not enough, they were taken by post-chaise out to Johnston to see a cotton mill with the latest machinery, worked very largely by children. Unlike the Minister of the parish, Mr Boog, they admired this 'profitable' use of children.

    Heading south-west towards Ayr, the road was all stone and rocks but became charming after Beith. From Irvine, the coastal plain looked very sandy and then was subsequently covered with sheep, a superb breed. Near Girvan, they came under the spell of Ailsa Craig's amiable shape, ten miles offshore, distracting them even from the sheep. They were further distracted by a terrible road, to Ballantrae, but saw some more hand-

some cattle and sheep. At Stranraer, exceptionally, they stopped for tea, found the town crowded for the May fair, and nowhere to stay. Their horses, especially the one who hauled the gig, were so exhausted that all four men had to walk their six last Scottish miles to Portpatrick, arriving so late that Alexandre could remember nothing of their arrival. Next day he described the perils of the rocky harbour, and cast his mind back over his five profitable weeks in Scotland.

On 3 May, we left Inveraray   and took the *Glasgow* road via Loch Lomond, spending the night at *Tarbet*, 24 miles from Inveraray. For the first ten, you follow Loch Fyne to its tip, the route superb all the way and the sheep also beginning to look better, a fine breed. I'm really glad to see sheep in such numbers and with such good wool. These are ten prosperous miles, well farmed and well forested. We dined 14 miles from Tarbet, and in the first 12 found ourselves amid crags, with the beginning of a small stream that was soon making a series of falls. These crags are uninhabited: in the whole distance, you come to just one solitary dwelling. There is nowhere the least sign of cultivation. Yet many such places do manage to grow something. The one agreeable sight on this part of our road is the very large number of little waterfalls which do give it some life. The horror of this route contains beauty of a kind. What must strike any traveller is the difference between this morning's route and this evening's: an enormous disarrangement of nature.

I'm infatuated [*toqué*] by what I've seen in these 12 miles. You arrive at the shore of Loch Long, a most beautiful stretch, both from its narrow length and from the nobility of the mountain shapes about its head. It's a salt-water loch with very large ships, an extension of the open sea. It's famous for its plentiful fish.

Round the loch you can see two or three pretty country-houses. The whole way to Tarbet is an avenue of trees, very welcoming and agreeable. Passing an oddly-shaped steep mountain[1] you arrive at the view of Loch Lomond, very near the village of Tarbet.

Tarbet, White Hut   It's a small place, built beside Loch Lomond, about which everyone has written and expressed a view. The one thing I'll impress on my reader is the need to have a map of Scotland. I'm afraid it's impossible to have any idea of the place, let alone a journey through it, without a map.[2] (I'm at the end of my 4th volume, and will leave Loch Lomond to the next. All I ask is the indulgence of the reader and his approbation when I have the good fortune to merit it.)

---

[1]   Ben Arthur (often known as the Cobbler).
[2]   They must have had maps, but never say whose: maddening. They were just too soon for Jn Ainslie's map of 1789, but never mention Taylor and Skinner's road maps, 1775, which might have been too bulky for them. If they used Taylor and Skinner's *General Map of the Roads of Scotland* they would have found it useless between Fort William and Bonawe, though using that map would certainly explain their original intention to travel due south along the military road that Alexandre followed on horseback and that would have been much too difficult for the gig. I think they did use that *General Map*.

On 4 May we left Tarbet and took a boat to explore *Loch Lomond*. It rained, but the wind was good and we sailed 8 miles down the loch, but then a mist developed and blotted out the entire view. It's a fresh-water loch, 24 miles long, and contains 28 islands.[3] It varies in width between 1 mile and 8. There are two very tall mountains; green to halfway, then naked rock.[4] Especially in summer, the verdure of the woods must greatly add to the beauty of the water. When the wood is mature it's used in boat-building: otherwise, in fencing and palisades, and sometimes for roofing.

This loch is more beautiful than I can say. I can't hope to give a true idea, but only a slight and general one. Through the dignities and beauties of its hills, and perhaps especially through their variety, this scenery is magnificent. When you come in sight of Luss (a small village), the loch becomes about 4 miles wide and there are several islands. The mountains are lower, but still noble. The islands are planted with trees, and the woods themselves look particularly well. At the end of our sailing-trip we had some very bad weather: the wind grew stronger and obliged us to go ashore at *Luss*. There we rejoined our horses, which we'd sent along by land. We dined, and during dinner the weather got worse, the wind blew with such strength that we didn't know whether we really wanted to return aboard our boat to sail down through the islands. In the end, we felt obliged to take to our horses and ride over-land to *Dumbarton*, where we were to sleep. The end of the day proved as agreeable as the beginning. You cover 8 miles alongside the *loch*, often through woods, through which you sometimes caught glimpses of the water, the boats and the islands, one part of which was covered with cattle, and there were the ruins of an old castle.[5] On another island one saw two or three very poor houses. This is a place where mad people are kept sometimes, indeed almost always. There is also an island on which, in the past, prisoners were sent. But although the island has kept its name as a prison, this use, which was common in the time of the kings of Scotland, has now been brought to an end.

But to return to our story, the view of all these different isles can't fail to please, and the 8 miles through fine woods likewise.

The rest of the route is superb on account of the goodness of the soil. And it is well supplied with gentlemen's houses.[6] The whole country is enclosed and well

---

3   The local books say 24 islands but some are very small: it's the largest freshwater lake in Britain.
4   This describes Ben Arthur (see footnote 1, above) but Ben Lomond, 3,192 feet, nearly oppo-site Tarbet, is green all over.
5   A century later, Murray's *Guide* noted that, on Inch Murrin, the largest, most southerly island, the duke of Montrose had a herd of fallow deer, and there were the ruins of Lennox Castle. Lazowski was taken with 'the setting of the lake against high wooded mountains': the most famous, Ben Lomond, spreads over six miles and stands 3,192 feet above the waters of the lake.
6   Ross-Dhu House, for instance, 2 miles south of Luss, which Sir Jas Colquhoun designed for himself, 1773–4, and which is now the magnificent Clubhouse of the Loch Lomond Golf Club. He also built Helensburgh, the pleasant watering-place on the Clyde, naming it after his pious wife. They entertained Boswell and Johnson at Rosedour, as Boswell called it, and whence the Colquhoun coach conveyed them on to Bonhill, seat of commissary Smollett, cousin of Tobias the novelist, who died in 1771. Johnson revised part of the Latin inscription on the tall Tuscan column erected above the Leven river to the novelist in 1774. The estate passed next year to the

farmed, especially as you come nearer to the town, where you find not only good farming but an abundance of manufacture. The view reveals a richness I haven't seen since we left Dundee: and on a most beautiful day. The houses are good: in about 3 miles I've seen about 8 or 10 gentlemen's houses and, what makes it all look the more flourishing, 3 villages are entirely new. Their existence depends on 3 manufactures and on [fullers for] muslins that are common and very cheap here.[7] This superb country led us right into Dumbarton, the capital of a shire.

Dumbarton, King's Arms[8]   This is a small town at the entrance of the river Lomond to the Clyde. It marks the end of the Highlands. We have left these aboriginal people, of whom I would still like to say a little more. I'm sure our travel through the mountains would have been extremely agreeable in summer weather. I'd advise anyone who is interested in seeing a pattern of ancient ways of living to come and visit, to observe the great changes that time, and civilisation, have brought about, so that we are so refined, so far removed from them, that we cannot really understand their wretched deprivation. And now I'm leaving these people whom I truly love: I'm perhaps biased towards

novelist's sister. She and her son responded to the growth of the printfield at Dalquharn by founding in 1782 a new village they named Renton, which by 1796 had developed several streets (*SAS*, XVII, p. 216). Another of the new villages that delighted Alexandre was perhaps what grew into Alexandria, named after a Smollett son. Part of the attraction for printing and bleaching linen and muslin was the softness and clearness of the Leven river-water, to which the loch seems to have acted as a strainer. *SAS*'s account of Bonhill (III, p. 446) gives a clear picture of the printing products here, 1768–92, from simple block-printed handkerchiefs to water-driven copper-plate presses, printing 20 or 30 dozen handkerchiefs an hour, in two or more colours, and leaving flower-patterns to be added by block-printers. In their delight at the spread of industry between the foot of Loch Lomond and Dumbarton, neither of them foresaw the desolate conditions that now characterise this sad district since their businesses went abroad, where the labour was even cheaper. Charles Ross of Greenlaw's *Map of Dumbartonshire*, c1777, already shows two printfields and a bleachfield along the west bank of the Leven river opposite Bonhill, amid trees and pleasantly scattered farms. Dorothy Wordsworth in 1822 noticed 'rows of white houses increased in number – and more factories' since her 1803 tour, 'yet the scenes as we pass along more pleasing than in my remembrance': *Journals*, 1959, II, p. 351: she, too, had no premonition of decay.

7   Lazowski noticed, as they rode along the river Leven down to the Clyde, 'a plain of great richness, where in the last 15 years bleaching works and manufactures of textiles and buttons have been established, employing very large numbers'. (Neither of them commented on Smollett's extremely handsome column.) In Dumbarton, 'the first thing I noticed on leaving the Highlands was the good building, houses stone-built, and a fine bridge; various workshops, one of them a glassworks'. The famous twin-peaked rocky hill (Pl 59, over) at the junction of Clyde and Leven, reminded him of Mont St Michel in Normandy. *SAS*, IV, p. 23, recorded, by 1792, the crown-and-bottle glassworks employing 130 hands, paying £3,800 a year in tax. It sharpened the picture of the textiles by referring to the extensive printfields (for staining cotton cloth) in the neighbourhood, employing 86 people from the town. Several families had moved out from Dumbarton to Renton, Bonhill 'and other new villages' to be nearer the printfields. 'About 2,000 tons of shipping belong to Dumbarton, employing 70 seamen.'

8   D. Macleod, *Dumbarton Ancient and Modern*, 1893, ch XXIII, 1st page: 'In 1828, it is the property of Mrs Currie, High Street.' It stood with its back to the river, on the site now numbered 117–127.

59. *Rock and castle of Dumbarton, published by Vernor and Hood, Poultry, May 1805, in* Beauties of Scotland, *III, Edinburgh, 1806.*

them by their beauty and the simplicity of their manners, which is perfected to such a high degree that it can't merely be a question of wisdom acquired in these mountains.

Back to *Dumbarton*. The castle stands nearby on a sort of sugar-loaf rock, broadly based and divided in two.[9] One is several feet taller than the other, which is so sheer that it needs no fortification, other than a wall all round and a tower above. It looks impregnable, the rock standing over 200 feet high, with waterfalls near the top. It is garrisoned by Invalids, under a captain, and serves as a prison. The king of England keeps it solely in case of Rebellion. It stands above the Clyde, which is a mile wide and navigable for small merchant-ships. From the top there are good views, and you can see *Port Glasgow* very distinctly, where the Glasgow merchants have their quays. Further out one can also see Greenock, another seaport.[10]

[9] Yes, really two sugar-loaves: see illustration.
[10] Perhaps word of Dr Johnson's prowess had put Alexandre and Lazowski on their mettle. 'Though the approach to the castle is very steep, Dr Johnson ascended it with alacrity, and surveyed all that was to be seen.' He was sixty-three, and 'could not bear to be treated like an old or infirm man'. If he reached the top, Boswell had reason to be proud of his 'alacrity', but my guess is that they were content to reach The Governor's House at the first stage. Two more stages involve about 350 more steps, and usually a stiff wind. Alexandre is right about the castle's extraordinary position. When Dorothy and William Wordsworth and Coleridge were here in August 1803, Dorothy noted a third distant view: up the Leven river to the mountains of Loch Lomond: *Journals*, I, 1959, p. 241.

The position of this castle is so much more extraordinary than all the mountains in the Highlands.

GLASGOW

On 5 May we left Dumbarton and arrived at *Glasgow*, 15 miles on. The route is charming. You cling almost all the way to river Clyde, broad and handsome, and where the tide floods in strongly. You go through farmlands, almost all of them enclosed, with very good soil and equally good farming, and with a large number of houses, mills and manufactures. Nothing could be finer than the whole of this route. There's a large number of country houses. This whole beautiful countryside leads you right up close to the town.

The entrance to Glasgow is much finer even than that into Edinburgh, which I remember praising enthusiastically. When you draw near to the first street, you find, for the last half-mile, gardens on both sides of the road, all very well kept; and this stretch of pretty scenes is most agreeable. I'll leave till tomorrow the description of Glasgow, where we shall stay two full days.

As we're here for 2 days, I shall devote (Saturday) the 6th May to a description of the town, and on the 7th I will give you some idea of the trade of the place.

Saracen's Head [11]   The town stands on the river Clyde, which is navigable up to here only for small boats of 7 or 8 tons. It is built at the edge of a pleasant level plain that's crossed by the river and ends in a low hill that causes an irregularity in one of the main streets.[12] The town is generally very well built. There are a great many excellent houses which (and this is what is so extraordinary) are all aligned and built on an almost regular plan – apparently without the proprietors being obliged by the burgh to conform. The churches seem well built and beautiful. Above all, one notices a taste for old styles which never fail to be light and agreeable.[13]

There are two towns, the new town[14] and the old. The old one is truly delightful,

[11] The Saracen's Head inn was where Boswell and Johnson stayed on 28/29 October 1773. Boswell described how Johnson put up a leg on either side of the coal fire 'in high glee'.
[12] He is presumably thinking of the High Street, which curves as it descends to the river from the ridge in the north-east, on which the medieval cathedral stands so memorably.
[13] Lazowski thought the streets 'perfectly well paved, better than in any other town I've seen'. Of the houses he noted many with 'gables surmounted by handsome urns and cornices and pilastered fronts and big square windows, the framing well proportioned'. He declared: 'The cathedral is an old Gothic building not worth going to find. But two modern churches are of a taste that pleased me infinitely (see Pl 60, over): they had only slender bell-towers above their porticos. One, especially, is modelled on the antique classical style, perfectly proportioned.' This is St Andrew's parish church, St Andrew's Square, set in the northern tip of Glasgow Green. 'The only building in Glasgow, 1739–56, intact enough to display the taste and affluence of her Tobacco lords' – Buildings of Scotland, *Glasgow*, 452 . 'In scale and sophistication a new departure for Scottish classical churches.' Lazowski's second church is close by, St Andrew's by the Green, Turnbull Street; converted to offices, 1988.
[14] Which is now known as 'the Merchant City'. Its development is described in Williamson, Riches and Higgs' Buildings of Scotland, *Glasgow*, n d, p. 104. It hadn't got far, by 1786, and was at least five years behind Edinburgh's.

60. *Glasgow, St Andrew's parish church, 1739–56, St Andrew's Square, by Allan
Dreghorn, after James Gibbs. Mungo Naismith was master mason. Alexandre: 'The
churches seem well built and beautiful . . . one notices a taste for old styles which
never fail to be light and agreeable.' One of 13 elegant engravings in James
Denholm,* History of the City of Glasgow*, 2nd edition, 1798. Notice the quality
of the paving; also the 'areas'. The church still adds to Glasgow's elegance.*

on account of its individually fine buildings and the width of its streets. All its
houses are built of freestone.[15] The streets are supremely well paved; without question, much better, even, than those of London. The old town is on a small scale, and
in that way like almost all old towns. The College is a large building, old and ugly,[16]
and is part of a university. There is a great number of professors in all subjects, paid
by the college, which however isn't rich. One curious feature of the college, or
university, is that all the professors, instead of dividing the year into three terms and

[15] Judith Lawson, in the Introduction to the *Glasgow* volume (p. 19) explains how the shallow
and seasonal flow of the Clyde limited the transport of bulky materials, like building stone,
restricting the early town to the local sandstone, 'which has continued to give Glasgow its distinctive appearance'. Light-grained, creamy-coloured, occasionally pink or red, weathering well, it was
quarried immediately west of the old town (see her map of the sites of the quarries, p. 20).
[16] He might at least have added: 'but very hospitable'. The original university was built in the
1460s, but replaced in the late 17th century after fires. What Alexandre found ugly is described in
the Buildings of Scotland, *Glasgow*, p. 335, as 'some of the most remarkable 17th-century architecture in Scotland, and their loss was a tragedy'. Unluckily, the area had become disreputable and the
University eagerly accepted an offer from the North British Railway Company, enabling them to
move out to the salubrious Gilmore Hill; but they provocatively commissioned an established
English architect, G. G. Scott, instead of the local Alexander ('Greek') Thomson. The railway
swept away Alexandre's 'old and ugly' university buildings and replaced them with the appropriate
name, College Goods Yard, itself now replaced.

three vacations, all at the same time, as they do in the other universities, here they do six months' work followed by six months' vacation. The professors of Latin and Greek, etc, have 8 months' work.[17] And there is yet another difference here; in England the young men who enter the university are obliged to know Greek, but here they don't need Greek, and only need a little Latin. Very few of the scholars live in the college: they mostly live in the town. Although the professors are paid by the college, the scholars pay them so much a year: the sums aren't fixed, but depend on the means of each scholar.[18]

At Glasgow, two bridges span the Clyde; one of them, very good, is old,[19] the other new, with seven arches, is flat and fairly wide, and what gives it its striking appearance is the way a large circular arch pierces the bridge over each pillar and between each pair of arches.[20] This reduces the weight of the bridge, lightens its appearance, and presents less resistance to the water when the river rises in flood. The size of the ships is restricted by the lowness of the bridges. Tolls are charged: the New Bridge was built 9 or 10 years ago. The town has spread very little across the bridges where the land is given over largely to a great many gardens, which can't fail to add agreeably to the view.

Above the two bridges and along the north bank of the river there is a most beautiful promenade, a smooth lawn with an alley of trees, enjoyed by the whole town in summer, especially on Sundays when it is quite crowded with every sort of people.[21]

Before leaving my description of Glasgow, I must say that the buildings are generally adorned by their architecture and rich, which sets this town apart: I have seen several very elegant private houses.[22]

The Town Hall is very impressive. It is backed by the Prison and the Sheriff's Court. Here the Sheriff serves as judge; not merely, as in England, someone who

[17] *SAS*, XXI, 1799, pp. 1–140, contains statistical accounts of the universities of Glasgow and Aberdeen: p. 34 gives a harrowing account of 'the uniform assiduity of the professors in the University of Glasgow'.

[18] Writing of the period 1700–60, T M Devine, *The Scottish Nation 1700–2000*, says student fees at Glasgow were £5, one-tenth the cost at Oxford and Cambridge.

[19] The Old Bridge, c1350, originally with 8 arches, was widened 1774–5 by Robert Mylne (Colvin, 682), then replaced in 1851–4 by Victoria Bridge (continuing Stockwell Street).

[20] The New (Jamaica) or Broomielaw bridge, 1768–72, was designed by Robert Mylne with his brother William, and built by John Adam (Colvin, 683). Both bridges have been supplanted. The circular openings between the main arches Alexandre had seen in Smeeton's bridge across the Tay at Perth: he would also have seen one in Robert Mylne's fine 2-arch bridge over the Aray at Inveraray if he hadn't been kept indoors by incessant rain. Glasgow Bridge is said to have cost nearly £9,000 (*Beauties of Scotland*, III, 1806, p. 199). Replaced by Telford's bridge in 1833–5, and again by the present one in 1895–9.

[21] Glasgow Green, open land bordering the river near the foot of the Saltmarket. Here, in 1806, *The Beauties of Scotland*, III, 1806, p. 196, still found 'on Sundays and holidays the citizens in great crowds wandering upon the banks of the river'. At the north-west corner of the Green, between the Greendyke and the Saltmarket, St Andrew's church in St Andrew's Square, 1739, was Glasgow's first leap across the burgh boundary: see pl 60, opposite.

[22] Glasgow is still distinguished by large merchants' houses in the outer parts of the town, many of them no longer serving their first purposes.

61. *Glasgow, the Town Hall and Exchange. 'Near the Town Hall is the Exchange, and there's a superb coffee house with a beautiful colonnade: the coffee house is there to aid the business negotiations.' In 1781 a famous coffee-room was built in Trongate to provide the merchants with more relaxed places to do business: very soon it became the Tontine Hotel. The piazza was designed to give them shelter against rough weather as they waited for news from London and beyond, and to catch the mail coaches. This building by Allan Dreghorn was begun in 1736, extended in 1758 and given the facilities of coffee-room and hotel in the 1780s. The mason Mungo Naismith carved popular grinning heads on the keystones of the colonnade. All burnt out in a fire on 4 September 1911* (Glasgow Herald, *9 September 1911).* Select Views of Glasgow and Environs, *Joseph Swan, 1828.*

accompanies the judge. Near the Town Hall is the Exchange, and there's a superb coffee-house with a beautiful colonnade: the coffee-house is there to aid the business negotiations.[23]

Mr Smith, whom I wrote about at Edinburgh, sent with us a letter for Mr Millar, who is Professor of Law at the University.[24] He told us so many things that were new

[23] See above: the colonnaded Tontine Hotel is Alexandre's 'superb coffee-house'. The Tolbooth Steeple still stands at Glasgow Cross, the hub of the city from the Middle Ages till the time of the French visit. You could then look W along Toongate and see some magnificent buildings: the Prison, 5 storeys high, and beyond it the Townhouse and Exchange.

[24] John Millar, 1735–1801, son of a Lanarkshire minister, went to Glasgow in his teens, became a friend of James Watt and attended Adam Smith's lectures on moral philosophy. Professor of Law in

to us about the laws and customs of this country, and something of its trade. I shan't forget to discuss all this when I come to write my general view of Scotland.

This Mr Millar was extremely kind and hospitable. He is the author, I was told, of a very good work on the economy and that he has a very high reputation throughout England. He is high spirited, a truly lovable man, talking about everything with enthusiasm and wide knowledge, speaking with warmth but always kindly. He showed us all over the college, including the library, which is large and increasing all the time: it's in a beautiful room, very tall, with a gallery.[25]

We also saw in the college various antiquities found in Scotland, some even found in the digging of a canal near the town. We dined with Mr Millar, at home with all his family, which is a considerable one. He seems a very happy man, always a pleasure to be with. He showed us so much kindness, even taking the trouble to come twice to our hotel to see if there was anything he could do for us. His acquaintance was, to say the least, helpful, and it was a pleasure to know a man of his reputation.[26]

1761: his lively lectures soon increased his pupils from four to forty. A Whig, he favoured, like his French visitors, American independence; also parliamentary reform (but he thought universal suffrage would lead to corruption). Alexandre describes the good-natured man his friends and his pupils loved: his 'considerable' family numbered 3 sons and 6 daughters. The book Alexandre thought was on 'the economy' was more on social theory, and influenced by Montesquieu and Hume. It was called: *The Origin of the Distinction of Ranks*, 1771, 4th edn 1806, and based on his well-developed lecture-notes. His other well-known book, *Historical View of the English Government*, appeared the year after this French visit, and was also based on his lectures.

[25] *Beauties of Scotland*, III, 1805, p. 229, described it as 'a handsome and lofty apartment containing about 20,000 volumes'. The only 'antiquities' it mentions are 'a considerable number of stones containing ancient inscription or figures brought from the Roman wall between the Forth and the Clyde'. Lazowski's reference to the library was devoted to his astonishment that the books seemed to have been shelved according to the height of the volumes rather than their subjects.

[26] Lazowski adds: 'He is a man of character: his face announces it, but his conversation proves it. He is profound, clear and extremely well provided with reasons. He is republican in principle, and his principles are severe: we talked a lot about political constitutions. In his company here in Glasgow I had pleasure such as I've rarely enjoyed.' Lazowski also added: 'For a very long time the printing of this town has been famous. The university's printer has recently invented a way of fixing the characters of a whole page permanently on a piece of metal; so that, without the expense of holding the types, you can re-use them; and, at the same time, you can undertake large editions of long works with the assurance that the whole pages of the text have been corrected and preserved ready for re-printing. He demonstrates that his method is economic, and I shall bring you a small example of his work.' This technique later became known as 'stereotype'. What follows I owe to the expert guidance of James Mosley, distinguished Librarian of St Bride Printing Library. Plates replicating pages of type were cast in moulds of plaster or a comparable material. In 1786, the Glasgow University Printing Office was run by Andrew Foulis. It was Alexander Tilloch, one of his partners, who developed this technique, though hardly 'invented' it. It was known in the Netherlands since the late 17th century; also in Edinburgh, where c1729 William Ged made plates for prayer-books. What was happening from the 1780s onwards was a spreading of the technique; particularly after Tilloch and Foulis interested the brilliant 3rd earl Stanhope in it. When he was a boy in Geneva, Stanhope had known Adam Smith; he became a firm friend and correspondent of Robert Simson, Glasgow Professor of Mathematics, who died when Stanhope was 15! Stanhope invented an improved printing press and promoted such improvements as 'stereotype'.

The town of Glasgow is provisioned by two canals, one of them small and not long, bringing coal from inland and returning with goods required in exchange. The other goes to Edinburgh and is a very impressive work of construction reaching from Glasgow to the Firth of Forth. It is 56 feet wide, 7½ feet deep, and comes within a mile of Glasgow, but doesn't yet reach the river Clyde.[27]

I ought to write about trade, and leave an account of these canals until tomorrow. But alas I've so far been able to hear very little about commercial matters, and that rather superficial. I can say that forty years ago the old town was very small, and now has at least 36,000 souls,[28] its trade being the principal reason for this great transformation.

On the 7th we scarcely went out and spent most of our time writing up our journals. However, in the evening we went out to supper with Mr Millar, where we found a large gathering of people, mainly several professors from the college.[29] So, after telling you more about Glasgow's commerce, I will pass on to our journey on the 8th, when we left the town.

The town's trade is very extensive, given a boost when Scotland became part of the United Kingdom:[30] it isn't Scotland's first town but it's the most commercial. It became so before the years of the American War that began in 1783, for I've been assured that in this town alone the tobacco imported was equal in amount almost to a third of all the tobacco going to the rest of the world. Many merchants have

He combined being Pitt's brother-in-law and friend (till 1789) *and* an unwavering radical till he withdrew from Parliament (in 1795) and was free to get on with experiments raging from safeguards against fire, to steamships, and stereotype printing.

[27] The Forth and Clyde Navigation was begun 1768 and mostly carried through by John Smeaton. It started some miles up the Forth from Edinburgh at Grangemouth, where the distance from Glasgow was only 22 miles as the crow flies. The lie of the land dictated a canal of 35 miles: nearly 11 miles from Grangemouth to the summit pool, a rise of 155 feet by 20 locks. Then 16 miles along the high level before a similar fall (156 feet) to the Clyde by 19 locks. It reached Stockingfield, where a small aqueduct of c1777 survives, in the Maryhill suburb of Glasgow, and then stuck at Hamiltonhill in Possilpark from 1777 to 1790. Port Dundas was building on a low ridge above the city in 1786. Completed under Robert Whitworth in 1790, it was later improved to take craft of 10 feet draught between the Irish Sea and the German Ocean. (Priestley's *Navigable Rivers and Canals*, 1831, pp. 266–73; *Beauties of Scotland*, III, 1805, pp. 479–87).
[28] This seems about right, if the Gorbals are included.
[29] This is Alexandre's only reference to Professor Millar's supper-party: Lazowski doesn't even mention it. The Professor may have overestimated the Frenchmen's appetite for academic conversation, but Alexandre did well to glean so much on Glasgow's commerce.
[30] It gave them free access to the American and West Indian markets, though merchants from the English ports did their best to stifle the Scots traders till about 1735. During the 7 Years' War, one Glasgow merchant owned 25 ships and traded for above half a million sterling. Glasgow merchants established factors in America and began to send them goods on credit. The amount of trade increased greatly but so did the risk of dishonoured debts described by Alexandre. The merchants who survived the crisis of the American war looked increasingly to the W Indies and Europe. In 1783 the Clyde merchants had 386 ships: by 1790 their ships had increased to 476, and their tonnage had doubled (*SAS*, V, 1793, p. 500, and Robert Forsyth, *Beauties of Scotland*, III, 1805, pp. 280–1).

become immensely rich but many others have become bankrupt through the infamy of the Americans who, after the war, have not honoured their debts to the British merchants: they have even, I'm assured, been authorised in this by the Congress, which is a very mean and truculent action (if it's true), legislating to encourage the dishonouring of debts to particular individuals, when the cause is a general one.

But after the Independence of America, the tobacco trade was lost to them, because all the other nations joined in and the Americans themselves exported it to the other nations and, increasingly, the English took over the trade which is widely extended. Despite the very considerable loss that the town sustained for a time, through lack of trade, I heard it said by Mr Millar (someone whose word one respects) that he didn't believe that it was even a bad thing for the town, for he claims that what was only a coastal trade wasn't anything like as useful to the nation in general as the manufactures into which the merchants have poured their energies, and which are being improved every day through new inventions, so as to equal, and in time surpass, the towns that for so long had only the trade.

So this leads one to think that the loss of America has not damaged England's purse so much as her pride, humbled by the loss of extensive territories that they have held for so long.

After losing the tobacco trade, the Glasgow merchants, most of them very rich, have established all sorts of manufactures. Here they've advanced at great speed, taking every opportunity; and, besides, they have another great advantage, for their traditional trade has always been the making of textiles. They have found workmen who have gone on making fine cloth, who have soon been able to make cotton goods, to the great advantage of the town.

Here all sorts of cotton manufactures flourish. They've even established a cotton mill, but they guard it jealously. We weren't allowed to see it at work.[31] All I know is that at Glasgow, they have, in a very short time, reached such perfection that they rival Manchester in the making of cotton goods: however, they haven't yet arrived at the same perfection in the making of cloths of thick cotton.

So they have created a most impressively successful trade. It is almost entirely based on goods made in the neighbouring countryside.[32] The merchants generally

---

31 Lazowski reckoned that there were 'three or more such mills as I described when we were in Derby, making use of as much cotton as Glasgow can spin as well as what it can import from India and Ireland'. He reckoned that Glasgow and the neighbouring district had no fewer than 14,000 looms working every day. 'On an average, the workers earn over 14 pence a day, and are usually paid by the piece.' At the end of the Scotland tour, Alexandre, summarising his impressions, wrote: 'Linen is a branch of the industry which is developed, I believe, as far as, if not further than, anywhere else.' Seven years later, the *Statistical Account* of Glasgow (V, p. 502) noted that the great cotton manufacture 'has, in some measure, supplanted the linen trade, which used to be the staple manufacture of the west of Scotland: there is yet a very great quantity of linens, lawns, cambrics &c still made . . .'

32 Robert Forsyth (*Beauties of Scotland*, III, 1805, 284–5) wrote: 'In order to carry this manufacture through all its branches, cotton-mills, bleachfields and printfields have been erected not only on all the streams in the neighbourhood, but even in situations more remote; and such is its prosperous state that, although the number of spinning mills has of late greatly increased, they are still

live in the town, but you have to go about 16 miles down river to reach the port of Glasgow,[33] a little town where all the ships are moored that belong to Glasgow. A little further down river is a little town called Greenock, separate from the port of Glasgow, but the same kind of small town: the difference between them is that the first is part of Glasgow, the second entirely independent.

Glasgow is a great outlet for cloths and muslins which are made all over this part of Scotland, and sent into England and many different places.

At present, what trade there is through the two canals is nothing of consequence, for the little one serves only to bring coals into Glasgow, and the other reaches the Firth of Forth and soon, at least, will be able to link the two seas. It will be of some use to the town, but much more to the whole of Scotland, for it will cut out the loss of great numbers of vessels that run great dangers in the stormy seas round the coast.

The commerce of this town is so considerable that this Clyde–Forth canal is, I suppose, the one major enterprise left to complete.

On the 8th (Monday) we left Glasgow   very late, after seeking letters of recommendation for *Paisley*, a manufacturing town where we slept the same evening. We crossed the new bridge[34] and, from there, we reached a beautiful plain, rich and well cultivated and with a great many country houses, until you arrive at a small town called *Renfrew*. Then the road was equally well supplied with the houses of peasant farmers, where the chief occupation was to create closes and paddocks for Glasgow merchants. All the pretty houses, too, that I found around the town, belonged to them, and some were pretty indeed. But what is more worth noting is the sense of real seclusion, or rather of comfort and ease, that one perceives among these people, the good quality of their clothes and of the building of their houses.

At about one and a half miles on from Renfrew, on the Paisley road, is a most extraordinary bridge, the first I've ever seen of its kind. I've tried to draw it on the next page. It has [10] arches, and in the middle you find another bridge branching out of it. It is built at the confluence of two rivers before they join the Clyde.[35] Each arm of the bridge spans a different stream.

unable to supply the necessary yarn, so that daily that article to a considerable amount is brought from England . . . The manufactures of Glasgow employ several thousand weavers who live in the district of the country around, and even to the distance of thirty or forty miles . . . This manufacture is not only important of itself, it is productive of work to many thousands of bleachers, tambourers, calico-printers &c.' (Tambourers were embroiderers working on material stretched ona tambour or hoop-frame: this gave way to machine-embroidery on a lappet-frame: see footnote 40, p. 210, at Paisley.)
33 Under an Act of 1771, navigation of the river was deepened so that by 1805, lighters of 70 tons could approach the Quay near Glasgow Bridge (then Broomielaw Bridge). But the larger vessels had to moor about 13 miles downstream near Dumbuck Ford.
34 Now Glasgow Bridge.
35 Alexandre was puzzled by this bridge, which was in the parish of Inchinnan. *SAS* (III, 1792, pp. 532–7) explains that 'every kind of soil is to be met with in this parish: in general it is good, especially near the rivers White Cart, Grise and Clyde . . . At the conflux of the rivers White Cart and Grise there is a very fine bridge, consisting of ten large arches. A large arch is thrown over from the centre of the bridge to the highway that leads to Paisley. When it was built, a toll was laid on all

62. *Alexandre's very rough sketch of Inchinnan Bridge.*

The bridge is rather handsome, and is said to have been built at a very reasonable cost.

After leaving the bridge you are more or less in the middle of a plain, with Paisley always in view ahead of you. In general, the land here is pretty good, worth 2 *louis* an *arpent*[36] and often more. Above all, it is well cultivated.[37] What is quite clear is that the better you are inclined towards gardening, the more you will approve of the town.

passengers to defray the expense, and the management was committed to trustees. In 1782 it was rented for £377 sterling. The tax was taken off in 1787.' In its account of Renfrew (II, 1791, p. 170) *SAS* continues the story: 'When the bridge of Inchinnan was built, the navigation to the town of Paisley was very much obstructed by it. Vessels were then obliged to pass through the arches, which could not be done without lowering their masts; the channel below the bridge became vastly wider, and of course very shallow. To render the navigation of the river fit for vessels with fixed masts, the town of Paisley obtained liberty to make a cut about half-a-mile in length, in which there is a very complete drawbridge in the turnpike road at the east end of Inchinnan bridge.' Sketching the bridge, Alexandre miscalculated and left himself with room for only six of the ten arches. He is looking downstream towards the Clyde. The bridge spans the confuence of the river Grise, flowing in from the left, and the river White Cart joining it and flowing on under the main bridge. The junction brings traffic from the Glasgow–Greenock road down into Paisley. Crawfurd and Semple's *History of the Shire of Renfrew*, 1782, pp. 41–2, says the middle arch is 60 feet wide, having a house built on either side of it. A toll-house was built outside the turnpike gate at the west (left) end of this bridge. The toll for a waggon drawn by one horse was fourpence, for a horse or ass, loaded or unloaded, twopence; foot passengers a halfpenny. A marble inscription on a pedestal named in Latin the bridge's architect, Mr Thomas Brown. Howard Colvin's *Dictionary of British Architects*, 1995 edn, p. 168, names Thomas Brown of Renfrew as director of the building, in 1773–4, of Ross-Dhu House, designed for himself by Sir James Colquhoun, Bart, on the shore of Loch Lomond, just south of Luss. The Frenchmen might easily have seen it when they were describing 'the route, superb, well supplied with gentlemen's houses': see p. 196 and footnote 6 above. Thomas Brown's bridge fell to a spring tide in 1809, and was replaced in 1812 by a different design by Robertson Buchanan.

36 10 shillings an *arpent*.
37 *SAS* (II, p. 173) says the soil, a deep rich loam, is exceedingly favourable to potatoes, 'though the soil has enjoyed no rest in the memory of the oldest man living'.

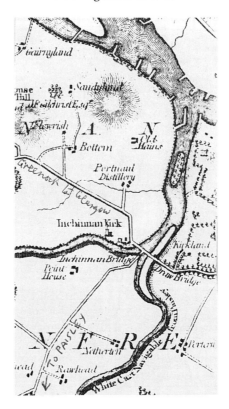

63. *J. Ainslie's map, 1796, explains Alexandre's very rough sketch of Inchinnan
Bridge on the Glasgow–Greenock road. It crossed the navigable White Cart
river at its confluence with the Grise just before they reached the Clyde. SAS,
III, 1792, p. 536, recorded its 10 large arches with a large arch thrown over
from the middle of the bridge to the highway leading to Paisley. After 1792 a
drawbridge was added for the benefit of sailing craft. It was a toll-bridge: a
toll-house stood beyond Alexandre's toll-gate on the left. The houses either side
of the junction to Paisley seem to have had a purely domestic function.*

Paisley, The New Inn   Paisley stands beside the river Cart, the old town on rising ground
above the west bank, with a view up to Glasgow, six and a half miles away, the new
town more regularly laid out on the east bank. The little river is unnavigable. The old
town bulks large and rather ugly on its higher ground; the new is built very simply and
well. This inn where we are is Lord Abercorn's,[38] who has a big estate here. It's beautiful and well-built. All around the town there are many very delightful merchants'

<hr />

38 James Hamilton, 8th earl of Abercorn, acquired the lordship of Paisley in 1764 and laid out a
new town here in 1779. William Chambers designed his splendid villa, Duddingston House, just
south of Edinburgh.

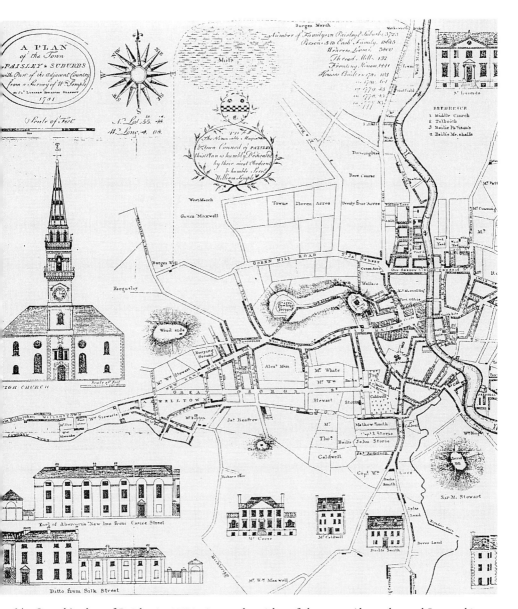

64. *Semple's plan of Paisley in 1781 gives a clear idea of the town Alexandre and Lazowski visited. Two elevations of the 'beautiful' New Inn they stayed in appear in the bottom left corner: they faced Silk Street and Gauze Street, on the extreme right edge of the map. At the top, a list records 3,723 families, and 3,800 looms in this town whose gauzes, 'developed to the greatest perfection', thrilled Alexandre.*

houses: they've made their fortunes in a short time. But their great trade has increased that of the country at large, and I must devote myself to giving you some idea of it today.

Years ago, before this century, Paisley was a small place and of so little consequence that anyone with 1,000 *louis* (£250) would have been regarded as a great merchant, and all that one could do in business was repeating what had been done, and in a small way. But since Glasgow lost its tobacco trade, in the American War, the merchants, as I've said, are occupied in transferring their funds not only into Glasgow business but also here. Furthermore, the merchants here, too, have established manufactures on a very large scale, and they have more or less achieved perfection: they seem to approach it more closely every day, something I shall perhaps describe elsewhere. The main point is that manufacture and trade here are partly run by merchants living in Glasgow, and partly by the merchants of this town.

The trade is in plain and ornamental gauzes – of cotton, of silk and cotton, and of silk – according to fashion, and what rules the trade. The merchants have shown an enormous number of samples, but they change everything as fashion changes, which creates great expense.[39] There are gauzes that are embroidered, on the looms, with different patterns – in which patterns I am no connoisseur: it's enough to say that these gauzes are developed to the greatest perfection, that the trade is very extensive and extremely profitable to the town.[40]

Cotton is another branch in which the trade has greatly expanded in this town,

---

[39] At the high point in Paisley's High Street, its Museum and Art Galleries has built up a most remarkable collection of looms and of samples of gauzes such as those very samples the town's merchants showed Alexandre and Lazowski in 1786. The collection is vividly presented and demonstrated by its enthusiastic keeper, Dan Coughlan, who was tremendously impressed by Alexandre's description of Paisley.

[40] The various cloths they refer to could be embellished and 'embroidered' on the looms: this 'embroidering' is known, Dan Coughlan tells me, as lappet weaving, a special weaving technique. See facing page and p. 221. *The Statistical Account* (VII, 1793, p. 65) backs Alexandre's superlatives: 'About the year 1760, the making of silk gauze was first attempted at Paisley, in imitation of that of Spitalfields in London . . . The inventive spirit, and the patient application of the workmen; the cheapness of labour at that time, and the skill and taste of the masters, gave it every advantage . . . such a vast variety of elegant and richly ornamented gauze was issued from that place as outdid everything of the kind that had formerly appeared. Spitalfields was obliged to relinquish the manufacture. Companies came down from London to carry it on at Paisley where it prospered and increased, it is believed, beyond any manufacture which any town in Scotland could boast of . . . it filled the country round to the distance of 20 miles; and the gentlemen engaged in it had not only warehouses in London and Dublin, but they had correspondents upon the continent, and shops for vending their commodities even in Paris itself!' By 1785, Professor Symonds, visiting the Rochefoucauld family in Paris in July, found it 'overwhelmed with English goods, and MARCHANDISES ANGLOISES written over all the shops' (*Innocent Espionage*, p. 235), and Calonne was reduced to prohibiting all foreign cottons, muslins, gauzes and linens from being imported into France in an effort to push Pitt towards the trade treaty of September 1786. The *SAS* writer on Paisley made Alexandre's point about the dependence of the trade upon fashion, and wrote specifically that 'in 1784, the manufactures of Paisley, in silk gauze, lawn and linen gauze, and white sewing thread, amounted to the value of £579,185. 16s. 6d; and that no fewer than 26,484 persons were employed in carrying them on'.

65. *Paisley. Mr Fullerton's pattern-book, late 18th-century: cotton and woollen in plain weave. The figuring, sometimes in silk yarn, was produced by means of a lappet device. This was just the process Alexandre and Lazowski watched with such admiration and envy. From the collection of the Paisley Museum, photographed through the kindness of the Assistant Keeper, Dan Coughlan.*

employing very many hands. They make a mixture of silk and cotton for dresses and waistcoats, and also make them just in cotton. In fact, in what one thinks of as light Manchester fabrics,[41] Paisley makes them so beautifully that she competes easily with Manchester: in the same way she hopes in a year or two to compete in the thicker coloured cloths.

[41] 'What one thinks of as light Manchester fabrics' may well be merely what they were able to see in Manchester in March, 1785: 'black cotton velvet such as I've never seen in France', garters and ribbons, flowered and unflowered, for the peasants (*Innocent Espionage*, pp. 65–6).

But before leaving the gauzes, it is pleasant to mention a new invention[42] which has made available fashionable gauze neckerchiefs, 3 ells for women [a little over a yard long]. I must make it clear that some weavers may not have long enough arms to work at the shuttle making these neckerchiefs, which are broad as well as long. In order to make them, they have developed the method sketched on the following page, which does exactly what is needed. The shuttle race (A) extends over the width of the loom. Over this shuttle race slides the shuttle. At each end of the beam there's a sort of box which receives the shuttle. From the box, a sort of hammer (called a picker) runs along the race and can't go beyond point (F). The points (C) and (F) touch one another when the shuttle leaves. The man holds the picking-stick (H) which begins the [word unreadably altered] by the cords (B C). When the man pulls one [of the?] cords hard, he pulls one of the pickers which is the one with the shuttle. Not being attached in the box when it is stopped at point (F), the shuttle escapes, traverses all the threads, and continues till it falls into the other box, which is at point (F) and is kept going by its impetus right to the end of the shuttle race at point (E).

This frame has taken a long time to bring to perfection. Its extreme value is acknowledged by everyone, for it was developed in this town for the benefit of everyone. I imagine it has become known by many other merchants since its invention.

Our friend Mr Millar was kind enough to give us a letter of recommendation to Mr Howle [presumably Mr Howell] who seemed to me a small labour agent [*petit négociant des mains*] to judge by the way he talks. He conducted us round all the industries in the town and then, when we'd seen all of them, he took us to see a demonstration of cotton-manufacture. It would have been difficult for us to see this; but as we had a letter from one of the proprietors we were admitted.

---

[42] Dan Coughlan at once saw, from Alexandre's description and tentative sketch, that what the Paisley weavers were using was not 'a new invention' but the fly-shuttle (or flying-shuttle) invented in 1733 by John Kay from Bury in Lancashire. What was new was certainly the *fichus* they were making with it. What Kay had done was create a mechanism for weaving cloth wider and faster than had been possible with the hand-thrown shuttle. This must have been Alexandre's first sight of a fly-shuttle, for its action is very impressive, even though it's hard for someone unskilled in weaving to understand fully, and explain intelligibly (as Alexandre demonstrates!): if he'd seen it before, in action, he would not have forgotten it. In the factories in Leicester and Derby the previous year, the machines he'd seen in action were stocking-frames and carding-machines: in the Manchester factory they'd been shown a piece of smooth, fine black cotton velvet, but *not* the machine it was made on. Despite Dan Coughlan's skilful instruction as he demonstrated what is quite conceivably the identical form of fly-shuttle that Alexandre and Lazowski were watching in Paisley, I could make no more successful a sketch and explanation of it than Alexandre did. Both it and his description show clearly that he was innocently describing the fly-shuttle mechanism on the assumption that it was the 'new invention' that made these sophisticated lappet-woven gauzes available. Of course Kay's 1733 invention had been perfected in various ways and *was* at the heart of the Paisley production, but I suppose it was the lappet-weaving technique that was the novelty Alexandre hoped he was sketching and describing. At any rate, his clear innocence about the already long service of the fly-shuttle is the best possible evidence of the innocent, completely unprofessional, nature of their industrial inquisitiveness.

66. *Alexandre's sketch of the fly-shuttle at Paisley. He mistook this for the 'new invention', the lappet-weaving mechanism that made machine-embroidery possible on gauzes, so making Paisley famous. 'The merchants have shown me an enormous number of samples, gauzes that are embroidered on the looms, with different patterns.' The fly-shuttle merely supplied speed and efficiency – impressive enough. His failure to identify the fly-shuttle says much for his technological innocence.*

This mill is a good 3 miles out of town,[43] so we took a post-chaise; for it was already late, we didn't want to stay on in Paisley, and it was too far to travel at the back of our vehicle. Anyway, it's enough to say that here at this mill is a number of machines that one would see ready to prepare and spin the cotton and perform many functions by means of very simple mechanisms.[44] The work of maintenance of the machines was also very simple and required no great strength, which brings about a saving of hands which are useful on the land and in other jobs; they employ

[43] Reading this, Dan Coughlan of the Paisley Museum at once thought of Johnstone (originally spelt Johnstoun). Sure enough, the Rev Robert Boog, in *SAS* VII, 1793, pp. 88–9, confirms: 'The spinning of cotton was introduced into this parish [Paisley Abbey parish] in 1783. The principal seat of that manufacture is at Johnstoun, a neat and regularly built village about 3 miles W from Paisley, upon the estate of Mr Houston of Johnstone. The village, begun in 1782, contained on Whitsunday last, 293 families or 1434 souls.' Alexandre, three paragraphs further on, said this mill 'has been able to provide itself with 2 or 300 houses, all new and attractive'. It's clear that Johnstone is where Mr Howell brought them to see a demonstration of an ambitious cotton miller in a new and growing village. Several houses that front on to Johnstone's main street are late 18th-century, some with modern shop-fronts let into the ground floor and with their chimney-stacks abbreviated.

[44] Dan Coughlan explains that this expansion was the result of introducing power-spinning. It involved a long series of operations on a sequence of machines, many of them called 'frames' – drawing frames, mule frames etc. The Frenchmen were trying to comprehend a very complex system, starting with the cotton bole, going on through the mixing room, carding room, etc. One wonders if the mechanisms themselves were as simple as they seemed to Alexandre, worked though they were by children. It is curious that he made no reference back to what they'd seen last year in Mr Swift's mill in Derby. When he says the machinery is entirely new, he must I think mean 'newly-made' or 'newly designed in some details'. All this exemplifies the successful technology transfer from England to Scotland.

girls and children. So this great number of machines of many kinds is worked only by children, of whom some work all day, and the others all night. In this way the work never stops, unless something goes wrong with the machine. These children are supervised and kept at work by two or three men in each room, who check that their work is well done.[45]

This machinery is entirely new and even not quite finished, for they are working daily to enlarge it. What is in place seems to be the last word in mechanical ingenuity,[46] until something new is discovered. The efficiency is such that, after they've prepared their cotton to the point where it is a round ribbon [*ruban rond*] like a perfectly finished thread [*achevan de fil*], they can then, on a single frame [*métier*], spin over 6000 ells from a pound of wool.[47]

To turn to more important issues, one must think not only of the enormous wealth this business pours into all this part of Scotland, but of the value of employing numbers of children, who couldn't make another industry thrive and who earn here from 2 to 3 shillings a week. This success can be seen precisely where we are: in the year or so that this mill has been working it has been able to provide itself with a small village of 2 or 300 houses, all new and attractive: their number increases every day and at present enough children are encouraged to work at the mill. These benefits accrue to the whole kingdom and there can be no regrets at the wealth this man can and will create.[48]

---

[45] Alexandre expresses no concern for the health of these children, any more than his brother did the previous year at Swift's mill at Derby, where the majority of the 200 factory-workers were small children and women, working ten hours a day (*Innocent Espionage*, p. 40).

[46] This hardly reads like 'very simple mechanism'.

[47] The word 'ribbon' is authentic, describing the stage in the process seen in the illustration of the Drawing Frame (of 1832, but showing the same process that they were watching). Dan Coughlan says spinning 6,000 ells from a pound of wool is not an exaggeration: indeed, it could be their misunderstanding of '60,000 ells'!

[48] Nevertheless, regrets were firmly expressed already in 1793 by the Minister of Paisley Abbey parish, the Rev Robert Boog (*SAS*, VII, pp. 88–9): 'It is painful to think that a manufacture which gives employment to so many hands, and which may be a source of great wealth to individuals, may be productive of very unhappy effects upon both the health and morals of the children employed in it. This there is some reason to apprehend. The numbers that are brought together, especially in the larger mills, the confinement, the breathing of an air loaded with the dust and downy particles of the cotton, and contaminated with the effluvia of rancid oil rising from the machinery, must prove hurtful in a high degree to the delicate and tender lungs of children. Add to this that mills which produce the water-twist are kept going day and night and children must be had who are willing to work through the night and sleep through the day. Tempted by the wages, parents send their children to this employment at a very early age when they have got little or no education. Ignorance, disease and mortality are but too likely to prove the effects of their manufacture if carried on by unfeeling and selfish men. The characters of the gentlemen engaged in it in their neighbourhood give reason to hope that every method will be employed which humanity and good sense can suggest to prevent these evils.' Thirty-seven years after the French visit, and only 14 miles east from Paisley, the 10-year-old David Livingstone went to work in Messrs Monteith's cotton-mill: from 6am to 8pm with 2 breaks for meals, with 2 hours afterwards for nightschool. He worked there till he was 23, fixing a Latin grammar on to the spinning jenny and able to study it in snatches of a minute. At 23 he was able to go on to read medicine, theology and

Three or four more of these mills are now established at various distances from the town, all contributing to the same prosperity, and certainly not failing to contribute to a big increase in the population of the area.

England, in the different branches of industry, has shown what can be done in one of them and, in consequence and in time, will be able to achieve it in others. London[49] backs the commerce of Paisley, which extends all over the different manufactures I've been telling about. The expansion here has been helped by Glasgow, which in turn they furnish with a big proportion of what they send out into foreign parts. This trade will probably become even more widespread, as it increasingly benefits the town which it has succeeded in doubling. So that one finds here more and more carriages and, very notably, an atmosphere of life and prosperity. Where 1,000 *louis* (£250) once seemed like riches to a merchant, he now thinks in terms of 25,000 (£6,250) and more. All that, however, is dependent on the ability of other nations to spend.

After getting back from our mill, to which Mr Howle had accompanied us, and gained us entry, we took tea with him. He stayed with us so late that our poor journal has once more been obliged to wait another day. I was touched.

On Tuesday 9th May   we left *Paisley*, dined at Beith and slept at *Ayr*: 36 miles. The first part of the route was not only very hilly but through country very bad for roads and for carriages: if it wasn't stones it was rocks. The countryside is mostly very agreeable, broken, and eventful, even a little mountainous, but by comparison with the higher mountains of Scotland, these, cultivated right up to the summit, are nothing very grand. Along this route, and coming up close to Paisley, we found a large number of peasant houses generally engaged in cloth-making. For most of the way, the countryside is enclosed and the land seemed to me pretty good and well maintained. In a very few places there seemed to be no effort at cultivation.

Greek in Glasgow. At 27 he was ready for the three most famous missionary expeditions of exploration of Africa in history.

[49] *SAS* (VII, 1793, pp. 64–6) gave a concise history of the Paisley industry at this time (the famous Paisley patterned shawls began only in 1805). Silk gauze started here c1760 on the model of Spitalfields in London, and succeeded 'beyond the most sanguine expectations.

SAS then relates this more nearly to 1786. 'It appears that in the year 1784, the manufactures of Paisley, in silk gauze, lawn and linen gauze, and white sewing thread amounted to the value of £579,185. 16s. 6d, and that no fewer than 26,484 persons were engaged in carrying them on.' The population of Paisley itself was then no more than about 12,000, which gives a clear picture of the industrialisation of the surrounding countryside.

Robert Forsyth's *Beauties of Scotland*, III, 1805, unlike so many *Beauties of* books, contains much serious information about the economic development of the countryside. Vol III starts with a beautiful frontispiece of Paisley Abbey's ruins, but adds to *SAS*'s information about the introduction of silk gauze manufacture to Paisley, in imitation of Spitalfields, that it was the work of Mr M'Kerral of Hillhouse in Ayrshire: it also adds that the Paisley manufacturers had their own design-draughtsmen and sent their patterns to London and Paris for approbation. 'By these means the inventive principle of modes and fashions, at least in respect of gauze, was transferred from Paris to Paisley.'

Beith is a very small town looking as if it has seen better days, its houses depressing. But from Beith to Ayr the road is charming. You go through a town called Irvine, the road here uneven without being hilly, the land rich and full of houses of gentlemen with gardens belonging to them: many of these proprietors have farms attached to their houses and have invested much money in those farms, and so given them a look of prosperity and husbandry.

When you have almost arrived at Irvine you cross a fine park.[50] I don't know its name but it lies about 2 miles from Irvine. The park looked new, coming on well, thoroughly looked after. *Irvine* is a pretty town, fairly big, and built in the middle of a plain beside the sea. The main street is quite well built and proportioned, and there is a considerable port where I saw large vessels, even 3-masted.[51]

From Irvine to Ayr you follow the coast road all the way. Here the sea forms a great bay,[52] with a sandy beach. The sea encroached and covered a part of the coastal plain with sand, rendering it completely uncultivable. It's only when you get a little further on that you realise that the coast has become covered with sheep, some of them superb and of a beautiful breed. We found close to Ayr, indeed as we entered, three fire pumps in the new square. One of them served, apparently, to pump water from the bottom of a coal mine. The other two, a lot bigger than the first, are for working bellows for a foundry: we were close to a large tile-works.[53]

Ayr, Kings Arms   Ayr is a seaport which has a busy trade with the *Isle of Arran*, being probably the port most conveniently placed for the job. She runs a regular packet-boat service to the island. She also carries on a small trade with Glasgow by way of spreading out into the country the goods this town produces. Its port is small: the day I was there, there were about 200 vessels, a great many of them fishing-boats.

They've built a fairly big jetty to protect the port from high winds and rough seas. Near the port are the remains of an old fortification, where there is still living at present a Pensioner. I'm not sure that he's up to defending it![54]

---

[50] ?Bourtreehill, the Hon Mr Hamilton's residence in 1793 (*SAS*, VII, p. 171).

[51] *SAS*, VII, 1793, p. 174, recorded 51 vessels belonging to Irvine in 1790, the largest 160 tons. *SAS* speaks (p. 170) of a row of houses on each side of the road leading to the harbour, mostly one storey high with finished garrets [*sic*] and occupied chiefly by seafaring people.

[52] It really is a great bay, curving round all the way from Saltcoats to Ayr, with a brief promontory at Troon.

[53] In 1796, the town council recognised that 'the fire engines' were inadequate and decided to order a new one from London, like the one from the new barracks that the army had used successfully to put out a conflagration in the town – John Strawhorn, *History of Ayr*, 1989, p. 85. The King's Arms, at Ayr, was rebuilt in 1833 and demolished in 1925. Its site at the bottom of High Street is occupied by a Woolworths store.

[54] Alexandre in good humour. This was the Citadel, built round the old parish church, next the sea. *SAS* (XXI, 1799, p. 42): 'Oliver Cromwell judging it proper to build a fortress at this place, for keeping the west country in awe, took possession of St John's church for an armoury. The walls of the Citadel enclose about 10 or 12 acres, originally surrounded with a wet ditch, with a draw-bridge over it on the side next the town: four bastions, three wells, a magazine and a sally port.' In ruins, it was rather a handful for a pensioner to hold.

The town itself is large, with several very pretty streets and good houses. It hasn't much in the way of manufacturing, though there is evidence of small businesses such as I noticed on entering the town.[55]

On the 10th   we left Ayr, lunched at Maybole and slept at *Girvan*, a journey of only 24 miles. Our route before lunch was good, though a bit hilly, the country absolutely fine, and yesterday's needed no recompense. But suddenly we reached a dreary desert, cultivated only in patches,[56] here and there. Approaching Girvan, one smelt the sea, and caught sight of an island, called Ailsa, at least ten miles out in the middle of the sea. From this shore, what is most irresistible is the shape of that island rock, very far off: I watched it all along as we rode (Pl 67, over). It's uninhabited except for some cattle someone's put ashore to graze.[57] When you approach Girvan the country becomes a little more cultivated. It is, at least, better that anyone who doesn't want to cultivate the land himself should let it well.

Girvan, Kings Arms   Girvan is a very small town which I think isn't famous, nor even remarkable for anything. It just furnishes fishermen and sailors, and the sea-shore of which it was built.[58]

On Thursday the 11th   we lunched at Ballantrae, then we got to *Stranraer*, and finally slept at *Portpatrick* (the New Inn). We travelled 39 miles, a long haul. We'd counted on

---

[55] He may have been too busy writing up Paisley to look seriously at Ayr. *SAS*'s author (XXI, 1799, p. 36) noted complacently: 'The town stands on a dry, sandy soil, and has fields adjoining, than which none can be fitter for walking, or for the diversions of racing, golfing, etc' – an early reference to Ayr's famous horse-races. It continues: 'Everyone has easy access to the turf, covered at all seasons with a beautiful verdure, and adorned in Spring and Summer with wild daisies and other flowers.'

[56] 'Even in the hilly parts of the parish they have begun to cultivate such spots of land as are capable of it' (*SAS* on Girvan, XII, 1794, p. 341).

[57] *SAS*, I, 1791, p. 104, under Ballantrae, described Ailsa as 'a most beautiful rock of a conical figure, 4 or 5 leagues NW of Ballantrae, refuge to an immense number of sea-fowls who breed on it, and stocked with rabbits and a few goats. It affords a fine object all around the coast . . . Opposite this coast the sea appears land-locked, for a most spacious bay of some 25 or 30 leagues diameter is formed by part of the coast of Galloway, of Down and Antrim in Ireland, east Argyllshire and Dumbartonshire, and about 80 miles of the coast of Ayrshire: all easily discernible by the naked eye on a clear day', together with half a dozen islands. No wonder Alexandre was excited by Ailsa and 'rock cliffs very far off'. It's a pity that at Ballantrae he was distracted by the awful state of the road.

[58] Alexandre was right about the origins: it seems that in the 1760s, considerable herring-fishing took place at the mouth of the river here. *SAS* (*ibid.*): 'By the concourse of people it drew together, and the wealth it produced, a sudden extension of the town was occasioned . . . The practice of smuggling, too, contributed in no small degree to the increase in the town of Girvan.' Alexandre was nodding on the subject of this staple trade. 'So happily is the harbour situated that vessels can get out to sea with a wind from almost any quarter.' Yet by 1794, no regular trade had developed (*SAS*, p. 345). That year, it recorded only 22 seamen, as against 203 handicraftsmen, 153 servants, 78 farmers. The Kings Arms is derelict in April 2000, and presumably awaits demolition.

CRAG OF AILSA.

67. *Ailsa Craig, 1776, from Thos Pennant,* Tour in Scotland and Voyage to the Hebrides, *1776 drawn Moses Griffiths, printed P. Mazell. Pennant landed 25 June 1772, found ruins of a chapel and fishermen's huts on the beach, and climbed an alarming path to a square 3-storeyed tower of the castle, 100 yards from a spring of fine water. Deafening chorus of grey gulls and kittiwakes, guillemots and razorbills. Throstles contributed their song 'as though they were in Hertfordshire'. Owner lets to people who take the young gannets for the table and other birds for their feathers. An amazing assemblage of precipitous columnar rocks facing mainland (lower engraving, with castle inset).*

spending the night in Stranraer, but could find nowhere to stay, neither for us nor our horses, on account of the May fair.[59]

Before lunch, the road was terrible; where it runs beside the sea, our wheels stuck in the sands, and then when the road climbed the hills it was also very bad, passing between rocks: a really dreadful road. The country, too, that we crossed seemed like the end of a chain of mountains, reminding us a bit of the Highlands. The breed of the cattle, however, is beautiful, especially of the sheep. The place where we lunched was insignificant: I pass it in silence.[60]

After lunch, setting off to Stranraer, the first 3 miles were horribly rough and hilly, the roads deplorable and the country wasted. After that short stretch was over, we found a good road, surprisingly smooth for seven miles; the bottom of a valley, well planted, and with the proud appearance of a great many beautiful trees. The little stream running along the valley is crossed by 3 or 4 very pretty, though very simple, bridges. At the end, you have reached *Loch Ryan* exactly at the place where its mouth opens into the sea. It is like a deep inland bay, but all these inlets are called lochs in this country. You ride more than half-way round this bay to reach Stranraer: the road runs close to the loch but rises and falls as the loch-edge rises and then falls. On the way, you pass through two very small villages, not well built, and involved in lochside trading.

We stopped to take tea at Stranraer, a small port at the far end of the loch. This town does a good trade. It has no artificial harbour, for the whole loch provides good, safe anchorage. I've even seen frigates and big 3-masted ships at anchor here, for the water's very deep.[61]

The fair prevented us from finding anywhere to stay in Stranraer. We could only ride through the town (fine, small and pretty),[62] and on 6 miles further to Portpatrick.

---

[59] Stranraer had two annual fairs, one in early May, the other in September. The 'Galloway plaiding' they'd sold for the Virginia market till the War of Independence gave way to increased flax growing and sales of coarse linen, both green and bleached, to the Glasgow and Kilmarnock merchants at these fairs (*SAS*, I, 1791, pp. 362–3).

[60] Alas, his indignation with the road has distracted him not only from the sensational views at Bennane Head and Lendalfoot, but, more seriously, from the purpose of their tour: *SAS* (I, 1791, p. 107) recorded neatly and vividly some of Ballantrae's real importance to Alexandre: 'The black cattle are of a small, handsome kind. The chief staple commodity is raising young cattle and sheep. The young cattle are for the most part sold to the grazier when two and a half years old, and changed from hand to hand till they are 4 or 5 years old when they are sent up to the St Faith and Hempton fairs in England [near Norwich and Fakenham respectively] and make part of what are called the fine *Scots Galloways*.' Great cattle fairs took place three times a year at Hempton, and at St Faith on 17 October for *three weeks*, for the sale of Scottish cattle.

[61] Ships of 300 tons came up into 'the Road', about half a mile from the town (*SAS*, I, 1791, p. 359).

[62] *SAS* (*ibid*) described in 1791 'the handsome town house and prison built c1773, with the many new houses built about the same time – well finished and adding greatly to the beauty of the streets'.

68. *Portpatrick: the packet-boat service to Donaghadee. Aquatint from William Daniell,* Voyage Round Great Britain in 1813, *1825. The tunnel to the left of the three moored packet-boats was probably the source of material for building the bright new quay.*

Our horses were so exhausted, especially the one drawing the gig, that we all had to walk those 6 miles. The country was hilly and wretched, the land very little cultivated and cheap. The cattle were poor little creatures, the price of a lean sheep 6 *francs*, and a cow 2 or 2.5 *louis*. The farmers are very poor, but better off than most people. The sole trade of the place is the making of common cloth. We arrived at Portpatrick so late that I can't remember any detail of our arrival.

Portpatrick, New Inn[63]   Portpatrick is a little town and the one where we have come in order to sail for Ireland. Its only business, and what gives it its life, is the packet-boats which sail daily for Ireland. It is the only place with regular communication between the two kingdoms.[64]

---

[63] *SAS* (I, p. 41) recorded in 1791 that 'almost every house is an inn'. According to Mackenzie and Cunningham, *Old Portpatrick*, the Blair Arms is Portpatrick's first inn. In 1698, Peter the Great of Russia is said to have stayed in it on his way to Ireland.
[64] He was overlooking the regular Holyhead–Dublin packet-boats, by which he later returned from Ireland.

The harbour is a mere opening between rocks cropping out of the water and is still recognised as very dangerous.[65] I'm about to leave Scotland, so I must write down for a moment the thread of my journey, and try to give a general idea of the resources and practices of the Scots against the background of their country.

A few more samples from Mr Fullerton's pattern-book at Paisley Museum, with figuring produced by means of a lappet device: cf Pl 65, p. 211 above.

[65] *SAS* (I, p. 39) recorded, only five years after this visit: 'There is now on the same spot one of the finest quays in Britain, with a reflecting lighthouse; and, instead of a few flat-bottomed boats, above a dozen trading-vessels of 40–60 tons . . . We have now four elegant vessels, fitted up with every accommodation, whose only object is to forward the mail and convey passengers from the one island to the other.'

10

Alexandre's General Observations on Leaving Scotland

On the strength of what he had seen and assiduously recorded during their great anticlockwise tour of Scotland's farms and towns, ending with their favourite textile technology in Glasgow and Paisley, we can now see the value of his day-by-day accounts, especially when they are supplemented by the 21 volumes of Sir John Sinclair's Statistical Account of Scotland's 938 parishes, in the 1790s, and by the Tours of Thomas Pennant, Louis Simond and others. It is greatly to Alexandre's credit that, as he reached the end of this phase of their tours, he should want to pause and try to summarise it, however briefly, for the benefit of his kind and encouraging father.

Lazowski, surprisingly and perhaps mercifully, forgot the general summary he promised in Edinburgh, though on his last day in Glasgow he composed a dozen or so paragraphs of old-fashioned French Jacobite obscurantism about the plight of the remaining highlanders in their glens. More of a romantic than the unfortunate clansmen themselves, Lazowski felt unable to forgive many of their chieftain/lairds for preferring London to the delights of the Highlands, nor could he forgive the Hanoverian government for encouraging the weakening of the clans in such ways.

What is perhaps seriously unforgivable is a letter Lazowski had composed the day before, in Glasgow, to Arthur Young: 'We run, instead of travelling. My companion wishes only to move from place to place. He counts every day how many miles we have done, and his satisfaction is all wais in proportion to the number . . . I write four hours at least every day.' *If Lazowski really was writing at least four hours every day, one sees one way in which Alexandre might have found him a tedious companion. One also wonders what on earth became of all that writing, and why what survives of it is sometimes much less interesting than Alexandre's observations, despite his dreadfully indecipherable handwriting: his interest in daily mileage, incidentally, he may well have acquired from Arthur Young!*

As Young would have done, he began with reflections on the quality of farming in Scotland and the evidence of its 'improvement'. From his recollection of their well-planned itinerary, he identified three distinctive divisions: first, all the lands round the wide and prosperous Firths of Forth and Clyde; second, almost all the rest of the east coast, including a part of the Moray Firth near Forres and Nairn, and, in the south-west, coastal Ayrshire and Galloway; third, the Highlands, 'where height and soil never allow the creation of good farmland'.

222

I've been about 5 weeks in Scotland, and I've seen a little of it all. Although I haven't been able to go deeply into several things I very much wanted to. I just wished I'd had more time. What I've sometimes managed to do is to give an idea not only of what there is, but what it might lead to. In these three different areas, there seem to be three very different regimes at work. For overall improvement to come about, it would require tremendous industry from the men themselves and from those making best use of them. What I'm sure of is this: in a country that was barbarous and without serious [agri]culture, and, generally speaking, without good soil, yet which at present is cultivated, that demonstrates the industry in these people and, at least, the will to work.

The people in the first of my divisions have proved themselves. They've cleared their lands, working daily to improve them, and have reached the point of taking on manufactures, and even of entering into rivalry with a people who are very accomplished, and famous for their commercial abilities of all kinds: the English.

In these richer parts, one has a sense of real opulence, and one sees Scots who seem to have risen rather above the business of manufacturing and trade: they use only sparingly and moderately what it has cost them such efforts to acquire.

The second of my divisions is the one that is at present coming into shape. The land is ungrateful, but the peasant gives everything to clear a part of it, and lives in hope that one of his clearings will be profitable, for his spirit is industrious and workmanlike. In the end, you can sense that these people are speaking to you with a positive pleasure, and you tell them of the visible difference they have wrought in the land since they began clearing it, and planting. I'm willing to bet that more than half the land they give to the plough will yield a crop, though at present it is wretchedly poor soil. The people are badly housed, but that they are used to. A sort of patriotism holds them to these ungrateful lands, when they would be so much better off if they moved, for example, to England.

My last division is the Highlands, which for arable purposes are virtually unclearable. The highlanders are a people apart, and act as though they are entirely different from the rest of the Scots. They have a little plot of land, from which they have just managed to scrape a living. They live on little. The idea of liberty makes them live, and that idea is so common and so strong that you'll find very few of these people working as servants or labourers. If they are obliged to earn their livings, they try to do a job of their own choosing. They are inseparable from their Highlands, and would never willingly leave them, even for the most beautiful place in the world.

They are frank and open about their habits, which are not exactly heinous, yet it is extraordinary that they are so given to theft: in their language, the word clearly signifies *stealing skilfully*, without the normal deplorable overtones of *theft*. In every way separate from the rest, this race of Scots is notably lazy: born to hunting, not husbandry. The rest of the Scots are good workers, not sparing themselves: mostly poor, and mostly good.

So there you see the destiny of Scotland. In 1707, Scotland came together with England in an Act of Union, to become Great Britain. They lost their own Parliament in Edinburgh, but sent members to the English Parliament. They were subject to the Acts of that Parliament, but greatly benefited by sharing in England's industrial and commercial supremacy, at home and overseas. Meanwhile Scotland remained mistress of her own internal affairs.

At this point, probably remembering his brother François' highly entertaining and illuminating general account of England based on their relatively static 13 months in an Assize town, and including a disquisition on the administration of law in England (A Frenchman's Year in Suffolk, 1784, pp. 79–90), Alexandre, after 5 weeks constantly on the move in Scotland, mistakenly felt emboldened to write five pages on the Scottish criminal law and administration of justice: we need not plunge after him. Nor is he adequately informed, of course, about the choosing of Scottish members for the English Parliament. He naturally remembered that here the Customs were in the hands of five Scottish commissioners, and that their host in Edinburgh had been one of them. Economic affairs were much more Alexandre's line. He continued:

In Scotland, which is what may be called a poor country, it's lovely to see quite a thriving commerce in the various places where it is now established; and to find in a land so empty and desolate, so sparsely endowed, towns as robustly commercial as Glasgow and Paisley: they on their own should have gained Scotland a much greater reputation. And it's curious that it's only in these two towns that commerce has been developed on a major scale. But there are several smaller towns, such as Leith, Aberdeen and Inverness, that cannot fail to be interesting in their economy.

Linen is a branch of industry which is developed, I believe, as far as, if not further than, anywhere else; and fine linen is so commonly available that, in all the inns, even the worst, you will find plenty of linen. The single article of linen is of very much greater importance to Scotland in general, even than the trade of Glasgow was before the American War. It adds to the spread of the general well-being.[1]

The character of this nation is tremendously enterprising. They make good soldiers and, above all, the very bravest ones. They are also straightforward, and in their inns, for example, they don't overcharge. They are fundamentally trustworthy and open, hardworking and intelligent. They speak a terribly corrupt version of English.

The main aspect of Scotland is discouraging: a mountain kingdom, and the mountains often covered by no more than 6 or 8 inches of soil, in which very little can grow. Often their cattle are unable to graze with any ease. It seems a land of great sadness; perhaps most of all because the dwellings are so scattered and, when you find them, they are so poor and depressing. Scotland could never become what one would call 'pretty' country, *un joli pays*, for even if one only planted forests of evergreen trees it would continue to convey an enormous feeling of sadness, and often of terrible monotony.

Yet the Highlands, which are something altogether apart, are certainly wonder-

---

[1]   Seven years later, the *Statistical Account* of Glasgow (V, p. 502) bears Alexandre out, but notes that the 'great cotton manufacture has, in some measure, supplanted the linen trade, which used to be the staple manufacture of the west of Scotland: there is yet, however, a very great quantity of linens, lawns, &c still made'.

fully agreeable for their beautiful variety, their setting among the lochs and the rivers: most delightful.

The religion of the Scots is Calvinist, very strict. On Sunday, for instance, whistling is a very grave sin. They detest all other religions, Anglican as much as Catholic. They worship in Kirks and chapels, among other sects, but their enthusiasm is always lively.[2] One of their laws concerns the independent manner in which people marry: that's to say, one isn't obliged to consult anyone in order to take whom one pleases; and the consent of parents is unnecessary, which is the reason why many English and Irish run away from home with young persons in order to get married; and why such a wedding seems increasingly attractive provided nobody succeeds in preventing it. This law is the cause in England of many family quarrels: I don't know why the English seem disinclined to declare such marriages void.[3]

The manners of the Scots [he means the lowlanders] are very little different from those of the English. They are perhaps a shade less polished. They may become more so when the nation throws itself into the arts etc: the differences are very small. The Scots receive all strangers [?foreigners] with the greatest courtesy and the minimum fuss. They are generally keener on drinking than the English, which is evident proof that they are not quite so polite. Then they are not so clean as the English, as one soon notices in their inns, and even in their houses; and I've been struck by much sad evidence of not only the untidiness, but also the inelegance, of the young women of this country, who are, with some notable exceptions, in Banff and parts of

2   As with the Scottish Law, it would have been surprising if Alexandre had been able to grasp the difference between the Scottish and English churches: the church of Scotland, 'the Kirk', being Presbyterian, the church of England being Episcopalian. In Scotland, the Episcopalians met in meeting-houses, like Catholics and the various sects of dissenting Presbyterians. The Presbyterian Kirk and its offshoots were Calvinist, and its congregations saw themselves as the 'elect', as distinct from the eternally damned. From 1694, all Presbyterian Kirk sessions were bound faithfully 'to exercise church discipline against all . . . scandalous offenders', not just whistling on the Sabbath, but 'fornication, adultery, drunkenness, blasphemy and other gross and abominable sins'. This must have led often to uncomfortable, as well as 'enthusiastic and lively' parish life. It should have led Alexandre to suspect the truth of his next statement.

3   The Rev Mr John Morgan, Minister of Graitney (now Gretna) in Dumfries, puts the record straight in *SAS*, IX, 1793, pp. 531–2. 'This parish has been long famous for the marriages of fugitive lovers from England. People living at a distance erroneously suppose that the established clergyman of this parish is the celebrator of those marriages; whereas the persons who follow this illicit practice are mere imposters, priests of their own creation . . . The greatest part of the trade is monopolised by a man who was originally a tobacconist, not a blacksmith as is generally believed; a fellow without literature, without principles . . . his life is a continued scene of drunkenness. Such is the man . . . who has had the honour to join in the sacred bonds of wedlock many people of great rank and fortune from all parts of England. It is 40 years and upwards since marriages of this kind began to be celebrated here [ie since c1750].' He added that there were at least 60 such charades a year, bringing in about £945 a year. When any ceremony was used, it was that of the Church of England, but when the 'parson' was intoxicated only a certificate was given, signed by the imposter and two witnesses, with fictitious signatures. The spelling of a specimen certificate is not very convincing: 'This is to sartfay all persons that my be conserned . . .' What was Morgan's Kirk session doing to allow the continuance of such a blasphemy? Could there have been sweeteners?

the Highlands, for example, rather plain. The habit of wearing neither stockings nor shoes is, I suppose, a distressing feature of poverty.

Scotland's poverty, of course, makes it a cheap country to live in; even luxury goods are relatively cheap. The Scots gentry enjoy fishing, hunting or shooting, but their country seems to me to be poor and disagreeable to shoot over. The Scots have great courage and would do anything for what they call 'a dram of whiskey', that is, about two glasses of whiskey, which is distilled from grain and of such potency that I could only manage half a glass. But the Scots drink great quantities and can do nothing without 'a drop'. Here they start drinking from the moment they wake up: a stable-boy can't start working with his horses until he's drunk the usual 'drop': very different from the stable-boys of England, where they don't drink till after dinner, but then make up for lost time. But I must say I find the Scots a fine, good people, fit for anything. They are free people, too 'new' to be extremely polished.

To conclude my reflections on this great part of the United Kingdom, I can't help seeing it as mainly a wild, uncivilised land, some of it scarcely able to support the lives of its people, who are in many parts working their hardest to transform it. The inns are not numerous and are apt to be not very agreeable, but you will find several places where we were well fed: in Edinburgh, we lived in luxury.

Despite inconveniences and temporary disagreements we have made virtually a complete tour of a Scottish kingdom, new at every point, which in 20 years' time will be unrecognisable, and very comfortably off. We have seen the Highlands, which we often talk about, inhabited still by a people of unique culture yet so near to our own home. Anyone with the curiosity to see them hurrying to catch up will see them spoiled all too quickly, by the alien world, and possibly by themselves.

Alexandre had no premonition that the highland clearances, begun by Cumberland in the 1740s, were about to be completed by the great landowners, who preferred to see their glens inhabited by sheep.[4]

---

[4] See John Prebble, *The Highland Clearances*, 1963, and T. M. Devine, *The Scottish Nation, 1700–2000*, chapters 9, 11 and 18.

11

Homeward Bound

*The beauties of Ireland; 'If only the poor Scots had this land'; the Boyne
valley and Slane; Dublin and neighbouring houses; a heatwave in the
Conway valley; Llansannan, 'un endroit perdu'; Whitchurch races;
Kidderminster tanneries; Worcester; Gloucester; the Cotswolds;
at Eton, journal's end*

*Towards the end of Alexandre's general reflections on Scotland, in the previous chapter, he
expresses his disappointment in the 'rather plain' looks of the young women. There were
notable exceptions, in and around Old Meldrum, and Banff, which I don't think were
mere symptoms of his youth and of the arrival of Spring (it was Shakespeare's birthday, 23
April, and, even north of Aberdeen, the weather was an improvement on the snow and
frost they'd set out in from Bury on 14 March). At any rate, by 15 May, three days after
crossing to Donaghadee from Portpatrick, they were driving from Lisburn to
Hillsborough, and found things quite different.* The girls here are all beautiful, fresh
complexioned and cheerful. They want nothing more than to laugh with all their
hearts . . . they are entirely appetising. We were followed along the road by one who
was pretty and *assez x x x* [*sic*!].

Here the houses are poorer, so are the people, though presentable. From
Hillsborough to Lurgan, the houses became wretched, only earth and straw, the
inside very dirty. It is extraordinary, the elegance and air of all the pretty girls lodging
in these awful hovels in which you'd scarcely kennel a dog.

And the landscape's quite different from what we've been seeing. The land: 1)
potatoes 2) oats, three times running 3) grass. I must say this rotation is deplorable,
not growing *something* between the 3 crops of oats. At Lurgan we stayed at the Black
Bear. Near the town is the very attractive house and garden of Mr Brownlow, with
Lough Neagh beyond; fresh water, and a fine effect from the house. *Arthur Young
described Mr Brownlow's view as it looked a decade earlier, from a bench on a gently
swelling hill. He advanced his tenants money for all the lime they chose, and took
payment in eight years with rent. Next day, Mr Brownlow and Arthur Young walked
into Lurgan market together.*

*Then Alexandre was thrilled by the magnificent farmlands of Rich Hill, well named,
as they approached Armagh, though he gave a poor mark to Mr Robertson, whose fine
park did* not *look properly maintained. In Armagh they stayed at the Molyneux Arms.
Arthur Young had stayed with the Archbishop, the public-spirited Richard Robinson,
and wrote of him: 'The buildings he's erected in seven years one would suppose to be the*

work of an [entire] active life' – the elegant palace, the barracks, the school and a new church, as well as three other churches, and a public library. And *'he has demonstrated what a fine, clean crop of wheat will grow here'. Alexandre criticised the Archbishop's farming and park ('needs enlarging'), but admitted that the public library, founded in 1771, was handsome: it was also remarkably well stocked. Finally:* He's more often in London than Dublin, which explains, I think, why his farming isn't taken seriously.

Alexandre was much better pleased by Newry, where they stayed at the Globe, 'another good inn' according to Arthur Young a decade earlier. The French were chiefly interested in the new canal, connecting Lough Neagh to the sea: 5 miles long, taking 2-masted vessels and is covered with ships of all sizes, its banks lined with warehouses. It trades not only with foreign parts and even direct to America, but still more she and her neighbours are swarming with manufactures of every kind, with special warehouse blocks for textiles, white and coloured: the whites sold weekly, the coloured four times a year. This in a town 5 miles from the open sea.

Staying at Drogheda White Horse on Sunday 21 May, they thought it was just the day to see the people in their best clothes. Not only were they shocked by the general impoverishment, they felt that the men looked like robbers and rogues. Nor did the girls look as nice as all those nearer Belfast. At Drogheda they made a delightful detour, following the Boyne, eating at Slane and going on to sleep at Navan. Along the river's rich lands, agriculture was being pushed to great perfection. The meadows made a beautiful landscape, often interspersed with country houses. Their gardens and parks had been given cascades and falls by the river 'which then retires to its original bed'. A very tall obelisk, raised to mark the site of William III's decisive victory here in these meadows, naturally became unacceptable to the Irish.

Alexandre made no reflection on the battle, but chose this moment to make his observations on what he thought of the Irish in relation to their agriculture. What is very striking is that despite the great richness of all this region, and its great natural fertility, it looks poor, which seems to be the result of the great idleness, and even more of the stupid simplicity, of the inhabitants. I have never yet seen a man here working what I call hard. They work as if they were toying gently with a pretty girl. Apart from that, they are charming. Gazing at our 'extraordinary' gig would, I'm sure, during the 15 days we've been travelling here, have lost the Irish whom we've passed anywhere near, more than 12 hours' work. From the time they've set eyes on us, they've stopped work and flocked over, like curious cattle, to come and see us. Even our dog trotting along beside the gig is to them an object of admiration, and they even try following us with words like 'grand-looking', 'splendid' etc. A favourite question was whether it was time to break off for dinner. Every day we were stopped 5 or 6 times in the middle of the road to be asked the time.

It's unfortunate that a people so stupid and idle goes with such lovely land. If only the poor Scots had such land they'd make a wonderful job of it compared with the Irish, whose sole aptitude is evidently drinking. [*Such generalisations always need qualifying. Only a decade earlier, in 1775,* An American Quaker in the British Isles *(ed K. Morgan, 1992, p. 60) allowed himself the observations that, from Edinburgh to Montrose, it was 'by no means a bad soil, but its whole Face discovers the Indolence of the*

People'. A glance at what Lazowski wrote just before reaching Blair Adam from Edin-burgh contradicts the Quaker, or reveals a rapid change in local behaviour.]

We've continued in this beautiful Boyne country as far as Slane. The village is built on a site above the river by a Monsieur Conyngham, a very rich landowner. [*Its creation has lately been described in the Buildings of Ireland volume on* North Leinster, *as 'a perfect example of the formally planned 18th-century estate village . . . solidly built and charming in a sober way, with four identical mansions and outhouses facing each other diagonally across the main crossroads'.*[1] *Mark Bence-Jones writes of the impressive approach to the castle from the village: 'the village cross-roads* [is] *transformed into a place worthy of the capital of a European princeling'.*[2]] *Alexandre:* Near the village is a superb water-mill that Monsieur Conyngham and two other people have had built: it cost 20,000 *louis*. They work only for themselves. The flour is I believe excellent. The machinery is simple but hard to see: it's kept in perfect condition. It's had the effect of encouraging arable farming, since the farmer has seen that they get a better price for their grain. What with the grandeur of the enterprise and the perfection of the product, I wager that everybody will be coming to see this fine mill.[3]

From Slane to Navan, the road continues along the river, and is the more charming because the farmlands are so good. We left Navan on the 23rd and slept in Dublin: 28 miles, following the banks of a delightful stream.

Gradually much more population towards the town. You come to what's known as Phoenix Park, extensive though not well tree'd. At its centre a very beautiful area with an obelisk[4] and lamps: the width and beauty of the roads crossing the park[5] and the number of country houses on all sides gives you the feeling of entering a large wealthy capital. In the middle of the park is the seat of the Lord Lieutenant of Ireland, the duke of Rutland. The house has a broad front, not well designed,[6] above a large garden. The park leads into Dublin, that's to say, to the first of its streets.

I stayed 5 full days in Dublin so as not to make a muddle of it: in consequence I spent some *very* full days.

DUBLIN

Harris Hotel.[7] *The 24th at Dublin*   We lost some sightseeing time looking for our servants who managed to arrive very late. Dublin is a fine town of 140,000 inhabit-ants, and well spread out: I reckon perhaps 5 miles broad by 2. It is built low, not

---

1   C. Casey and A. Rowan, 1993, 471. It was laid out in the 1760s by Henry, 1st baron Conyngham, who died in 1781. Alexandre's Monsieur Conyngham was his nephew, the 2nd baron, who died at Bristol Hot Wells in 1787. He was kind to Alexandre and Lazowski in Dublin.

2   *A Guide to Irish Country Houses*, 1988, pp. 260–1.

3   This enormous mill survives: its photograph in Casey and Rowan does it little justice.

4   The present one was erected to the duke of Wellington in 1817.

5   It's more than twice as big as Hampstead Heath (*Rough Guide to Ireland*, p. 91).

6   See Mark Bence-Jones, *A Guide to Irish Country Houses*, 1988, pp. 6–7, with illustrations.

7   Colette O'Daly, at the National Library, found me Wilson's Dublin Directory for 1786. It listed R. G. Harris's Hotel at 103, Capel Street, running north from the Liffey. It was then one of Dublin's most fashionable streets. Now there are pawnbrokers.

much above sea-level, and is traversed by the river Liffey. The river is crossed by six bridges in the town: four of them are very old and ugly; one of the others, the Queen's bridge, has only 3 arches but is elegant; the other, which the big ships reach, has 5 arches and is very beautiful. From this bridge to the place where there are no longer jetties on either bank, a great many ships are moored, creating a forest of masts, which mingle with all the houses and have a charming effect. It's not a large river: I doubt if you could find room for more than four vessels abreast.

Returning to the town, it's large and beautifully built. I'm sure that this elegant and proper manner of the English is very difficult to acquire by other people. There's a street called *Dame Street* which is truly superb, as much on account of the general beauty of its shops as of the width of the street itself.[8] It is not absolutely finished, but already it is very handsome.[9] One's general idea of Dublin is that it's a body of blocks of houses built on a regular plan, their situation isolated by the streets and the width of the streets, making it a place that must be healthy: also by its maritime position, its nearness to the sea, and then by the convenience of a river, bringing all sorts of shipping to a town of great commerce and great magnificence; exuding wealth so ostentatiously that one could easily nod off to sleep just looking at a quantity of the fine horses, handsome carriages and beautiful houses in this town.

So on the 24th after a preliminary look at the town and quays we went into more detail, and first the barracks, begun in 1704, a block of buildings giving on to the river, and square: a uniform block of buildings, agreeable to look at. In these barracks, the regiments of infantry could be stationed, and the dragoons and the garrison ordnance of the town. I find it difficult to believe that a garrison contains seven regiments, so close-packed that they haven't room on the page, so to say.[10] After looking at the barracks, we went to Phoenix Park, which I mentioned yesterday.

Outside the town, on the other side of the river, we found the hospital 'of the invalids', a good building of brick. There were other hospitals; for orphans, for maternity, for the sick, one for the town of Dublin, and for the children of sailors, one for foundlings, one for incurables: there were a great many other hospitals for the sick and the old: some have been established by subscription. Many of the buildings are very good.

The Castle is largely of old red brick. One sees the remains of the ancient castle, but the present one hasn't long been built. There's one long square court where the Lord Lieutenant has his official residence (his house in Phoenix Park is for recreation). His official residence has the appearance of an excellent private house with fine rooms, and which could easily hold 500 persons.

After dinner we went to see the College, which is at the same time a university, in

---

8 It is now really wide, as an A road, leading the N81 into the two major traffic roundabouts at the heart of Dublin, between Dublin Castle and College Green!
9 It is now absolutely finished.
10 Arthur Young, in 1774 (*A Tour in Ireland*, 1892 edn, I, p. 18) wrote: 'The barracks are a vast building, raised in a plain stile, of many divisions, the principal front is of an immense length. They contain every convenience for ten regiments.'

a building extraordinarily grand and beautifully built in stone. Its facade on College Green is very fine. The College seemed to be on the same footing as Oxford or Cambridge. It has its professors and young people, as in England. This College, a little town on its own, is superb. Returning to our hotel we passed the Customs, the old building: they're raising another at the end of the town.

On the 25th   we stayed in Dublin. We'd brought a letter of recommendation which we sent, but the person addressed wasn't in town. Today, therefore, we hired a four-wheeled cab (*fiacre*) and went to a place called the Black Rock. It's a seaside village, 3 miles from Dublin, in Dublin Bay. The road you take is through a country-side of small country houses, mostly very pretty. The land sells at 5 *louis* the *arpent*. These prosperous areas are very pleasant to drive through and gave me a pleasure greater (I find) than I can properly express. Arrived at *Black Rock*[11] we found a cluster of pretty houses making up a village. The view of it is delightful: on one side the sea, covered with sailing ships, their masts mixed with one side of the village. On the other side, the village and fertile surrounding country and more pretty small houses. Nothing could be more exhilarating.

After enjoying the view for a long time, we returned to the town, crossing another part of the plain, still very rich, and returning through *Ranelagh*, 2 miles from town: it's a public garden where the whole town takes tea in the Spring. There's a big room as well as the garden, where one can promenade: it's open every day, all day.[12] Back in the town we saw the Parliament House, where the members meet, as in London.[13]

On College Green, a triangular space, a bronze statue of William III on horse-back stands in the middle. The parliament building's facade is a half H with a peri-style formed of 12 columns; the frieze and entablature are uniform with the columns, in great simplicity. Inside, on one side, is the house of commons. The other chamber is for the Lords. The rooms shared between the two houses are large, handsome and comfortable: what's most remarkable is the high elegance and the beauty. After the parliament we dined, and after that the *Comedy*. The theatres were exactly as in London, dirty and wretched,[14] and what might be thought passable for

[11] 3 miles south-east of the town, in Dublin Bay, between Booterstown Marsh (a bird sanctuary in 1999) and Dun Laoghaire. On the shore towards Black Rock was a favourite bathing-place for Dubliners.

[12] 'The Ranelagh Gardens, about a mile to the south of Dublin, was opened as a place of amuse-ment by William Hollister, organ-builder from London, in 1766. He erected a burletta theatre there, which he supplied with singers and an orchestra, and laid out the gardens in alcoves and bowers for tea-drinking parties': (Constantia Maxwell, *Dublin under the Georges*, 1946, pp. 95–6). It was eclipsed at the end of the century by the Rotunda Gardens and Assembly Rooms, opened in support of the Lying-In Hospital (itself opened in 1757).

[13] Young (see footnote 10 above) thought it 'grand . . . the apartments spacious, elegant and convenient, much beyond that heap of confusion at Westminster'.

[14] Alexandre's brother François was clearly interested in the theatre and gave a full and interesting account of his experience of it in London (*Innocent Espionage*, pp. 202–7). He certainly gave no indication that the London theatres were '*sales et vilaines*'.

69. *Dublin, St Stephen's Green, James Malton, 1792–99.*

a small town but not for Dublin. The exits were so narrow and bad that ladies could scarcely pass, and there would be great danger in a fire.

The 26th   we had this letter of recommendation for someone, and now we traced him, Monsieur Conyngham[15] who had been employed as Treasurer of Ireland,[16] a Court appointment. He is very polite and cultivated and, happily for me, he'd arranged for us to go to an evening ball. We naturally accepted. We'd already seen the duke of Leinster's house, which is most handsome, the courtyard especially, and with a big garden at the back of the house, very rare in the town.[17]

Across the road we came to *St Stephen's Green*, a large square green of very great distinction, with good buildings lining it, and then an avenue of fine elms parallel with one side, and all within the green, and a lawn and a lake and the statue of King James.[18] The avenue of trees is a mile long, which gives you some idea of the gran-

[15] Francis Pierpoint Conyngham, nephew and heir of the Lord Conyngham whose work Arthur Young, and they, had admired at Slane. He succeeded his uncle in 1781: see footnote 1, above.

[16] Alexandre was on the right lines: he was MP for County Clare and Teller of the Exchequer for Ireland (Burke's *Peerage*, unconfirmed in *The Complete Peerage*).

[17] The duke of Leinster built his town house to the design of Richard Cassells in 1745, on Kildare Street (its back view looks out at Merrion Square). They sold Leinster House c1815. The whole site, with 1890s additions, now houses the Dail, the National Library, the National Gallery and the National Museum.

[18] The equestrian statue displayed George II, *not* King James! Arthur Young, in Dublin in 1776, recorded: 'The houses in general, and what they call their two-roomed ones, are good and convenient. Mr Latouche's, in Stephen's Green, I was shown as a model of this sort. I found it well contrived and finished elegantly' (*op cit*, I, p. 19). The Green was re-laid out by a Guinness in 1880. Many of the Georgian houses have been replaced in our own depressing day. On the north

deur of this place.[19] The houses are mostly beautiful, and comfortably lived in. This seems to be the 'best' part of the town.

Going from there to the Archives we crossed a part of the town we didn't know, which was absolutely like the rest, although newer, indeed still being built. The Archives building will be magnificent when it's finished. It stands beside the river. We've also seen the new Custom House, also not quite finished. It will be large and extensive but I don't like the architecture.[20]

We dined with Monsieur Conyngham at his house. After a good dinner,[21] and much wine, he obliged us to go to the Comedy and gave us a rendezvous for the ball that evening. After returning home, we were to meet at about half past ten for the ball given by Lady *Ely*, a rich lady who spends her money on things of this kind.[22] The first moments were a little embarrassing, but after that it got rather better. The ballroom was a good 90 feet long, with columns, and in the finest taste: it was magnificent. There we found the whole of the grandest company in Dublin, and what was notable was that they were so elegant and so brilliant. I have *never* seen so many pretty women so beautifully dressed as I saw there. It was a charming ball for the eyes, but I was bored at not really knowing anybody.

At about 2 o'clock there was a magnificent supper, an abundance of everything one could desire. There were 200 people at the supper. The duchess of Rutland, wife of the Lord Lieutenant of Ireland, was there: a charming woman, quite as pretty as the best of all that Dublin could provide in the way of pretty women. After supper the ball began again, and lasted till 5 in the morning. We slept, exhausted, for we'd been walking all day, and to be awake all night was too much. However, I was enchanted to see the best society of Dublin all together.

On the 27th   we were taken by Mr Conyngham on a tour of the country houses round Dublin. We were in his carriage with our horses following: we often mounted. Six miles from the town we saw two very good houses, one of which, belonging to a Mr Clement,[23] is very pretty and stands beside the Liffey: from there we went on to several more houses beside the river, all of them attractive and in rich country, the land almost growing crops by itself and the river delicious, converted with cascades of perhaps 12

side, the Shelbourne holds its own. On the south side, numbers 85 and 86, built c1738 by the architect Cassells, belong to the Catholic University, who show them as fine examples of Dublin's early-Georgian living.

19   It was known as 'the Beaux Walk' at the time of the Rochefoucauld visit (see facing page).
20   On Custom House Quay, on the north bank of the Liffey. It was James Gandon's finest work, built 1781–91. It's often described as Dublin's counterpart to London's Somerset House. Ironically, he was 'looking to French neo-Classicism to reinvigorate Palladianism' (Colvin).
21   More of a lunch.
22   Writing of the influence of the Adam brothers, Constantia Maxwell said: 'Ely House, for instance, with its beautiful wrought-iron staircase, mahogany doors, silver handles and lock-plates, carved chimney-pieces and walls decorated with stucco, is obviously inspired by their taste.' She also records an 'attic theatre' in the marquess of Ely's mansion.
23   Mark Bence-Jones at once identified him as Nathaniel Clements, banker, politician and amateur architect. This house, Killadoon, at Celbridge, Co Kildare, has a notably fine interior.

feet at one of the houses we saw: they say you can see the salmon leap here, but that we didn't see.

Finally, after seeing many country houses of which the interior and the views increased our sense of the beautiful, we went to a large house called *Carton*. It belongs to the duke of Leinster: the park is very big, covering 3,000 *arpents*, all enclosed by a wall. It still lies fallow but is crossed by a river which is pleasant, or at least improves the setting. The house is old, but very considerable. We saw the duke there, who politely pressed us to dine, and even to stay if we had the time: we were obliged to accept at least the dinner. We went to look at the little garden, which is pretty enough but it isn't kept with the same care as English gardens.[24]

After dinner we took leave of the duke in order to visit another house: one more that remained on our list. We crossed another part of his park and saw what's called the cottage. It's a place designed in the rustic, countrified manner, in the vernacular, and there is not another single park where you would fine one. This one is very pleasantly arranged, with great simplicity. The little garden is very well cared for and charming, above all, for the pictureque view that one has of the water and woods.

From this park we went to another called Castletown. The park is extensive and there are many fine trees, but the house is superb, quite magnificent, all in freestone and in the new taste:[25] the view from the house is pleasant enough but the house is more worth seeing than any other thing. A mile further on from Castletown House, the *maison dieu* is poor and neglected . . . but it is situated on the bank of a very well

[24] Arthur Young visited the duke of Leinster here on 27 June 1776, almost exactly 10 years earlier. At that time Young thought, and wrote, that 'the park ranks among the finest in Ireland. It's a vast lawn, which waves over gentle hills, surrounded by plantations of great extent, and which break and divide in places, so as to give much variety. A large but gentle vale winds through the whole, in the bottom of which a small stream has been enlarged into a fine river, which throws a cheerfulness through most of the scenes: over it a handsome stone bridge.' More details of a large shrubbery, a cottage and a prospect tower: all kept in the highest order by 1,100 sheep. One wonders if Alexandre or Lazowski mentioned Young to the duke: it seems more than likely that they would have read his *Tour of Ireland* (*op cit*, I, pp. 31–2).

[25] By 'the new taste' he means Palladian. It was built for William Conolly, a publican's son from Donegal, which he represented in the Irish House of Commons. Backing the Hanoverians, he became Speaker in 1715, and in due course the richest man in Ireland. In 1714, John Molesworth, finishing his term as envoy to Tuscany and hoping to steer British architecture away from baroque, brought a Florentine architect, Alessandro Galilei, to London with him; and home to Ireland in 1718. Speaker Conolly commissioned him in 1718 and the work began in 1722, four years after he'd returned to Florence. Galilei's design was therefore realised by Edward Lovett Pearce who was in Italy studying architecture in 1723–4. 'By 1731, he had become the leading Palladian architect in Ireland' (Colvin, *Dictionary*, p. 745). Mark Bence-Jones, in his splendid *Guide to Irish Country Houses* (1988, p. 75), describes its 13-bay front, 'reminiscent of the façade of an Italian Renaissance town palazzo' and says: 'Despite the many windows and lack of a central feature, there is no sense of monotony or heaviness: the effect being one of great beauty and serenity.' The wings and curving colonnades are presumably Pearce's design. The story of the interior is notorious, the work of a Lady Louisa Lennox, who married Tom Conolly, William's great-nephew: together they employed excellent craftsmen, and possibly Sir William Chambers. By *maison dieu*, below, he presumably means the church?

planted river: the breadth and beauty of the water have a most charming effect, and so do several bridges.

There is a great number of fine rooms in the houses we've seen. There was a lot of company in the last house and we were invited to supper, but were so tired that we couldn't have responded to the company, which was some of the same crowd we had seen at the ball.

On the 28th   we've done virtually nothing. We've been to the home of our acquaintance who made us undertake two more visits. We went to look at a smart house in the town with a garden of 10 *arpents*: very rare in a town. In the evening we walked to the canal which brings all provisions into Dublin, the centre of the kingdom. [*Sketch omitted.*]

It has roughly the shape sketched on the opposite page. You must see the shape of the basin and the opening of the circuit which is curved and very narrow, and then of the canal itself which is 50 miles long and a regular 50 feet wide. On each side it is well planted with elms, can carry all sorts of boats and is of great use to the town. The canal has several locks and must have cost a great deal of money. It hasn't long been finished and already it is said to have increased Dublin's trade.

29 May. We have left Dublin and have set sail for Holyhead   in England,[26] but before leaving Ireland I must attempt a brief general reflection.[27] There are 5 packet-boats in service, those boats that carry the letters. The passage is 74 miles. We've exchanged our horses and we've only 14 hours to make the crossing. I wasn't ill, and on the boat I was with some very friendly people. We arrived at Holyhead towards 1 in the morning. The night was superb. Entering the port was difficult and a fairly large détour was necessary, but experience has ensured that boats have never been lost in living memory.

Holyhead, Mr Jackson, 30 and 31 May   We stayed at Holyhead. Holyhead's on its own little isle off the isle of Anglesey on the west of Wales.

1 June   We dined at the house half on the road at Bangor Ferry. The isle of Anglesey abounds in history, and the cows and bullocks are fine. The sheep, though small, are also very good: I saw an excellent breed. A sparsely-populated island.

Bangor Ferry, The George[28]   The town of Bangor was only 2 miles from where we slept. The country very well cultivated. A brief view of the sea and of a park near Bangor.[29]

26 Wales was still an indistinct idea to these Frenchmen.
27 Alexandre's intentions are admirable, but he has not really been in Ireland long enough – fifteen days – to philosophise about her. His strength is in direct reporting. I have regretfully cut the general reflection. As a reporter, though, he had acquired his brother's acumen.
28 'George very good; Castle comfortable' – Murray's *Handbook to North Wales*, 1868. The Castle promised views of the mountains of Conway, and from an eminence, the loftiest mountains of the Snowdon range. The George, on the banks of the Menai, later had full view of Telford's suspension bridge of 1819–26.
29 Penrhyn Castle.

The town's ugly but quite big. Very hilly road from Bangor to Conway, much of it running by the sea and high rocks. The land, we were told, fetches 6 *louis* the *arpent*.

Conway, Harp Crown[30]   The town of Conway is tiny and all in the walls of an old castle: its walls are still preserved. The entries are two gates defended by two towers, and the wall is strengthened by 44 towers apart from those of the castle. It stands above an arm of the sea and above the rock, and is an assemblage of towers.[31] The walls go up to 12 feet thick. The castle dominates on all sides and is dominated by nothing. At present it is almost a ruin, and a part has been demolished.[32] One looked at the walls of some of the rooms, but knowing nothing of what this place was, I could only think it served to reduce opposition. There is a little trade, feeble. The town is very sparsely inhabited: it's the road that keeps it alive.

The farming is fairly good round here, the land hilly: it works out at 8 shillings the *arpent* – dear. They keep a lot of cows, graze them on pastures in summer and in winter on hay. They don't give much milk. One handsome cow, that at this time might cost 6 or 7 *louis*, yields no more than 18 quarts: not enough, and much less than the Irish cows. Crop rotation: 1) wheat; 2) cabbages; 3) barley; 4) grass. I must be sure to say that the profitable growing of cabbages round here is almost general and most useful. Turnip growing is very little known.

They raise here a great many good-looking beasts which they fatten for sending to London. Some farmers here are very rich, and in consequence capable of living on their land. There's a gentleman-farmer here who spends all his income on experimenting with wheat. I think it's impossible for him to succeed here.

On the 3rd of June   dined at *Llanrwst* and slept at *Llansannan*: 24 miles. The first part we rode in the bottom of the [Conway] valley, half a mile wide between steep slopes,[33] and crossed by 2 or 3 torrents falling from the hills. All the rest is only a superb lawn, smooth as ice: very good soil. The only drawback was the sun. Full above us, it created a terrible heat. We arrived at Llanrwst in the valley of the Conway river and stayed from ten in the morning till 4, as it was too hot to attempt the new route we'd planned through the mountains.[34] In the evening we went on, knowing that the mountains would be a test for the horses, over very bad tracks. We had found an area of the country that is partly deserted, just a few farms, and in consequence little agriculture. But everywhere terrible mountains till we drew near Llansannan. There the hills

[30] Did Alexandre mean Harp *and* Crown? By 1868 you could choose between the Castle and the Erskine Arms, which was 'indifferent'.
[31] 'Each tower is isolated by a timber bridge so that it could fight alone': Elisabeth Beazley and Lionel Brett, *North Wales: A Shell Guide*, 1975, p. 30. They recommend climbing the Chapel Tower to a groyne-vaulted oratory. I think the walls have only 21 towers: a question of definition?
[32] Alexandre thought it was built by William I, and had of course no idea of the part it and the other Edwardian castles played in holding Wales for Edward I.
[33] Of the Cambrian mountains.
[34] It may perhaps be put down to the great heat that in Llanrwst Alexandre failed to notice the broad, graceful river-bridge (1663): with reason, Beazley and Brett reckon it the most elegant stone bridge in North Wales (*North Wales: A Shell Guide*, p. 117).

seemed a little lower and wooded, which brought us into another view, much more agreeable.[35]

Llansannan, Twa Key [*sic*]   Llansannan's a very small place on the banks of a little river that's more a torrent. Its situation, amid very high hills and in very wooded country, makes it delightful: a lost place [*un endroit perdu*].

On 4 June   we dined at *Denbigh* and slept at *Mold*. We were scarcely able to climb up the hills even though we dismounted. The countryside's lovely and a little more culti- vated. Just as you arrive in the valley below Denbigh,[36] the road flattens out. The valley's richness is extraordinary and you find a beautiful house with a park near the town.[37] Denbigh's a fair-sized town at the junction of 2 valleys, the long broad street leads steeply up to the ruins of an old castle. There were 3 walls, one behind another and all very thick. Remains of fortifications, and also of a very extensive church, never completed.[38] View superb, and you find a plain running 3 miles between hills – woods and enclosures, the land worth at least 20 shillings an *arpent*. A certain opulence – the numbers of houses of all kinds that you notice have an effect. From Denbigh to Mold, the last 15 miles were very warm work, through charming country. Houses were now extremely frequent. One in particular we passed was that of Mr S . . . Maurice, who owns a manufactory, or rather a bleaching business, a very extensive one.

Mold, The Griffon[39]   Mold is an attractive small town, its main street respectably and even well built, in brick, below a hill. The surrounding lands seem very productive. On 5 June we left Mold and arrived at *Chester* in one stretch: only 13 miles, but hilly and not a good journey. The higher parts are sandy, full of small stones, and there is lime, very advantageous for Chester. There are various mines, above all coal. The mines are close to Chester, the roads are damaged terribly by the great carts.

  After climbing and descending these awful roads for about 7 miles you suddenly find yourself on a high point in full view of Chester and the river Dee, not far from its entrance into the sea, and creating a mist in the warm weather, slightly spoiling our view. There is no sign of arable enclosure for all the enclosed fields are in pasture: butter and cheese are the rich products of this landscape. We entered a suburb, built of an ugly brick. We shall stay here tomorrow.

---

35 Beazley and Brett (*North Wales: A Shell Guide*, pp. 117–18) describe Llansannan as 'the only sizeable community in the Aled valley, which is of extreme and unspoilt charm, both above and below the village, though more accessible below'. In 1868, Llansannan's inn was the Saracen's Head. About 5 miles up the valley are two picturesque waterfalls.
36 The Clwyd valley.
37 Probably *Plas Clough*, 1595, step-gabled and stuccoed.
38 'Leicester's church.' The castle was 'slighted' under Charles II.
39 It had given way to the 'Black Lion' by 1868.

Chester White Lion[40]   We've been all day in Chester and saw the town in the morning. It is overlooked by a hill but lies mostly in the plain of the Dee and is virtually an island, with the Dee on one side and, on the other, a canal going to Liverpool.[41] The town's old walls provide a walk-way all round, and charming views over the prosperous countryside. The town is built of brick, even the bridge.[42] The bridge is the first English bridge we've crossed from Wales, marking the separation of the two kingdoms.[43] The streets are handsome but uneven, on account of their situation. They are built in the form of arcades, which gives them rather a melancholy appearance.[44] Chester's a bishopric. The palace is nothing, a mean and wretched house.[45]

The cathedral is large and famous for its long existence:[46] they say it's one of the oldest in England. It's built of a red freestone and sandstone: the surfaces are badly affected by time. The whole town is built upon this stone: the misfortune is that there is no place where it can be regularly renewed.[47] There are several other public buildings, for the corporation and for the market, but there is nothing at all remarkable.[48]

The trade of the town is twofold: one is a direct river trade, maritime after crossing the country for 12 miles; the other is trade with Liverpool, which is altogether more considerable.

The number of meanders in the river before arriving at its mouth, and the lowness and lack of water, means that the tide must be full before the ships can get

40 Not listed by Murray in 1868.

41 The hill, with its castle and little town, is Hawarden, 2 miles to the west. The Shropshire Union Canal runs along beneath Chester's north wall, the river under her south wall. Alexandre demonstrates this observation on one of his primitive sketch-maps.

42 He was mistaking the pink sandstone of the (essentially Roman) town walls and the 14th-century Dee Bridge with brick, which came to be the chief building material in the 18th century. The remains of the sandstone quarry that was being used as early as AD 100 are on the south side of the Dee at Handbridge (Pevsner and Hubbard, *Cheshire*, 1971, p. 134). Alexandre is overlooking the famous 'black and white' timber-framed medieval structures that survive, notably in 'the Rows', Shoemaker's Row, for instance.

43 Chester, like Shrewsbury, was certainly a fortified 'Marcher' (Welsh border) town.

44 So much for Chester's pride in its 'Rows'.

45 It had been the abbot's lodging until the Reformation, and was on the south side of Abbey Square.

46 In 1868, Murray's *Guide* asserted confidently that as far back as the 2nd century a monastery was erected here to SS Peter and Paul, and re-dedicated to St Werburh c907 by Aethelflaed. The last part is true: her remains were brought here from Staffordshire and her church was re-founded as an abbey in 1092 by the second Norman earl of Chester. The Benedictine monastic buildings for 40 monks were established to the north of the church, which probably explains why the large south transept, with its four double-aisled bays, now gives the cathedral a slightly lop-sided appearance.

47 He is showing an unusual interest in building-materials, but hasn't noticed the contradiction of what he wrote about the town and the bridge.

48 Alexandre was just a decade or two too early to see Thomas Harrison's extraordinary group of buildings from 1788 to 1822 for the county on the site of the castle: they have reasonably been described as 'one of the most powerful monuments of the Greek Revival in the whole of England'. At least he wouldn't have said it wasn't 'at all remarkable'.

moving: this is why the port is so difficult and so little frequented. I've seen only 10 ships in the port and 3 under construction, but perhaps it's because we're here at a bad season. There are at Parkgate, 12 miles from Chester, regular packet-boats for Dublin.

Alexandre's handwriting is particularly maddening in some of these pages. It had been quite a strenuous tour, and he may have been tired or not feeling well. He still manages to scrawl some very interesting observations. At Whitchurch, the ball was 'too late for us'.

Whitchurch, The George   We arrived at Whitchurch very early. We were happy to arrive here on the day of the races. The town's in a dip near two very attractive hills and between them a great many country houses. The town's fairly big but ugly.[49] The church is a simple building but very elegant.[50] The races ensure a good crowd. That evening at 5 we went, and there was certainly a crowd. Only two horses were needed to run for the race to take place. There was much disputing before the start, but in the end, after two hours of wrangling, they were off. The race over, we returned to our hotel. That evening, we were told, there was a ball but we didn't go: it was too late for us. These races were a great time of festivity for all the inhabitants of the district.

On the 8th   we left and arrived, without break, at *Shrewsbury*, 20 miles and the roads generally good, the landscape magnificently rich. We're still in Shropshire. If you want more details you can find them in one of the volumes I wrote last year [see *Innocent Espionage*, pp. 90–1]. There's no point in my repeating what I wrote then. [He does, of course, but we needn't.]

Shrewsbury, The Talbot   On the 9th we left Shrewsbury on the route we followed last year and dined at *Coalbrookdale*, beside the iron bridge (see last year's journal). From Coalbrookdale we went on to *Bridgnorth*, where we slept. The road was generally hilly, but beautiful, and rather tiring.

Bridgnorth, Pig and Castle[51]   Bridgnorth is up on high ground, indeed a cliff, and above all in a landscape cultivated right up to the town. The town itself is too abrupt and vertical, but the road at the top is broad and well-built, well-peopled and prosperous.

49 Michael Moulder, a better judge (*Shell Guide to Shropshire*, 1973), says it's 'undoubtedly the most handsome town in North Shropshire, too often by-passed by the traveller to Wales or the North'. Perhaps this is why the centre has remained comparatively unspoilt and keeps its character as a busy, thriving market-town!
50 Rebuilt in 1712–13 after a fire, it seems to have been built by William Smith, brother of the more celebrated master builder Francis, of Warwick. Here he used the 'simple but very elegant' plan of John Barker, of Rowsley.
51 Byng, *Torrington Diaries*, I, 1970, p. 185, on 20 July 1784, arrived at 3 o'clock from Ironbridge and wrote: 'The sign of our inn has certainly been the old one of the *Elephant & Castle*, tho' now chang'd to, and written, Pig and Castle. We dined tolerably'.

There's an old castle built in the rock, so old that it's in ruins.[52] It overlooks the river above the little port. The lands all round the town are so rich that they justly astonish a stranger.

On the 10th   we left Bridgnorth and rode to *Kidderminster*: only 13 miles but the roads were so bad we could go no further. It was little more than shifting sand, and good patches were rare. The first 6 miles were detestable. However, the surrounding light lands are cultivated, and almost all are enclosed. The farmers make fairly good extensive use of turnips, their lands being light. They sow very little wheat.

Alexandre has four pages of farm-details that are so illegible, from slovenly writing, that I have to abandon them. It's a pity, for he appears to be enthusiastic about a particular farmer's methods.

We left the farm and got almost to Kidderminster without being held up. The route, only on sand, though hard on the horses, was agreeable, the cultivation rich. You could see Kidderminster spread out, in a valley.

Kidderminster, The Lion[53]   A biggish town, crossed by a little river, a mere stream, not navigable, but working 2 or 3 mills.[54] These are for the tanneries which are here in some numbers. Everywhere we go, we see felled trees, stripped of their bark and being carried to the river. The whole road is covered with these carts. It seems to be a branch of industry at least well protected, even if it isn't pushed to great perfection. That's something I don't know about.[55]

The canal is to join up this district with the river Severn, which passes some three miles from the town. It carried heavy craft that bring all the coal for the consumption of the whole countryside, also the materials the town's staple trades in wool and cotton require. The town's paving is horrible. There are 2 or 3 good streets, more or less well-built. The whole town belongs to Lord Foley,[56] who has had a very handsome inn built, much more like a private house than an inn.

The farms here are very rich, although still on sandy soil: they fetch good prices. The farmers complain that the recent drought is yellowing all the crops. The town's

[52] It was captured from the Royalists by the Parliamentarians in the Civil War, who then scored a direct hit on the Royalist ammunition dump with the result that many Bridgnorth buildings date from soon after that disaster in 1646.
[53] It formerly stood at the top of the High Street.
[54] The Stour, rhymes with shower.
[55] Miss Hart, the Reference Librarian at Kidderminster, very kindly tells me that the tanneries were more closely associated with Bewdley and the Wyre Forest just beyond the Severn. It's interesting that Alexandre found tanneries in Kidderminster, whose main industry was of course the textile one, already making carpets but concentrating on them more exclusively a century later. Byng, *op cit*, I, 87, refers to the carpets: 'There is a great demand, both at home and abroad, for its carpets, silks, shags and bombazeens; 300 looms were constantly employed in the carpet business.'
[56] Thomas, 2nd baron Foley of Kidderminster, 1742–93, descended from a successful Jacobean ironmaster of Stourbridge.

trade is very extensive and it's a pleasure to see the quantity of new buildings, all for the manufacturers. They make carpets here in great quantity, selling them by the square foot, or by *languettes* [swatches] of silk cloth, and they sell silk and cotton. They send all these goods manufactured here elsewhere. They send them from here to *Gloucester*, which has the secondary trade, extended to the ports of London, *Bristol*, and the outlets of the river Severn.

On the 11th we left Kidderminster   and dined and slept at *Worcester*. Our gig horse was tired and we were obliged to hire one to put in front of ours. Of our 14 days, only the first 6 were really bad and the rest were as good as the rest were hard-going. Daily we ride over a superbly rich and prosperous country and all these rich parts deserve a river that's navigable.

We follow this magnificent plain through a great many small villages until we've reached Worcester. One arrives through an avenue of trees and country houses and enters the town itself by a superb road, almost straight but magnificently built.

Worcester, Hop-Pole[57]   It's an old town in the middle of a very rich plain, and beside the river Severn which brings here enough large vessels to establish a considerable trade. Two small ports are separated, one from the other, by a superb freestone bridge.[58] All new, it has 6 arches, almost all of the same fine size, which is what makes it very handsome.

The high street is broad and very well built. I've never seen such a large number of fine inns in one town. The cathedral is an ancient Gothic building that was an abbey,[59] of which one still sees some of the walls. The church is very grand – broad and with a beautiful vault. It's one of the most beautiful I've seen in England, as much for its length as for its beautiful proportions. The town was also walled but one sees few remains. Outside the town to the north there's a promenade, quite long, and very pleasant in the summer. It's the only walk there is for the whole town and it's too small, which is a pity.

Worcester's trade is only in porcelain: I've seen some quite beautiful pieces.[60] The river provides perhaps a little *cabotage* [? coasting trade], but I don't know about it. All I know is that the river Severn is the greatest benefit to the whole area which would be a much poorer place without it.

---

[57] 'A noisy, dear, inn': Byng, *op cit*, I, 188.

[58] It was the work of John Gwynne, 1771–80, whose bridges at Shrewsbury and Oxford they'd also admired.

[59] A 7th-century cathedral, it became an abbey in the 10th century, destroyed by the Danes. It was re-founded as cathedral and priory by St Wulfstan, and maintained mostly 40–50 monks. At the Dissolution the monks were replaced by secular canons.

[60] He doesn't mention, as Byng surprisingly does, its making of gloves and carpets at this time (*loc cit*) as well as porcelain: 'the colours are very fine and their imitation of old Japan excellent; but I think there is a want of taste and of good painters'.

On the 12th   we left Worcester and dined at an isolated inn[61] near a common; from there we went on to Gloucester for the night: 26 miles, 16 of them before dinner.

After a rather desultory ride I at last saw a man from whom I extracted the following information. The land here is all 25 *livres* an *arpent*. He spoke of a farm of 100 acres, of 20 or 30 cows, and 50 or 60 sheep: the cows are rather too small but of a good breed, and they give 18 quarts of milk a day. The ordinary rotation of crops was 1) [blot]; 2) wheat; 3) turnips; 4) barley; 5) meadow, which is usually only a simple artificial meadow etc. From the inn where we ate, to arrive at Gloucester you continue along the same common, which is seven miles long.[62] At the end of this common is a mature wood from which you have a superb view of the Severn, and you see *Gloucester* in front of you in the bottom of the valley. The country's rich and enclosed. You cross the Severn on a very new bridge[63] and arrive at the West Gate.[64] You follow a causeway which on one side has the river and on the other goes by the watermeadows, in one part of which is the racecourse.[65] It's to communicate with these watermeadows and the river that there is a causeway through the flooded area which is marked out by 12 bridges.[66]

Gloucester, The King's Head. On the 13th   we stayed all day at *Gloucester*, and occupied the day with sight-seeing. This morning we went to a farm nearby to see the making of Gloucester cheese, which is famous. They distinguish between the single and the double Gloucester. The first is made with the morning's fresh milk at exactly the best moment for the cow. The double Gloucester's made with that of the previous morning and evening with the cream removed. The single is about half as thick as the double. It is richer, having the cream; and the other, not having the cream, doesn't keep half so well. Apart from the ingredients, both are made in the same way. *Voilà.*

The river surrounds the town and enters the sea not far away and brings up increasing numbers of hefty ships, some of 50 tons. This is the port for all the merchandise of the hinterland, which naturally gives it some interest in the general commerce. I've seen in what's called the port about 15 ships, all of them fairly powerful.[67]

The cathedral and the college: these two buildings are in an ancient precinct

[61] Andrew Houldey, Librarian, Gloucester Collection in Gloucester Reference Library, thinks this was the Green Dragon, which has changed its name to the Corse Lawn: see note 62 below.
[62] This identifies the common as Corse Lawn, now reduced from 7 miles long to about 3, and shows that from Worcester they followed the (B4211) Upton-upon-Severn road, keeping west of the Severn, and missing Tewkesbury. Andrew Houldey helped resolve this.
[63] This was the Maisemore Bridge, by Thomas Dudford across Over causeway: you then crossed Westgate Bridge over the Eastern channel of the Severn; then Foreign Bridge over the Old Severn.
[64] Andrew Houldey has very kindly explained to me the complex watermeadows and bridges and culverts as you approached Gloucester from Upton-upon-Severn. You can see the sequence of bridges and causeways in Kip's North-West Prospect of the City of Gloucester, 1734.
[65] The races coincided with the Three Choirs Festival.
[66] They were really just arches or culverts to allow the marsh-drainage.
[67] Kip's North-West Prospect shows already in 1734 'a large and commodious key and wharf' hard up against the bridge on its south side, ie below the bridge and towards the estuary.

separated from the town. The cathedral was built between 1047 and 1060, in the time of William the Conqueror. It's a fine old building but too long, and the pillars are much too stout.[68] There is in this church a window of quite extraordinary lightness, and 73 feet tall; all in stonework, it's an astonishing achievement.[69]

In front of the cathedral is a small close,[70] hardly less agreeable. The College stands beside the church on another place surrounded by other houses. That of the College is nothing remarkable and is not particularly big, and in order to distinguish it, it is well built. The river that winds through the beautiful meadows can't fail to enhance a beautiful view.

On the 10th we left Gloucester   and slept at *Cirencester*,[71] 17 miles. The first 7 miles, all handsome country, rich, abundant, well covered with woods, but *rich*. Several very pretty country houses along these 7 miles. You climb a very long hill, perhaps a mile, but here our servants missed their way.[72] I was obliged to ride after them and go and bring them back off their route to join up with us again, and then to halt at an inn just as Mr de Lazowski, who was waiting for me, came and rejoined me. One part of the land is good, but another is a chalky soil which we followed all the way to our inn. *Voilà* the general manner in which I gather they make such a good living from this indifferent land.

First they distinguish two sorts of soil: what will grow wheat and what won't. They obviously treat each sort differently – the first valued at 12 shillings, the second 9. The first are worked like this: 1) wheat; 2) turnips; 3) barley; 4) grazing. The second: 1) oats; 2) grazing; 3) turnips; 4) barley; 5) grazing.

They have a great many sheep, all of them superb. They'll improve the land, which without them would not do well at all. The land's enclosed, partly by drystone walls, for the land's all stony. It's a miracle that it yields excellent harvests. The rest of our journey was through fairly poor-looking land.

The town is set in a bottom with a lot of woodland and a river. The town is an

68 Pevsner says it was rebuilt in 1058, but that Abbot Serlo responded to the increase to sixty monks by rebuilding the church, 1089–c1120, ie under William II and Henry I. Alexandre can only give us the impression of a late 18th-century Frenchman with little idea of the aspirations and limitations of Romanesque church builders. We, too, tend to feel surprised at the unusual height (30 feet 7 inches) of the massive circular columns of Gloucester's nave, about twice the height of those at Norwich; and certainly one way of expressing the awesome majesty of the Norman church.

69 He curiously doesn't refer to the wonderful white, blue, yellow and red glass in this great east window. It seems to have been finished shortly before 1350, but no one has, I think, related this window to the contemporary tragedy of the Black Death. It shows Edward II with orb and sceptre as on the masterpiece of his tomb near the window, which may very well have been financed from the vast proceeds of the pilgrimages to the tomb: miracles were reported soon after its installation c1330.

70 'College Green' is the cathedral close, now entered from the south by College Street, containing some pleasant Georgian houses.

71 In Cirencester, for almost the only time on this long tour, Alexandre forgot to note down where they stayed. I suspect they were beginning to grow tired, and had had enough.

72 Presumably at Crickley Hill, they failed to fork right and headed straight on towards Oxford.

assemblage of beautiful houses. The roads are not at all good. The town has an air of great prosperity, with a great many excellent shops and I imagine a considerable trade derives mainly from its road traffic. The surroundings of the town are green and beautiful. Near the town is the house and park of *Lord Bathurst*.[73] The house looks old and not at all remarkable. The view of the park, although very dry, is delightful. The house is built of the local freestone and forms part of the agreeable views of the park, which is very extensive. It seems divided into two. One, called the little park, is 3 miles long.[74] On each side there are angles from which run very pretty promenades. The best part is where the deer come: it's natural, and covered with great quantities of mature woodland. The great park is no more than a wood surrounded by long walls – 18 miles of them. The park is famous for its beautiful woods and for several smaller scenes, which are very picturesque, and delightful on that account.[75]

In one walk in the park I encountered a cow that had two calves, both of which looked like young red-deer; which interested me greatly and seemed more than extraordinary. I was thinking that there was nothing left to see in this country.

On the 15th   we left *Cirencester* very early and arrived, without breaking our journey, at *Burford*. It was only 17 miles but all of it rough going, the road covered with small bits of [Cotswold] stone and sand, and very hilly. The little valley roads were better, but rare: very agreeable though.[76] But the road was quite hard enough for our horses.

[73] Henry, 2nd earl Bathurst, became (incompetent) Lord Chancellor in 1771 and died here in 1794. His father, 1st earl, son of a Governor of the East India Company, was a Tory opponent of Walpole and friend of Pope, who came here in 1718 and soon became a leading collaborator in Bathurst's creation of this park. There is a beautifully illustrated description of the park in Mavis Batey and David Lambert's invaluable book, *The English Garden Tour*, 1990. John Byng came here with a summer chill the July after the Rochefoucauld visit, and was disposed to carp. But he admitted 'an immense and princely enclosure of ground, containing a deer-park and sheep-walk, 1000 acres, a wood planted by him (1000 acres) and 2000 acres of old wood'. It would take 3 days to see properly. He described a great column 'on which is perch'd Queen Anne, looking towards the house, over which appears the church steeple'. And he visited 'old ruins, amidst groves in the centre of the wood, where I alighted to see a great room where an annual music meeting is held; to which all the country come and pass the day in dancing and dining in these shady cool retreats'.
[74] Puzzling: the whole park is four and a half miles long, running due west from the town.
[75] See footnote 73 above.
[76] Through Arlington and Bibury, with its little trout stream; it's one of the most agreeable roads in the world. When Byng arrived to stay at the George, it was Burford Fair day in July 1785. 'The inn was so crouded that I could scarcely find room for my horse and a chair at a public table for my tea, amidst a crew of farmers, etc. The fair was the gingerbread sort, with the usual clamour; but not one shew at which I could give a peep. A book of ancient customs says: "At Burford was a yearly procession of great jollity on midsummer's eve, when a painted dragon and a painted giant were carried about the town"; but all such exhibitions are lost in the poverty and distress of the lower people, and a fair is now no more than a large market. Let's hear what Goldsmith rightly imagined:
"Ye friends to truth, ye statesmen who survey
The rich man's wealth increase, the poor's decay;

Burford, The George[77]   where we've slept, is a little town with no trade. It's traversed by a
fine road, but badly built: you find only one rather beautiful house.[78] It is former trade
that caused six roads to converge on Burford, and explains the large number of former
inns, of which several still survive even today. I have counted in this town 300
post-horses.

On the 16th   we left *Burford*, dined at *Oxford* and slept at *Dorchester*. From Burford into
Oxford the landscape was much like yesterday's. Five miles from Oxford we came to
the Thames valley, and Oxford lay before us, in a rich and beautiful plain. The
meadows occupy the greater part of the plain, and an enormous number of trees,
which have disappeared in all the surrounding countryside: they enhance still more
the great beauty of the general view.

One arrives over one of the causeways that cross these immense meadows. We've
already been here, and at Dorchester, in our journey last year. You will find my
description in my journals, also that of Nuneham, and indeed the road to
Dorchester and the general view of the countryside. This year it's embellished, not
only by the beautiful weather, but even more by the season, so that everything is
green and alive and seen to its best advantage. It was not at all like this the first time
we were here.[79]

On the 17th   we left *Dorchester*, dined at *Henley* and slept at *Eton*.

Those are the last words Alexandre wrote in the journals of his travels in Britain.

Tis yours to judge how wide the limits stand
Betwixt a splendid and a happy land."
I re-bridled my nag, and . . ., trotted over a staring newly-enclosed country to Aldsworth.'
[77] The George survives as offices in the High Street, next to Barclays Bank.
[78] It even lost its fine road when it was by-passed in 1812. The irony of Alexandre's apparently
grotesque comments lies in our knowledge that Burford's wealth of beautiful houses, not to
mention her church, springs from her successful medieval merchants and her coaching trade into
the 18th century. Unluckily, when Alexandre was moving on every day, his *'bien-bâti'* normally
meant 'recently well built'. The 'one rather beautiful house' must have been Speaker Lenthall's
'The Priory', 3-storeyed, 7 gables, but severely reduced in 1809.
[79] They were here on 27 March 1785, Easter Day. It rained so hard that they couldn't leave their
inn. Next day it snowed, but they had some sun in the afternoon (*Innocent Espionage*, p. 137).

Epilogue

Alexandre, 18, had kept his travel-journals going in foul weather and fair throughout his 3-month tour of farms and towns all over the United Kingdom; signs of flagging, of probably physical tiredness, appeared only in the last stages; at Chester, Whitchurch and Kidderminster. The signs are obvious in his very variable handwriting and orthography: from being generally hard to decipher, it becomes finally baffling. To my surprise and relief, though, the scanty travel-notes of the 16-year-old of 1784 had, by 1786, come close to the competence, if not quite the natural ability, of his elder brother François. Their *précepteur*-companion, Maximilien de Lazowski, 38, whose own handwriting and spelling are perhaps excused by a Polish background, contributes only to the Scottish section of this tour: it is likely that his manuscript for the whole UK tour exists, but I have been unable to track it down. I'm the more grateful for Mlle Françoise Marchand's gift to me of a surviving typescript of that Scottish section. Between them, they presented Alexandre's father with a curiously memorable report on their long journey.

When my friend John Rogister sent word of a manuscript *Tour of Switzerland* by Lazowski, deposited in the Town Library of Versailles, my first hope was that there might emerge from it some personal details of his life: there's a notable lack of them in his tours of the UK. That there *was* a tour of Switzerland we knew, and that it occurred in September 1786, three months after the return home from Scotland (*Innocent Espionage*, p. 241). Lazowski wrote in August to press Arthur Young to join him where Alexandre's elder brother François had been stationed with his Regiment, at Pont-a-Mousson, just south of Metz in Lorraine: 'You would live with a Regiment, and your insatiable curiosity would be furnished with a manner of living and some military details unknown in England. You would travel with us in the next month through Switzerland that you should be very amiable.'

It may be that Young's curiosity about French Regimental life was not insatiable. I think he would have enjoyed Lazowski and François's tour of Switzerland, though it is not even clear from Lazowski's 537 quarto pages of description whether François was there with him or not. The first person singular gives way to the first person plural on, I think, one occasion only! The book is of course packed with details of Swiss agriculture and the trade of its towns, the remarkable scenery, but above all, he is carried away, over and over again, by Swiss politics and by political theory generally (Bibliothèque de Versailles, Collection Jean & Henriette Lebaudy, MS 47, 4°).

Twice in Switzerland he was reminded of Scotland. The second time (pp. 234–5), between Thun and Lucerne, he noticed: 'They collect in the forest all the moss they can find, put it in a heap near the house, and during the winter it will come in as useful addition to the compost until the season for planting potatoes, for which this moss compost is found excellent. Sometimes one also uses moss on its own, and it's successful planted immediately with the potatoes. It seemed rather extraordinary to find in Switzerland a method I'd seen in use in the Highlands of Scotland.' If he did see moss used with the planting of potatoes in highland Scotland, it didn't seem at the time extraordinary enough to record the fact; eg on 2 April where he described potato-planting. His earlier reference (p. 140) to his recent Scotch tour came at Langnau-in-Emmental, which had an 'immense' manufacture of cloth and coloured cottons: 'they never use water in bleaching their cloths. I've seen them using water in France, England, Scotland and Ireland, where bleaching is very well understood. They say "No water" succeeds better, and they got the idea from Geneva!'

At Geneva and Ferney, Lazowski's Swiss tour ended with passion. Voltaire had died there only ten years earlier, yet 'it's now painfuly, shamefully dilapidated. Today the workroom of Voltaire is a servant's bedroom: one may judge the rest from that one fact. I don't know another example in the world of such shabby, disgraceful meanness.' 'Calvin's reform, in spirit like Presbyterianism, admits no other principle of government, any other power, than that of the people. A single reading of *Lettres de la Montagne* makes it impossible not to believe that what is coming to pass is a real revolution.' After another paragraph along those lines, Lazowski's *Tour of Switzerland* ends, probably through inadequate book-binding, mid-sentence, at the bottom of p. 537. He has expressed his private political belief, which François, his close friend in 1792, can never, I think, have understood, or even suspected: nor could François's father, the duke, nor Arthur Young.

Next year, in April 1787, Lazowski pressed Young again, and he came. They made Young feel infinitely more at home at Liancourt than his famously disagreeable wife could make him feel at Bradfield. He approved the duke's manufacture of linen and stuff in nearby villages: he welcomed the employment of great numbers of idle hands, and probably didn't even think of 'industrial espionage' and 'technology transfer'. We now know that as soon as Lazowski arrived in Edinburgh he sent off to the duke in Paris 'the most superb memorial on the agriculture of the two kingdoms' (England and Scotland). The duke forwarded this treatise to an early French equivalent of our Board of Agriculture, of which Young became Secretary when we went to war with Revolutionary France. The duke's efforts to help French agriculture came to nothing: Lazowski's memorial reached the Minister, Calonne, just as his government collapsed.

There's no doubt that the duke was using Lazowski to interest his sons in improved industrial technology over here for the benefit of their education, much as fathers encourage their sons' interest in technology today. That Alexandre might have profited by this in the spinning mill and cotton factory he set up at Mello, not far from Liancourt, in 1795, cannot alter the essential 'innocence' of Alexandre's responses, ten years earlier, to the excitement he experienced in Derby.

I've described these developments at some length in the Epilogue to *Innocent Espionage*, and shall not repeat myself here. The late Professor J. R. Harris embodied his unrivalled knowledge in *Industrial Espionage and Technology Transfer: Britain and France in the Eighteenth Century* (1998), a definitive book if ever there was one. He was characteristically kind and helpful when I was working on *Innocent Espionage*, and has shown his general approval by summarising very valuably in chapter 21 the various and distinctive technological experiences they recorded. For instance, at Broseley, John Wilkinson was ill, and the Rochefoucauld trio was taken round by his manager. 'The resulting description is the only good one of Wilkinson's works at New Willey . . . later they saw Wilkinson's works at Bradley in the Black Country, and quickly appreciated that the operation of both blowing engines and hammers by steam-power freed the iron industry geographically from water-power sources.'

Especially where agriculture is concerned, Arthur Young and the duke and Lazowski show themselves good human beings as well as good economic patriots; they urgently wanted to see the improvement of French technology. Nobody did as much as Arthur Young to promote French farming improvement. His instrument was the publication of his incomparable *Travels in France*. When a French translation appeared in 1793, complete with its 'General Observations' on the French economy, and the progress of the Revolution to the beginning of 1792, the far-from-Anglophile *Convention* ordered 20,000 copies to be printed and distributed free all over France.

I often think what a strange coincidence it is that two of the central figures in the La Rochefoucauld visit to England in 1784 and 1785 became two of the leading witnesses of the fall of the French monarchy – Young in the crucial first stages in June and July 1789, and François on 10 August 1792. I have rehearsed all that in the *Innocent Espionage* epilogue: how Young conveys the imminence of Revolution, which adds such vividness to his description of so much of France; and how in June 1788, Alexandre, not quite 21, married, more fortunately than he could have known, Adélaïde de Chastullé, a cousin of Joséphine de Beauharnais. In December 1790 he bought the *ci-devant* priory of the Madeleine at Mello, a picturesque mill-village, 7 miles from his childhood home at Liancourt. It presumably became their country seat. He joined Lafayette briefly as a Lieutenant-Colonel, but resigned in dismay in 1792. Their first three children were born in Paris, the second arriving during the September massacres. In 1794, they withdrew to her family estate in Domingo, but, perhaps as early as next year, 'the citizen Delarochefoucauld' was setting up his factory and spinning-mill, starting to take on several hundred hands, and bringing his English experience to the benefit of the Republic. They made, '*à la manière anglaise*, quilting, muslins, etc, more beautiful than those of all the other factories', and hired, very expensively, the services of John McCloude, a specialist weaver and former Manchester foreman, who'd been working at Sens, Amiens and elsewhere since 1790.

From 1801, Napoleon was developing his grandiose court with the aid of Alexandre's wife, as *dame d'honneur* of Joséphine. Alexandre became *chargé d'affaires* in Saxony in 1802, ambassador in Vienna in 1805. How splendid he looks as Grand Officier de la Légion d'Honneur (pl 71, p. 250).

How his elder brother François did his best to stay close to the king on 10 August 1792, and was lucky to get away, and to be able to get his father away, to England with their lives, is told fairly fully in *Innocent Espionage*. François, too, had a humiliating experience with the army, in his case, the Bourbon army. He retreated with his

70. *David's signed preliminary sketch of Josephine kneeling for her coronation as Empress by Napoleon. The* dame d'honneur *bearing the right (near) side of her train is her kinswoman, Mme de La Rochefoucauld, Alexandre's wife. This black-lead pencil sketch is in the Louvre, with the famous oil-painting,* Le Sacre de Napoléon 1er, 1806–7, *for which it was made. By 1802, Alexandre was Napoleon's* chargé d'affaires *in Saxony; in 1805, ambassador to Vienna.*

delightful wife Marie de Tott to Altona, near Hamburg. There they brought up their first five children. She did a simple watercolour painting of their rustic home. It is in the collection of the Marquis de Amodio at Verteuil sur Charente.

Lazowski's fate is hard to establish. At about 6 on the morning of 10 August 1792, François, who chronicles the whole awful day so vividly, went down with the king into the courtyard of the Tuileries, 'and there I was glad to see my close friend, M de Lazowski, with his brother'. (He had six brothers: this was probably the Inspector of Manufactures Young had met.) François then found a bench in the corner of the Assembly and sat watching the grisly events leading to the proclamation of the end of the monarchy. Before that, he'd been worried about Lazowski and was overjoyed when suddenly he appeared – 'for one loves one's friends a hundred times more in the midst of great danger than in ordinary times'. At 7 that evening, François made a last offer to try to help the king, who told him it was too dangerous to think of. So he left to find a bed in his brother Alexandre's house, in case his own was watched. There he found Alexandre and his wife, eight months pregnant, and Lazowski. It was the last time all three were together, the brothers

71. *Portrait of Alexandre, Comte de La Rochefoucauld, Comte d'Empire (1809), Pair de France, Ambassadeur, Grand Officier de la Légion d'Honneur.*

and Lazowski, who had spent all of 1784 and much of 1785 together in England. Next day, someone came to warn them that mobs with pikes were coming to search Alexandre's house, normally occupied by one of the hated Swiss Guards officers.

François made his way to the Ecole Militaire, talking loudly to his English servant Charles in the hope that he'd be mistaken for an Englishman. There his servants had brought his horse. He leapt on to its back, sent messages to his family and friends, drew a pistol and left at a trot for Versailles, avoiding towns and villages. At Rouen he managed to persuade his father of the danger, and to get over to England after him. From Bury St Edmunds on 30 October 1792, the duke wrote to Lazowski in Paris, discussing with him the actions of François, and showing his complete trust in Lazowski's discretion. The next direct reference to Lazowski comes in another of the duke's letters, this time from Philadelphia and writing to his duchess in Switzerland, expressing delight in the news of François's service under the duke of York as a squadron commander in various actions across NW Europe. This 1796 letter refers to '*la pauvre Lazowski*' (*sic*) and is the only suggestion that Lazowski was dead. It is curious, in view of Lazowski's warm friendship with both François and his father, that neither of them makes any more reference to either the time or circumstance of his death. Otherwise there are just one or two references, back in the autumn of 1792, when François, in despair about the incompetence of the Bourbon army he'd joined and, marching round in circles in the plain of Fleurus, noted: 'On this march, I recognised one of the foot-sloggers, the brother of M de Lazowski, and formerly an officer in the Regiment of Darmstadt . . . Their company had always served in the vanguard of our army, so that I had never seen him, though I knew that he was there. I found him sturdier, and even taller: a fine lad. All he wanted was to get to the firing-line – to see what we could do.'

A little later, on 9 November 1792, as François left the duke of Bourbon with his certificate of 'unlimited leave' he saw young Lazowski again. On the 14th, at Maastricht, he heard that Brussels had fallen: nothing now seemed impossible to the French army. He made for England as fast as possible. With François settled in Altona and Alexandre in Mello, it is disturbing to have only that reference to '*la pauvre Lazowski*' in 1796 to give any suggestion of Lazowski's end. It may be that his attempts to improve French agriculture, in association with the chemist Lavoisier, and the Physiocrat Du Pont de Nemours, in response to the drought of 1795, was too much for Fouquier-Tinville. That seems precisely the kind of worthy cause that would bring out the blood-lust in the infamous Jacobin Public Prosecutor. At present all we actually know is that, in about 1795, poor Lazowski disappeared from the records.

The circumstances of Lazowski's death remain surprisingly obscure. The duke's mention in 1796 of '*la pauvre Lazowski*' was presumably a reference to his widow: he should strictly have said '*la pauvre Lazowska*' but that was a Polish habit he overlooked: the use of *la* is enough. There isn't even a hint of a wife in these years when he is serving as *précepteur* and bear-leader, but that was nine and ten years earlier, plenty of time for him to have married.

Apart from much obscurity, there is one confusion about his 'death' that can be resolved without more ado. At the front of the hefty quarto manuscript volume of Lazowski's *Voyage en Suisse en 1786* in the Bibliothèque de Versailles, a slightly shocking note has been added, in a separate hand, which I translate:

> Lazowski, a friend of Marat, was one of the sad heroes of the 10th of August, 1792. He was interred in the Place de Carrousel, and his tombstone is sheltered within the patriotic shadows of two trees of Liberty.

The trouble with this is that it refers to Maximilien's brother Claude, not to the friend of les La Rochefoucauld who wrote the excellent *Voyage en Suisse en 1786*. The confusion is not cleared up by a footnote in the *Autobiography of Arthur Young* (ed M. Betham-Edwards, 1898), p. 119. Young was devoted to Maximilien, and says here: 'His brother must not be wholly judged from Mme Roland's portrait, penned in prison . . . It is true that Lazowski threw himself into the very heart of *Sans-culottisme*, and that his funeral oration (1792) was pronounced by Robespierre. His alleged share in the September massacres requires stronger evidence than that of his bitterest enemies at bay.' Young had forgotten that *two* of Lazowski's brothers were caught up in the Revolution. Claude, jacobin and *sans-culotte* was killed on 10 August and praised by Robespierre. So it was a third brother who was alleged to have taken part in the horrors of September. A fourth, 'a fine lad', we saw on the previous page doing well in the doomed Bourbon army. Maximilien himself stands unaffected by his brothers' reputation.

It is hardly a surprise. He and Arthur Young shared some of the most hopeful preliminary scenes of the Revolution together. For instance, at Versailles, by 8 o'clock on the morning of 15 June 1789, they'd secured good seats in the gallery of the great chamber that held 2,000; 'the representatives of 25 millions of people just emerging from the evils of 200 years of arbitrary power, assembled with open doors under the eye of the public'. What a wonderful political, as well as agrarian, *reporter* Young was (Schama's *Citizens* made very good use of him).

'On 28 June, I left Paris on my travels, taking leave of my excellent friend Mons Lazowski, whose anxiety for the fate of his country made me respect his character as much as I had reason to love it for the thousand attentions I was in the daily habit of receiving from him . . . The want of bread is terrible . . .' At Lunéville, Young was being made welcome by Lazowski's old father; at Sélestat in Alsace being warmly greeted by François, his new Regiment happily entitled the Champagne Light Horse. At Besançon, he wrote to Lazowski, who replied on 2 August: 'I never was so uneasy in my life. The outcry against the English has been very high for a time. The people was convinced that you were paying *banditti* for creating disturbance . . . Every traveller is stopped and in the provinces they do not know what is to travel for the sake of travelling . . . You are a giddy head.'

Young's last evening in Paris, 19 January 1790, when he saw quite clearly what was coming, he spent with Lazowski, 'he endeavouring to persuade me to reside upon a farm in France; and I enticing him to quit French bustle for English tranquillity'.

One last vignette depicts the close friendship of Young with Lazowski and Liancourt. It is told by Young in an essay entitled 'An English Farm established in

France'. (It would now come under the heading of Technology Transfer!) Young published it in his most famous work, usually given the short title of *Young's France* or *Young's Travels in France*, but properly titled *Travels with a View of ascertaining the Cultivation, Wealth, Resources and National Prosperity of the Kingdom of France*. (With that title, it's a wonder Young hasn't been automatically accused of industrial espionage.) A second edition appeared in 1794, two handsome quarto volumes, vol I from London, vol II from Bury St Edmunds. The essay on the English farm in France appeared as Chapter XX in vol II, and since 1794 has never been reprinted.

It is too long to reprint here. I can't resist reproducing Young's opening paragraph, in the proud manner with which in the 1830s Sir William Napier immortalised the history of the Peninsular War! Abbreviation follows.

> Among the most interesting observations which the Duke of Liancourt has made in the various visits he paid to England, was that of the superiority to which the industry of that kingdom was carried beyond the practice of France; and above all, to what a degree of perfection agriculture had attained, founded on experiment, and manifest in an infinitely greater production of corn and of live stock than is to be found in almost any other country, extent and quality of soil considered. Impressed with this fact, he had long cherished the hope of introducing into his own country this source of increasing wealth, but sensible, at the same time, that the most useful innovations could be introduced by example only . . . he determined to attempt, as soon as it was in his power, an essay of English agriculture; but as he was desirous of having his example followed, it was necessary that these essays should be so conducted as to ensure success.
>
> His friend Mons de Lazowski's residence during three years in England, whither he consented to accompany the sons of the Duke, facilitated these means. Mons de Lazowski, whom I had the pleasure of knowing intimately, acquired that knowledge in agriculture which much inquiry, assiduous application, and frequent conversation with the best farmers, could give to a mind very capable of, and much accustomed to, observation: he was likewise no stranger to the projects of Mons de Liancourt; and in this instance, as on every occasion, his unexampled friendship made him eager to second his views.

Now it begins to read like the 'systematic colonisation' that was soon being preached for the benefit of South Australia by Edward Gibbon Wakefield. I abridge and abbreviate. M de Liancourt inherited his father's estate at Liancourt in 1789 (not an entirely auspicious year), engaged an English farmer, Richard Reeve, to come over from Suffolk with his family, and a farm labourer; they brought with them every kind of farming implement, likewise 5 oxen, a bull and 5 cows from Sussex to perpetuate that breed, and added a Suffolk polled bull and 5 cows. The farm provided at Liancourt had yielded about £200 a year, but was considerably enlarged by land taken from the park and other farms. Fortunately some land was suited to sheep and other land for cattle-grazing: it was in a country surrounded by great markets and very near to that of Paris.

The English set to work, training local labourers to use their new English plough and other tools, and the women servants in dairy management. Two young Frenchmen were placed by Young with good farmers near Bradfield so that, if the English family tired of living in France, they could be replaced, or assisted if they decided to remain. The stock was improved from Normandy and Switzerland: by 1792 it amounted to a fine herd of 105 head, with a planned rise to 300. Mr Reeve thought only of continuing his farming at Liancourt and the young French labourers from England joined him. The culture of turnips and cabbages as cattle food was introduced throughout the neighbourhood. 'Some proprietors enclosed their fields, several made farm implements on the English model, many more hands were employed, and the English were received with pleasure and treated in the most cordial manner. These successes were in great measure due to the indefatigable and enlightened vigilance of Mons Lazowski, whose heart is equal to his capacity.' Printed in 1794, this use of the present tense suggests that Lazowski was alive that year, though in dangerously useful company.

Young concluded his chapter on 'An English Farm in France' by recalling how Liancourt's grandfather had, in 1754, established mulberry-trees and silk-worms at Verteuil-sur-Charente, in Angoumois, and lived to see the success of his enterprise – unlike the duke, at Liancourt, who has the mortification of seeing the destruction of 'an establishment that would have been a germ of national prosperity, and was unique in France'.

Liancourt now boasts a mean little square named *Place La Rochefoucauld*. In it stands a bronze statue of 1861 commemorating the duke. As founder of France's '*Ecoles d'Arts et Métiers*', he stands with his back to an anvil, a set-square and other tools. His introduction of vaccination in France in 1800 is noted, as is his co-founding of the Savings Banks, the '*Caisses d'Epargne*' in 1818, after the Napoleonic Wars and the Restoration. The statue is dedicated *Au bienfaiteur de l'Humanité*. We now have clearer ideas of his respect for the English Farm, his devotion to Arthur Young, and the educational value, not only to his two sons, of travelling in Britain with Lazowski.

The timing of those travels was most fortunate: no one, at one time, saw more of the changes being put into practice in England than the two young aristocrats and their tutor, and no one has left clearer records of those changes. Their itineraries were very cleverly devised (mainly, I think, by Arthur Young). For instance, France had no network of coalfields and canals, and there at Worsley in 1785 stood the three young Frenchmen, contemplating (with dismay in Lazowski's case) a boat-trip along the duke of Bridgwater's amazing subterranean canal-system. François Crouzet (whose book *Britain Ascendant*, 1990, demonstrates every aspect of the economic ascendancy Britain gained in the 18th century over France, and who so kindly agreed to write the Foreword to this final volume in my 'La Rochefoucauld in Britain' trilogy) reinforced John Harris's conclusions on the way the long progress of our coal-fuel technology familiarised practical men, employers and shop-floor workers, with the day-to-day experience of technology-change: in this way, it made the transfer to France of our coal-fuel technology almost impossible, for 'only the men who were used to it were capable of introducing it abroad, and they only arrived in sufficient numbers after 1815'.

This was at the heart of Liancourt's thinking when, apparently in 1789, he transferred Richard Reeve and his English farm from Suffolk to Liancourt. He had already set up small textile manufactures in nearby villages (J.-D. de La Rochefoucauld, *Le Duc de La Rochefoucauld-Liancourt*, 1980, pp. 106–39); for Alexandre's ambitious establishment of a spinning-mill and cotton manufactory at Mello, see J. R. Harris's *Industrial Espionage and Technology Transfer*, 1998, pp. 390–2.

Liancourt's sons toured Britain at a most favourable time for their studies: they were interested in everything, but already it was too late for an aristocrat and courtier to make serious attempts to contribute to the improvement of France's industry and farming. In the Hall of the Assembly on 10 August 1792, François heard the proclamation of the end of the monarchy: he managed to persuade his father to seek safety in England. Liancourt would have liked to become a naturalised Englishman, but shortage of funds forced him to cross the Atlantic. In France his ideas of improved industry and farming were postponed till his return, c1800. The implacable *Ultras* precipitated a deporable scene at his funeral at the Madeleine in 1827, in which his coffin was knocked into the gutter: he was thought to have encouraged the lower orders to find skilled work. His statue at Liancourt was not erected till 1861, well into the Second Empire.

THE LA ROCHEFOUCAULD ROAD TO SCOTLAND AND BACK VIA IRELAND

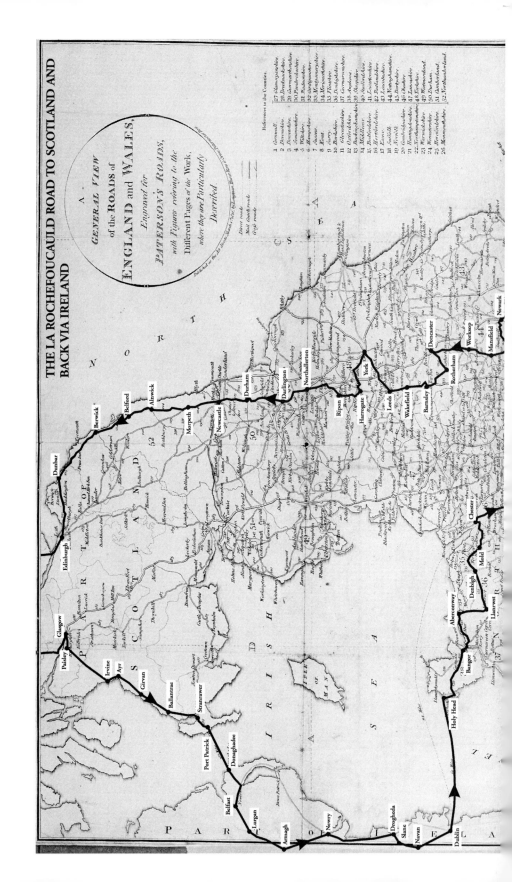

A
GENERAL VIEW
of the ROADS of
ENGLAND and WALES,
Engraved for
PATERSON'S ROADS,
with Figures referring to the
Different Pages of the Work,
where they are Particularly
Described

Direct roads
Mail Coach roads
Cross roads

Published as the Act directs, March 1811, by Longman Hurst Rees & Co.

References to the Counties.

1 Cornwall.
2 Devonshire.
3 Dorsetshire.
4 Somersetshire.
5 Wiltshire.
6 Hampshire.
7 Sussex.
8 Kent.
9 Surry.
10 Berkshire.
11 Gloucestershire.
12 Oxfordshire.
13 Buckinghamshire.
14 Middlesex.
15 Bedfordshire.
16 Hertfordshire.
17 Essex.
18 Suffolk.
19 Norfolk.
20 Cambridgeshire.
21 Huntingdonshire.
22 Northamptonshire.
23 Warwickshire.
24 Worcestershire.
25 Herefordshire.
26 Monmouthshire.

27 Glamorganshire.
28 Brecknockshire.
29 Carmarthenshire.
30 Pembrokeshire.
31 Radnorshire.
32 Cardiganshire.
33 Montgomeryshire.
34 Merionethshire.
35 Flintshire.
36 Denbighshire.
37 Caernarvonshire.
38 Anglesea.
39 Shropshire.
40 Staffordshire.
41 Leicestershire.
42 Rutlandshire.
43 Lincolnshire.
44 Nottinghamshire.
45 Derbyshire.
46 Cheshire.
47 Lancashire.
48 Yorkshire.
49 Westmorland.
50 Durham.
51 Cumberland.
52 Northumberland.

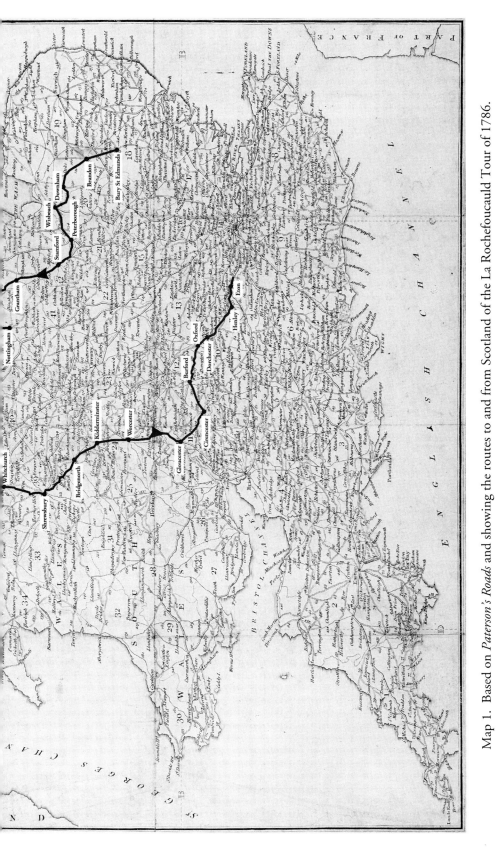

Map 1. Based on *Paterson's Roads* and showing the routes to and from Scotland of the La Rochefoucauld Tour of 1786.

A
GENERAL MAP
of the Roads of
SCOTLAND,
made out from actual Surveys taken
By Geo. Taylor
& Andw. Skinner.
1775.

N.B. The figures on the Roads, shew the
distances in Miles and Furlongs.

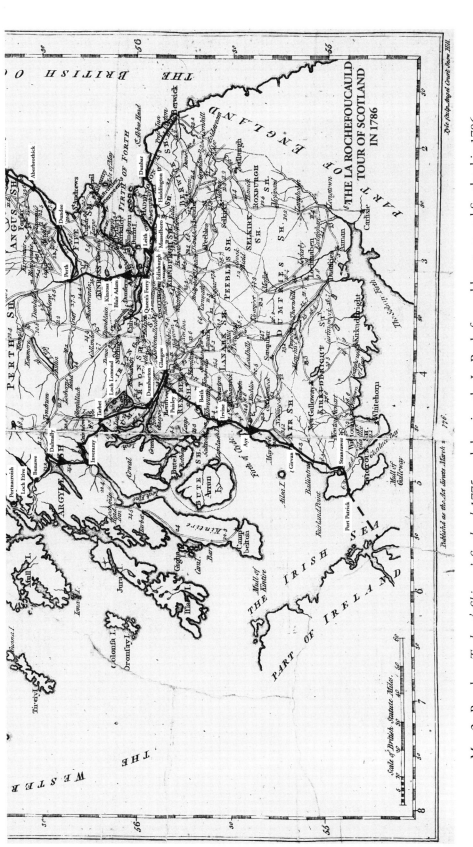

Map 2. Based on *Taylor & Skinner's Scotland*, 1775, and showing the La Rochefoucauld route round Scotland in 1786.
A line of dashes represents Lazowski's boat-trip from Fort William to Bunawe via Loch Linnhe and Loch Etive.

Index

Note: page references in *italics* indicate illustrations

Armagh: Molyneux Arms 227
  new buildings 227–8
Armstrong, William George, baron 92 n.31
Arran, Isle of (N. Ayrs) 216
Ayr 215, 216–17
    Citadel 216 n.54
    King's Arms inn 216
Ayton castle (Ber.) 99 n.6

Bailey's British Directory 55 n.54
Bakewell, Robert 4, 19, 76–7 n.64, 78 n.73,
  79
Balgownie Bridge, Aberdeen *iii, 157*
Ballantrae (Ayrs.) 217 & n.57, 219 n.60
Bamburgh (Northumberland) 92
    castle 92–5, *93*
    Swan inn 92 & n.30
Banff 155–6, 225
    battery 156–7 n.92
    castle 157 n.95
    Cross Keys inn 156 & n.90
    Duff House 155–6
    manufacturing 156
    and women 5, 156, 225, 227
Bangor Ferry 235–6
    inns 235 & n.28
banking, in Scotland 117–18
Banks, Sir Joseph xxii, 184
Barber, Andrew 34 n.47
Barker, John, of Rowsley, architect 239 n.50
barley: in England 17, 39, 61, 68, 77, 87
    in Scotland 129, 142, 147
Barnbougle estate (Midlothian) 127 n.4
Barney, John 9 n.7
Barnsley (Yorks.) 50
Barrie, Andrew 143 n.51, 144 n.54
Batey, Mavis & Lambert, David 75 n.58, 244
  n.73
Bathurst, Henry, 2nd earl 244
Baxter, John *158,* 158–9 n.97
beans: in crop rotation 39, 61, 77, 136, 159
    sowing 137 n.33
Beauharnais, Joséphine de 248, *249*
The Beauties of Scotland see Forsyth, Robert
Beazley, Elisabeth and Brett, Lionel 236
    nn.31,34, 237 n.35
Beckett, J. 27 n.27
Bedford, Francis Russell, 4th earl 13
Beith (Ayrs.) 215, 216
Belford (Northumberland) 95–6
    Bluebell inn 81, 95, *95,* 96 n.36
Bell, Mervyn 88–9 n.17
Ben Arthur (mountain) 195, 196 n.4
Ben Cruachan (mountain) 189–90

Ben Lomond (mountain) 196 nn.4,5
Bence-Jones, Mark 229, 233 n.23, 234 n.25
Bennett, K. 78 n.73
Bervie (Inverbervie; Kincardine) 144–5
Berwick 96–7, 98–100, 101
    Red Lion inn 97, 98
    salmon fishery 97, 100
    Tweed bridge 99
    walls 99
Bethune, Andrew 106–7 n.35, 115 n.74, 120
    n.94
Black, Joseph, chemist xx, 114 & n.71, *122,*
    124
Black Rock (Dublin) 231
Blackett, Sir William 83 n.5
Blair Adam 129–31
Bodt, General Jean de 50–1 n.42
Bombelles, Marc de, *Journal de Voyage en
    Grande Bretagne et en Irlande* xxiii
Bonawe (Argylls.) 165, 179, 186–8, 189
    iron furnace 189 nn.54,55
Bonhill, (Dunb.) 196–7 n.6, 197 n.7
bonnet, Highland 104–5 n.28, 161, *161,* 162
    n.106, 176
Boog, Rev Robert 194, 213 n.43, 214 n.48
Boswell, James
    and Jacobites 174 n.21, 181–2 n.39
    Journal of a Tour to the Hebrides xxii
    in Lowlands 196 n.6, 199 n.11
    in north-east Scotland 163 n.109, 166 n.2,
    168, 170 n.10
bothies 128, 182
Bourtreehill park (Irvine) 216 n.50
Bower, Joseph (father & son) 51 n.43
Boyne, river 228–9
Brand, John (historian of Newcastle) 81–2 n.2
Brander, James (Nairn bathing-machine
    proprietor) 160–1 n.102
Brandon (Suffolk) 8, 9
Breckland (Suffolk and Norfolk) 8 & n.4
breeches xix, 165, 166, 174 n.22, 175
Bridge of Don (Brig o'Balgowine) *iii, 153*
Bridge of Tay, Aberfeldy 169 n.7
Bridgnorth (Shrops.) 239–40
    Pig and Castle inn 239 & n.51
Brig o'Balngownie (Bridge of Don) *153*
Brown, Lancelot 'Capability' 1, 28, 29 n.41,
    37 nn.55–7, 90 n.25
Brown, Patrick, of Dryburgh 144, n.54
Brown, Thomas, Edinburgh 119 n.92
Brown, Thomas, Renfrew 206–7 n.35
Brownlow, Mr 227
Bruce, Rev George 101 n.14

Lowlands 216
Newcastle 83–6, 150
Northumberland 98
Yorkshire xvii, 54
Coalbrookdale (Shrops.) 239
Cockburn, Henry 123 n.103
Coleridge, S. T. 198 n.10
Colling, Charles & Robert, cattle-breeders,
Ketton (Co. Durham) 78 n.73
Colquhoun, Sir James 196 n.6, 206–7 n.35
Colvin, Sir Howard: *Biographical Dictionary of
British Architects* xxiii
and England 8 n.1, 22 n.21, 48–9 n.29,
49 nn.31,32, 62 n.6, 82 n.3
and Ireland 233 n.20, 234 n.25
and Scotland 113 n.66, 128 n.7, 143 n.51,
148 n.64, 158 n.97, 191 nn.59–60,
201 n.20, 206–7 n.35
Conolly, Tom 234 n.25
Conolly, William, Speaker of the Irish House
of Commons 234 n.25
Conway, Harp Crown inn 236
Conway Castle 236
Conyngham, Henry, 1st baron 229 n.1
Conyngham, Francis Pierpoint, 2nd baron
229 & n.1, 232, 233
Cook, Olive, *see also* Smith, Edwin 8 n.4
Coote, Sir Eyre xxii, 163 n.109
Cope, Sir John 181 n.38
Coquet river (Northumberland) 88
Cordiner, Charles, *Antiquities & Scenery of the
North of Scotland* xxii–xxiii
Cordiner, Rev Charles *158*, 158 n.97
corn, white 61
Cornwallis, Charles, 1st marquess 8
Corse Lawn (Glos.) 242 n.62
cotton industry: Banff 156
Dundee 140 n.38
Glasgow xix, 205, 224 n.1
Johnstone xvii, 194, 213–15
Kidderminster 241
Nottingham 22
Paisley 210–13, 215
Perth 134
Coughlan, Dan 210 nn.39,40, *211*, 212 n.42,
213 nn.43,44, 214 n.47
Craig, John, Edinburgh architect 108 n.38
Crawford Wm, Dundee surveyor 140 n.37
Crawfurd and Semple, *History of the Shire of
Renfrew* 206–7 n.35
Creech, William, financial writer 118 n.86,
119 n.87
Crew, Nathaniel, 3rd baron 93–4 & n.33
Croft Bridge (Durham) 77 n.70, *78*

crofters 138, 166, 171–2, 181, 223
Cromwell, Oliver 62 & n.9, 102, 216 n.54
crop rotation xvi
in England 13, 17, 32, 38–9, 42, 43–4,
61, 70, 77, 87, 91, 242–3
in Ireland 227
in Scotland 129, 136, 138, 154, 159
in Wales 236
Cross Guns inn, nr Guyhirn (Cambs.) 12–13
& n.15, 13 nn.17,18, 14
Crouzet, François, Professor Emeritus xv–xx,
254
Culford (Suffolk) 8 n.1
Cullen (Banffs.) 157
Cullen, William, Glasgow professor 114 n.71
Culloden, battle of (1746) xix, 165, 173 n.20,
174, 178, 181
Cumberland, William Augustus, duke of 134,
166 n.1, 181 n.33, 226
Cure, Cornelius, sculptor 18–19 n.8

Dalhousie, 8th earl of 140 n.41
Dalmally (Argylls.) xxiii, 171 n.16, 186,
189–90
Dalrymple, Sir John, historian 137
Daniell, William, *Voyage round Great Britain
iii*, 159 n.99, *190, 220*
Darby, H. C. 15 n.22
Darling, Grace 94 n.35
Darlington (Yorks.) 76, 77
St Cuthbert's church 78 n.71
Talbot Inn 78 & n.71
Darnley, Henry Stewart, lord 112 & n.60
David, Louis, French painter under the
Empire *249*
Davilers, A. C., French architectural writer 49
n.32
Davy, H., Suffolk antiquary 8 n.2
Day, J. Wentworth, writer of the Fenland 12
n.15, 14 n.20
Dee, English river 237, 238
Dee, Scottish river 148, 149–50
Deering, C., Nottingham historian 22–3
n.23, 26 n.25
Defoe, Daniel: in England 58 n.59, 58–9
n.61, 59 nn.62,63, 62 n.6, 82 n.3, 97 n.40
in Scotland 102 n.18, 103 n.23
Denbigh 237
Denholm, James *200*
Denton Lodge, Feltwell (Norfolk) 9 & n.7
Denton, Osbert 9 & n.7
Denver Sluice *x*, *10*, 10 n.11, 11
Derby, silk and cotton industry 4, 22, 212
n.42, 213 n.44, 214 n.45, 247

Hollister, William, entertainment supplier
231 n.12
Holyhead (Anglesey) 235
Home, Francis, medicine professor 114 &
n.72, 146
Hooper, S. *90, 93*
Hope, John, Regius Keeper, Edinburgh
Botanic Garden 115 n.74
Hopetoun, Charles Hope, 1st earl 128 n.7
Hopetoun House (Lothian) 128 & n.7
horse-racing 45, 217 n.55, 239, 242
horses 77, 100, 128, 137 n.33, 176
Houldey, Andrew, librarian 242 nn.61,62,64
houses:
in England 239, 243, 245
gentry 27, 28, 29, 54, 96
rural 45
urban 21, 54, 55, 63, 76, 100
in Ireland 227, 228, 231, 233–5
in Scotland
gentry 101, 105, 140, 169, 181, 194,
195–7, 199, 216
Highland xviii, 166–7, 171–2, 178,
181
Lowland 194, 195–7, 199, 206, 216
rural 104, 128, 138, 159, 161, 163
urban 102–3, 133, 143, 150, 152, 160,
178, 197 n.7, 199–200, 201
stone 21, 29, 150, 200
see also turf
Howle (?Howell), Mr 212, 215
Humber, river 54
Hume, David, philosopher on human
understanding 114 & n.70, 116, 121
n.97, 124
Hunter, Dr Alexander 65–6, 66 n.32, 68
Hutcheson, John, architect 143 n.51
Hyde, Ralph 99 n.7, 100 n.10

Inch Garvey (Firth of Forth) 127 nn.5, 6
Inchinnan Bridge 206–7 & n.35, *207, 208*
industry see cotton industry; linen industry;
silk weaving; textile industry
inns, quality of xv–xvi, 144, 147, 178, 184,
224–6
Inveraray (Argylls.) 130 n.9, 165, 189, 191–3
New Inn 191, 194
Inveraray Castle 129 n.8, *190*, 191–3, 194
Inverbervie (Kincardine) 144–5
The Ship Inn xv, 145
textile industry 145–6
Inverkeillor (Angus) 142 n.48
Inverness 161, 163
manufacturing 164, 170 n.9, 223

Masons' Inn 164
Ireland 227–45
general observations 235
and poverty xx, 227, 228
iron industry 46–7
Irvine (Ayrs.) 216

Jacob, F. H., hospital historian 22 n.21
Jacobite Rebellions
1715 146–7 n.59, 191
1745 41 n.4, 99 n.4, 110, 134, 165, 166
n.1, 174 n.22, 177, 181–2
Jacobites xix, 174, 181
Jacomy, M. Bruno 22–3 n.23
James I and VI 107, 109, 134
James II and VII 137 n.34
Jeally Brans Inn (Aberdeens.) 147 n.62
Jefferys, Thomas, surveyor 42 n.7
Johnson, Samuel 196 n.6
and Flora Macdonald 174 n.21, 182 n.40
in Highlands 163 n.109, 166 n.2, *168*,
169 n.6, 170 n.10, 174 n.22
and Jacobites 181–2 n.39
Journey to the Western Islands of Scotland
xxii, xxiii
in Lowlands 198 n.10, 199 n.11
in north-east Scotland 104, 127 n.3,
150–1 n.70, 161 n.104
Johnstone (Renfrews.), cotton industry xvii,
194, 213 n.43, 214–15
Jones, John Paul 127

Kali 185
Kay, caricaturist *122*
Kay, John, inventor 212 n.42
Kedleston Hall (Derbys.) 4
keels 84–5
Kent, Sir Charles 8
Keppel, Augustus, 1st viscount 8
Kidderminster (Worcs.) 240–1, 246
carpet-making 240 & n.55, 241
cotton and silk manufacture 241
tanneries 240
The Lion inn 240 & n.53
Killiecrankie, Pass of (Perths.) 137
kilt xix, 161–2, *175*
Kinfauns (Perths.) 138
Kinfauns Castle (Perths.) 139 n.35
Kingoody quarry (Perths.) 139
King's College Chapel (Cambridge) 15 n.29
Kingston, Elizabeth Chudleigh, duchess of 29
n.37
Kinlochlaich House, Appin (Argylls.) 183
n.45

Kinneff (Kincardine) 146
Kinnoul (Perths.) 138
Kinross (Perths.) 131
Kip, *Britannia Illustrata* 21 n.19, 83 n.5, 242
    n.64
Kirkwood, J. (Edinburgh surveyor) 106–7
    n.35, *107*, 126 n.1
Knaresborough (Yorks.) 68
Knight, C. B., York historian 62 n.3
Knox, John 105 n. 31, 133 n.21

La Rochefoucauld, Adélaïde, comtesse de
    248–9, *249*
La Rochefoucauld, Alexandre comte de,
    principal narrator xv, *passim*, *250*
    general observations of Ireland 235
    general observations on Scotland and
        Scotsmen xvii–xviii, 222–6
    handwriting and spelling 96 n.37, 97 n.42,
        222, 239, 240, 246
    and industry xv–xvi
    marriage 248–9
    and Napoleon 181–2 n.39, 191, 248, *249*,
        251
La Rochefoucauld, François, comte de
    in Cambridge 15 n.29
    in Derby 22 n.23, 214 n.45
    escape from France 248, 251, 255
    in Leicester 135 n.28
    and Louis XVI 181–2 n.39, 248–9
    and post-chaises 104 n.27
    in Suffolk 1–2, 224
    and theatres 231 n.14
    tour of Switzerland 246
    travel-notes 246
La Rochefoucauld-Liancourt, duc de 1, *3*
    and agriculture 4, 5, 247–8, 253, 255
    escape from France 5, 248, 251
    and Adam Smith 121 n.97, 123 n.99
La Rochefoucauld-Liancourt, Sophie de
    Lannion, duchesse de *2* (caption), *3*
Labelye, Charles (drainage engineer) 11
lairds 173, 222
Lambert, John, Parliamentarian general 102–3
    n.21
land clearances 8, 27, 69, 118, 146, 154, 223
land drainage: East Midlands 20
    fenland 9–14
    Scotland 139
land improvement: in England 27–8
    in Scotland 128
    see also enclosure; land clearances
land values: in England 15, 42–4, 50, 68, 76,
    87, 91, 101, 242, 243

in Ireland 231
in Scotland 102, 129, 136, 138, 141–2,
    155, 157, 159, 164, 172, 207
in Wales 236, 237
landowners 129, 173
landscape:
    English 37–8, 53, 68, 70, 73–5, 239
    Highland 170, 181, 193
    Irish 227
    Lowland 194, 196
    north-east Scots 105, 132, 155, 157
    reactions to xvi–xvii
language, Gaelic 174–5
Lauderdale, James Maitland, 8th earl 102 n.19
Lavoisier, Antoine Laurent, French chemist
    114 n.71, 251
Lawson, Judith, Glasgow historian 200 n.15
Lazowski, Claude 252
Lazowski, Maximilien de, principal narrator
    passim, xv, 1, 222, 246
    death 251–2
    on Dr Johnson xxii
    and French Revolution 249–51
    and studies of agriculture 4–5, 247, 248,
        251, 253, 254
    Tour of Switzerland xxiv, 246–7, 252
Leach, Peter, architectural biographer 35 n.51,
    41 n.4, 89 nn.21,22, 96 n.36
Leeds 55–60
    Cloth Halls 55 nn.53,56, *56*, 58–9, *58*,
        59–60
    General Infirmary 55, *56*, *57*, 66
    Old Kings Arms inn 55 & n.53
Leeds and Liverpool Canal 56 n.58
Leicester: spinning industry 135
    stocking industry 4, 151 n.71, 212 n.42
Leinster, James Fitzgerald, 2nd duke 234
Leith (Lothian) 106, 111, 119–20, 121, 224
Lennox, Lady Louisa 234 n.25
Lenthall, William 245 n.78
Lesage, Alain René, *Gil Blas* 142
Leslie, Alexander, 1st earl Leven, general
    102–3 n.21
Leven, river (Dunbartons.) 197 n.6
Liancourt (La Rochefoucauld home) *2*, 247,
    253–5
Lincoln 54
Lindley, William, architectural engraver 64
    n.15
linen industry: in Highlands 191 n.61
    in Lowland Scotland 196–7 n.6, 205 n.31,
        219 n.59, 224
    in north-east Scotland 105, 131 & n.16,
        134, 136, 140 n.38, 142, 145–6

Index